The Psychology of Acute Trauma

A Clinician's Guide to Healing and Recovery

The Psychology of Acute Trauma

A Clinician's Guide to Healing and Recovery

David A. Moore

Henry Ford Hospital, Detroit, MI, United States; Michigan State University College of Human Medicine, East Lansing, MI, United States

Greg Mahr

Henry Ford Hospital, Detroit, MI, United States; Michigan State University College of Human Medicine, East Lansing, MI, United States

ELSEVIER

ACADEMIC PRESS

An imprint of Elsevier

Academic Press is an imprint of Elsevier
125 London Wall, London EC2Y 5AS, United Kingdom
50 Hampshire Street, 5th Floor, Cambridge, MA 02139, United States

For accessibility purposes, images in electronic versions of this book are accompanied by alt text descriptions independently provided by Elsevier, generated with the aid of AI. For more information, see https://www.elsevier.com/about/accessibility or Radarweg 29, 1043 NX Amsterdam, Netherlands.

Books and Journals published by Elsevier comply with applicable product safety requirements. For any product safety concerns or queries, please contact our authorised representative, Elsevier B.V., at productsafety@elsevier.com.

Publisher's note: Elsevier takes a neutral position with respect to territorial disputes or jurisdictional claims in its published content, including in maps and institutional affiliations.

Notices

Knowledge and best practice in this field are constantly changing. As new research and experience broaden our understanding, changes in research methods, professional practices, or medical treatment may become necessary.

Practitioners and researchers must always rely on their own experience and knowledge in evaluating and using any information, methods, compounds, or experiments described herein. In using such information or methods they should be mindful of their own safety and the safety of others, including parties for whom they have a professional responsibility.

To the fullest extent of the law, neither the Publisher nor the authors, contributors, or editors, assume any liability for any injury and/or damage to persons or property as a matter of products liability, negligence or otherwise, or from any use or operation of any methods, products, instructions, or ideas contained in the material herein.

ISBN: 978-0-443-33212-8

For Information on all Academic Press publications
visit our website at https://www.elsevier.com/books-and-journals

Publisher: Megan Ball
Acquisitions Editor: Simonetta Harrison
Editorial Project Manager: Himanshi Yadav
Production Project Manager: Gomathi Sugumar
Cover Designer: Mark Rogers

Typeset by MPS Limited, Chennai, India

Dedication

This book is dedicated to the trauma survivors who have shared their pain, their joy, and their stories with us. Their courage has been our best teacher.

David A. Moore and Greg Mahr

Contents

About the authors

Dr. David A. Moore, PsyD is a senior staff clinical health psychologist and the director of Trauma and Acute Care Surgical Psychology Services at Henry Ford Hospital, in the Department of Surgery, Division of Trauma and Acute Care Surgery, and the Department of Psychiatry. He is the past chair and current vice chair of the Henry Ford Hospital Ethics Committee, and a clinical assistant professor in the Department of Psychiatry at the Michigan State University College of Human Medicine. He has extensive clinical and research experience in academic medical centers across the United States, including three Level I trauma centers. He has served in leadership roles at all stages of training with a deep interest in facilitating the integration of psychology programs into medical settings and providing education to community and professional audiences alike. Dr. Moore can be contacted on his website doctordavidmoore.com.

Dr. Greg Mahr, MD is a graduate of the Wayne State University School of Medicine and has served as director of Consultation Liaison Psychiatry at Henry Ford Hospital for over 20 years. He has many publications and presentations in trauma, psychosomatic medicine, nightmares, and sleep medicine. He is on the faculty at Michigan State University and Wayne State University. He currently provides psychiatric support for the Henry Ford Trauma Recovery Center and runs a nightmare clinic in the Sleep Medicine Department. Dr. Mahr can be contacted on his website gregmahr.com.

Acknowledgments

The authors acknowledge Andrea Weiss for her outstanding editorial work and Amy Beth Edwards for editorial support.

The authors also acknowledge Kimberlyn Lott and Amy Beth Edwards, as well as David H. and Denise Moore, for their emotional support, kindness, and generosity throughout the writing process.

Endorsements

"In early 2025, I found myself under ICU care as a result of trauma from a serious bicycle accident. The support provided to me by Dr. Moore allowed me to process my emotions related to this trauma and to process and manage the post-injury anxiety that I was feeling. Wholistic care at its finest. *The Psychology of Acute Trauma: A Clinician's Guide to Healing and Recovery* provides an outstanding overview of the emerging field of trauma and acute care surgical psychology. This book will serve as an invaluable resource for both clinicians and hospital administrators alike. Drs. David A. Moore and Greg Mahr crystalize decades of experience providing care to acutely injured individuals into a thoughtful and easy-to-read guide to caring for patients and developing cutting-edge trauma psychology programs."

Bob Riney
President and CEO
Henry Ford Health

"*The Psychology of Acute Trauma: A Clinician's Guide to Healing and Recovery* offers a comprehensive guide for clinicians working in medical settings with patients experiencing acute trauma. With clarity and depth, the authors outline evidence-based assessment and timely interventions, while emphasizing the importance of interdisciplinary collaboration grounded in a biopsychosocial framework. This book provides clinicians with a practical roadmap for delivering effective, trauma-informed care in high-acuity hospital environments."

Kelly L. Gilrain, PhD, ABPP
Chief Psychologist
Cooper University Health Care

"*The Psychology of Acute Trauma: A Clinician's Guide to Healing and Recovery* is a practical and thoughtful guide that honors the lived experience of patients and demonstrates the expertise of its authors. It offers deeply informed insight and perspective into an important and underdiscussed area of healing. This work is an important addition to the field that will undoubtedly benefit countless patients."

Rana Awdish, MD
Best-selling author of *In Shock: My Journey From Death to Recovery and the Redemptive Power of Hope*
2021 Pushcart Prize Nominee

Chapter 1

What is trauma?

At the end of the day, we can endure much more than we think we can—Frida Kahlo

Acute trauma

This book is about acute trauma, the kind that Kahlo experienced that day in 1934. Kahlo came eventually to a place of healing and integration through her courage, her authentic acceptance of her pain, and through her art. This book is about the heroic people who have experienced acute trauma and their path to recovery. This book is about how clinicians and caregivers can guide them to the kind path that Frida eventually found. Like most people who have experienced acute trauma, Kahlo had no expectation that the day of the tram collision would be anything but a normal day. Many people awaken in the emergency department or the intensive care unit with no idea of how they got there. Many trauma survivors start their story with words like, "It was just an ordinary day ..." This book is about the next day, the first day of the long process of recovery.

Frida Kahlo's Story.

At 14 years old, Frida Kahlo was traveling home with her classmates on a tram. In one devastating moment, a bus collided with the tram, leading to the deaths of seven people. A 4-foot metal spike was thrust through Frida's pelvis. Her boyfriend bravely grasped the spike and pulled it out of her body, saving her life. She suffered permanent injury, both physically and emotionally.

Frida recovered for several months in the hospital, then many more months after her return home. Her recovery was complicated by the polio she had contracted as a child. She had preexisting disability, but also preexisting coping skills. To the surprise of her medical team, she regained the ability to walk, though with a significant limp that always reminded her of her trauma. Chronic pain plagued Frida for the remainder of her life. During this arduous recovery process, she began to paint, a process that allowed her to both express and transcend her suffering. "My painting carries within it the message of pain," she wrote (as quoted in Herrera, 1984, p. 148). Trauma transformed Kahlo. "If you knew how terrible it is to know suddenly, as if a bolt of lightning elucidated the earth. Now I live in a

The Psychology of Acute Trauma. DOI: https://doi.org/10.1016/B978-0-443-33212-8.00016-6

(Continued)

painful planet, transparent as ice, but it is as if I had learned everything at once in seconds" (as quoted in Herrera, 1984, p. 75).

What did Kahlo know suddenly? What did she learn from her acute injury?

Trauma- and stressor-related disorders

Although the psychological literature about chronic trauma and posttraumatic stress disorder (PTSD) is vast, much less has been written about acute trauma. Clinicians and support networks struggle with what to say to patients after acute trauma and how to stay present with them in their grief.

Adjustment disorder and acute stress disorder are the official diagnostic terms for the kind of symptoms Frida Kahlo may have been experiencing after her trauma. Diagnostic symptoms, as described in the Diagnostic and Statistical Manual of Mental Disorders, Fifth Edition, Text Revision (DSM-5-TR), include distressing memories, nightmares, flashbacks, intense mental distress, dissociative symptoms (feelings of being detached from oneself or periods of amnesia), avoidance, and emotional hyperarousal (American Psychiatric Association, 2022).

While diagnostic criteria have their value, a strict focus on criteria can distance clinicians from the lived experience of their patients. The focus of the work can become checking boxes instead of caring. In this book, we will avoid technical issues and jargon as much as possible and focus instead on the actual experiences of patients and clinicians. Our patients' words and experiences matter just as much as diagnostic criteria.

Who are the authors?

We have been providing psychological and psychiatric care for patients with acute trauma for more than a decade. We work at Henry Ford Hospital, a large urban teaching hospital in Detroit, Michigan. In 2012, the hospital decided to implement an innovative program for the psychological care of its growing number of survivors of acute trauma, with the specific aim of preventing the development of PTSD. Dr. David A. Moore, funded by the Level I trauma center, joined in 2017 as the first full-time director of Trauma and Acute Care Surgical Psychology (TACS Psych) services. Dr. Greg Mahr is the director of the Consultation Psychiatry service that also provides acute trauma care. We work as a team and have authored this book collaboratively.

Collaborative work with trauma and acute care surgery teams, nursing staff, and support networks is essential to our job. The challenges of working with this population require a team effort, and this collaboration is one of the great joys of this work. The trauma surgeons have come to deeply value the work that we do. As we explain to the team sometimes, "Words are our scalpel." Words can open wounds when necessary, and words can heal.

Trauma and acute care surgery is a busy clinical service, with over 2000 patients with traumatic injuries treated each year. We try to see each patient as soon as possible after their injury. We provide assessment and treatment while patients are hospitalized. In our work with nightmares, we collaborate with the Thomas Roth Sleep Disorders & Research Center.

A Note on voice and orientation

The work we do is personal. Writing this book was also personal as well as collaborative. Indeed, each chapter was crafted jointly by the two of us. While sometimes we use the third-person singular, in order to emphasize the personal nature of the work, we also sometimes write in the first-person singular voice of "I." The "I" is either of us in our clinical roles.

The clinical interventions described in this book do not always fall into a particular school or type of therapy. They are designed to be practical, clinical, and respectful of the suffering person in front of us that we are trying to help. Interventions described will be evidence-based when possible, or evidence-supported when feasible. Most importantly, we will try to honor the inner experience of the trauma survivor.

What is trauma?

Traumatic injury has always been part of the human experience, and people have long attempted to describe and understand the psychological impacts of trauma. Jean Laplanche and Jean-Bertrand Pontalis defined trauma as "an event in the subject's life defined by its intensity, the subject's incapacity to respond adequately to it, and by the upheaval and long-lasting effects it brings about in the psychical organization" (Laplanche & Pontalis, 1988). Bessel van der Kolk similarly described the experience of trauma as one that is unable to be integrated, which leads to a reliving of the experience rather than solely remembering it (van der Kolk, 2014).

Remembering is a subtle process: Many traumas are remembered cognitively, but the emotions associated with them are unintegrated, so they are relived and reenacted. In a case of childhood physical abuse, for instance, a person may consciously remember the abuse they experienced as a child. But because they have not integrated the emotions into memory, the trauma can express itself as anger, sadness, or somatic symptoms. Trauma survivors are often shocked by their own feelings or behaviors, as if they came from some other place or person. Indeed, they do; they come from an unintegrated aspect of the self.

The three components of the Laplanche and Pontalis definition of trauma are an event, a response, and the long-lasting effects (Laplanche & Pontalis, 1988). These components are crucial to most definitions of trauma, including the DSM-5-TR definition and the definition used by the Substance Abuse and Mental Health Services Administration (SAMHSA).

A definition of trauma

The SAMHSA is the U.S. government agency that monitors and regulates mental health services. SAMSHA developed a consensus definition of trauma using an expert panel:

> *Individual trauma results from an event, series of events or a set of circumstances that is experienced by an individual as physically or emotionally harmful or life threatening and that has long- lasting adverse effects on the individual's functioning and mental, physical, social, emotional or spiritual well-being (Substance Abuse and Mental Health Services Administration, 2014).*

The three e's—event, experience, and effect—are further described. The event must involve the actual or extreme threat of physical or psychological harm. Yet it is not the event itself but the experience of the event that matters. The same event might be traumatic for one individual but not another. As in many medical illnesses, such as those involving inflammation, the body's reaction is part of the trauma phenomenon.

The third e, effect, is also complex. Effects can be immediate or delayed, short- or long-lasting. Effects can include inability to cope with stress, anxiety, problems with memory and attention, loss of trust in others, and problems regulating emotions. People might be hypervigilant about future trauma or withdrawn and emotionally numb. As in Kahlo's case, effects can be both negative and positive.

The American Psychiatric Association (APA) publishes the official diagnostic guidebook in mental health, the DSM-5-TR. The DSM-5-TR does not explicitly define trauma, but a description of traumatic events is embedded in the criteria for and discussion of PTSD (American Psychiatric Association, 2022). War, physical assault, sexual assault, kidnaping and severe motor vehicle collisions are cited as examples of trauma. Incarceration, but only as a prisoner of war, is also included. Life-threatening or debilitating medical illnesses are not necessarily considered traumatic, but sudden catastrophic events like awakening during surgery are. Witnessing trauma, in person, can be considered traumatic. Learning of trauma experienced by a close family member or friend can be considered traumatic. The DSM-5-TR also requires, for the diagnosis of PTSD, symptoms of intrusion, where the trauma imposes itself on ordinary life with intrusive memories or nightmares.

How common is trauma?

Trauma is ubiquitous. In 2020 there were more than 43.5 million injury-related emergency department visits in the United States (Cairns & Kang, 2022). Additionally, there has been a significant increase in exposure to firearm injuries beginning with a rise in 2018 with with an increase of nearly 20% between 2019 and 2022 (Zwald et al., 2023). Acute trauma deeply affects the survivor, with 6% to 30% of survivors with orthopedic injuries developing acute stress disorder (Warren et al., 2016). Approximately 69% of Americans will experience a minimum of one traumatic event within their lifetime (Goldstein et al., 2016). Worldwide, more than 40 million individuals sustain permanent injuries as the result of trauma each year (Miclau et al., 2025).

What makes trauma traumatic?

Some kinds of trauma are more likely to leave emotional scars than others. Assaults by people we know are often more traumatizing than assaults by strangers. Sexual assaults are more traumatic than other kinds of assaults. When trauma creates feelings of powerlessness and betrayal, it is particularly likely to cause psychic damage. Thus, childhood traumas perpetrated by parental figures are particularly damaging. This parent, who is supposed to love me and whom I of necessity depend on is, in fact, harming me. Traumatized children often feel that no one loves them, that no one can validate their pain.

It is the relationship between the event and the person experiencing the event that makes trauma traumatic. Prior trauma can make people more susceptible to a new trauma. Other factors that increase the level of distress after trauma include a prior psychiatric history. Some kinds of trauma are more likely to cause acute stress disorder, including sexual trauma, gunshot wounds, assaults, motor vehicle crashes, traumatic limb amputations, and spinal cord injuries. Emotional support and close loving relationships can mitigate the effects of trauma. In essence, it is the presence of an intense psychological response, in tandem with the life-threatening event, that leads the event to be experienced as "traumatic."

Acute trauma versus posttraumatic stress disorder

Trauma has been the subject of intensive study, but most of the literature has focused on chronic posttraumatic stress. Acute trauma, especially in nonmilitary settings, has received less research attention. Also, the practical aspects of how to talk to people who have experienced acute trauma have not been clearly elucidated. The American College of Surgeons Committee on Trauma (ACS COT) now requires that verified Level I, II, and III trauma centers provide appropriate mental health screening and referrals. Due to its chronic nature, PTSD, by definition, can only be diagnosed one month after the experience of a traumatic event. For the first month after a trauma, the proper diagnostic terms would be adjustment disorder and acute stress disorder. For instance, in Frida Kahlo's case, shortly after the tram collision, she would have been diagnosed with acute stress disorder. Then, if symptoms persisted, she might have met criteria for PTSD.

That first month after trauma is thus a period of unique opportunity. By working with patients with acute trauma, we might better understand how the mind integrates and processes trauma. Even more importantly, we might help relieve human suffering and possibly prevent PTSD and other adverse mental health outcomes.

Why this book?

This book is intended as a practical treatment guide for clinicians involved in the management of acute trauma survivors. We have tried to convey what our patients have taught us about how trauma feels from the inside. When we begin with that understanding, we can be more effective with patients and accompany them on their journey of trauma recovery.

Each chapter will begin and end with a clinical narrative, and extensive clinical material is woven through each chapter. One entire chapter is devoted to examples of clinical dialogs with patients; another chapter is devoted to historical and literary examples of trauma and trauma recovery. Narratives help convey inner experience and help build empathy, and it is ultimately through modifying our internal life narrative that we process and heal from trauma.

This book is intended for all members of the clinical team, as well as the administrators and leaders who guide those teams. Patients and caregivers can benefit from the information we will explore, which is evidence-based and clinically informed. Trauma affects all of us, and, guided by empathy and understanding, we are on this journey together.

Chapter summary

Acute trauma is very common and causes deep psychic wounds. Definitions of trauma are described and are important to consider, as well as the impacts of trauma on the psyche. Adjustment disorder and acute stress disorder develop soon after trauma, but after one month, if symptoms persist, the term PTSD may be used to describe those symptoms. The authors also describe their background and clinical work.

References

American Psychiatric Association (2022). *Diagnostic and Statistical Manual of Mental Disorders* (5th ed., text rev.). American Psychiatric Association Publishing. https://doi.org/10.1176/appi.books.9780890425787.

Cairns C., Kang K. (2022). 10.1562/cdc:12911 National center for Health Statistics (US) National Hospital Ambulatory Medical Care Survey:2020 Emergency Department Summary Tables.

Goldstein, R. B., Smith, S. M., Chou, S. P., Saha, T. D., Jung, J., Zhang, H., Pickering, R. P., Ruan, W. J., Huang, B., & Grant, B. F. (2016). The epidemiology of DSM-5 posttraumatic stress disorder in the United States: results from the National Epidemiologic Survey on

Alcohol and Related Conditions-III. *Social Psychiatry and Psychiatric Epidemiology, 51*(8), 1137–1148. https://doi.org/10.1007/s00127-016-1208-5.

Herrera, H. (1984). Frida: A Biography of Frida Kahlo. *Harper Perennial, Harper Perennial,* 45.

Laplanche, J., & Pontalis, J.-P. (1988). *The language of psychoanalysis.* Routledge.

Miclau, T., Balogh, Z. J., Miclau, K. R., Bernstein, B., Kojima, K. E., Kurozumi, T., Leighton, R. K., Lundy, D. W., Putzeys, G., Schipper, I. B., Vandesande, W., de Camargo Leonhardt, M., Miranda Goncalves, M. A., Pelosini Gaiarsa, G., & Pape, H.-C. (2025). Trauma systems: a global comparison. *OTA international: the open access journal of orthopaedic trauma, 8*(3 Suppl). https://doi.org/10.1097/OI9.0000000000000376.

Substance Abuse and Mental Health Services Administration. (2014). *SAMHSA's Concept of trauma and guidance for a trauma-informed approach.* https://library.samhsa.gov/sites/default/files/sma14-4884.pdf.

van der Kolk, B. A. (2014). *The body keeps the score: Brain, mind and body in the healing of trauma.* Penguin.

Warren, A. M., Jones, A. L., Bennett, M., Solis, J. K., Reynolds, M., Rainey, E. E., Viere, G., & Foreman, M. L. (2016). Prospective Evaluation of Posttraumatic Stress Disorder in Injured Patients With and Without Orthopaedic Injury. *Journal of Orthopaedic Trauma, 30*(9). https://doi.org/10.1097/BOT.0000000000000623.

Zwald, M. L., Van Dyke, M. E., Chen, M. S., Radhakrishnan, L., Holland, K. M., Simon, T. R., Dahlberg, L. L., Friar, N. W., Sheppard, M., Kite-Powell, A., & Mercy, J. A. (2023). Emergency Department Visits for Firearm Injuries Before and During the COVID-19 Pandemic - United States, January 2019-December 2022. *Morbidity and Mortality Weekly Report, 72*(13), 333–337. https://doi.org/10.15585/mmwr.mm7213a2.

Chapter 2

The next day: beginning the process of recovery

Kevonte's Story

The morning started like any other for Kevonte as he made his way toward the front door and started to walk to the grocery store. Halfway through his walk, he heard the sound of screeching tires. A black sports utility vehicle was speeding toward him, back windows open. Seconds later, guns blazed.

Kevonte was unconscious when he arrived at the trauma bay, with multiple gunshot wounds to his abdomen, chest and back. He required emergent operative intervention and ultimately was discovered to have multiple bowel and gastric perforations. Imaging revealed a retained projectile located in his spine. The surgeons worked tirelessly to stabilize him, controlling bleeding and repairing lacerations, and kept his abdomen open to prevent compartment syndrome. Kevonte was alive, although he required mechanical ventilation to assist with his breathing. After his transition to the surgical intensive care unit, he developed paraplegia, a consequence of the bullet that had severed his spinal cord. It was there that we met, over his open abdomen, as he began to open his eyes, the next day.

The Next Day

Instead of the cold concrete of the street, Kevonte felt an unfamiliar pressure. As he attempted to raise his arm to investigate his face, he realized that his wrists had been bound. Straining to open his eyes and blinded by bright lights, he attempted to call for help but found himself unable to speak because of the endotracheal tube. He panicked and wondered, "What happened? Am I dead?"

A few hours later, when I stepped quietly into his room, Kevonte turned his head and met my gaze, over his open abdomen. Understanding that he would be unable to communicate via traditional means, my goal was simple: To introduce myself and orient him to the recovery efforts while trying to identify his support system. Our first meeting was brief, with Kevonte communicating via basic hand signals: a thumbs up for yes and sideways for no.

I asked Kevonte if he recalled any of the events surrounding his admission, and he signaled that he had little knowledge of why he was currently in the hospital. I shared basic details related to his injuries and the recovery efforts, then stated, "It's

The Psychology of Acute Trauma. DOI: https://doi.org/10.1016/B978-0-443-33212-8.00009-9

(Continued)

very common to have strong feelings and thoughts when these unexpected events turn our worlds upside down. Have you noticed any such thoughts or feelings?" I closely observed his behaviors as he intently listened to me. Slowly closing his eyes, sitting still for a moment, he then hesitantly shifted his thumb upward toward the ceiling. While I typically ask open-ended questions during my evaluations, I was conscious of the frustration that could cause Kevonte, since he could not speak. "One of the common emotional changes people may experience is sadness," I shared, followed by a description of common symptoms of anxious distress. Kevonte signaled that he was both sad and scared, with periods of confusion and panic often occurring in the evening. He felt that less staff were available in the evenings and worried that he would be unable to call for help if he needed to. Tears welled up in his eyes, and I asked if I could hold his hand, a gesture that he later stated made him "feel like a person again."

The foundations of inpatient acute care

The trauma- and stressor-related disorders are by their nature acquired conditions, caused by a discrete traumatic event. This unique element allows clinicians to engage in psychiatric secondary prevention, potentially preventing the development of more chronic forms of distress such as posttraumatic stress disorder (PTSD) through well-timed psychological interventions during the acute phase of recovery. Consequently, the path toward optimal psychological recovery following trauma should begin in the hospital, immediately after an individual sustains an injury. Despite this, few trauma centers offer early psychological interventions (Bulger et al., 2022; Moore et al., 2019; Ridings et al., 2022). Our integrated program affords us the opportunity to engage patients anywhere in the hospital, including the emergency department, intensive care units, general practice units and even in the preoperative area and post anesthesia care unit.

Comprehensive trauma care is evolving, and the importance of systematically addressing the need for psychological services in trauma centers was recently reinforced by the American College of Surgeons. The 7th edition of the Resources for Optimal Care of the Injured Patient 2022 Standards, Revised July 2025 includes several novel requirements aimed at addressing the psychological well-being of the traumatically injured patient (American College of Surgeons, 2025). Specifically, all verified Level I and II trauma centers must now develop and implement screening protocols for patients at high risk for mental health concerns with Level I, II, and III programs requiring a referral to a mental health provider for patients identified as high risk. The information contained within this book will allow you to develop and implement a program to both meet and exceed these requirements.

Practicing in a fast-paced acute care setting, such as a trauma center, offers both logistical and technical challenges that differ greatly from ambulatory settings because traditional approaches to psychodiagnostic assessment and intervention may not be feasible. The initial phases of managing the therapeutic alliance following acute injury offer special challenges, including potential barriers to empathy.

Therapeutic psychodiagnostic assessment in acute care settings

Providing effective treatment requires accurate assessment. When new trainees begin rotations with me, I always share that the goal of effective consultation is to get the answer rather than an answer to the consultation question. Without accurate assessment, treatment planning will lack a substantive foundation, oftentimes leading to ineffective interventions and a frustrating experience for patients and clinicians alike. In the following sections approaches to effective assessment in acute care settings will be discussed, as well as techniques to transform your assessments into therapeutic experiences.

Special considerations related to assessment in acute care settings

Conducting effective assessments in acute care settings begins with understanding the key differences between inpatient settings and their ambulatory counterparts. Unlike traditional outpatient behavioral health settings, a vast majority of patients with trauma present for treatment emergently with acute medical and surgical needs as their primary concern. Few, if any, expect to engage with a specialized behavioral health team during their admission, which may sometimes elicit concerns that they have "done something wrong" to warrant a visit from a mental health specialist. Such reactions afford clinicians a rare opportunity to educate individuals about the process of providing mental health services as a part of comprehensive trauma recovery. By providing supportive psychoeducation at the onset of the initial clinical encounter, the goals of both normalizing the psychological responses to trauma and validating the patient's emotional experience can set the tone for the entire hospitalization. The trauma survivor receives the message that the trauma team is here to help them recover as a whole person and that their emotional experience is important. This in turn allows the clinician to proactively address avoidance-based coping, a key mechanism for the maintenance of posttraumatic psychological distress, prior to behavioral patterns becoming deeply engrained. Healthy recovery usually involves experiencing rather than suppressing emotions.

In acute care settings the inpatient behavioral health team rarely knows how long the patient will be in treatment. Patients with lower-acuity injuries may only require 24 hours of care, whereas those with more severe injuries may require many months of intensive medical and surgical management. For this reason, one of the core competencies associated with successful functioning as a consultation liaison provider is developing an ability to rapidly clarify the consultation question posed by the referring team while also identifying the patient's most pressing concerns, all while under significant time pressure. Assertive interdisciplinary collaboration will help the clinician identify an estimated length of stay, which in turn will inform the structure of the assessment and future interventions.

Because of the unpredictable nature of scheduling procedures, imaging studies, and other medical and surgical interventions, assessments are often interrupted to allow for patient transport for medical care. It is imperative that the clinician maintain flexibility while attempting to prioritize critical elements of their assessment at the beginning of the clinical encounter. Discussing the patient's planned schedule with their primary treatment team prior to attempting to assess the patient may reduce the likelihood of interruptions.

Privacy and confidentiality are important aspects of care, as many assessments occur in the context of shared spaces or in the presence of members of a patient's social support network. Evidence suggests that the presence of positive social support may mitigate the development of PTSD (Keane et al., 2006), although the presence of third parties may limit the patient's ability to be fully engaged in an assessment. Clinicians should utilize informed consent related to the nature of the proposed assessment, notifying patients of the voluntary nature of the encounter and inquiring about their preferences related to the presence of third parties (e.g., engage in assessment in private, with visitors, or wait until visitors leave), all while attempting to ascertain whether the presence of third parties may have impacted the patient's ability to provide accurate information related to their current symptom experience and psychosocial history.

Oftentimes patients have sustained injuries or require therapies that may impair their ability to communicate via speaking or writing, which poses a special challenge to the completion of psychological evaluations. Psychological evaluations typically rely heavily on patient self-report. Clinicians practicing in acute care settings must develop confidence utilizing creative forms of communication that capitalize on each patient's strengths while minimizing potential pitfalls that may increase frustration or lead to demoralization of the patient. Specifically, if the patient is unable to communicate via speaking, writing, or typing, approaches that utilize inventive combinations of mouthing words, nodding, body signals, communication boards, or eye movements may help the clinician communicate with the nonverbal patient. Clinicians are encouraged to first consult with the referring provider to discuss whether an effective approach to communication has been identified and, if not, to discern any functional or cognitive impairments that may limit communication. After assessing the patient's current functional capabilities, clinicians may offer patients a range of options in terms of communication approaches, which may serve the dual purpose of increasing a sense of control. If concerns related to cognitive impairment exist, incorporating a brief assessment of mental status (e.g., confirming name, birthday and basic logical reasoning queries such as "Do rocks typically float on water?") will assist in identifying the reliability and validity of the patient's responses. Teach-back strategies, which incorporate reflective listening techniques, are critical to ensure that the clinician is accurately interpreting the patient's communications and that the patient is comprehending the clinician's communications.

Finally, all assessments should include discussions related to risk, with a particular focus on both suicidal and homicidal ideation. Patients who have sustained injuries as a result of the actions of another may be at an elevated risk to experience a desire for retaliation, whereas individuals whose own actions have led to the unintended death of another may be at an elevated risk for suicidal ideation. Death and dying can be an important issue in the acute care environment, and open and honest discussions may help destigmatize the topic. Patients may have legitimate concerns about their survival. Candidly discussing issues related to death and dying may allow them to respond in an authentic manner while feeling validated that their experiences may be common in the context of exposure to trauma.

Building rapport and the therapeutic alliance in acute care settings

Unlike traditional outpatient treatment, building rapport and establishing the therapeutic alliance may be challenging to accomplish in acute care settings characterized by the presence of large multidisciplinary treatment teams who are caring for patients who have initially presented for the management of physical health concerns. Because of shorter courses of treatment and abbreviated encounter times, it is imperative that clinicians strive to establish rapport quickly to optimize patient outcomes. The following strategies may assist clinicians in developing rapport and maintaining the therapeutic alliance.

Warm handoffs and cultural brokers

Although the presence of large teams may make establishing rapport a challenge, prior trusting relationships with team members may prove beneficial in the context of large team interactions. Identifying trusted team members during the pre-consultation process may allow for the completion of warm handoffs, where the identified team member may introduce the clinician at the onset of the assessment in hopes of more rapidly establishing rapport. For patients whose background may be different than the clinicians, cultural brokering may prove effective in facilitating increases in rapport and enhancement of the therapeutic alliance. A cultural broker may be an individual who is well known to the patient or retained through the health care organization to assist with navigating culturally related health care decisions (National Center for Cultural Competence, 2004).

Rehumanization

Unexpected admission to the hospital after sustaining a traumatic injury is oftentimes a dehumanizing experience. Clothes are cut off to quickly identify injuries, and the frenetic pace of emergency care can be overwhelming to the conscious patient. Medications for pain may dull the senses, or lead to the presence of an altered sensorium, impairing the ability to discern reality from fantasy. Interventions to increase safety, such as restraints, eliminate bodily autonomy, and ventilator dependence takes away the voice. Depending on their injuries, patients may be unable to eat, drink, or control bodily functions. In a cruel twist of fate, dignity and independence are revoked in an instant, without permission. In this setting, it is imperative for us to strive to rehumanize those we work with, which may also have a secondary benefit of building rapport and strengthening the therapeutic alliance. Genuineness of intent is critical. Recommendations for basic interventions to preserve the autonomy, dignity and independence of patients with acute trauma are summarized in Table 2.1.

Communicating empathy

Empathy heals. Empathy is a crucial element of healing in psychotherapy and clinical care. In situations where the integrity of the self is damaged, as in acute trauma, empathy is a crucial factor in restoring hope and regaining trust in the world. When the bodily and psychological integrity of the person has been damaged, the experience of human caring is restorative. Communicating empathy is important from the very first contact with the trauma survivor; that is why the next day is so important.

Empathy is different than sympathy. Sympathy resembles sorrow and pity; it is a favor granted from the outside. The sympathetic person is outside or even above the situation. Empathy is being with the suffering person and connecting with their pain, not observing it safely from outside. While there are strategies for communicating empathy, including those illustrated in Table 2.1, the best way to communicate empathy is to feel empathy. Empathy can be painful to experience, and an important way to allow oneself to experience empathy is to take care of oneself emotionally. If we are tired, stressed, or unhappy, it is difficult to allow the experience of empathy to develop. Empathy also involves acceptance. It is important not to over-identify with the patient. Over-identifying has an inauthentic element; the patient's trauma is the patient's trauma, not yours. It has be accepted, and it can't be undone.

TABLE 2.1 Basic interventions to preserve the autonomy, dignity, and independence of patients with acute trauma.

Autonomy

- Introduce self and all team members
- Ask for permission to engage
- Ask to sit, when able

Dignity

- Ensure the patient is clothed or covered
- Ask about comfort if the patient appears to be in pain
- Offer to assist with completing basic tasks, such as refilling a water cup, as appropriate
- Respond in a compassionate manner, offering assistance with emotionally related responses, such as wiping the tears of a patient who has functional limitations or is restrained
- Use therapeutic touch, such as holding the hand of a patient when delivering difficult information, with patient permission

Independence

- Maximize choice by providing options related to care (e.g., "Would you like to meet now or in 10 minutes?")

Advocacy-Related Interventions

- Serve as a liaison

Active listening conveys empathy. Avoid trying to provide solutions; listen to understand, not solve. Validate feelings; be patient and present. Accept patients where they are, even when they are angry or in denial. There is no script for recovery, especially in the acute phase of trauma recovery where emotional responses can be highly variable. Empathy can be nurtured and to some extent taught. In Chapter 19, Teaching the Next Generation of Clinicians, we will review strategies for teaching empathy to trainees.

Issues that may impact empathy

Empathy is both essential to providing effective care and a complicated construct with both cognitive and emotional components (Delgado et al., 2023; Figley, 2002). Acute care settings are intense and challenging practice environments; as such, it is important to acknowledge the inherent potential obstacles, ranging from the psychological to the physical, that may impact our ability to maintain and enhance empathy. While such obstacles can occur in any clinical care setting, they are especially important in the acute care setting, where distress is severe and tensions can run high.

Burnout and compassion fatigue

Burnout and compassion fatigue can interfere with clinician empathy and the development and maintenance of the therapeutic alliance (Delgado et al., 2023; Figley, 1995). Burnout is a phenomenon observed in individuals who are exposed to chronic stress in the work environment and is increasingly common in health care workers (Delgado et al., 2023). Burnout syndrome has been associated with a wide range of negative experiences, including helplessness, likely influenced by the oftentimes uncontrollable nature of working in demanding and fast-paced work environments (Maslach et al., 2001). Other effects exhibited by clinicians experiencing burnout syndrome include fatigue, emotional depletion, and negative cognitions surrounding their patients, work in general and themselves (Maslach & Jackson, 1981). The Maslach Burnout Inventory is considered the gold standard assessment for measuring burnout (Maslach & Jackson, 1981).

Compassion fatigue is a parallel yet separate process that may result from the experience of secondary traumatic stress (Figley, 1995). Specifically, it is a form of caregiver-specific burnout that has been defined by (Figley, 2002) as "a state of tension and preoccupation with the traumatized patients by re-experiencing the traumatic events, avoidance/numbing of reminders and persistent arousal (e.g., anxiety) associated with the patient" (p. 1435). Due to the high levels of secondary traumatic stress inherent in our work, clinicians practicing in trauma centers must proactively work to address the experience of both burnout syndrome and compassion fatigue to prevent the erosions in empathy that may otherwise occur.

Confronting reality and the just world hypothesis

The "just world" is a place where one's actions correlate with outcomes, where "good things happen to good people and bad things happen to bad people." In reality, traumatic events may impact anyone. The trauma survivor must eventually come to accept the injustice of the trauma that they experienced, but caregivers can unconsciously use the just world hypothesis to distance themselves from and "other" the trauma survivor. The belief in the just world hypothesis serves as a protective mechanism that provides distance from the suffering experienced by the trauma survivor. This natural tendency to devalue another's suffering is likely rooted in an attempt by observers to insulate themselves from the harsh reality of the world (Lerner & Simmons, 1966). This mindset impacts both patients and clinicians alike and may negatively affect clinician empathy when caring for individuals whose circumstances challenge our belief in the just world. It may also cause us to blame the victim when they "deserve" what happened to them; for instance, if they were engaged in an illegal activity when they sustained their injury.

Trauma-informed care

Increased attention has been paid in recent decades to the psychological impacts of trauma and the special issues faced by trauma survivors who are seeking medical or mental health care. To create a unified approach to addressing the impact of traumatic experiences on the individuals and communities served by our health systems, general principles and guidelines have been developed under the rubric of trauma-informed care. The central principles of trauma-informed care, as outlined by the Substance Abuse and Mental Health Services Administration (SAMHSA) include safety; peer support; trustworthiness and transparency; collaboration and mutuality; and empowerment, voice and choice (Substance Abuse and Mental Health Services Administration, 2026). These guidelines emphasize collaboration and emotional safety, shifting the focus of health care from "What's wrong with you?" to "What did you experience?" These principles are at the core of good trauma care and are the essence and spirit of the interventions described in this book.

Environmental factors

Environmental factors are also important to consider, as acute care settings offer unique challenges that may impact the ability to maintain empathy as compared to traditional ambulatory settings. Obvious factors such as the fast pace of the work and limited time with patients may impact the clinician's ability to connect with them on a deep empathic level, with intensive care settings providing their own unique challenges inherent to treating individuals with critical care needs.

Contact precautions may also introduce unique barriers to developing empathy due to the need for personal protective equipment (PPE), such as gloves, gowns, respirators, surgical masks, and face shields. While PPE serves a critical purpose in protecting the clinician from pathogens, it may introduce literal and metaphorical barriers that impact our ability to connect with our patients. For scenarios that require face coverings, simple interventions such as affixing an easily decontaminated or disposable photograph of the clinician to the exterior of the protective gown may serve to humanize the clinician. Self-reflection is critical as clinicians navigate complex personal experiences when asked to potentially compromise their own health while providing care to another.

Translating theory into practice

Refining the formulation

During the course of our first several meetings, Kevonte and I spent hours of time discussing his emotional experiences and how different his world was now compared to the way it was prior to the assault. He had no history of psychological concerns or previous treatment. He described strong feelings of sadness and fear. Despite difficulties with communication, I began to develop my diagnostic formulation and treatment plan, which included assertive liaison work with his primary surgical and intensive care teams.

The assessment process should be ongoing, especially in situations such as Kevonte's, which necessitate flexibility. He was eventually extubated, although the placement of a tracheostomy and ongoing ventilator support were still required. The removal of the endotracheal tube, which also enabled the removal of the restraints since unintentional self-extubation was no longer a concern, opened up additional avenues to refine the diagnostic formulation via mouthing words and writing. Kevonte described patterns of fluctuating mental status that were very distressing, although these began to fade as his physical recovery progressed. His affect began to brighten, and we started each of our sessions with a fist bump, at his request. He would later describe the impact of our early interactions, stating, "You helped me understand that I wasn't broken; there was nothing wrong with me. And you didn't give up when I couldn't talk to you. I'm a normal person who had something terrible happen to them." Kevonte embodied the aspirational goal of early intervention, to strive to integrate the traumatic experience in a healthy manner, not struggle to erase it.

Chapter summary

The principles of mental health care in the setting of acute trauma include conducting an accurate psychodiagnostic assessment and building rapport. Medical and surgical issues, as well as environmental factors can create special challenges for the provision of mental health services. A comprehensive trauma program that includes mental health services as a standard of care can avoid the stigma associated with mental health care while providing effective interventions early in the recovery process.

References

American College of Surgeons (2025). *Resources for optimal care of the injured patient 2022 standards, revised July 2025* (7th ed.). American College of Surgeons. https://www.facs.org/quality-programs/trauma/quality/verification-review-and-consultation-program/standards/.

Bulger, E. M., Johnson, P., Parker, L., Moloney, K. E., Roberts, M. K., Vaziri, N., Seo, S., Nehra, D., Thomas, P., & Zatzick, D. (2022). Nationwide survey of trauma center screening and intervention practices for posttraumatic stress disorder, firearm violence, mental health, and substance use disorders. *Journal of the American College of Surgeons, 234*(3), 274–287. https://doi.org/10.1097/XCS.0000000000000064.

Delgado, N., Delgado, J., Betancort, M., Bonache, H., & Harris, L. T. (2023). What is the link between different components of empathy and burnout in healthcare professionals? A systematic review and meta-analysis. *Psychology Research and Behavior Management, 16*, 447–463. https://doi.org/10.2147/PRBM.S384247.

Figley, C. R. (1995). *Compassion fatigue: Coping with secondary traumatic stress disorder in those who treat the traumatized.* Routledge.

Figley, C. R. (2002). Compassion fatigue: Psychotherapists' chronic lack of self care. *Journal of Clinical Psychology, 58*(11), 1433–1441. https://doi.org/10.1002/jclp.10090.

Keane, T. M., Marshall, A. D., & Taft, C. T. (2006). Posttraumatic stress disorder: Etiology, epidemiology, and treatment outcome. *Annual review of clinical psychology, 2*, 161–197. https://doi.org/10.1146/annurev.clinpsy.2.022305.095305.

Lerner, M. J., & Simmons, C. H. (1966). Observer's reaction to the "innocent victim": Compassion or rejection? *Journal of Personality and Social Psychology, 4*(2), 203–210. https://doi.org/10.1037/h0023562.

Maslach, C., & Jackson, S. E. (1981). The measurement of experienced burnout. *Journal of Organizational Behavior, 2*(2), 99–113. https://doi.org/10.1002/job.4030020205.

Maslach, C., Schaufeli, W. B., Leiter, M. P., & Burnout, J. (2001). *Annual Review of Psychology, 52*(1), 397–422. https://doi.org/10.1146/annurev.psych.52.1.397.

Moore D.A., Peltzer-Jones J., Snipes C., Hughes J.B., Johnson J., Fasbinder B., Nathens A. (2019, November). *Are verified trauma centers providing trauma informed psychological care?: A national survey of mental health service availability in Trauma Quality Improvement Program verified trauma centers.* Presented at 10th Annual Trauma Quality Improvement Program Scientific Meeting and Training, Dallas, TX.

National Center for Cultural Competence (2004). Bridging the cultural divide in health care settings: The essential role of cultural broker programs. Available from: https://nccc.georgetown.edu/documents/Cultural_Broker_Guide_English.pdf.

Ridings, L. E., Espeleta, H. C., Streck, C. J., Davidson, T. M., Litvitskiy, N., Bravoco, O., Kassam-Adams, N., & Ruggiero, K. J. (2022). Assessing service quality and access in trauma centers through behavioral health screening, education, and treatment after pediatric injury. *Journal of Pediatric Surgery, 57*(11), 632–636. https://doi.org/10.1016/j.jpedsurg.2022.01.014.

Substance Abuse and Mental Health Services Administration (2026). Trauma-informed approaches and programs. Available from: https://www.samhsa.gov/mental-health/trauma-violence/trauma-informed-approaches-programs.

Chapter 3

The neurobiology of acute trauma

Derrick's Story

Derrick had struggled with violence all his life. His father was physically abusive. When Derrick was 14, he joined a gang. By the time he was 21, he had been involved in several shootings and stabbings, both as a victim and perpetrator. He described these events matter-of-factly as "part of the job," and denied any symptoms of anxiety until the age of 25. By then he had left gang life and was working part-time as a security guard. We saw him after a different kind of trauma. He had been sitting in a parked car when a drunk driver struck his vehicle. He sustained a fractured clavicle and some other minor injuries but said that he suddenly felt overwhelmed by anxiety. The side window of his car had shattered, and the sudden feeling of the shards of broken glass on the skin of his neck and arms, in his words, "stirred something." He was awake all night, fearful, hypervigilant, and afraid to drive. "What's wrong with me, Doc? This accident was nothing. I knew I was fine. Why am I so upset by it?"

Event and experience

Derrick's case beautifully illustrates the difference between the event and the experience. This motor vehicle crash, which was relatively minor, was perceived by Derrick to be more traumatic than the shootings and stabbings he had previously been exposed to, even though in some objective sense he was less at risk of serious injury. As we will see, trauma can prime the brain for future trauma, and certain physical and emotional details can trigger a full trauma response, such as being trapped in a parked car while watching a crash unfold. In Derrick's other traumas he felt agency; he was armed and with friends, and although he was injured, he felt in control of the situation. The tactile quality of the glass on his skin became a particular trigger, as if the distinct tactile sensation of glass on skin bypassed somatosensory processing and became emotionally charged.

The Psychology of Acute Trauma. DOI: https://doi.org/10.1016/B978-0-443-33212-8.00002-6

Trauma and the brain

From an evolutionary perspective, managing trauma is an important function of the brain. Attacks by predators, injuries, and sudden death have been part of human heritage. To maximize survival, the brain must heighten awareness and vigilance in times of danger, then dampen those responses when danger has passed.

When danger is perceived or trauma occurs, a cascade of neurophysiological events takes place. The hypothalamus initiates a response to stress along two distinct pathways. First, the autonomic nervous system initiates the well-known fight-or-flight response involving adrenaline and noradrenaline release from the adrenal gland. These molecules increase heart rate and contractility, redirect blood flow away from the skin to vital organs, open and relax airways, increase metabolic rate, and boost blood sugar. In response to adrenaline and noradrenaline, we feel hyperalert and focused, as well as frightened.

Secondly, the hypothalamic-pituitary-adrenal (HPA) axis responds in a slower way to stress. It begins with the release of corticotropin-releasing hormone (CRH) from the hypothalamus. CRH stimulates the pituitary to release adrenocorticotropic hormone (ACTH), which stimulates the adrenal gland to produce glucocorticoids, such as cortisol. Glucocorticoids, which maintain the stress response, have complex effects on metabolism, generally leading to the breakdown of fat and muscle to produce glucose. Glucocorticoids also suppress the activity of insulin, again causing glucose levels to increase. Like adrenaline and noradrenaline, glucocorticoids can cause heightened alertness and anxiety. At sufficient levels they also inhibit the autonomic response to stress by suppressing the production of adrenaline and noradrenaline. Other parts of the brain secrete CRH. The CRH secreted by the amygdala is especially important in terms of suppressing the autonomic fight-or-flight response (Herman et al., 2016).

The amygdala

The amygdalae are a pair of almond-shaped bodies within the temporal lobes of the brain (amygdala means "almond" in Greek). It is part of the limbic system, which processes emotions, and is a complex body with multiple nuclei and subnuclei. The amygdala has an important role in the processing of emotions, as well as in memory, emotional learning, and decision-making based on emotional salience. To describe its role in simplified, anthropomorphic terms, the amygdala "decides" what actions to take based on their emotions and "chooses" what to remember as well as the feelings associated with those memories. The amygdala has an important role in what are called "flashbulb memories," the vivid and highly detailed recollections associated with traumatic events, as if traumatic scenes were illuminated and recorded by the flash of a camera bulb (Khan and Messiri, 2025). In Derrick's case, the shattered glass was a tactile form of a flashbulb memory, initiated by his most recent and comparatively minor trauma.

Prefrontal cortex

The prefrontal cortex has an important role in trauma regulation and recovery. The prefrontal cortex suppresses the trauma response in a top-down manner. It is closely connected to both the amygdala and the hypothalamus but also to the parts of the brain directly involved with language and awareness. Again, speaking simplistically and anthropomorphically, one might say that after acute trauma, the prefrontal cortex says to the rest of the body, “We’re safe now. The danger is gone, and people we love are around us. You can let down your guard.”

After a trauma, the brain exhibits conditioned responses. After a motor vehicle crash, for instance, a trauma survivor may avoid the street or intersection where the accident occurred. That response may then generalize, and the person may avoid driving altogether. The prefrontal cortex dampens those conditioned responses, assessing the reality of the current danger and the appropriate level of response.

Other modulating factors

The neurobiology of the trauma response is very complex and involves other hormones, including thyroid hormone, oxytocin, and growth hormone. Oxytocin is particularly interesting because it is the hormone associated with social bonding and feelings of affiliation. Clinically, we know that some individuals respond to trauma by seeking solitude while others seek support and solace from others. These response patterns may correlate with baseline oxytocin levels (Herman et al., 2016; Rahmani et al., 2022).

Neural networks

The emergence of functional imaging technology like functional magnetic resonance imaging (fMRI) has enhanced our understanding of the brain’s response to trauma. Neural networks are complex webs of neurons that are activated as a group in certain brain states. The important networks involved in the brain’s trauma response are the default mode network (DMN), the external control network (ECN), and the salience network (SN). When the brain is “at rest,” with no tasks to attend to, the DMN becomes activated and is involved in daydreaming, creativity, and the formation of autobiographical memories. After a stressful event, the DMN shows less connectivity with other brain regions and can become overactive and associated with ruminations. The SN relates to vigilance and activates the ECN, which attends to tasks and activities (Duval et al., 2015). When the DMN is "stuck" in a pattern of ruminations, the brain has a difficult time attending to other tasks.

Treatment and the brain

Since trauma leaves its imprints on the brain, perhaps so does treatment. Finding proven markers for therapy-related brain changes has been a long-standing goal for neuroscientists (Gabbard, 2000), one that has been only partially realized (Manthey et al., 2021; Schumacher et al., 2018). For instance, pharmacological treatment for posttraumatic stress disorder (PTSD) and anxiety has been shown to normalize the functioning of the HPA axis (Tafet & Nemeroff, 2020), so psychotherapeutic interventions are presumed to do the same, although this has been difficult to demonstrate. In addition, the study of neural networks in trauma recovery has shown promising results, including increased DMN connectivity after effective psychotherapy (Schlumpf et al., 2019). Mindfulness training in particular has been shown to increase DMN connectivity (Boyd et al., 2018).

Sleep physiology and trauma

Sleep is not simply a state of rest but a complex process of coordination between multiple areas of the brain. For sleep to occur, brain vigilance must be reduced, wakefulness must be suppressed, and drowsiness must occur. Anxiety, hypervigilance, intrusive thoughts, and nightmares are a hallmark of the response to trauma. Furthermore, sleep symptoms like insomnia and nightmares are diagnostic features of the chronic sequelae of trauma like PTSD.

Sleep disturbance at the time of trauma is predictive of poor outcomes on the development of PTSD (Neylan et al., 2021). The precise brain mechanisms that mediate poor sleep after acute trauma are not well understood. Sleep reactivity is important as it predicts vulnerability to insomnia after an acute stressor occurs. The trait of sleep reactivity may be a marker of a vulnerable brain system that is prone to failure and disorganization in response to an acute stressor. The vulnerability of the system in combination with the severity of the stress may lead to an asymptomatic stress response of insomnia in response to trauma (Kalmbach et al., 2018).

Acute trauma may cause unique sleep issues. Trauma-associated sleep disorder has been proposed as a parasomnia. Besides nightmares, it includes behavioral issues like thrashing and tossing, rapid eye movement (REM) sleep without atonia, and dream enactments like vocalizations. These observations, if validated, suggest disturbances in multiple areas of sleep physiology (Swift et al., 2022).

Sleep has an important but poorly understood role in the processing of acute trauma. Some of the prefrontal cognitive processing that underlies trauma recovery, like the retention of safety memories and the extinction of overgeneralized fear responses are enhanced by sleep (Pace-Schott et al., 2015). REM sleep may have a specific role in trauma processing, especially in the development of new semantic associations, which may facilitate the processing of the internal trauma narrative (Cai et al., 2009). REM sleep will be discussed in more detail in Chapter 8, Understanding and Treating Nightmares, when nightmares are explored.

Complex trauma

Complex trauma, the focus of Chapter 4, appreciating the impact of complex trauma, affects, on a neuronal level the trauma networks of the brain. This is especially true in childhood trauma. Brain trauma networks may have a critical period where trauma exposure has a major impact on trauma processing mechanisms. Chronic stress reduces connectivity between the prefrontal cortex, amygdala, and hippocampus, causing dysfunction across the trauma processing system (Cerqueira et al., 2007). Fear responses become difficult to modulate because the prefrontal cortex is unable to integrate new learning and use it to modify existing fear responses (Acheson et al., 2012). With childhood trauma the HPA axis is upregulated, resulting in future vulnerability to stress (Tarullo & Gunnar, 2006). The brain is designed to process and integrate trauma, but in limited doses.

The neurobiologically based trauma narrative

Our knowledge of neurobiology, although incomplete, allows us to construct a narrative of the experience of trauma based in neuroscience. The experience of trauma is ubiquitous, and the brain is designed to handle and process it. Trauma activates the danger centers of the brain. We go on "high alert" with the activation of the sympathetic nervous system. Soon (after about 10 minutes), the slower HPA axis is activated, which both dampens the activity of the sympathetic nervous system and prepares the organism for a longer-term stress response by initiating a catabolic state of muscle breakdown and glucose release. Eventually, we begin to recover, and with input from the prefrontal cortex the trauma response subsides. In this case the response to trauma is entirely adaptive.

Sometimes the response to trauma becomes maladaptive. In severe extended trauma, for instance, the prefrontal cortex can never realistically coach the amygdala and HPA axis that the situation is now safe. In Man's Search for Meaning, Viktor Frankl (1959) tells a powerful story related to his concentration camp experiences (Frankl, 1959). A fellow prisoner was having a nightmare, screaming and crying in his sleep. Frankl's inclination was to awaken and reassure him, but then he realized that the world he would awaken to was just as nightmarish as his dream; there was no point in awakening him. In such situations, the prefrontal cortex can never send that "all clear" message. The only solution is to "wall off" the trauma, which sometimes involves walling off the emotional aspects of the human experience. Many survivors left the camps silent, emotionally numb, and withdrawn. This response produces the affective numbing and social withdrawal seen in PTSD, and it can be well described in terms of brain function, as the DMN is narrower in its range of brain connectivity than prior to the trauma.

In other cases, the acute autonomic response never shuts down. The person remains on high alert, anxious, hypervigilant, watchful, and avoidant. This anxious state does not lend itself to sleep; in acute danger the organism stays awake to protect itself, and emotions and memories are inadequately processed. The SN sees danger everywhere, and the DMN is never able to construct an autobiographical narrative that allows for trauma processing.

Part of the value of the neurobiologically based trauma narrative is that it provides a shared language that deepens both the patient's and the clinician's understanding of the trauma response. It provides a shared language and deepens empathy, especially the empathy the trauma survivor has regarding their own trauma responses. Acceptance and understanding are the first steps toward healing and growth.

Derrick's surprising emotional response

Derrick had a history of chronic trauma exposure. He had probably walled off these recurrent experiences, storing them somewhere outside of his awareness so that he felt they had no ill effects upon him. When he was safe, his prefrontal cortex reminded him for several years that there was no need for the constant vigilance that was so protective in his younger years. Then suddenly he faced a new trauma, admittedly minor compared to his old traumas but symbolically important because it was so unexpected. There was no way to prepare for it, no weapons or friends that could have protected him. The odd tactile detail of the shards of broken glass was important. We might imagine that that sensation, involving a sensory modality other than vision and hearing, somehow bypassed the protective walls built around his past traumas and reopened them. The novel minor trauma invoked profound forgotten major trauma and became major trauma because it reopened a world of unprocessed trauma. The part became the whole.

Treatment described in neurobiological language

Pharmacological treatments are designed to suppress the persistent acute autonomic response and potentially normalize the functioning of the HPA axis. Psychotherapy engages the internal coach and strengthens the top-down suppression provided by the prefrontal cortex. It allows the DMN to integrate traumatic memories into a broader associative network and construct an autobiography that includes the trauma and frames it in a meaningful context.

Psychotherapeutic intervention in acute care settings involves both direct anxiety reduction through techniques such as centering and relaxation and by encoding the trauma in a narrative framework.

Understanding the neurobiological model can itself be therapeutic. We explained the neurobiological model to Derrick, and he understood the mechanisms behind the brain's responses to trauma; he was less embarrassed about his traumatic response. His emotional reaction was destigmatized. He could readily accept the idea that his present traumatic response was related to his prior traumas. Instead of being frustrated at his "silly" response to minor trauma, he could begin the painful work of facing his prior traumas. Although the neurobiological model as we have described it is an oversimplification, it provides a model that both the clinician and trauma survivor can believe in. In that way, the model itself contributes to the therapeutic process and directly informs biopsychosocial case conceptualizations.

Chapter summary

Our expanding knowledge of neurophysiology has deepened our understanding of the trauma response. Subcortical responses from the HPA axis, especially the amygdala, are modulated by cortical input from the prefrontal cortex. The neurophysiological model provides a narrative for the trauma survivor that destigmatizes the trauma response and aids in trauma processing. Psychotherapy can be viewed as a kind of brain training that facilitates healing.

References

Acheson, D. T., Gresack, J. E., & Risbrough, V. B. (2012). Hippocampal dysfunction effects on context memory: Possible etiology for posttraumatic stress disorder. *Neuropharmacology, 62*(2), 674–685. https://doi.org/10.1016/j.neuropharm.2011.04.029.

Boyd, J. E., Lanius, R. A., & McKinnon, M. C. (2018). Mindfulness-based treatments for posttraumatic stress disorder: A review of the treatment literature and neurobiological evidence. *Journal of Psychiatry and Neuroscience, 43*(1), 7–25. https://doi.org/10.1503/jpn.170021.

Cai, D. J., Mednick, S. A., Harrison, E. M., Kanady, J. C., & Mednick, S. C. (2009). REM, not incubation, improves creativity by priming associative networks. *Proceedings of the National Academy of Sciences of the United States of America, 106*(25), 10130–10134. https://doi.org/10.1073/pnas.0900271106.

Cerqueira, J. J., Mailliet, F., Almeida, O. F. X., Jay, T. M., & Sousa, N. (2007). The prefrontal cortex as a key target of the maladaptive response to stress. *Journal of Neuroscience, 27*(11), 2781–2787. https://doi.org/10.1523/JNEUROSCI.4372-06.2007.

Duval, E. R., Javanbakht, A., & Liberzon, I. (2015). Neural circuits in anxiety and stress disorders: A focused review. *Therapeutics and clinical risk management, 11*, 115–126. https://doi.org/10.2147/TCRM.S48528.

Frankl, V. (1959). *Man's search for meaning*. Beacon Press.

Gabbard, G. O. (2000). A neurobiologically informed perspective on psychotherapy. *British Journal of Psychiatry, 177*, 117–122. https://doi.org/10.1192/bjp.177.2.117.

Herman, J. P., McKlveen, J. M., Ghosal, S., Kopp, B., Wulsin, A., Makinson, R., Scheimann, J., & Myers, B. (2016). Regulation of the hypothalamic-pituitary- adrenocortical stress response. *Comprehensive Physiology, 6*(2), 603–621. https://doi.org/10.1002/cphy.c150015.

Kalmbach, D. A., Anderson, J. R., & Drake, C. L. (2018). The impact of stress on sleep: Pathogenic sleep reactivity as a vulnerability to insomnia and circadian disorders. *Journal of Sleep Research, 27*(6). https://doi.org/10.1111/jsr.12710.

Khan, Z., Messiri, N. E., Iqbal, E., Hassan, H., Tanweer, M. S., Sadia, S. R., Taj, M., Zaidi, U., Yusuf, K., Syed, N. I., & Zaidi, M. (2025). On the role of epigenetic modifications of HPA axis in posttraumatic stress disorder and resilience. *Journal of Neurophysiology, 133*(3), 742–759. https://doi.org/10.1152/jn.00345.2024.

Manthey, A., Sierk, A., Brakemeier, E. L., Walter, H., & Daniels, J. K. (2021). Does trauma-focused psychotherapy change the brain? A systematic review of neural correlates of therapeutic gains in PTSD. European Journal of Psychotraumatology, *12*(1). https://doi.org/10.1080/20008198.2021.1929025.

Neylan, T. C., Kessler, R. C., Ressler, K. J., Clifford, G., Beaudoin, F. L., An, X., Stevens, J. S., Zeng, D., Linnstaedt, S. D., Germine, L. T., Sheikh, S., Storrow, A. B., Punches, B. E., Mohiuddin, K., Gentile, N. T., McGrath, M. E., Van Rooij, S. J. H., Haran, J. P., Peak, D. A., ... McLean, S. A. (2021). Prior sleep problems and adverse post-traumatic neuropsychiatric sequelae of motor vehicle collision in the AURORA study. *Sleep, 44*(3). https://doi.org/10.1093/sleep/zsaa200.

Pace-Schott, E. F., Germain, A., & Milad, M. R. (2015). Sleep and REM sleep disturbance in the pathophysiology of PTSD: The role of extinction memory. *Biology of Mood and Anxiety Disorders, 5*(1). https://doi.org/10.1186/s13587-015-0018-9.

Rahmani, E., Lemelle, T., Sharp, H., Smarbafzadeh, E., & Kablinger, A. (2022). A descriptive analysis of pharmacological management of aggression and/or agitation in patients with traumatic brain injury in a Southwest Virginia inpatient population. *Journal of Clinical Pharmacy and Therapeutics, 47*(12), 2083–2090. https://doi.org/10.1111/jcpt.13754.

Schlumpf, Y. R., Nijenhuis, E. R. S., Klein, C., Jäncke, L., & Bachmann, S. (2019). Functional reorganization of neural networks involved in emotion regulation following trauma therapy for complex trauma disorders. *NeuroImage: Clinical, 23*. https://doi.org/10.1016/j.nicl.2019.101807.

Schumacher, S., Niemeyer, H., Engel, S., Cwik, J. C., & Knaevelsrud, C. (2018). Psychotherapeutic treatment and HPA axis regulation in posttraumatic stress disorder: A systematic review and meta-analysis. *Psychoneuroendocrinology, 98*, 186–201. https://doi.org/10.1016/j.psyneuen.2018.08.006.

Swift, K. M., Thomas, C. L., Balkin, T. J., Lowery-Gionta, E. G., & Matson, L. M. (2022). Acute sleep interventions as an avenue for treatment of trauma-associated disorders. *Journal of Clinical Sleep Medicine, 18*(9), 2291–2312. https://doi.org/10.5664/jcsm.10074.

Tafet, G. E., & Nemeroff, C. B. (2020). Pharmacological treatment of anxiety disorders: The role of the HPA axis. Frontiers in Psychiatry, *11*. https://doi.org/10.3389/fpsyt.2020.00443.

Tarullo, A. R., & Gunnar, M. R. (2006). Child maltreatment and the developing HPA axis. *Hormones and Behavior, 50*(4), 632–639. https://doi.org/10.1016/j.yhbeh.2006.06.010.

Chapter 4

Appreciating the impact of complex trauma

Gina's Story

Gina was exposed to significant childhood trauma, including regular exposure to adverse childhood experiences. Her father, a frequent misuser of alcohol, physically abused her from the age of 4 until 12, when he left the family. Gina's mother, the person whom she looked to for support, ignored the abuse and was also neglectful of Gina. Gina left home at 17 and moved in with an older boyfriend whom she had only briefly known. Gina's boyfriend also frequently misused alcohol, and after a few months, he became physically abusive as well. After two years of enduring his abuse she left the relationship and quickly married a man who seemed to Gina to be different and genuinely caring. Soon after the marriage, he accused Gina of infidelity and assaulted her, resulting in both a fractured rib and clavicle. We worked with Gina during her hospitalization and then after discharge. Gina described that she was disgusted with herself and felt she was a failure. She would say, "I'll always end up being abused by someone. I'm good for nothing, I deserve it." Her family provided little or no support.

Acute trauma in the context of complex trauma

When meeting with a trauma survivor in the context of an acute traumatic event, it is natural to focus on the recent event and not the prior trauma history. Good screening and assessment tools, as discussed in Chapters 5 and 20, will facilitate a richer consideration of the overall context of trauma in the survivor's life. For those experiencing acute trauma in the context of complex trauma it can seem that trauma never ends, and there is no safety or solace.

We have described some of the existential challenges to the sense of self, meaning, and identity that can occur in acute trauma. Such issues are heightened when acute trauma impacts a patient with a history of complex trauma. In those cases, a sense of self-worth and self-efficacy are already damaged. For a healthy individual, exposure to acute trauma challenges the sense of identity and purpose; for the complex trauma patient, the acute trauma confirms an already existing sense of emptiness and purposelessness.

The Psychology of Acute Trauma. DOI: https://doi.org/10.1016/B978-0-443-33212-8.00003-8

Clinical features of complex trauma

While not officially included as a disorder in the Diagnostic and Statistical Manual of Mental Disorders, Fifth Edition, Text Revision (DSM-5-TR) (American Psychiatric Association, 2022), complex posttraumatic stress disorder (CPTSD) was recognized as a distinct diagnostic category in 2022 by the World Health Organization (World Health Organization, 2019). CPTSD is distinguished from posttraumatic stress disorder (PTSD) by the presence of notable emotional dysregulation, negative self-cognitions, and interpersonal difficulties. Complex trauma can occur when there are repeated and inescapable traumatic events that deeply affect personality, relational capacity, and sense of self. Complex trauma usually occurs in the context of a close interpersonal relationship, like that between a parent and child, as seen with Gina. Complex trauma typically, but not always, involves adverse childhood experiences like neglect and abuse. Furthermore, exposure to adverse childhood experiences has been shown to be positively related to more severe CPTSD symptoms in adulthood (Zhang et al., 2021). Situations in adulthood where complex trauma can occur include forced captivity, human trafficking, or ongoing intimate partner violence. Nosologically, CPTSD can be considered as part of a spectrum of trauma-related disorders. In addition to CPTSD, borderline personality disorder and PTSD can be considered to exist on this spectrum of disorders based on the degree of personality involvement, with borderline personality disorder exhibiting the most personality involvement and PTSD the least (Giourou et al., 2018). Because of the chronic nature of the trauma inherent to CPTSD, as well as its typical occurrence in childhood, it has more of an impact on personality than PTSD. Oftentimes, the traumatic events, leading to noncomplex PTSD occur in adulthood when personality is more stably formed and after exposure to a single traumatic experience.

Diagnostically, it is helpful to consider the possibility of CPTSD in patients with a history of childhood trauma or sustained and repeated exposure to trauma in adulthood. When acute trauma occurs in the context of CPTSD, psychotherapeutic techniques can be modified to address the special issues faced by the individual experiencing CPTSD. Potential modifications should include:

1 The patient is more likely to require long-term treatment and support. Due to this, short-term approaches used within acute care medical settings should include early discussions related to the expectations regarding acute care as well as the likelihood that outpatient services will be needed after discharge, oftentimes with a different clinician.
2 The patient will likely have difficulties in developing trust. These difficulties related to trust and perceived abandonment are important to consider when approaching the treatment planning process. Slow and thoughtful approaches to care aimed at fostering a sense of autonomy are

important. The complex trauma patient is likely to view their acute care clinician as a representative of all professionals associated with their specialty. A rupture in the therapeutic relationship at this stage in treatment may prevent the individual experiencing CPTSD from seeking care in the future.

3 Disruptions in the therapeutic relationship, especially loss of trust, are more likely to occur. If this loss of trust does occur, it is important to make space for the survivor to explore the experience in a nonjudgmental manner, if they are amenable. If the patient declines interest in the therapeutic exploration of the rupture, the clinician may suggest less intense "social" follow-up visits, with the patient's permission. These visits may be as brief as a few minutes and are conducted primarily to show genuine caring and to demonstrate that the clinician will be there "on good days and bad" without abandonment. For many survivors experiencing CPTSD or borderline personality disorder, relationships are intense, and self-preservation mechanisms such as pushing away those close to them may prevent the pain of abandonment. When the clinician shows they are there for the survivor "no matter what," true therapeutic progress may become possible.

Preemptive psychoeducational interventions, including basic therapeutic skills, may be of benefit. Preemptive interventions might include those emphasizing basic emotional identification skills, validation and normalization of the survivor's experience, and the early integration of acceptance-based skills. If possible, cognitive behavioral therapy skills, integrating thought records (see Appendix) and rational responding, may be helpful. Preemptive statements like, "Because of all the things you've been through, you are likely to feel discouraged sometimes and want to give up. Sometimes, the more we struggle with our dislike of the situation, the more we get stuck in those thoughts. Accepting doesn't mean that we like what happened, or that we are happy with the outcome. It just means that we understand it did happen, and that gives us the space to let go so we can focus on living." may be helpful in reducing ruminative distress while setting appropriate expectations related to the emotional responses that are common following exposure to trauma. Additional therapeutic approaches are discussed at length in Chapter 6, Psychological Interventions for Hospitalized Trauma Patients.

The trauma experience in complex posttraumatic stress disorder

According to trauma theorists like Peter Walker, complex trauma may be considered a type of attachment disorder (Walker, 2013). In the typical complex trauma scenario, childhood abuse and neglect precludes the formation of stable attachment bonds with parenting figures. The abusive or neglectful parent is too dangerous to bond with. If the other parent is not abusive, bonding may still be difficult because of the outrage of feeling not loved enough to be protected. Acute trauma raises questions like "Do I matter?" and "Am I loved?" as well as "How could this happen?" While those questions are difficult to answer for anyone after a serious acute trauma, for a complex trauma, patient, the answers are even more difficult to come by. They lack the prior context of a loving relationship; meaning is more difficult to find when one has never felt loved. The new trauma is more likely to be faced with passivity and despair rather than outrage. The new trauma is "more of the same" rather than a violent, unexpected intrusion.

To compensate for the attachment deficits in CPTSD Walker (2013) suggests an emphasis on four key aspects of the therapeutic relationship. These are empathy, authentic vulnerability, dialogicality and a collaborative relationship repair. Rigidly scripted therapies, like cognitive behavioral therapy, can be perceived by CPSTD patients as lacking in empathy. Kohut defines empathy as "vicarious introspection" (Kohut, 2011). Empathy is conveyed by careful listening and thought exploration, and is deepened by techniques like mirroring and paraphrasing. Authentic vulnerability, according to Walker (2013), involves being comfortable enough as a clinician to reflect emotions and even to reveal, when appropriate, one's own emotions. Modeling vulnerability for the patient can be therapeutic in and of itself because individuals experiencing CPTSD are rarely comfortable with feelings of vulnerability. Dialogicality refers to the normal give and take of speaking and listening. Individuals experiencing CPTSD are often accustomed to one-sided "monological" conversations where their listening is exploited by the monologues of a narcissist. They must unlearn such maladaptive patterns and learn to speak with the expectation of being listened to. Collaborative relationship repair refers to the genuine closeness that develops when interpersonal disagreements and conflicts are resolved through discussion and collaboration. In collaborative relationship repair, the minor conflicts and disappointments that occur in any relationship, including the therapeutic relationship, can be used for building trust.

Walker's (2013) techniques, though designed for the long-term outpatient setting, are simple and natural enough to apply to the acute care trauma setting in the treatment of acute trauma patients experiencing CPTSD.

Transgenerational trauma

Transgenerational trauma, though distinct from CPTSD, shares some clinical features with CPTSD. Transgenerational trauma refers to the emotional impacts of trauma on the next generation. The children of Holocaust survivors, for instance, though they were not personally impacted by the index trauma, may grow up with traits of affective blunting and relational difficulties. Transgenerational trauma is distinguished from complex trauma because direct exposure to trauma was not involved, and distinguished from vicarious trauma in that the trauma was not directly witnessed (Salberg & Grand, 2024).

Significant segments of the population are transgenerational trauma survivors, including groups that are at high risk for exposure to acute trauma. Black Americans, for instance, are victims of transgenerational trauma, beginning with the experience of slavery and then generations of racism and discrimination. Some immigrant subgroups also have exposure to transgenerational trauma and have emigrated to the US because of chronic persecution in their countries of origin.

How is transgenerational trauma transmitted to the next generation? Part of the mechanism is likely to be through the attachment difficulties of the parent who experienced the trauma. For the trauma survivor, attachment and parenting are often difficult and conflictual. The traumatized parent wants to love their child but struggles with the intimacy and the emotional give and take that parenting requires. The trauma is perpetuated and becomes transgenerational because the attachment is uncertain and conflictual. Also, the child of the trauma survivor is heir to a trauma narrative. By words and actions, they are taught that the world is dangerous and uncertain, love is fleeting, and anything and everything can be taken away at any time. Finally, transmission may occur genetically, through epigenetic changes in the DNA of the trauma survivor.

Responses to acute trauma in the survivor affected by transgenerational trauma resemble those of the survivor experiencing complex trauma, and require the same attention to empathy, authentic vulnerability, dialogicality, and a collaborative relationship repair that are required in the CPTSD patient.

Caregiver issues in complex posttraumatic stress disorder with acute trauma

Survivors of acute trauma experiencing CPTSD present special challenges and opportunities for both professional and family caregivers in the management of acute trauma. Some common issues are as follows.

1. Family support is often lacking, or if present, is conflictual. The family structures that led to abuse or neglect in childhood are usually still present when an acute traumatic event occurs in adulthood. Support is given reluctantly or conflictually, and the trauma survivor feels that any help from family has "strings attached."
2. Professional caregivers are often viewed suspiciously by the complex trauma survivor. They fear and expect both abandonment and poor care. They may experience preemptive anger in expectation of poor care and create a situation where care is difficult to provide because of excessive angry demands, creating a self-fulfilling prophecy of abandonment.
3. The emotional distress associated with complex trauma is often experienced somatically, so the individual experiencing complex trauma may have

increased reports of pain and bodily distress. Medications become a symbolic substitute for emotional connection, so such patients may present as "drug-seeking." Paradoxically, because their expressions of distress can seem exaggerated, complaints of pain or anxiety in the individual experiencing complex trauma are more likely to be ignored, so they may get less care and comfort.

4 Caregivers may be alternately idealized and devalued. One minute they, might be greeted with tears of gratitude, minutes later, they might be screamed at. Mistrust, fears of abandonment, and emotional isolation drive these storms of affect, which can be overwhelming both for the caregiver and for the trauma survivor.

5 Sometimes the vivid expressions of distress shown by the complex trauma patient can lead some caregivers to try to "rescue" the complex trauma patient by bending milieu rules and policies or pharmacologically over-treating emotional distress. In the end, such attempts at rescue often lead to poor care.

6 The devaluation and idealization may be personalized, so that some staff may be seen as terrible and others as wonderful. This behavior is sometimes described as "splitting." It is important for the treatment team to be aware of this tendency and to act and speak in a coordinated and consistent manner, sometimes using a single spokesperson for the team as a whole. Staff must be attentive to limits and boundaries and speak with one voice about issues like pain medications and milieu rules.

7 Self-report may be distorted in patients experiencing complex trauma. Such patients often don't trust that they will get the help they need, so they amplify symptoms in the hope of getting help and support. Instead, they may get inappropriate care. For instance, they may report high levels of depression and suicidality when they are not actually suicidal, expecting more empathy. Instead, they are placed on suicide precautions and are further isolated from support as they must give up phones and be confined to their rooms.

8 While the Trauma and Acute Care Surgical Psychology (TACS Psych) service will necessarily be focused on the most recent trauma, the complex trauma patient may express distress related to multiple past traumas at the same time. For the survivor, these multiple traumatic events are all related; for example, the recent acute trauma may cause them to remember and relive childhood abuse. This may give the false impression to the treatment team that the current acute trauma is less distressing than it actually is; the team might feel that the current trauma must not be so bad if the patient keeps focusing on other traumas. For the individual impacted by complex trauma all of the traumas are often experienced as one unending traumatic event.

The behavioral and milieu issues seen with patients affected by complex trauma are akin to those observed in patients experiencing borderline personality disorder. These disorders, as we have seen, are both conceptualized to exist on the trauma-related disorder spectrum along with PTSD. Clinically, patients often meet criteria for both diagnoses. The diagnosis of CPTSD, however, is less stigmatizing than that of borderline personality disorder because it emphasizes the relationship between the behavioral concerns and the traumatic experiences. When the diagnosis of borderline personality disorder is emphasized, the behavioral concerns are more likely to be seen as volitional and/or characterological, and this diagnosis can interfere with care by making empathy and caring seem futile. Despite the challenges, empathy and caregiving are the cornerstones of the treatment of the survivor affected by complex trauma. Empathy, tempered by wisdom and clear boundaries, yields good results in the care of the complex trauma patient who has sustained an acute injury.

Pharmacological intervention in the acute trauma patient with complex posttraumatic stress disorder

For many patients, medications are a tangible, concrete symbol of caring. For the CPTSD patients grappling with issues of mistrust and abandonment, this symbolic connection between medication and caring is even stronger. The prescribing clinician often feels caught in a trap, facing an acute trauma patient with CPTSD who is in distress. Not treating will be experienced by the patient as a lack of caring and empathy, but to offer pharmacological treatment is to enact a rescue fantasy with medications that may not be appropriate. A complex middle ground is the best strategy, using medication appropriately but still conveying caring and empathy. It is important to base medication decisions as much as possible on observable objective findings on labs, imaging, or physical exam rather than just patient self-report. This is especially challenging when treating pain, which is intrinsically based on subjective self-report. The prescriber must be aware of and balance internal issues of genuine empathy, rescue fantasies, and fear of an angry response from the patient. Prescribers can react to "med-seeking" behavior with anger or frustration, mistrusting all self-reports from the patient and ultimately under-treating pain. There are no simple formulas to manage these challenging situations. Self-reflection can help the clinician make thoughtful, ethical, and caring decisions.

Gina's Hospitalization

Following her admission, Gina was initially very isolative and withdrawn. Her mother visited and, at first, seemed very supportive. She frequently engaged members of the care team and told staff at length about Gina's problems and previous difficulties. One night Gina, and her mother had a shouting match. Gina was heard to scream, "You hate me," to her mother, after which her mother left and never visited again.

(Continued)

Gina demanded increased pain medication that night. Her request was refused, and Gina demanded to see the night manager. In her frustration, Gina voiced suicidal feelings. She was placed on suicide precautions, and then became enraged that she had lost her phone and had to have a one-to-one observer in her room. "No one is listening to me!" Gina screamed.

Eventually, the overnight surgical resident became involved, and to rapidly de-escalate the situation, they ordered a one-time 2 mg dose of lorazepam. The TACS Psych team assessed the patient the next day, discontinued suicide precautions, and negotiated strategies for the appropriate expression of distress.

Over the next few days, Gina demanded more lorazepam. She continued to complain that "no one cares about me." The TACS Psych team met regularly with the surgical and nursing staff as well as the patient. Hydroxyzine was started instead of lorazepam. Nursing developed a plan to provide consistent staff members whenever possible. The TACS Psych team saw her daily to reinforce coping skills and provide consistent support and psychoeducation. The primary Trauma and Acute Care Surgery service became the spokesperson for all medical and surgical decisions. With a firm but supportive milieu structure, Gina became less angry and more pleasant and interactive. As she recovered physically, her distress diminished. A warm handoff was made to the outpatient trauma recovery center team. She left the hospital expressing gratitude to the treatment team.

Chapter summary

This chapter describes common issues in treating the individual experiencing CPTSD with acute trauma. Such patients present special opportunities for providing good trauma informed care to a population with special needs and issues. The internal experiences of the CPTSD patient are described, especially mistrust and fear of abandonment. Those special issues require that clinicians pay focused attention to empathy in the acute care setting. Recommendations to both clinicians and members of the patient's support network are provided.

References

American Psychiatric Association (2022). *Diagnostic and Statistical Manual of Mental Disorders* (5th ed., text rev.). American Psychiatric Association Publishing. http://doi.org/10.1176/appi.books.9780890425787 .

Giourou, E., Skokou, M., Andrew, S. P., Alexopoulou, K., Gourzis, P., & Jelastopulu, E. (2018). Complex posttraumatic stress disorder: The need to consolidate a distinct clinical syndrome or to reevaluate features of psychiatric disorders following interpersonal trauma? *World Journal of Psychiatry, 8*(1), 12–19. https://doi.org/10.5498/wjp.v8.i1.12.

Kohut, H. (2011). *Search for the self: Selected writings of Heinz Kohut: 1950–1978*. Routledge.

Salberg, J., & Grand, S. (2024). *Transgenerational trauma: A contemporary introduction*. Routledge. http://doi.org/10.4324/9781003087762.

Walker, P. (2013). *Complex PTSD: From surviving to thriving*. CreateSpace Independent Publisher.

World Health Organization, International Classification of Diseases, Eleventh Revision (ICD-11). (2019), Available from: https://icd.who.int/browse11.

Zhang, L., Ma, X., Yu, X., Ye, M., Li, N., Lu, S., & Wang, J. (2021). Childhood trauma and psychological distress: A serial mediation model among chinese adolescents. *International Journal of Environmental Research and Public Health, 18*(13). https://doi.org/10.3390/ijerph18136808.

Chapter 5

The psychology of acute trauma: assessment and case conceptualization

Javon and David's Stories

Javon and David, both 17-year-old males raised in an underresourced urban environment in the midwestern United States, stopped at a neighborhood block party. As the evening progressed, a fight broke out between two different groups of boys. One of the boys brandished a pistol and leaped into a nearby car, firing as it sped off. Javon and David were standing next to each other and suffered similar injuries. The moving line of fire was at chest level, and multiple gunshot wounds caused spinal cord injuries resulting in paralysis at the T4 level in both boys. Neither would ever walk again, but Javon and David had very different psychological responses to their injuries, and very different trajectories of recovery.

The internal experience of trauma

An understanding of the internal experience of trauma guides the assessment, conceptualization, and ultimately treatment of the patient with acute trauma. Because effective care might prevent posttraumatic psychopathology, it is important to understand the conceptual models that describe the psychological impacts of acute trauma. Some models are theoretical, some are empirically based, but all are important. Conceptual understandings help guide our earliest interventions, support our feelings of empathy, and foster the development of a supportive therapeutic relationship.

One theoretical conceptualization is Mardi Horowitz's (1986) five-stage model of response to a sudden serious traumatic event (Horowitz, 1986). Stage 1 is the outcry, or the immediate feelings of confusion and distress. After outcry comes denial and numbness (Stage 2), then intrusive repetition (Stage 3), working through (Stage 4), and finally completion and integration (Stage 5). Progression through the stages is nonlinear, and individuals may oscillate between stages. In fact, significant differences in response occur between

The Psychology of Acute Trauma. DOI: https://doi.org/10.1016/B978-0-443-33212-8.00022-1

individuals, and progression through the five stages is based on history, genetics, and prior response habits.

Acute trauma can also include a foreshortened sense of the future, loss of hope, and a change in the internal expected life narrative. Trauma survivors may feel that they will fail to attain usual life milestones, such as work, school, and family, or feel that they may lose those achievements if they have already attained them.

Initial emotional responses can include sadness, agitation, anxiety, and numbness. Unless complicated by issues like delirium or functional impairment, such experiences are considered common nonpathological responses to an abnormal and highly stressful situation. Emotions after trauma can be powerful and feel overwhelming, leading to defensive responses such as denial, which refers to not accepting, on a conscious level, emotional or empirical realities, and isolation of affect, which refers to the defense mechanism of putting feelings in a box and pretending they don't exist. Both denial and isolation of affect are examples of avoidance-based coping mechanisms.

Narrative theory and the "full" story

Narrative theory can be a useful tool for understanding some aspects of coping with trauma. One way trauma is integrated is through narrative. Narrative is the structure, the story with which we frame our experiences, especially our traumatic ones (Mahr et al., 2025).

Arthur W. Frank (1995), a prominent medical sociologist at the University of Calgary, described three types of narratives that patients, families, and care providers tell themselves: Chaos, restitution, and quest (Frank, 1995). The chaos narrative describes the confusion, fear, and doubt that occurs early in the trauma recovery process. The restitution narrative involves a full recovery and return to life as it was prior to the trauma. A minor accident, a fall, or a simple fracture can be framed as a restitution narrative when a full recovery is expected. Television commercials for health care products are often mini restitution narratives: The man in the antidepressant commercial wrings his hands and looks depressed, then takes the latest antidepressant. In the next scene, he is happily walking along the beach with his family. All is well, for all time. In cases like Javon and David's, however, full restitution is not possible; nothing will be the same as it was. To insist on a restitution narrative requires denial and avoidance and creates incomplete narratives that do not include the information necessary for full emotional processing.

The quest narrative begins with acceptance-informed hope and then involves the gradual development of a new life narrative that incorporates the trauma and its effects. A quest narrative facilitates recovery and can lead to posttraumatic growth.

Resilience

Resilience refers to the ability to adapt and recover from trauma and other adversity. Resilience has characterological and genetic components but is also influenced by environment and culture (Maul et al., 2020). Resilience tends to be protective against the adverse emotional consequences of trauma, and an assessment of resilience can be an important component of the trauma evaluation.

Hope and acceptance

Hope is the expectation of a better future. Hope can be difficult to maintain after the shock of acute trauma, but it is associated with resilience and posttraumatic growth. Loss of hope leads to avoidance-based coping and is correlated with helplessness, depression, suicidality, and posttraumatic stress disorder (PTSD) (Gallagher & Lopez, 2018).

Avoidance-based coping can masquerade as hope. When a trauma survivor or, more commonly, a family member, insists that "everything is going to be all right," they may not be expressing genuine hope, but rather avoidance rationalized as positive thinking. Genuine hope requires acceptance and develops, after severe trauma, in the context of a restitution narrative. True hope takes time. The opposite of hope is despair, and despair can occur early in trauma recovery. Facing this despair can be a first step toward acceptance, hope, and posttraumatic growth. True acceptance includes acceptance even of the despair that can accompany trauma recovery, moving the survivor closer to the genuine psychological integration of the traumatic experience itself.

The evaluation

Exposure to trauma affects individuals with varying past histories, life narratives, and genetic loading differently, so an individual risk factor–focused assessment is always necessary. Important goals of integrated Trauma and Acute Care Surgical Psychology (TACS Psych) programs include the identification of individuals at risk for developing psychological distress following injury, as well as those already experiencing acute psychological distress. Special attention must be paid to assessing past trauma and established patterns of coping, as well as prior history of mental illness. Delirium is common in the acute phases of trauma recovery, especially in intensive care settings, and must be recognized early. The deficits in cognition and attention that characterize delirium often affect on how the trauma survivors process information and emotions.

While a complete and thorough assessment is important, as we saw in Chapter 2, The Next Day: Beginning the Process of Recovery, the earliest clinical contacts necessitate a focus on building rapport and establishing the therapeutic relationship. Trauma survivors are often suffering, ill, and in pain. Respect for their suffering should be prioritized over completing symptom checklists; a sensitive and trauma-informed evaluation focuses on gathering necessary information rather than seeking complete information. The trauma survivor and the therapeutic relationship are always more important than a clinical form.

Assessment in acute care settings should also involve risk assessment, which will be reviewed later in this chapter, and triage. While many trauma survivors have no past psychiatric history, such a history, when present, can indicate important risk factors. Individuals with a psychiatric history are at higher risk for psychiatric complications, including the development of novel trauma- and stressor-related disorders and depressive disorders (Breslau, 2012). Certain types of mechanisms of injury tend to have a stronger psychological impact. The psychological impacts of an assault, for instance, are likely to be more serious than those after a mechanical fall with the same level of physical injury.

Unless they have preexisting trauma, most patients with acute trauma will not meet the duration criterion of one month of continuous trauma symptoms (American Psychiatric Association, 2022) required to make a new diagnosis of PTSD, but knowledge of risk factors associated with the development of posttraumatic psychopathology is important for prevention. Keane et al. (2006) described an etiological model for the development of PTSD, with emphasis on considering factors related to both risk and resilience. Factors commonly identified as related to posttraumatic distress broadly fall into one of three categories: (a) pretraumatic factors, (b) peritraumatic factors and (c) posttraumatic factors (Jones et al., 2024). Of these, peritraumatic factors identified as highly predictive of future psychological distress (Howlett & Stein, 2016; Keane et al., 2006) include: sexual assault or rape (Breslau, 2012), gunshot wounds (Breslau, 2012; Brewin et al., 1999), assaultive violence (Breslau, 2012; Brewin et al., 1999), motor vehicle collisions (Beck & Coffey, 2007), traumatic limb amputation (Sahu et al., 2017) and spinal cord injury (Otis et al., 2012). In addition to event-related factors, several pretraumatic factors have been shown to predict the development of psychological distress, including: prior psychiatric history (Breslau, 2012; Keane et al., 2006), previous exposure to traumatic events (e.g., prior assault, sexual or physical abuse, witnessing community violence, adverse childhood experiences, forced migration or exposure to terrorism or combat) (Keane et al., 2006). Posttraumatic factors that predict psychological distress include negative emotional response following the novel traumatic event (Breslau, 2012; Brewin et al., 1999; Keane et al., 2006) and financial hardship as a result of the traumatic injury (Murphy et al., 2019). Protective factors are important as well. Posttraumatic distress may be moderated by positive social support following injury (Keane et al., 2006), suggesting the potential importance of postevent psychological interventions.

Depressive disorders can occur after acute trauma. Kendrick et al. (2018) identified several factors associated with increased risk for depression following injury (Kendrick et al., 2018). Like Keane et al. (2006) model, the factors that were identified as associated with increased risk for depression fell into pretraumatic and peritraumatic categories. Specifically, the pretraumatic factors included prior psychiatric diagnosis, higher preinjury depression and anxiety severity scores, lower preinjury quality-of-life scores, lower socioeconomic status, and age (45 to 64 years old). Peritraumatic factors included only injury severity, although it is important to note that this study sample consisted solely of patients who sustained unintentional injuries and was conducted in the United Kingdom, where guns and firearm injuries are uncommon.

While both PTSD and major depressive disorder may develop as discrete disorders, growing evidence indicates that a bidirectional etiological relationship between the two disorders may exist (Wang et al., 2023). Specifically, the presence of a premorbid depressive disorder places an individual at increased risk for the development of PTSD following trauma exposure. Those with no history of premorbid depression are at increased risk for developing a depressive disorder if they have already developed PTSD following trauma exposure. Additionally, it has been suggested that trauma-related depressive disorders potentially have different neurobiological underpinnings than depressive disorders with endogenous origins (Wang et al., 2023). While trauma- and stressor-related disorders, major depressive disorder and substance use disorders are the most commonly identified forms of chronic psychopathology following traumatic injury, additional forms of psychopathology such as anxiety disorders can also develop after trauma.

To assist with our process of risk factor–informed triage, we have developed a novel screening tool modeled after the three levels of risk factors described above, called the Psychological Vulnerability Screening Questionnaire (P-VSQ) to assist with rapidly identifying individuals at risk for developing mental health concerns following exposure to trauma. The application of the P-VSQ and triage process will be discussed when we review the process of building an effective TACS Psych program in Chapter 20, Building an Effective Trauma and Acute Care Surgical Psychology Program.

Risk assessment tools

Assessment of suicidality, now required in most clinical settings, is critically important to prioritize when assessing the trauma survivor. Trauma survivors, especially those experiencing nightmares, are at a substantially higher risk of developing suicidal ideation (Reffi et al., 2024). In addition to a thorough clinical interview, common screening tools for suicidality include the Columbia-Suicide Severity Rating Scale (C-SSRS) (Posner et al., 2011), Patient Health Questionnaire-9 (PHQ-9) (Kroenke et al., 2001), and Beck

Scale for Suicide Ideation (BSS) (Beck et al., 1979), which are used in many clinical settings. In addition to suicidality, it is also important to screen for substance misuse, homicidality, psychosis, mania, and, especially in older adults, cognitive impairment.

Homicidal ideation must be sensitively assessed, especially for survivors of interpersonal violence who often experience context-appropriate frustration and anger regarding their assailants. Clinical interviewing strategies aimed at differentiating contextual nonpathological assaultive ideation versus homicidal intent should include a thorough review of the patient's history, including history of actualized assaultive violence or homicide, history of urges to engage in violence, verbal threats, threats directed toward an identified victim versus vague threats to an unidentified individual, specific plan, access to means, impulsivity, and substance use. Utilizing aids such as the Assault & Homicidal Danger Assessment Tool (Hoff et al., 2009) and STAMP (staring and eye contact, tone and volume of voice, anxiety, mumbling, and pacing) model (Luck et al., 2007) may help to structure the risk formulation and reduce uncertainty related to determining the risk potential. Should an individual be identified as posing an acute risk for assaultive violence, follow all local laws and professional standards related to ensuring the safety of the patient and identified target, as well as initiation of in-hospital safety protocols such as one-to-one observation, visitor restrictions, and environmental safety precautions.

Other assessment tools

In addition to risk assessment tools, validated measures of other clinical phenomena can be integrated into the assessment process as applicable. The selection of appropriate tools depends on the consultation question and may range from enhancing an understanding of symptom severity related to specific forms of psychopathology to gross cognitive functioning. When evaluating whether to integrate measures into your assessment process, it is imperative to ensure that they have been validated for use in your setting and patient population. Table 5.1 illustrates the range of commonly used assessments and screening tools that may be useful in acute care settings. Measures should be used to support the process of case conceptualization and diagnostic formulation in conjunction with the clinical interview and should not be relied on as the primary source of information supporting the assignment of a diagnosis. Finally, some measures may require additional training and certification processes prior to being able to administer, score, and interpret results.

Case conceptualization and diagnosis

Assessment leads to both case conceptualization and diagnosis, which then inform treatment planning and clinical interventions. Case conceptualization,

TABLE 5.1 Sample measures and assessment tools for acute trauma treatment settings.

Treatment Setting	Measure/Assessment
Suicidality	Beck Scale for Suicide Ideation (BSS) Columbia-Suicide Severity Rating Scale (CSSR) Patient Health Questionnaire-9 item number 9 (PHQ-9)
Homicidality and assault risk	Assault and Homicidal Danger Assessment tool
Mood	Hospital Anxiety and Depression Scale (HADS) Hamilton Depression Rating Scale (HAM-D) Patient Health Questionnaire-9 (PHQ-9) Hamilton Anxiety Rating Scale (HAM-A)
Trauma-related	Severity of Acute Stress Symptoms—Adult National Stressful Events Survey Acute Stress Disorder Short Scale (NSESSS) PTSD Checklist for DSM-5 (PCL-5) Short Posttraumatic Stress Disorder Rating Interview (SPRINT) Brief Resilience Scale (BRS) Posttraumatic Growth Inventory (PTGI)

also known as case formulation, is a structured and theory-driven approach to organizing and synthesizing relevant information related to an individual case. Case conceptualization is the basis for the diagnostic formulation and treatment plan. Conceptualizations formulated in acute care settings differ from those formulated in traditional outpatient settings in several important ways. Because of the abbreviated nature of inpatient care, conceptualizations in the inpatient setting must necessarily rely heavily on clinician judgment and informed clinical intuition. Conceptualizations are living models that evolve as additional information related to the individual is discovered throughout the consultative and treatment process. Conceptualizations sometimes lead to therapeutic approaches that are easily adapted to acute care settings, such as cognitive behavioral therapy or acceptance and commitment therapy.

In addition to conceptual models associated with specific therapeutic modalities, the biopsychosocial approach developed by Engel (1977) is one of the most widely utilized models in hospital settings (Engel, 1977). The biopsychosocial approach aims to understand the individual's biological, psychological, and social issues, both in isolation and in tandem with each other. The model emphasizes consideration of contextual factors to inform the provision of multidimensional treatment.

Common diagnoses that may affect individuals during the peritraumatic period include the trauma- and stressor-related disorders such as acute stress disorder and adjustment disorder as well as other diagnoses, such as delirium, neurocognitive disorders, and substance use disorders. History may reveal other psychiatric disorders, such as depressive disorders, bipolar disorder, schizophrenia spectrum disorders, or anxiety disorders, which are important to consider in case conceptualization and treatment. While it is not within the scope of this text to review detailed diagnostic information for each possible clinical outcome seen in acute care settings, it is important for those treating acutely injured patients to familiarize themselves with the major diagnostic categories of the Diagnostic and Statistical Manual of Mental Disorders, Fifth Edition, Text Revision (DSM-5-TR) commonly associated with acute trauma, (American Psychiatric Association, 2022). Because of the dynamic and oftentimes time-sensitive nature of evaluations in this setting, it is not uncommon to refine the diagnostic formulation and case conceptualization regularly as care progresses. Finally, as all evaluations in acute care settings occur in the context of ongoing medical and surgical care, it is imperative to rule out all biomedical causes that could potentially be influencing the expression of psychologically related symptoms before definitively assigning a psychiatric diagnosis.

The diagnosis does not, of course, capture all the relevant factors in the case conceptualization. Severity of distress is often not captured in the diagnosis, nor are the important pretraumatic, peritraumatic, and posttraumatic factors. While often not documented in brief consultation notes, a thorough case conceptualization, utilizing an appropriate model based on the patient's individual characteristics, is essential to formulate prior to engagement in disposition and treatment planning.

Differentiating normal versus pathological psychological adjustment

An essential component of assigning an accurate diagnosis is the differentiation of normal psychological responses to trauma from psychopathological responses to trauma. As alluded to above, many acute psychological responses to trauma are considered normative. To pathologize such responses would not only constitute poor practice but also increase the likelihood of further stigmatizing the patients with whom we work. Inappropriate pathologization of normative emotional responses runs the risk of reinforcing the idea that the experience of sadness, fear, and frustration after injury may be aberrant, leading to an increased risk for the development of detrimental avoidance-based coping mechanisms and true psychopathology in the future. Additionally, core to the assignment of nearly all DSM-5-TR diagnoses is the determination of the level of functional significance associated with the symptoms experienced by the individual (American Psychiatric Association,

2022). The determination of functional significance relies on two criteria: (a) the distress that is experienced is disproportionate to the severity of the stressor, and (b) the distress causes functional impairment, which is often measured by its impact on the individual's social, occupational, or other areas of functioning. After reviewing these criteria from the lens of the clinician functioning in an inpatient medical setting, it is immediately apparent that these definitions highly favor those undergoing psychodiagnostic assessment in traditional outpatient settings, as nearly all of our patients have experienced a stressor with a severity great enough to require admission to an inpatient surgical service. Furthermore, many patients experiencing acute distress during hospital stays will be unable to demonstrate impairment related to social and occupational functioning due to the nature of the acute onset of the distress during a controlled hospital stay. As such, we must rely on the "other areas of functioning" when determining functional significance.

Assessing the impact on other areas of functioning requires the clinician to adopt a mindset informed by the standard of care for the setting in which the patient is receiving care in. In inpatient general practice medical and surgical units, impacts on other areas of functioning may include: Engagement in physical and occupational therapy, participation in recovery efforts by adhering to medical recommendations (e.g., medication adherence, use of incentive spirometer, receiving medical and surgical interventions, allowing for lab work and imaging studies, etc…), engaging staff during rounds, engaging and participating with nursing staff, maintenance of personal hygiene, and active engagement with visitors (when present). Assessment of functional impairment in intensive care settings, especially when patients are intubated, is particularly challenging. In these settings, especially when delirium is present, a lack of engagement in care is often related to altered mental status rather than solely related to underlying adjustment processes. While it is important not to discount the impact of emotional distress while completing the diagnostic formulation in this context, it must be weighted appropriately, and oftentimes, erring on the side of caution is recommended.

Case conceptualization and diagnostic formulation in practice

While David and Javon were good friends and grew up in the same neighborhood, they were very different in terms of posttraumatic adjustment.

David's Story

David was an only child who came from a background of complex trauma, who had endured multiple adverse childhood experiences prior to sustaining his current trauma. His father, who frequently misused alcohol, had been physically abusive in David's early years and left the family when David was 10. After his father left, David's mother developed depressive symptoms and withdrew emotionally from the family. David had problems at school related to behavioral outbursts and

(Continued)

truancy, and had recently begun using cannabis heavily on a regular basis "to deal with stress."

In the immediate posttraumatic period, David presented as unemotional and flat. Although he denied depressed mood, his answers to questions tended to be brief and monosyllabic, and he reported a lack of interest in previously valued activities such as listening to music and talking to his friends. His appetite had decreased substantially, and he began reporting difficulties falling asleep in the evenings after several days in the hospital. He frequently refused TACS Psych follow-up visits, sometimes saying he was sleepy, sometimes saying, "I'm fine. I don't want to talk today."

David's family visited the hospital frequently and tried to be supportive, but tended to promote avoidant coping. Avoidant coping will be reviewed in more detail in Chapter 14, The Support Network, but it refers to an ineffective strategy of "looking away" from emotionally charged issues. When David expressed distress, his family often responded to him by saying things like, "You just have to be strong," or "Don't worry, you'll be fine. God's going to perform a miracle." They frequently told David, "Don't cry."

David and his family were told many times, in as thoughtful a way as possible, that he would never walk again. They appeared to understand this information on a cognitive level and could provide teach back, but they never accepted the information on an emotional level. David would ask repeatedly, "So when am I going to walk again?" His overall length of stay was 28 days, with a worsening of observed symptoms as time passed.

Javon's Story

Javon was raised in a single-parent household headed by his mother, with notable food insecurity. He and his two older siblings did well both academically and socially, with Javon describing a large social network comprised of extended family members, community members from his Baptist church, and friends who provided high-quality social support. Javon stated that his favorite subject in school was English and that he enjoyed writing poetry, especially when he needed to express his emotions. There was no family history of mental health concerns or substance misuse. Javon reported social use of cannabis once or twice a month but no other substances, including alcohol.

Javon had notable distress in the immediate posttraumatic period. He was frequently tearful and described experiencing intrusive images and memories during the daytime, as well as nightmares of the shooting, leading to frequent nighttime awakenings that impaired his ability to get consistent restorative sleep. He reported significant difficulties discussing the events surrounding his admission and stated that he preferred not to think about or talk about what happened. During periods of time when he was unable to avoid confronting the reality of his situation, for example, prior to dressing changes, he became visibly upset. Javon explained, "I don't know, when I have to see my wound, it just makes it so real. My heart feels like it's going to jump out of my chest, and I feel out of breath." He shared considerable difficulties related to concentration and often became irritable

(Continued)

when unable to complete tasks that had previously been viewed as trivial. Later he shared concerns that he would be unable to achieve highly valued life milestones, such as having a family and working, stating that no one would ever be able to love him because of his paralysis.

Javon's family visited frequently. When Javon grew tearful, his mother would hold him and grieve with him, normalizing and validating his emotional experience while modeling context-appropriate displays of emotions herself. Javon was highly engaged in care and participated in all scheduled follow-up visits. He actively utilized coping skills based on previously enjoyable life activities, such as writing poetry. These activities provided comfort and solace. His overall length of stay was 22 days. His distress was severe for the first 10 days, then gradually and steadily improved.

Application of the biopsychosocial model

On a biological level, David had genetic loading for substance use and depressive disorders. His prior history of complex trauma increased his psychological vulnerability for subsequent trauma, like the one he suddenly faced after sustaining the gunshot wounds leading to his admission. His social support network, though well-intentioned, reinforced maladaptive coping patterns that encouraged avoidance-reliant hope. This avoidance-based approach to coping led to clinically significant functional impairment, as evidenced by his disengagement from the rehabilitation process and worse functional outcomes related to his physical and psychological recoveries due to lack of participation.

David's case conceptualization considers his unique biological, psychological, and social factors, also including appreciation of his pretraumatic, peritraumatic, and posttraumatic risk factors. The clinical narrative suggests that following exposure to a life-threatening event that was associated with interpersonal violence, David experienced notable stress that was unable to be adequately addressed by existing coping styles, which ultimately led to the expression of psychopathology that would best be classified as an adjustment disorder with depressed mood. Furthermore, the encouragement of avoidance-based coping from his support system in tandem with his own preexisting avoidant style of dealing with stress via the heavy regular use of cannabis, will strongly influence the types of treatment that might be helpful for David. Although David had less initial distress than Javon, his distress increased throughout his hospital stay.

Although Javon and David faced similar socioeconomic barriers and were raised in the same neighborhood, Javon had not experienced childhood abuse and did not have a genetic loading for mental illness. Javon and his support system faced the traumatic event with significant grief and anxiety, including Javon's development of clinically significant distress. Because of the combination of intrinsic factors and the quality of his social support system, he eventually developed acceptance-informed hope that allowed him to participate fully in the physical and psychological recovery processes. This integration of acceptance was consistent with his strong religious beliefs. To the casual observer, Javon appeared to be doing "worse" than David early in his hospital course, as he expressed more distress. This early distress actually facilitated long-term recovery.

Javon's case conceptualization suggests a higher likelihood of a positive prognosis despite his significant early distress. Specifically, the lack of biological and psychological vulnerabilities, when paired with positive social support, should serve as a buffer when faced with his acute trauma. Diagnostically, Javon both reported and displayed symptoms that eventually supported a diagnosis of acute stress disorder with an initial differential diagnosis of adjustment disorder with anxiety. His experience of notable physiologic distress and his high level of engagement were important considerations in developing his initial treatment plan. Although Javon had high levels of distress initially, his distress improved significantly over the course of his hospital stay.

Case conceptualization as a guide to treatment

The comprehensive case conceptualization guides treatment interventions. For both Javon and David, the type of injury (gunshot wounds resulting in complete spinal cord injury at T4) and the severity of injury (paralysis below the nipple line) suggested that they were both at high risk for psychological complications. David had the further risk factors of prior traumatic experiences and a family history of psychological issues.

In David's case, for instance, his family history as well as his clinical presentation suggested that pharmacological interventions with an antidepressant might be of benefit. Because of his extended stay, we were able to initiate psychotherapy, although his avoidance-based coping often limited participation. His difficulties with being aware of and expressing feelings suggested that he might benefit most from adapted acceptance and commitment therapy interventions, which will be discussed in Chapter 6, Psychological Interventions for Hospitalized Trauma Patients, during his hospitalization, as well as motivational interviewing interventions to increase participation in the rehabilitative process.

Although Javon lacked a past psychiatric history and family history of trauma and mental illness, he had a high-risk mechanism of injury and significant emotional distress. His healthy coping style and good insight suggested that he might benefit from initial treatment targeting his physiologic arousal via relaxation training and mindfulness meditation, with later transition to insight-oriented or existential therapies, which were both paired with psychoeducational interventions related to common responses following traumatic injury. Therapy in Javon's case focused on reducing distress and facilitating posttraumatic growth.

The treatment planning process includes post-discharge planning. After the acute care phase in the inpatient setting, many trauma survivors will need follow-up therapy based on the overall assessment and the identification of risk factors. The goals of outpatient follow-up care include the treatment of underlying psychiatric illness, the relief of distress, and, to the extent possible, the prevention of PTSD. While David obviously needs outpatient follow-up for a variety of reasons, Javon would still benefit from outpatient follow-up. That decision is partially based on the severity of injury and the presence of initial distress, but also because his healthy coping suggests the possibility that further therapy might facilitate posttraumatic growth.

Javon and David: Clinical Course

Javon did well in treatment and had a good recovery. After a 22-day hospitalization in the acute care setting, he was transferred to a specialized inpatient spinal cord injury rehabilitation center for further rehabilitative treatment. Javon was realistic but remained hopeful. He was beginning to develop a restitution narrative.

David did not fare as well. He remained isolative and withdrawn. He was started on antidepressant medication but showed little benefit. He participated only minimally in physical and occupational therapy. Efforts at psychotherapeutic interventions with both David and his support system were rejected, sometimes angrily, "I really just need you to tell me when I am going to be able to walk again." Unlike Javon, he was reluctant to accept the recommended transfer to a rehabilitation center, demanding to stay in the hospital until he could walk again.

In terms of narrative theory, there is no right story or correct narrative, but there are incomplete narratives. David and his family, for instance, could not accept a trauma narrative that included the terrible reality of permanent paralysis. They knew that fact cognitively, but could not incorporate it into their trauma story. They insisted on a restitution narrative when such a narrative was not possible. Sometimes trauma survivors insist on restitution narratives to avoid facing the full pain and grief associated with the trauma. This protective fantasy can be adaptive very early in recovery, but can quickly, as in David's case, become maladaptive.

Chapter summary

Acute trauma can have lasting emotional and psychological impacts. The trauma survivor faces a sudden and unexpected intrusion into their life situation and must adjust psychologically to that intrusion. The trauma treatment team can facilitate that adjustment with careful and empathetic diagnosis and psychological assessment, which can then inform the case conceptualization and treatment phases of recovery.

References

American Psychiatric Association (2022).*Diagnostic and statistical manual of mental disorders* (5th ed., text rev.). American Psychiatric Association Publishing. https://doi.org/10.1176/appi.books.9780890425787.

Beck, J. G., & Coffey, S. F. (2007). Assessment and treatment of PTSD after a motor vehicle collision: Empirical findings and clinical observations. *Professional Psychology, Research and Practice, 38*(6), 629–639. https://doi.org/10.1037/0735-7028.38.6.629.

Beck, A. T., Kovacs, M., & Weissman, A. (1979). Assessment of suicidal intention: the Scale for Suicide Ideation. *Journal of Consulting and Clinical Psychology, 47*(2), 343–352. https://doi.org/10.1037/0022-006X.47.2.343.

Breslau, N. (2012). In J. G. Beck, & D.M.Sloan. (Eds.). *The Oxford handbook of traumatic stress disorders* (pp. 84–97). Oxford University Press. https://doi.org/10.1093/oxfordhb/9780195399066.001.0001 Epidemiology of posttraumatic stress disorder in adults.

Brewin, C. R., Andrews, B., Rose, S., & Kirk, M. (1999). Acute stress disorder and posttraumatic stress disorder in victims of violent crime. *American Journal of Psychiatry, 156*(3), 360–366. https://doi.org/10.1176/ajp.156.3.360.

Engel, G. L. (1977). The need for a new medical model: A challenge for biomedicine. *Science (New York, N.Y.), 196*(4286), 129–136. https://doi.org/10.1126/science.847460.

Frank, A. W. (1995). *The wounded storyteller: Body, illness, and ethics*. University of Chicago Press.

Gallagher, M. W., & Lopez, S. J. (2018). *Oxford handbook of hope*. Oxford University Press.

Hoff, L. A., Brown, L., & Hoff, M. R. (2009). *People in crisis: Clinical and diversity perspectives* (6th). Routledge. https://doi.org/10.4324/9780203893234 Available from.

Horowitz, M. J. (1986). Stress-response syndromes: A review of posttraumatic and adjustment disorders. *Hospital and Community Psychiatry, 37*(3), 241–249. https://doi.org/10.1176/ps.37.3.241.

Howlett, J. R., & Stein, M. B. (2016). Prevention of trauma and stressor-related disorders: A review. *Neuropsychopharmacology Official Publication of the American College of Neuropsychopharmacology, 41*(1), 357–369. https://doi.org/10.1038/npp.2015.261.

Jones, K., Boschen, M., Devilly, G., Vogler, J., Flowers, H., Winkleman, C., & Wullschleger, M. (2024). Risk and protective factors that predict posttraumatic stress disorder after traumatic injury: A systematic review. *Health Sciences Review, 10*. https://doi.org/10.1016/j.hsr.2023.100147.

Keane, T. M., Marshall, A. D., & Taft, C. T. (2006). Posttraumatic stress disorder: Etiology, epidemiology, and treatment outcome. *Annual Review of Clinical Psychology, 2*, 161–197. https://doi.org/10.1146/annurev.clinpsy.2.022305.095305.

Kendrick, D., Baker, R., Hill, T., Beckett, K., Coupland, C., Kellezi, B., Joseph, S., Barnes, J., Sleney, J., Christie, N., & Morriss, R. (2018). Early risk factors for depression, anxiety and post-traumatic distress after hospital admission for unintentional injury: Multicentre cohort study. *Journal of Psychosomatic Research, 112*, 15–24. https://doi.org/10.1016/j.jpsychores.2018.06.008.

Kroenke, K., Spitzer, R. L., & Williams, J. B. (2001). The PHQ-9: validity of a brief depression severity measure. *Journal of general internal medicine, 16*(9), 606–613. https://doi.org/10.1046/j.1525-1497.2001.016009606.x.

Luck, L., Jackson, D., & Usher, K. (2007). STAMP: Components of observable behaviour that indicate potential for patient violence in emergency departments. *Journal of Advanced Nursing, 59*(1), 11–19. https://doi.org/10.1111/j.1365-2648.2007.04308.x.

Mahr, G., Moore, D., Drake, C., & Reffi, A. (2025). Depth psychology and acute trauma. *Journal of Jungian Scholarly Studies, 20*(1), 46–55. https://doi.org/10.29173/jjs253s.

Maul, S., Giegling, I., Fabbri, C., Corponi, F., Serretti, A., & Rujescu, D. (2020). Genetics of resilience: Implications from genome-wide association studies and candidate genes of the stress response system in posttraumatic stress disorder and depression. *American Journal of Medical Genetics Part B: Neuropsychiatric Genetics, 183*(2), 77–94. https://doi.org/10.1002/ajmg.b.32763.

Murphy, P. B., Severance, S., Savage, S., Obeng-Gyasi, S., Timsina, L. R., & Zarzaur, B. L. (2019). Financial toxicity is associated with worse physical and emotional long-term outcomes after traumatic injury. *Journal of Trauma and Acute Care Surgery, 87*(5), 1189–1196. https://doi.org/10.1097/TA.0000000000002409.

Otis, C., Marchand, A., & Courtois, F. (2012). Risk factors for posttraumatic stress disorder in persons with spinal cord Iijury. Topics in Spinal Cord Injury. *Rehabilitation, 18*(3), 253–263. https://doi.org/10.1310/sci1803-253.

Posner, K., Brown, G. K., Stanley, B., Brent, D. A., Yershova, K. V., Oquendo, M. A., Currier, G. W., Melvin, G. A., Greenhill, L., Shen, S., & Mann, J. J. (2011). The Columbia-Suicide Severity Rating Scale: initial validity and internal consistency findings from three multisite studies with adolescents and adults. *The American Journal of Psychiatry, 168*(12), 1266–1277. https://doi.org/10.1176/appi.ajp.2011.10111704.

Reffi, A. N., Cheng, P., Kalmbach, D. A., Moore, D. A., Mahr, G. C., Seymour, G. M., Solway, M., & Drake, C. L. (2024). Understanding nightmares after traumatic events in Detroit (UNiTED): prospective associations with interpersonal violence and posttraumatic stress disorder symptoms. *European Journal of Psychotraumatology, 15*(1). https://doi.org/10.1080/20008066.2024.2409561 Available from.

Sahu, A., Gupta, R., Sagar, S., Kumar, M., & Sagar, R. (2017). A study of psychiatric comorbidity after traumatic limb amputation: A neglected entity. *Industrial Psychiatry Journal, 26*(2), 228. https://doi.org/10.4103/ipj.ipj_80_16.

Wang, S.-K., Feng, M., Fang, Y., Lv, L., Sun, G.-L., Yang, S.-L., Guo, P., Cheng, S.-F., Qian, M.-C., & Chen, H.-X. (2023). Psychological trauma, posttraumatic stress disorder and trauma-related depression: A mini-review. *World Journal of Psychiatry, 13*(6), 331–339. https://doi.org/10.5498/wjp.v13.i6.331.

Chapter 6

Psychological interventions for hospitalized trauma patients

The Intern

An important part of our program's mission is to train the next generation of psychologists, psychiatrists, and psychologically minded surgeons. Jesse is a clinical psychology doctoral candidate who is completing a training rotation with us as part of their predoctoral internship. Every morning, we triage cases, assigning consults to different team members, with the requirement that all trainees receive direct supervision for every case they manage. These case presentations encompass a review of the case conceptualization, diagnostic formulation, care up to that point, and the treatment plan. Each daily supervision experience culminates with the supervising attending staff member visiting the patient with the trainee for a confirmatory review of the patient's experience. Today has been a very busy day, and Jesse has just presented to my office to begin our review of cases.

Integrating therapeutic interventions

As discussed in Chapters 2 and 5, practicing in acute care settings requires that we adapt our approaches to clinical care so that we may thrive in these fast-paced environments. As in psychodiagnostic assessment, case conceptualization and treatment planning, psychotherapeutic interventions deployed in this setting require significant adaptation. Traditional evidence-based protocols delivered in outpatient settings are often structured to provide between eight and 16 sessions of psychotherapy at regular weekly time intervals, with each session typically being between 1 and 2 hours in duration. In inpatient settings lengths, of stay are short, and patients are ill. Flexibility in both the duration and frequency of follow-up visits is required. Yet psychotherapeutic interventions are important. While some patients may have lengths of stay of sufficient duration to deliver a full course of evidence-based psychotherapy, frequently admissions are brief, and the evolving nature of patients' adjustment responses necessitate the compression of treatment timelines, often to one to two

The Psychology of Acute Trauma. DOI: https://doi.org/10.1016/B978-0-443-33212-8.00010-5

sessions. Also, because patients are ill, they can often only tolerate brief sessions.

In addition to the need for flexibility related to session duration and frequency, special consideration of service context is necessary to ensure the feasible implementation of recommendations contained in the treatment plan. Specifically, different models of service delivery, which will be discussed in further detail in Chapter 20, Building an Effective Trauma and Acute Care Surgical Psychology Program, may influence which recommendations will be feasible or not. Internally embedded clinicians who have been incorporated into the patient's surgical team, compared to external consultants who are part of an independent consultation-liaison service, may see a higher likelihood of success in recommending behaviorally based interventions that teams must assist with, such as behavior plans/contracts or modifications of surgical plans of care such as including the Trauma and Acute Care Surgical Psychology (TACS Psych) service clinician during dressing changes or painful bedside procedures where behavioral pain management interventions may prove helpful. The embedded clinician also destigmatizes psychological interventions.

In the hospital setting, it is important to view both the clinical teams and the patient as our clients. While we are providing direct clinical care to our patients, we must also consider that these patients are primarily managed by the medical and surgical teams. These teams often have specific consultation questions or goals for care that must be considered when formulating our treatment plan and associated recommendations. By formulating a range of feasible recommendations for both our patients and their primary medical or surgical team, we may not only increase the effectiveness of our treatment but also empower the medical and surgical teams to view themselves as essential partners in our patients' emotional recovery processes.

Evidence supported treatments: adapting approaches to inpatient settings

Because standardized protocols for hospitalized patients usually are not available, evidence-based interventions that have been shown to be efficacious in outpatient settings must be adapted for the acute care setting. We call these adaptations of evidence-based treatments and interventions evidence-supported treatments and evidence-supported interventions. Because of the need to develop treatment plans that are dynamic and adaptable to short-term hospital stays, the focus of treatment is often directed toward applying an eclectic mix of evidence-supported interventions with the goal of mitigating current distress, minimizing future distress, and promoting posttraumatic growth. In addition, the inpatient TACS Psych team must also consider requests from the primary medical or surgical team, such as assessing decision-making capacity to consent to treatment or engage in the disposition planning process, as well as specific questions related to differential psychodiagnostics, such as discerning whether psychological distress or altered mental status is indicative of a preexisting condition or novel to the hospital stay.

The development of brief treatment protocols aimed at addressing the unique needs of acutely injured trauma survivors who are admitted to the hospital has been identified as an under-researched area. Most of the limited research relates to early intervention and the prevention of posttraumatic psychopathology conducted after the patient's discharge (Roberts et al., 2010, 2019). While some studies have attempted to adapt structured outpatient protocols to inpatient hospital settings via randomized trials (Fauerbach et al., 2020; Larsen et al., 2021), many studies lack the scientific rigor of their counterparts that have been conducted in traditional outpatient settings. The most recent systematic review of randomized clinical trials conducted in this area identified just six studies out of an initial pool of 633 that met review criteria, with only three of the six trials being conducted solely while the patient was admitted to the hospital (Grant et al., 2025). All six were delivered within three months following injury, and a majority incorporated components of cognitive behavioral therapy.

Related to the prevention of posttraumatic stress disorder (PTSD) in outpatient settings, the International Society of Traumatic Stress Studies (ISTSS) PTSD Treatment and Prevention Guidelines suggested that only two single time point interventions (the 512 Psychological Intervention Model and single-session eye movement desensitization and reprocessing [EMDR]) and two multiple-session interventions (brief dyadic therapy and self-guided Internet-based intervention) have emerging evidence for preventive efficacy when deployed within 3 months of trauma exposure (International Society of Traumatic Stress Studies, 2019). For patients where emerging traumatic stress symptoms are a concern, such as those associated with acute stress disorder (ASD), the ISTSS (2019) standard recommendations for outpatient management are cognitive behavioral therapy with a trauma focus, cognitive therapy, or EMDR. The definition of cognitive behavioral therapy with a trauma focus includes, but is not limited to, modalities such as cognitive therapy for PTSD (CT-PTSD), cognitive processing therapy (CPT), and prolonged exposure (PE). While the literature surrounding the prevention of PTSD is scant, especially for patients remaining hospitalized in acute care settings, the rigorous scientific study of the prevention of other forms of posttraumatic psychopathology, such as depressive disorders, anxiety disorders, and sleep-wake disorders, is even more limited.

Flexibility and moving targets

The need for dynamic adaptation of the treatment plan and provision of evidence-supported interventions is also impacted by additional factors related to the physical and social environments. Many hospital settings lack privacy and require providing treatment in areas where clinical conversations may be overheard, including by an unrelated roommate for patients in shared rooms, by the patient's visitors, by other team members, or even by law enforcement and correctional officers if the patient is in police custody or incarcerated.

The presence of these unpredictable environmental factors poses unique challenges to developing and implementing structured treatment protocols. Clinicians often find themselves in positions where they are unable to execute carefully crafted plans because of the presence of unexpected visitors or the need to transport a patient for an urgent procedure or imaging study. Planned interventions may be derailed if significant stressors, such as pathology reports with unwanted results or worsening of disease states, occur between intervention sessions.

Clinician flexibility is required, and while some challenges may be posed by the environmental factors themselves, they do offer unique opportunities to enhance treatment and build strong therapeutic relationships with patients and their support systems. Specifically, by modeling flexibility, we may set an example for dealing with unexpected stressful situations that may arise during the normal course of inpatient hospital care. Additionally, unlike many traditional outpatient settings, the presence of visitors may provide unique opportunities for the clinician to model prosocial communication and support adaptive behaviors. While some studies suggest increased benefit from incorporating support systems into the patient's psychosocial recovery processes (Grab, 2025), clinicians must honor patient autonomy and attain informed consent from patients prior to conducting any evaluations or treatment with any third parties present at the time of visit. If visitors must remain present, as may be the case for patients who are in police custody or who are incarcerated, the clinician's judgment should inform the approach to assessment and treatment with these vulnerable groups.

Therapeutic modalities

Adapting traditional outpatient treatments to inpatient settings is an art that requires considerable clinical experience and skill. A majority of the modalities highlighted in the following sections have either shown significantly positive empirical outcomes or promise related to the management of a wide range of posttraumatic psychological sequelae. Clinicians are encouraged to utilize discretion and clinical judgment when attempting to adapt treatments, while engaging in peer case consultation or supervisory oversight when necessary.

Psychoeducational interventions

While we don't recommend psychoeducational interventions as the sole approach to treatment, we strongly encourage clinicians to incorporate psychoeducational interventions into nearly all treatment plans.

Psychoeducational interventions increase patients' favorable perceptions of engagement with mental health providers following intervention (Brooks et al., 2021). Additionally, psychoeducational interventions may decrease uncertainty and provide a sense of control related to the recovery process, facilitating adherence to behaviorally related components of their plan of care, such as physical and occupational therapy and adherence to the recommended medication regimen.

Initial patient contacts should be warm and supportive in recognition of the distress initially faced by trauma survivors navigating the acute phase of their recovery. In addition to nonstandardized approaches, Psychological First Aid is an evidence-informed series of modular interventions that was jointly developed by the National Child Traumatic Stress Network and National Center for PTSD (Brymer et al., 2006). Access to the field operations guide is available through either organization at no cost (Brymer et al., 2006). While initially developed to assist individuals immediately following exposure to a disaster or terrorism, many of the core components and interventions contained within the Psychological First Aid approach are applicable to the survivors of traumatic injuries. For instance, interventions aiming to assist survivors by understanding their immediate needs while providing practical help and information related to the event and recovery efforts align closely with the Keane et al.'s (2006) model for the development of PTSD, where the presence of high-quality social support and information related to recovery efforts may mitigate the development of PTSD in at-risk individuals (Keane et al., 2006).

In addition to orientation to recovery efforts and identifying immediate patient needs, psychoeducational interventions related to the provision of information about common responses following exposure to trauma are recommended. Intense emotions are common after acute trauma, even though they may seem foreign to the patient. Information on how to differentiate nonpathological emotional responses from those that may be considered pathological is important as well, with the presence of functional impairment often indicating that emotional responses have progressed to the point of clinical significance.

Education related to functional impairment, as defined by the American Psychiatric Association and discussed in Chapter 5, The Psychology of Acute Trauma: Assessment and Case Conceptualization, assists patients in understanding when formal psychological treatment may prove beneficial both during their hospital stay and following discharge (American Psychiatric Association, 2022). Timing related to the provision of this information is important to consider, as one does not wish to inadvertently bias the patient's responses to open-ended questions regarding current symptoms of distress. Typically, this information can be provided at the close of the initial session or at the onset of the first follow-up visit if it cannot be completed following the initial assessment. Using teach-back strategies, such as asking the patient to provide you with information related to the reviewed education in their own words, will allow clinicians to assess patient comprehension and may assist with clarifying concepts related to the recovery process. In addition to verbally reviewing information with each patient we encounter, we've also created a "What to Expect During Your Admission" guidebook, which contains information related to the physical and psychological recovery processes that is provided to all patients seen by our service.

Communication skills training

Many times, patients will share difficulties related to ineffective communication both with their medical team members and their family members or social support system. While not technically a psychotherapeutic intervention, communication skills training may prove helpful in increasing the collaborative nature of care between the patient and their medical and surgical teams, as well as reducing tension and promoting high-quality social support from family members. If patients are amenable, communication skills training sessions may also be conducted with their caregivers, including the utilization of interventions such as observe and clarify skills or the stoplight metaphor (Chapman, 2012).

Observe and clarify skills attempt to remove observational and confirmation biases from conversational partners, instead focusing on observing shifts in behavior that are correlated with changes in emotional expression. This allows team members to elicit the true underlying emotional experiences of the patient and facilitate a conversation that will allow for productive discussion surrounding how the caregiver can best provide functional assistance to the patient. The stoplight metaphor centers on teaching the red light, yellow light, green light skill and focuses on proactively identifying topics of conversation that the patient has reported as being related to increased relational stress or conflict (Chapman, 2012). Topics are then grouped into three categories: red light signifying a topic that should not be discussed, yellow light signifying a topic that is leading to heightened arousal and should be diverted, and green light indicating that the conversation has returned to a place of comfort for the patient. The patient is encouraged to utilize skills such as the stoplight metaphor during conversation, and based on developmental level, can even be provided with color-coded physical representations of these lights to visually cue their conversation partner (see Appendix for printable handout). These techniques can prove particularly helpful if patients experience difficulties with emotion dysregulation due to relational distress and can give caregivers a clear understanding of the patient's emotional state and boundaries to avoid unnecessary relational difficulties.

Motivational interviewing

Motivational interviewing is a key modality that has been shown to be effective at promoting behavior change in many medical settings (Bischof et al., 2020). At its core, motivational interviewing is a collaborative, nonlinear series of interventions that holds the ultimate goal of promoting contemplative and personally driven behavior change in patients (Miller & Rollnick, 2023). Motivational interviewing techniques emphasize "rolling with resistance" and avoiding prescriptive interactions related to target behaviors and instead take an inquisitive approach centered on understanding the patient's experience and the reasons that behavior change may be important to them. Targets can include premorbid health behaviors, such as alcohol or substance use, or novel behaviors that have developed during the hospitalization, such as engaging with physical therapy or rehabilitation services.

Due to their highly dynamic nature, motivational interviewing techniques may be interwoven with most of the other therapeutic approaches presented in this chapter. Motivational interviewing can have a high potential for significant therapeutic impact in a short period of time. Conversations incorporating motivational interviewing skills center on the utilization of four core techniques described as OARS skills. OARS is an acronym for open-ended questions, affirmations, reflections, and summaries. Communications utilizing OARS skills attempt to elicit change talk from our patients with the goal of identifying four key types of statements indicating beliefs around change. Change talk typically falls into DARN statements, which stands for statements indicating a desire, ability, reason, and need to change. Throughout the interaction clinicians, are encouraged to "pick flowers" by listening for the presence of identified DARN statements the patient may make. Incorporating OARS skills to facilitate change, the clinician then provides a narrative summary to the patient with a "bouquet" of the identified DARN statements in the patient's own language (Miller & Rollnick, 2023).

The change ruler is an effective strategy to not only identify the patient's desire to engage in behavior change but also their realistic expectations about whether behavior change is likely to occur or not (Miller & Rollnick, 2023). Change rulers utilize a 0 to 10 scale, with 0 representing the lowest importance/confidence and 10 representing the highest importance/confidence. After orienting the patient to the anchor points, the clinician then queries them about a specific behavior that has been identified, asking them to rate their perceived importance of changing that specific behavior utilizing the 0 to 10 scale. To facilitate the highest likelihood of success related to behavior change, follow-up questions are encouraged to explore with the patient why their score wasn't lower. This provides them with an opportunity to reflect on the importance of their own self-described behavior change instead of giving excuses as to why behavior change may not be possible. Finally, the clinician will utilize a second change ruler incorporating the general approach described above, this time asking the patient to rate how confident they are that they will change the targeted behavior (Miller & Rollnick, 2023).

Mindfulness interventions

Mindfulness approaches that are utilized in acute care settings represent a spectrum of interventions that range from basic relaxation training to more complex guided imagery and meditation interventions. Approaches such as mindfulness-based stress reduction and mindfulness-based cognitive therapy have been shown to be effective for the management of PTSD-related avoidance, physiologic arousal, and negative emotional states such as shame and guilt (Boyd et al., 2018). Adapting these treatments to inpatient settings offers the opportunity to highly individualize interventions to the patient's preferences, which may increase efficacy and overall engagement in treatment. Mindfulness meditation may be paired effectively with relaxation training that incorporates diaphragmatic breathing. This combination of interventions may quickly and effectively address symptoms of anxiety-related physiologic arousal, such as tachycardia, shortness of breath, and diaphoresis, as well as other symptoms of panic such as an impending sense of doom, restlessness, and racing thoughts. For patients who ruminate, mindfulness-based centering techniques or guided imagery may prove helpful.

Guided imagery interventions utilizing prewritten scripts may assist the clinician, although tailoring the intervention to familiar locations based on the patient's experiences often enhances efficacy while pairing it with core components of prescripted interventions. For example, "leaves on a stream" is a common intervention aimed at reducing distress regarding intrusive thoughts while promoting mindfulness-based acceptance of the current moment. During the exercise, the patient is instructed to activate all five of their senses, while the image of being on the banks of a stream watching leaves slowly fall from the tree branches into the water is described in detail. The patient is then asked to place any thoughts they may be experiencing on the next leaf, describing it without judgment while watching it float downstream out of sight and out of mind. In this example, the movements of the leaves, when paired with the guided imagery, allow for cognitive defusion and acceptance of the idea that thoughts are just thoughts. Cognitive defusion refers to the process of detaching oneself from one's thoughts and identifying that thoughts are not always an accurate reflection of reality.

Some patients may not identify with the rural stream setting, especially if they live in an urban environment. Clinicians may tailor this intervention to each specific patient's needs. If the patient prefers a setting other than one based in nature, it is important to incorporate the sense of movement, which is the core element that allows defusion to be successful. Examples from my clinical practice include facilitating guided imagery interventions where the patient is sitting on their own porch watching cars drive by, in their backyard watching clouds drift overhead, or even in their bed at home watching a pet enter and exit the room.

Prior to engaging in these interventions, patients are asked to describe and name their current emotions, while rating them on a 0 to 10 scale, with 0 being the least intense and 10 being the most intense. Patients then re-rate their emotional experience following completion of the intervention to assess the efficacy of the intervention. I encourage patients to practice at least twice per day, one time being immediately before bedtime. Other particularly beneficial times to encourage practice would be immediately prior to situations that cause pain or anxiety, such as dressing changes or physical or occupational therapy.

These interventions must be used with caution if the patient has reported reexperiencing symptoms, such as significant intrusive memories or flashbacks during relaxation, because of the potential for increased distress related to intrusive thoughts upon attempting to induce a state of relaxation. Clinicians may start with utilizing relaxation training and grounding or centering techniques with the patient's eyes open, asking them to focus on a specific point in the room to optimize efficacy. Patients may also attempt to engage in interventions with their eyes closed if they so wish, although they should be encouraged to open their eyes and immediately notify the clinician should distress develop during the intervention.

Mindfulness-based behavioral pain management interventions are also important to consider when providing care to acutely injured trauma survivors (Miller-Matero et al., 2019). Psychological pain management strategies can be used in addition to, not instead of, other pain interventions, such as pain medications. Psychological pain management approaches capitalize on the combination of relaxation training and guided imagery techniques described above, with a specific focus on reducing pain and discomfort. Patient suggestibility and a willingness to participate are notable predictors of efficacy, and these interventions are often paired with encouragement from the primary surgical team in combination with psychoeducation related to the gate control theory of pain. Similar to mindfulness interventions aimed at reducing psychological distress, conducting pre- and post-ratings on the 10-point scale of both physical pain and identified emotions is required, with ongoing practice strongly encouraged between follow-up sessions.

Behavioral interventions

Behavioral activation is known to be an effective treatment for depression. In a small clinical trial, behavioral activation has shown promise in hospitalized trauma patients by reducing symptom severity related to PTSD (Wagner et al., 2007). Behavioral activation is well-suited to acute care settings because it is simple and easy to deliver. It can also easily be paired with acceptance and commitment therapy (ACT). Clinicians must be creative when formulating behavioral activation plans, as some previously enjoyed life activities, like running, may not be feasible after acute trauma.

When we understand the core values associated with a particular life activity, we can, in collaboration with the patient, modify the activity in a way that is appropriate to the current situation. For example, if the patient states that they love hiking as a primary stress management activity, mindfulness-based guided imagery interventions can assist the patient in visualizing their favorite trail. Not only can this accomplish the goals of the mindfulness intervention itself, but it also leads to enjoyment via behavioral activation. When formulating behavioral activation plans, it is also important to consider the potential re-traumatizing effects of some previously enjoyed life activities. For instance, if the patient states that they enjoy playing video games or watching movies and are admitted after sustaining multiple gunshot wounds, we may encourage playing games or watching movies as a form of behavioral activation while discouraging engagement in media that may replicate the traumatic event (e.g., media that involves violence or firearm use).

"Enjoyment experiments" can also be helpful. If patients share that they are experiencing difficulty identifying any activities that they may enjoy due to new functional impairment or the limitations of being confined to a hospital room, clinicians may incorporate "enjoyment experiments" where the patient engages in novel activities in an attempt to identify new areas of interest. Each of our surgical units contains behavioral activation toolkits, including colored pencils, a mindfulness coloring book, and a deck of cards. Clinicians are encouraged to identify resources available in their health systems to support developing their own behavioral activation toolkits.

Some individuals who are exposed to trauma can develop an adjustment disorder with disturbance of conduct that may lead to verbally or physically aggressive behaviors. Behavior plans or contracts can be helpful in addressing such issues. Behavioral plans can also address behavioral issues associated with preexisting cluster B personality disorders or traits. If traditional approaches to modifying behavior prove unsuccessful at mitigating disruption, a behavior plan may be deployed to provide a structured set of expectations that both the teams and the patient can follow until the target behavior is extinguished.

The first step in completing a successful behavior plan is to conduct a functional behavioral analysis, where the clinician identifies stimulus-response relationships between the patient and their interoceptive and external environments. The process should be non-punitive. It is essential that clinicians adopt a growth-focused mindset that prioritizes collaboration with the patient and emphasizes the impact of the recent trauma. Following completion of the functional behavioral analysis, identification of patient-stated goals should be prioritized, with the attainment of these goals serving as the foundation for the behavior plan itself. Expectations related to conduct are reviewed, as well as the integration of proactive coping skills and helpful communication patterns that have been exhibited by staff. Multiple contingencies should be prepared, each clearly outlining expectations and the consequences of escalating behavior, especially if a physical threat to self or others is present. Aligning with the patient will allow for a higher likelihood of adoption of novel prosocial behaviors, and it is often helpful to encourage the patient to teach new team members how to utilize the plan so that the collaborative nature of the process is preserved. Special considerations include developing sensitive plans with individuals who may be impacted by intellectual or developmental disabilities. Goals and target behaviors should be both feasible and attainable and should be formulated with a culturally sensitive approach utilizing developmentally appropriate language.

Cognitive behavioral therapy interventions with a trauma focus

Cognitive behavioral therapies (CBT) are well established as the gold standard for treating trauma survivors in outpatient settings and include specific therapeutic approaches such as CT-PTSD, CPT, and PE (International Society of Traumatic Stress Studies, 2019). Because of the highly efficacious nature of PE in treating chronic PTSD, Rothbaum et al. (2012) adapted it to be suitable for use in an abbreviated timeframe immediately following exposure to trauma, trialing modified prolonged exposure (mPE) in patients who had been treated and discharged from the emergency department following traumatic injury. The outcomes of this trial indicate that mPE was found to be effective in reducing the severity of symptoms of distress related to PTSD and depression in patients discharged from the emergency department (Rothbaum et al., 2012). Attempts to replicate these results via the deployment of mPE in an inpatient hospital setting failed to present evidence of improved efficacy as compared to standard of care that involved the delivery of non-standardized psychological interventions, such as those described in this chapter, for some patients in the control arm (Larsen et al., 2021).

While CT-PTSD and CPT have shown considerable efficacy in outpatient settings, they have not been formally studied in acute care settings. Only three randomized clinical trials have incorporated traditional CBT interventions into the care of hospitalized trauma survivors (Grant et al., 2025). These studies, which included interventions such as anxiety management training, imaginal exposure, and cognitive restructuring, saw improvements in patients' self-rated symptom severity scores related to ASD, depressive disorders, and state-based anxiety (Fauerbach et al., 2020; Pirente et al., 2007). Furthermore, patients participating in traditional trauma-focused CBT identified that the collaborative nature of CBT led to feelings of empowerment and a sense of increased control that facilitated therapeutic change (Lowe & Murray, 2014).

In clinical practice, I have found several traditional CBT interventions, as described by Beck, to be effective (Beck, 2020). Basic psycho-educational interventions related to assisting patients in understanding the connections between thoughts, emotions, and behaviors provide a foundational understanding for navigating the emotional recovery process as well as fostering a sense of control over their own emotional experiences. Additional therapeutic techniques, such as identifying automatic thoughts and underlying core beliefs, may grant greater insight into the nature of distress, should distorted cognitions be present. With longer hospital stays, utilizing an adapted trauma-informed thought record (see Appendix for printable handouts) provides an opportunity to explore the nature of stimulus-response relationships as well as the ability to engage in cognitive restructuring interventions, including rational responding to distorted automatic thoughts. Teaching these foundational skills during the inpatient stay may also facilitate transitioning into an effective outpatient therapy program.

Acceptance and commitment therapy interventions

CBT traditionally addresses distorted cognitions, but sometimes, after severe trauma, psychological distress is not the result of distorted cognitions. The trauma survivor may be facing truly difficult situations, like the unexpected loss of a limb or paralysis. ACT addresses such events not as distortions but as painful realities. ACT is a values-driven series of behavioral interventions that link the utilization of mindfulness-based techniques with acceptance and a behavioral commitment to living one's life according to their values (Hayes et al., 1999).

ACT as an applied treatment for assisting trauma survivors has six components: (a) creative hopelessness, (b) the problem of control, (c) willingness and defusion, (d) the self as context, (e) value living, and (f) committed action (Walser & Westrup, 2007). ACT has shown considerable promise in addressing suffering associated with PTSD in outpatient settings because of its unique combination of interventions aiming to increase experiential acceptance, which directly address core symptoms of experiential avoidance (Walser & Westrup, 2007; Wharton et al., 2019).

Because of the nature of ACT, it is particularly well-suited to address additional common difficulties associated with hospitalizations, such as a lack of perceived control. In addition to effectively treating symptoms of PTSD, ACT has also been shown to be effective in treating symptoms of trauma-related depressive disorders and reducing the likelihood of suicidal ideation in trauma-exposed veterans (Walser et al., 2015). Increased mindfulness was associated with significant reductions in depression severity. Increases in experiential acceptance were associated with a lower likelihood of suicidal ideation (Walser et al., 2015).

ACT easily adapts to acute care settings and can be used with other approaches discussed in this chapter, including discrete mindfulness interventions like leaves on a stream, as well as behavioral activation. Patients have found values-based card sorting activities (see Appendix for printable handouts) helpful, not only in identifying and ranking their own personal values but also in pairing them with creative problem solving and the development of novel coping skills. Clinically, acceptance-based interventions have led to notable decreases in distress and promoted positive coping and growth.

Acceptance is a rich and complex concept. Acceptance is not, of course, "being happy" that the event occurred. Acceptance does not mean we like what has happened; acceptance means that by "leaning into" the reality of our life situation as it is now, we may let go of the struggle with the injustice of our situation and events we cannot change. Acceptance gives us the power to take control by acknowledging that some things are out of our control, which in turn gives us the ability to choose to live a life filled with value and meaning.

Ideally, family members and loved ones share in acceptance. When family members are productively involved in the plan of care a new "normal" is easier to attain. Shared acceptance allows the patient and loved ones to approach suffering jointly. They can understand together that nothing will ever be the same, but that life still has meaning and purpose.

Existential and solution-focused interventions

As discussed throughout this text, in addition to the alleviation of suffering, the promotion of posttraumatic growth should be considered a potential goal for treatment. While not typically thought of in traditional outpatient settings, deploying evidence-based practices, the incorporation of existential and solution-focused approaches has proved highly effective as an adjuvant when combined with other therapeutic modalities discussed in this chapter. The utilization of existential approaches has a rich history related to their application as a treatment for survivors of trauma. Viktor Frankl (1962, 1967), a survivor of horrific trauma endured in concentration camps during World War II, developed an existential approach to treatment that he termed logotherapy (Frankl, 1962, 1967). Logotherapy, as Frankl described it, sees the central issue in the human experience as a search for meaning. Acute trauma makes this search for meaning more acute and poignant. Contemporary extensions of Frankl's work include the school of existential analysis, which expands on his belief that man's ultimate motivation in life is the search for meaning to include three additional existential motivations (Längle et al., 2003). These three additional motivations can be described as fundamental questions: the question of existence, the question of life, and the question of the person.

Humanistic approaches that incorporate these existential questions as primary prompts can assist us in navigating the patient through the process of developing greater posttraumatic growth (Vachon et al., 2016). The humanistic-existential approach views growth and healing through the lens of attempting to increase an individual's sense of completeness, integrity, and self-coherence (Vachon et al., 2016). It emphasizes the understanding of posttraumatic strengths rather than focusing on symptoms and posttraumatic distress. Solution-focused approaches have shown strong efficacy and large effect sizes, particularly related to the development of posttraumatic growth and sleep disturbance (Eads & Lee, 2019). Interventions such as the miracle question can be easily intertwined in both clinical assessment sessions, or follow-up psychotherapy sessions. The miracle question is, "Suppose you went to sleep tonight and a miracle happened that solved your problem. When you woke up tomorrow, what would you notice that would be different?" Because solution-oriented problem-solving approaches are future-focused, these interventions also pair well with motivational interviewing interventions if behavior change is a primary goal.

Interpersonal and relational aspects of care

The most important aspects of psychological care are the most difficult to measure and manualize. The therapeutic alliance, which is influenced by caring and empathy, may be the most important aspect of psychological care (Tschacher et al., 2015). Psychotherapy is not a product; it is a relationship. The language used to describe and differentiate the multiple types of therapies can seem to suggest that they are unique and separate products to be delivered. They are not. They are operationalized strategies to effectively convey understanding, knowledge, and caring. The similarities between therapeutic techniques far overshadow their differences. Caring and empathy are difficult to operationalize, but are the key to effective psychological interventions. Sometimes, an excessive focus on differentiating between therapies can obscure the existential aspects of facing a suffering human and trying to help them navigate the unfamiliar and difficult terrain of acute trauma.

End-of-life issues in acute trauma

End-of-life issues can be especially poignant in acute trauma cases. Often, trauma survivors are young and in good health prior to the traumatic event. In these cases, death is often totally unexpected. Trauma can deeply influence the experience of death, and when trauma results in death within days or hours, there is little time or opportunity to process both the experience of the traumatic event itself and consider end-of-life issues. The setting of acute trauma care is typically less focused on end-of-life issues than a geriatric or oncology setting might be; trauma surgeons prioritize life-saving measures and are less oriented towards end-of-life issues. The end-of-life issues that can appear in the acute trauma setting are powerful examples of the flexibility required in the psychological treatment of the patient with acute trauma.

Exposure to trauma can shake our trust in the world around us. Those impacted by PTSD are more likely to refuse care, mistrust clinical interventions, and report increased levels of pain and emotional distress (Johnston et al., 2024). Trauma survivors sometimes express a wish to die alone, and this wish seems to be colored by bitterness and despair, as well as a feeling of being betrayed by the world. This feeling can be acknowledged and normalized, and brief interventions based on the principles of narrative therapy and ACT can be beneficial.

While end-of-life accounts from acute trauma patients have not been systematically studied, Johnston et al. (2024) reported that individuals diagnosed with PTSD sometimes relive their traumatic experiences at the end of life. In these cases, a more comprehensive life review could be considered, especially including concepts of forgiveness and self-compassion. The end of life, while a time of grief and sadness, can also be a time of reconciliation and personal growth. Palliative care and hospice interventions can be useful in cases where acute trauma results in terminal injury (Esquibel et al., 2020).

Therapeutic interventions at the end of life often involve legacy work. Legacy work focuses on prioritizing issues of meaning and purpose and thoughtful consideration of what one leaves behind at the end of life. If time is limited, legacy work can be done mentally; if time is sufficient, consideration can be made of physical mementos such as cards, notes, gifts, audio and video recordings for loved ones or descendants. Legacy work is related to the Dignity Model, which has been shown to be effective in the care of patients who have terminal conditions (Chochinov et al., 2011). End-of-life care involves the liminal space between life and death and necessarily involves existential issues of meaning, purpose, and spirituality.

What makes therapy therapeutic?

Different schools and types of therapy are sometimes misrepresented as if they were different products. For purposes of research and marketing, they are sometimes presented as products, each with its own rules and manualized interventions, competing for validation in the research and commercial marketplace. The similarities between different types of therapies far outweigh their differences. When clinicians are videotaped, the way they describe what they do is very different than what they actually do. The clinician's descriptions of their therapy make it sound like they are delivering unique products, but skilled clinicians from one school, when they are actually doing the work, sound very much like skilled clinicians from another school of therapy. For instance, a good CBT-focused clinician can sound very much like an ACT-focused clinician when they are actually delivering interventions. Certain key common elements are shared by all good clinicians, one of the most important of which is empathy (Norcross & Lambert, 2019). Rather than thinking of different therapies as different products, it is more meaningful to think of each type of therapy as emphasizing a different aspect of a therapeutic intervention. Good therapy focuses on the empathic connection with the patient and builds on that connection to offer useful skills and insights. The empathic connection is actually the crucial aspect of the intervention, but it is sometimes neglected in academic literature because it is difficult to operationalize. That is especially true in the ultra-short-term therapies that must be used in the acute care setting. The real work in that setting is connecting and caring, and conveying that caring.

Treatment planning: a teaching exercise with Jesse the intern

Meeting With Jesse

Jesse entered my office, hanging their wrinkled lab coat on my coat rack and placing their cup of coffee on the table before taking a seat in one of the chairs directly across from me. Despite the busy day, they brought an air of enthusiasm to our supervision discussion, eagerly stating, "I can't wait to get your input on these cases!"

Always organized, Jesse prepared their case discussions in a standardized and structured manner so that we could succinctly review all relevant clinical information prior to discussing recommendations related to the treatment plan. Today, Jesse wanted to present their patients' relevant symptom experiences and proposed diagnoses, asking for my input on how to best assist each patient from a treatment planning perspective, considering individual interventions in addition to the standard recommendations.

The treatment plan is the culmination of our clinical assessment process and includes a wide range of recommendations. Some interventions are standard and necessary for each patient; others, such as the specific therapeutic modality or recommended psychological interventions, are unique to the individual case. Standard recommendations include the provision of developmentally appropriate psychoeducation related to common experiences following exposure to trauma, as well as the available psychosocial recovery services that patients may utilize during their hospital stay. Additionally, each treatment plan includes information related to the recommended disposition or whether ongoing mental health care is recommended following discharge. An integral component of each treatment plan is also the emphasis on collaborative communication with the patient's primary medical or surgical team, documenting that information related to the assessment and associated recommendations has been directly conveyed to them. Let's look at some of Jesse's cases to illuminate the process of developing the treatment plan and adapting interventions to the individual.

Jesse's Case Description of Mr. Jones

Mr. Jones is a 35-year-old man, currently on hospital day 10, who presented to the emergency department by ambulance with concerns related to significant right leg pain with obvious deformity following a 9-foot fall from a ladder while intoxicated on alcohol. On admission, his blood alcohol level was 0.25, and following imaging, he was found to have multiple fractures in his right lower extremity requiring surgical fixation.

(Continued)

The patient described new-onset symptoms of intermittent sadness as well as shame and guilt related to his recent fall and ongoing hospitalization. He also reported that he was worried about the impact that his injury might have on his ability to return to work as a roofer. The patient denied experiencing functional impairment related to his emotional shifts and has been participating in physical and occupational therapy.

Mr. Jones described a pattern of significant alcohol use, with daily drinking beginning approximately 1 year prior to this admission. He reported that he drank approximately 1 pint of vodka daily. He denied symptoms of withdrawal on cessation in the past and is not exhibiting any symptoms of withdrawal during this admission. He described frequent unsuccessful attempts to stop consuming alcohol, as well as often consuming more than intended, increased tolerance, and cravings for alcohol. His recurrent alcohol use resulted in failures to fulfill personal obligations, as evidenced by frequent call-offs from work due to hang-overs, and recurrent alcohol use in situations where it is physically hazardous. He denied using any other substances, including cannabis and tobacco.

He had no prior psychiatric history or history of mental health treatment. He denied any current or past suicidal ideation, intent or plan as well as any symptoms of mania or perceptual disturbances such as auditory or visual hallucinations. There was no family history of psychiatric illness, although he did share that his father had also experienced difficulties related to alcohol misuse. He had strong family support from his wife of 10 years and no children. My diagnostic formulation included a primary alcohol use disorder, severe, in a controlled environment.

My conceptualization includes consideration of his emotional distress as context appropriate and not leading to functional impairment. He is currently medically cleared for discharge and expected to be transferred to an inpatient physical rehabilitation program within 1 to 3 days.

Jesse's case presentation for Mr. Jones paints a picture of an individual with preexisting concerns related to alcohol use disorder that occur in the context of insight into his psychopathology. When beginning the process of treatment planning, one of the critical steps is analyzing the potential length of time available to provide care to patients while they are hospitalized. In the case of Mr. Jones, Jesse shared that we would only have 1 to 3 days prior to his discharge. Additionally, his discharge plan revolves around transition to an inpatient rehabilitation program, so we cannot transition him directly to a substance use disorder treatment program.

With this information in mind, my initial approach would incorporate psychoeducational interventions with motivational interviewing as my primary intervention to promote intrinsically driven behavior change related to substance use cessation. Currently, his emotional distress is subclinical in nature, although education related to symptoms of both depressive disorders and anxiety disorders would prove helpful should the patient develop increased distress following discharge. Additionally, I would recommend a consult for our trauma social work team prior to the patient's discharge so that they may assist with reviewing options for ongoing substance use disorder treatment after completion of his inpatient rehabilitation stay. I would also ask the patient if he would like to meet with our addiction medicine team prior to discharge so that they may discuss psychopharmacologic interventions to assist with sobriety.

Jesse's Case Description of Ms. Newton

Ms. Newton is a 22-year-old woman, currently on hospital day 2, who presented to the emergency department via private vehicle after sustaining multiple stab wounds to her upper extremities and abdomen. On presentation, she was found to be hemodynamically unstable. Her injuries include multiple lacerations to her hands and forearms, as well as several penetrating wounds in her abdomen requiring an emergent exploratory laparotomy with subsequent colostomy. I saw her in the surgical intensive care unit, where she was sleepy but oriented to self, time, context, and location, and able to fully participate in my evaluation. Her sister was initially present but left the room to make sure she had maximal privacy. She described remembering the details surrounding her assault and that her ex-boyfriend had stabbed her in her home shortly after she terminated the relationship. Additionally, she reported recalling her sister carrying her to her car and driving her to the hospital, stating that she thought she wasn't going to survive.

She described the development of significant psychological distress upon waking up this morning in the hospital and beginning to process what had happened. Specifically, she reported notable new symptoms of anxious distress, including intrusive images and memories, related to her assault, hypervigilance, and physiologic symptoms of distress, including racing heart, shortness of breath, and diaphoresis when male team members are in the room. This is also supported by the surgical team's observations, who shared that she appears to be very uncomfortable when male team members are tasked with providing care to her. She stated that she was very scared that her ex-boyfriend might attempt to harm her because she survived, and the police have not yet apprehended him.

Ms. Newton reported socially using cannabis once or twice a month and denied any other substance use. Additionally, she denied any prior history of psychiatric treatment or clinically significant mental health concerns, although she did share that she is a "worrier" at baseline. She described a strong desire to live and denied any current or past suicidal ideation, intent, or plan, as well as any symptoms of mania or perceptual disturbances such as auditory or visual hallucinations. Despite anger directed towards her ex-romantic partner for assaulting her, she denied homicidal ideation, intent, or plan. She denied any family history of any psychiatric concerns or treatment. She reported that her sister is a good support for her, but that outside of her sister, she has limited contact with her other family members and only a handful of trusted friends.

My diagnostic formulation includes a primary diagnosis of an adjustment disorder with anxiety. She is currently expected to have at least 1 to 2 weeks

(Continued)

remaining in her hospital stay if she does not experience complications, and she is open to regular follow-up during that time.

Jesse's case presentation for Ms. Newton describes new-onset psychological distress in an individual with multiple risk factors for the progression of adjustment disorder to ASD and the potential development of PTSD. These risk factors include genetic loading for anxiety disorders, a high-risk mechanism of injury (i.e., interpersonal violence) perpetrated by a former romantic partner, the presence of significant emotional distress and a fear of dying shortly following the assault, and limited social support. We know that we have at least 1 to 2 weeks to provide intervention to this patient. At the time of the evaluation, no recommendations had been made as to disposition.

Considering the patient's multiple symptoms of distress, my initial treatment focus following the delivery of trauma-related psychoeducation would be on providing high-quality proactive coping mechanisms to mitigate the most disruptive symptoms. In this case, that likely would be the physiologic distress associated with male team members entering the room. To begin addressing these concerns, I would provide psychoeducation, teaching mindfulness-based interventions with an initial focus on relaxation training. Because of the presence of significant re-experiencing symptoms, I likely will begin with a mindfulness centering or grounding exercise, encouraging the patient to keep their eyes open to mitigate the potential for intrusive thoughts or images during treatment. To increase the likelihood of active engagement and ongoing practice related to the mindfulness interventions, I would request permission from the patient to educate her nurses and care team members about the plan of care so that they may encourage utilization of coping skills proactively should distress develop.

Additionally, we can recommend environmental interventions. In the case of Ms. Newton, two primary environmental changes may be helpful. As she was assaulted by a known individual who is not in police custody, I would encourage our team to enact heightened safety precautions for the patient, including modifying the electronic medical record to make Ms. Newton unsearchable, restricting visitation to a list of individuals authorized by Ms. Newton, and placing the patient in a room in the visual field of a nurses' station. Because of Ms. Newton's fear of men entering her room, we would recommend assigning female staff when possible. If female staff are not available to care for the patient, we would encourage that all male staff are accompanied by a female team member when performing any direct care. Additionally, with Ms. Newton's permission, we could place reminder signs on her door requesting that all care team members announce their name and role prior to entering the room. We will plan to see Ms. Newton 2 to 3 times per week until symptoms improve. Discussions related to a transition to outpatient behavioral health care will begin once disposition recommendations are finalized.

Jesse's Case Description of Mr. Williams

Mr. Williams is a 47-year-old man who is currently on hospital day 35, who presented as a direct transfer to the surgical intensive care unit from an outside hospital for escalation of care and management of an open abdomen after sustaining multiple gunshot wounds to the torso and lower extremities. Following the closure of his abdomen, he was transferred to the surgical general practice unit. I have been following him for 2 weeks and have conducted the initial evaluation and three follow-up sessions with him.

He continues to report the experience of context-appropriate sadness related to his assault and prolonged hospitalization, with the presence of some guilt, stating, "I know I shouldn't have been in that neighborhood, I just feel so guilty putting my family through this." Mr. William's treatment was initially focused on his guilt, which was severe. He has been appropriately utilizing his social support network by spending time with his wife and children daily when they come to visit. Additionally, he has been using the behaviorally based pain management interventions that we discussed during our first treatment session to good effect, with pain ratings consistently decreasing 4 to 5 points out of 10 following utilization. After the provision of behavioral pain management interventions, the patient was amenable to integrating acceptance and value-based interventions into his plan of care. To date, we have completed a values card sort activity to identify highly valued life activities.

Currently, Mr. Williams is not reporting any clinically significant symptoms of distress and has been using the combination of skills offered in therapy. He has no prior psychiatric history or history of mental health treatment, although he did report daily cannabis use and social alcohol use prior to admission, neither of which caused functional impairment. He has continuously expressed a strong desire to live, and despite his fluctuating sadness and guilt, he has consistently denied any current or past suicidal ideation, intent, or plan as well as any symptoms of mania or perceptual disturbances such as auditory or visual hallucinations. Of note, he described being raised in unsafe neighborhoods as a child with exposure to frequent community violence and the unexpected deaths of several friends at a young age.

My diagnostic formulation concludes that the patient does not currently have any diagnosable psychological disorder. He will require transfer to an inpatient physical rehabilitation program once medically cleared. I would appreciate any feedback you might have about potential interventions that might be helpful so that I can refine my treatment plan.

Jesse's case presentation for Mr. Williams illustrates how we can dynamically adjust our treatment plans as targets for treatment change during our patients' hospital stays. As the patient is not currently reporting clinically significant distress and has responded well to beginning acceptance-based treatments, I would encourage Jesse to continue to focus on this as the primary approach to treatment. Additionally, the eventual incorporation of existential approaches when combined with acceptance-based interventions may prove helpful in promoting posttraumatic growth and further reducing symptoms of distress related to guilt. The values card sort activity that the patient completed can be utilized for discussions about behavioral activation interventions. These can be used to reinforce effective coping skills that the patient may utilize during periods of time when he does experience a sad mood. As the patient nears discharge, it would be important to discuss different options for ongoing psychological support after he completes his physical rehabilitation.

Applying psychological treatment options

As we have seen, a range of psychological treatment options are available to assist and support the acute trauma patient. These should be chosen flexibly and thoughtfully. Patients' needs will vary over the course of their recoveries. Treatment planning is a dynamic process, and options must be chosen in collaboration with the patient. The therapeutic relationship itself is the most important ingredient of effective psychological treatment. Maintenance and development of that relationship should take precedence over any specific treatment choice or plan. The human empathic bond with a suffering individual is central to any psychological intervention.

Chapter summary

The authors describe the array of therapeutic interventions that can be helpful in the psychological management of patients with acute trauma. The acuity of severe trauma and the distress it can cause creates challenging issues for the inpatient treatment teams. Methodological issues make psychotherapy research challenging in the acute care settings, so many interventions are evidence-informed rather than evidence-based.

References

American Psychiatric Association (2022). *Diagnostic and statistical manual of mental disorders* (5th ed., text rev.). American Psychiatric Association Publishing. https://doi.org/10.1176/appi.books.9780890425787.

Beck, J. S. (2020). *Cognitive behavior therapy: Basics and beyond*. Guilford Press.

Bischof, G., Bischof, A., & Rumpf, H. J. (2020). Motivational interviewing: An evidence-based approach for use in medical practice. *Deutsches Arzteblatt International, 118*(7), 109–115. https://doi.org/10.3238/arztebl.m2021.0014.

Boyd, J. E., Lanius, R. A., & McKinnon, M. C. (2018). Mindfulness-based treatments for posttraumatic stress disorder: A review of the treatment literature and neurobiological evidence. *Journal of Psychiatry and Neuroscience, 43*(1), 7–25. https://doi.org/10.1503/jpn.170021.

Brooks, S. K., Weston, D., Wessely, S., & Greenberg, N. (2021). Effectiveness and acceptability of brief psychoeducational interventions after potentially traumatic events: A systematic review. *European Journal of Psychotraumatology, 12*(1). https://doi.org/10.1080/20008198.2021.1923110.

Brymer M., A. Jacobs, C. Layne, R. Pynoos, J. Ruzek, A. Steinberg, E. Vernberg, P. Watson (2006). *Psychological first aid: Field operations guide* (2nd ed.)., National Child Traumatic Stress Network. https://www.nctsn.org/sites/default/files/resources//pfa_field_operations_guide.pdf.

Chapman, S. G. (2012). *The five keys to mindful communication: Using deep listening and mindful speech to strengthen relationships, heal conflicts, and accomplish your goals.* Shambhala Publications.

Chochinov, H. M., Kristjanson, L. J., Breitbart, W., McClement, S., Hack, T. F., Hassard, T., & Harlos, M. (2011). Effect of dignity therapy on distress and end-of-life experience in terminally ill patients: a randomised controlled trial. *The Lancet Oncology, 12*(8), 753–762. https://doi.org/10.1016/S1470-2045(11)70153-X.

Eads, R., & Lee, M. Y. (2019). Solution focused therapy for trauma survivors: A review of the outcome literature. *Journal of Solution Focused Practices, 3*(1). https://doi.org/10.59874/001c.75083.

Esquibel, B. M., Waller, C. J., Borgert, A. J., Kallies, K. J., Harter, T. D., & Cogbill, T. H. (2020). The role of palliative care in acute trauma: When is it appropriate? *American Journal of Surgery, 220*(6), 1456–1461. https://doi.org/10.1016/j.amjsurg.2020.10.002.

Fauerbach, J. A., Gehrke, A. K., Mason, S. T., Gould, N. F., Milner, S. M., & Caffrey, J. (2020). Cognitive behavioral treatment for acute posttrauma distress: A randomized, controlled proof-of-concept study among hospitalized adults with burns. *Archives of Physical Medicine and Rehabilitation, 101*(1), S16. https://doi.org/10.1016/j.apmr.2018.11.027.

Frankl, V. E. (1962). *Man's search for meaning.* Beacon Press.

Frankl, V. E. (1967). Logotherapy and existentialism. *Psychotherapy: Theory, Research & Practice, 4*(3), 138–142. https://doi.org/10.1037/h0087982.

Grab, J. (2025). Psychological and social aspects in orthopaedics and trauma surgery, challenges and solutions in trauma: a didactic overview. *EFORT Open Reviews, 10*(6), 431–438. https://doi.org/10.1530/eor-2025-0054.

Grant, E., Bowman, A., & Johnson, L. (2025). Effectiveness of interventions for psychological distress following traumatic injury: A systematic review. *Injury, 56*(2). https://doi.org/10.1016/j.injury.2024.112090.

Hayes, S. C., Strosahl, K. D., & Wilson, K. G. (1999). *Acceptance and commitment therapy: An experiential approach to behavior change.* Guilford Press.

International Society of Traumatic Stress Studies. (2019, March 19). *Posttraumatic stress disorder prevention and treatment guidelines methodology and recommendations.* https://istss.org/wp-content/uploads/2024/08/ISTSS_PreventionTreatmentGuidelines_FNL-March-19-2019.pdf.

Johnston, N., Chapman, M., Gibson, J., Paterson, C., Turner, M., Strickland, K., Liu, W.-M., Phillips, C., & Bail, K. (2024). Re-living trauma near death: an integrative review using Grounded Theory narrative analysis. *Palliative Care and Social Practice, 18.* https://doi.org/10.1177/26323524241277851.

Keane, T. M., Marshall, A. D., & Taft, C. T. (2006). Posttraumatic stress disorder: Etiology, epidemiology, and treatment outcome. *Annual Review of Clinical Psychology, 2*, 161–197. https://doi.org/10.1146/annurev.clinpsy.2.022305.095305.

Längle A., Kirchbach G. v, Wurm C. (2003). https://www.researchgate.net/publication/292412091_Existential_analysis_-_The_search_for_an_approval_of_life (Original work published 1999).

Larsen, S. E., Hunt, J. C., Geier, T., Heyrman, K., Schumann, N., Brandolino, A., Timmer-Murillo, S., Bergner, C., Larson, C., & deRoon-Cassini, T. A. (2021). A randomized trial of modified prolonged exposure to prevent the development of posttraumatic stress disorder in patients hospitalized with traumatic injuries. *Journal of Traumatic Stress, 34*(1), 104–115. https://doi.org/10.1002/jts.22580.

Lowe, C., & Murray, C. (2014). Adult service-users' experiences of trauma-focused cognitive behavioural therapy. *Journal of Contemporary Psychotherapy, 44*(4), 223–231. https://doi.org/10.1007/s10879-014-9272-1.

Miller, W. R., & Rollnick, S. (2023). *Motivational interviewing: Helping people change and grow*. Guilford Press.

Miller-Matero, L. R., Coleman, J. P., Smith-Mason, C. E., Moore, D. A., Marszalek, D., & Ahmedani, B. K. (2019). A brief mindfulness intervention for medically hospitalized patients with acute pain: A pilot randomized clinical Ttial. *Pain Medicine (United States), 20*(11), 2149–2154. https://doi.org/10.1093/pm/pnz082.

Norcross, J. C., & Lambert, M. J. (2019). In J. C. Norcross, & M. J. Lambert (Eds.). *Handbook of psychotherapy integration*. Oxford University Press.

Pirente, N., Blum, C., Wortberg, S., Bostanci, S., Berger, E., Lefering, R., Bouillon, B., Rehm, K. E., & Neugebauer, E. A. M. (2007). Quality of life after multiple trauma: The effect of early onset psychotherapy on quality of life in trauma patients. *Langenbeck's Archives of Surgery, 392*(6), 739–745. https://doi.org/10.1007/s00423-007-0171-8.

Roberts, N. P., Kitchiner, N. J., Kenardy, J., & Bisson, J. I. (2010). Early psychological interventions to treat acute traumatic stress symptoms. *The Cochrane Database of Systematic Reviews*(3). https://doi.org/10.1002/14651858.CD007944.pub2.

Roberts, N. P., Kitchiner, N. J., Kenardy, J., Lewis, C. E., & Bisson, J. I. (2019). Early psychological intervention following recent trauma: A systematic review and meta-analysis. *European Journal of Psychotraumatology, 10*(1). https://doi.org/10.1080/20008198.2019.1695486.

Rothbaum, B. O., Kearns, M. C., Price, M., Malcoun, E., Davis, M., Ressler, K. J., Lang, D., & Houry, D. (2012). Early intervention may prevent the development of posttraumatic stress disorder: A randomized pilot civilian study with modified prolonged exposure. *Biological Psychiatry, 72*(11), 957–963. https://doi.org/10.1016/j.biopsych.2012.06.002.

Tschacher, W., Haken, H., & Kyselo, M. (2015). Alliance: A common factor of psychotherapy modeled by structural theory. *Frontiers in Psychology, 6*. https://doi.org/10.3389/fpsyg.2015.00421.

Vachon, M., Bessette, P. C., & Goyette, C. (2016). Growing from an invisible wound": A humanistic-existential approach to PTSD. In G. El-Baalbaki, & C. Fortin (Eds.). *A multidimensional approach to post-traumatic stress disorder–from theory to practice*. InTech.

Wagner, A. W., Zatzick, D. F., Ghesquiere, A., & Jurkovich, G. J. (2007). Behavioral Activation as an Early Intervention for Posttraumatic Stress Disorder and Depression Among Physically Injured Trauma Survivors. *Cognitive and Behavioral Practice, 14*(4), 341–349. https://doi.org/10.1016/j.cbpra.2006.05.002.

Walser, R. D., Garvert, D. W., Karlin, B. E., Trockel, M., Ryu, D. M., & Taylor, C. B. (2015). Effectiveness of acceptance and commitment therapy in treating depression and suicidal ideation in veterans. *Behaviour Research and Therapy, 74*, 25–31. https://doi.org/10.1016/j.brat.2015.08.012.

Walser, R. D., & Westrup, D. (2007). *Acceptance & commitment therapy for the treatment of post-traumatic stress disorder and trauma-related problems: A practitioner's guide to using mindfulness and acceptance strategies*. New Harbinger Publications.

Wharton, E., Edwards, K. S., Juhasz, K., & Walser, R. D. (2019). Acceptance-based interventions in the treatment of PTSD: Group and individual pilot data using Acceptance and Commitment Therapy. *Journal of Contextual Behavioral Science, 14*, 55–64. https://doi.org/10.1016/j.jcbs.2019.09.006.

Chapter 7

Psychopharmacologic interventions for trauma patients

Pharmacotherapy in acute traumatic stress disorders

Pharmacological interventions are an integral part of mental health treatment for most psychiatric disorders. Medications can provide not only symptom relief but also specific treatment for the neurophysiological dysregulation that can accompany acute traumatic stress disorders (ATSDs), which include both acute stress disorder (ASD) and adjustment disorder. Such dysregulation might, in theory, be responsive to psychopharmacological intervention. Medications ideally can relieve distress and may help prevent the development of posttraumatic stress disorder (PTSD).

But the pharmacological therapy of patients after acute trauma has special challenges. The large double-blind clinical trials that established the efficacy of psychopharmacological agents in disorders such as PTSD and major depressive disorder have not been attempted in ATSDs because of the special clinical issues involved in treating this population. These disorders are time-limited, and patients with ATSDs often require acute medical and surgical interventions, making research trials difficult to perform and consents for research challenging to obtain. Yet these patients have a high level of distress and may experience severe insomnia, nightmares, and grief. There is a strong impetus to relieve distress, but a lack of clear guidelines and algorithms for treatment.

Also, these patients may have other issues that complicate pharmacological treatment. They are often in pain and may require pain medications. They may have previous psychiatric disorders that may be untreated or inadequately treated. Substance misuse, intoxication, or substance withdrawal may complicate the clinical and diagnostic presentation and affect the choice of medications. Patients, families, and other clinicians may have unrealistic expectations about what medication can be provided. Many patients have asked, "Doc, can you give me something to make this all go away?" Obviously, no medicine can do that.

This chapter will focus on specific pharmacological treatments of trauma- and stressor-related disorders and associated symptoms, such as insomnia, nightmares, anxiety, and intrusive thoughts. Two aspects of ASD treatment

The Psychology of Acute Trauma. DOI: https://doi.org/10.1016/B978-0-443-33212-8.00025-7

need to be considered, namely symptom relief and PTSD prevention. Most treatments, except for some insomnia treatments, purport to do both. The pharmacological management of traumatic brain injury (TBI) is discussed briefly later in this chapter. The pharmacological treatment of nightmares is reviewed in Chapter 8, Understanding and Treating Nightmares. Fig. 7.1 is a flow chart summarizing the psychopharmacological interventions discussed in the chapter.

Pain and withdrawal are indications for urgent pharmacological treatment. The management of these issues is well described in standard medical and surgical texts, and the discussion of such treatment is beyond the scope of this book except to remind the reader that pain is a subjective experience. Distress heightens the experience of pain, and relieving general distress can help with pain and vice versa.

When to consider psychotropic medications

Psychotropic medications should be considered in cases of a prior psychiatric disorder. Patients with acute trauma are likely to have experienced prior trauma, and the acute trauma may have occurred on top of a preexisting PTSD or complex posttraumatic stress disorder (CPTSD). In those cases, pharmacological intervention for PTSD or CPTSD is appropriate because we are treating an underlying disorder rather than an ATSD. Similarly, with other underlying psychiatric disorders, such as depressive disorders, bipolar disorders, or schizophrenia spectrum disorders, treatment of the underlying disorder may be appropriate and may help to relieve overall distress. Additionally, acute

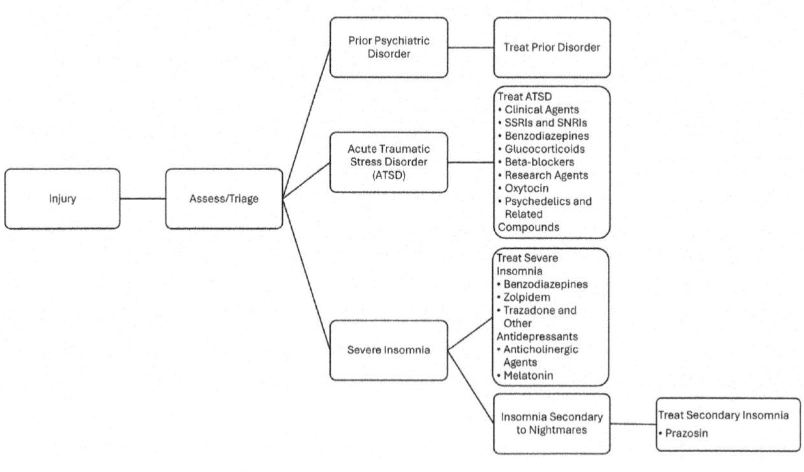

FIGURE 7.1 Flow chart for psychopharmacological interventions.

trauma can be a significant stressor that leads to relapse of the underlying illness.

Memories are a complex issue in ATSDs. Intrusive memories are an important trauma symptom. Some potential interventions, such as benzodiazepines or beta-blockers, might suppress memory formation. Theoretically, forgetting or not remembering a trauma may seem beneficial, but it may also contribute to avoidance-based coping and interfere with processing the traumatic experience and potential posttraumatic growth. Further, if we apply the ideas of theorists like Bessel van der Kolk, memories may be dissociated, that is, stored outside of conscious awareness or in the body itself (van der Kolk, 2014). A memory not stored in conscious awareness may still affect behavior and emotions, but may be less accessible to integration and processing. Memories that are not stored in conscious narrative form may be stored by dissociative mechanisms, and drugs that interfere with memory formation may have a risk of increasing this kind of dissociated storage. Dissociated memories are less accessible for the integration and processing that is part of recovery.

Selective serotonin reuptake inhibitors and serotonin-norepinephrine reuptake inhibitors

Selective serotonin reuptake inhibitors (SSRIs) and serotonin-norepinephrine reuptake inhibitors (SNRIs) have been extensively studied in PTSD and are moderately effective. Response rates in patients receiving SSRIs were significantly higher than in those receiving placebo, so SSRIs are a natural choice for the treatment of ATSDs (Bertolini et al., 2024). The specific SSRIs and SNRIs recommended by the U.S. Department of Veterans Affairs for PTSD are sertraline, paroxetine, and venlafaxine (Alexander, 2012).

Benzodiazepines

Benzodiazepines are commonly used sedative-hypnotic drugs and are effective in reducing anxiety and inducing sleep. Benzodiazepines affect the widely distributed inhibitory neurotransmitter system known as gamma-aminobutyric acid (GABA). Benzodiazepines are typically safe and well-tolerated and, unlike SSRIs, which begin to work only after a period of 2 to 4 weeks, are effective immediately. Benzodiazepines are habit-forming and should be avoided in patients with substance misuse issues or strong family histories of substance misuse. Benzodiazepines have amnestic properties and can interfere with long-term memory storage (Barbee, 1993). There is no evidence from controlled clinical trials that benzodiazepines aid in recovery from ASD (Howlett & Stein, 2016). Benzodiazepines also suppress rapid eye movement (REM) sleep, and REM sleep has an important role in trauma processing.

Benzodiazepines may have a limited role in the acute management of severe insomnia, agitation, or hypervigilance. In one small case series, temazepam was effective in improving sleep and reducing symptoms of ASD, but in another small case series patients treated with benzodiazepines were more likely to show symptoms of PTSD after 6 months than those not treated with benzodiazepines (Davidson, 2006). Davidson (2006) reported that clinically he uses a short-term course (2 to 4 weeks) of benzodiazepines in patients with acute agitation, anxiety or sleep disturbance. Benzodiazepines are, of course, standard treatment for alcohol withdrawal.

Zolpidem is a commonly used hypnotic drug that is not a benzodiazepine but instead a unique class of drugs known as Z-drugs. Zolpidem is a GABA agonist and has a side effect and dependency profile that is similar to the benzodiazepines. There has been minimal research on zolpidem in the acute trauma setting.

Other hypnotics

Concerns about dependency have made clinicians reluctant to prescribe benzodiazepines for anxiety or sleep. Instead, low-dose sedating antidepressants such as trazadone, amitriptyline, or doxepin are used, although the best clinical evidence suggests that they are ineffective (Everitt et al., 2018). Trazodone is very commonly used for insomnia despite evidence suggesting that it is not effective (Yi et al., 2018).

Insomnia can be considered from two points of view, which suggest different pharmacological interventions. The most traditional view is to consider insomnia as a lack of sleepiness, and to treat it with sedating agents like benzodiazepines and related drugs, as discussed above. The other framework is to consider insomnia as an excess of wakefulness and to treat it with drugs that suppress wakefulness. Wakefulness is mediated by orexin, also known as hypocretin, and newer hypnotics like Suvorexant, Lemborexant, and Daridorexant target the orexin system and improve sleep not by causing sleepiness, but by suppressing wakefulness (Żełabowski et al., 2025). Orexin antagonists have not been used extensively in hospital or acute trauma settings, but they have the important advantage of not causing sedation and not suppressing REM sleep.

Prazosin, the alpha-1-adrenergic receptor agonist used to treat nightmares, has been shown to improve sleep in PTSD (Taylor, 1997). Hydroxyzine, an anticholinergic drug, and the anticonvulsant gabapentin have been shown to improve sleep in PTSD as well. Gabapentin has a complex mechanism of action involving the modulation of GABA and glutamate synthesis (Taylor, 1997). None of these drugs has been studied in ASD.

Melatonin is commonly used as a hypnotic because it is safe, cost-effective, and available over the counter. Melatonin regulates the circadian rhythm, but unlike other hypnotics, does not cause sleepiness. People who take melatonin describe a state of quiet wakefulness, which seems to predispose them to sleep. Melatonin has shown some promise in improving sleep quality, but it has not been systematically evaluated in a trauma population (Brzezinski et al., 2005; Zhdanova, 2005). Melatonin is secreted by the pineal gland during normal diurnal hormonal rhythms. It is best thought of as a "clock-reseter" rather than a hypnotic agent.

Glucocorticoids

Steroid hormones have a central role in modulating the body's response to stress. PTSD is associated with abnormalities in the hypothalamic-pituitary-adrenal axis. Exogenous steroids suppress the body's steroid response to stress and might, in theory, prevent the hypothalamic pituitary changes that result in PTSD. Animal models suggest that steroids might be most effective in a narrow 6-hour window after an acute trauma (Zohar et al., 2011). Human trials that have been attempted have been small and have shown mixed results. Some have suggested that steroids might be of benefit as late as 3 months after an acute trauma, but such interventions remain experimental (Florido et al., 2023).

Beta-blockers

Beta-blockers, like corticosteroids, can suppress elements of the stress response. Beta-blockers block the effects of epinephrine and norepinephrine. For instance, the increases in heart rate that occur in stress reactions will be blocked by drugs like propranolol. The beta-adrenergic system has been shown to have a role in the storage of memories associated with emotional arousal. Beta-blockers have shown some promise in the treatment of PTSD, especially when used early in the course of the disorder and in combination with psychotherapy (Giustino et al., 2016). Beta-blockers have not been adequately studied in ASD and must be considered experimental but promising at this time.

Opioids

Opioids are commonly used in the management of posttraumatic pain. A large multicenter study of patients with acute trauma showed that the median exposure to opiates in acute trauma patients is 30 mg of oxycodone. Most exposure occurs in the first 72 hours after trauma, and a significant degree of variability in exposure exists not only between trauma centers but especially within trauma centers (Alexander, 2012). Animal studies have shown that opioids may cause retrograde amnesia, perhaps by altering the way the hippocampus consolidates memories or by activating NMDA receptors

(McNally & Westbrook, 2003). Opioids have shown some promise in observational studies in the acute care setting (Mouthaan et al., 2015).

Oxytocin

Oxytocin enhances feelings of social bonding, trust, and safety. Animal data on the potential benefits of oxytocin have shown some promise, but the use of oxytocin after acute trauma remains experimental in humans.

Psychedelics and dissociative drugs

Psychedelic drugs like mescaline and lysergic acid diethylamide (LSD) and dissociative drugs like ketamine and 3,4-methylenedioxymethamphetamine (MDMA) have shown increasing promise in the treatment of a variety of psychiatric disorders, including PTSD. Psychedelic drugs can produce a dissolution of the sense of the separateness of the individual self and a sense of oneness with the universe. This mystical feeling or awareness, which Freud discussed as the "oceanic feeling" (Freud, 1961), can be an emotionally transformative one that changes the emotional perspective on trauma. On a neurophysiological level, psychedelic drugs suppress the default mode network and enhance associativity between different brain areas. In this way, they resemble REM sleep, and we might speculate that both dreaming and psychedelic experiences can lead to integrative experiences (Mahr & Sweigart, 2020). The tuberculosis drug D-cycloserine is closely related to the potent drug MDMA and has shown initial promise in the treatment of ASD, especially when combined with exposure therapy (Difede et al., 2014).

Psychedelics may have a role in trauma therapy in the psychological management of trauma responses in the postacute phase. Such interventions are not appropriate in the setting of acute inpatient care, but are of important theoretical interest in deepening the understanding of trauma processing and recovery.

Traumatic brain injury

A TBI is a head injury that involves damage to the brain. Most TBIs are mild and do not cause permanent brain damage, and are called concussions (although repeated concussions can cause long-term brain damage resulting in chronic traumatic encephalopathy). Worldwide, 69 million TBIs occur annually, and 25% are severe enough to cause long-lasting brain damage (Dewan et al., 2019). Often, such injuries occur in the context of polytrauma, or multiple severe trauma-related injuries. TBI is discussed in more detail in Chapter 10, Neurocognitive Disorders and Delirium, but patients with TBI present special issues in terms of psychopharmacological management. Common behavioral issues in these patients include agitation, aggression, disinhibition, irritability, impulsiveness, anxiety, and depression (Plantier & Luauté, 2016). Recovery tends to be slow and arduous.

While a complete review of this literature is beyond the scope of this book, the acute phase of TBI management often includes barbiturates and propofol, which lower intracranial pressure, prevent seizures, and depress cerebral metabolism, as well as antiseizure medications (Tani et al., 2022). In the postacute phase, antidepressants and buspirone can be helpful for depression and anxiety. Aggression and agitation can be difficult to manage in the cognitively impaired patient. Atypical antipsychotics such as olanzapine can be helpful. Amantadine, beta-blockers, antiepileptics, and methylphenidate can also be considered. Haloperidol and benzodiazepines may interfere with brain healing and should be avoided (Rahmani et al., 2022).

Polytrauma

TBI is often associated with polytrauma, which involves multiple injuries in multiple organ systems. TBI patients often have multiple orthopedic injuries, organ damage, and acute medical complications like shock, and may be facing issues of acute withdrawal or intoxication as well. Such cases require multiple medical and surgical interventions; life-threatening issues must be handled first. These patients often face a lengthy course of hospital treatment and extensive medical trauma in addition to their severe index trauma.

The psychology of prescribing

The pharmacological treatment of patients with acute trauma presents certain special challenges. The prescriber is often faced with a patient in significant distress, but in a setting where treatments that are well proven, safe, and highly efficacious are lacking. Medication therapy is a collaborative process. The development of a strong therapeutic alliance is essential to effective prescribing, and the prescriber must understand the therapeutic issues involved in the act of prescribing medicine (Mintz, 2022).

In addition to their therapeutic benefits, medications have symbolic power for both the prescriber and the patient and can represent caring in concrete form. Every prescription, in addition to its potential pharmacological benefit, has an important symbolic meaning for both the patient and the clinician. For the prescriber, giving a medication alleviates the powerful feeling of helplessness that a patient with acute trauma can stir in the prescriber. "At least I can do something," the prescriber tells themselves, and the feeling of helplessness is resolved. Countertransference feelings can be very powerful; it is important to be aware of them so that we give a prescription for the right reasons.

For the trauma survivor, being given a prescription has important symbolic meanings as well. It can potentially be experienced as a dismissive "medicalization" of their emotional distress. Every prescription is an implied promise, and every medication failure can be experienced as a broken promise. Alternatively, a tangible intervention like a medication can be experienced as a concrete manifestation of caring. Each time the medication is held and taken, that caring is internalized.

This symbolic power of medication is demonstrated by its placebo effect. While we try to minimize placebo effects in research, in clinical medicine, we can augment placebo responses by conveying genuine caring, hope, and empathy.

Selma's Story

Selma is a 40-year-old woman admitted after she was stabbed by an acquaintance during a fight. Selma has a long psychiatric history and has been diagnosed with schizoaffective disorder, bipolar type, and borderline personality disorder. She has been treated with antidepressants, mood stabilizers, and antipsychotics, without clear benefit. She has never been psychiatrically hospitalized. Selma also has a history of chronic alcohol and cocaine use. She reported that she has not consumed alcohol for several weeks, but last used cocaine 1 week ago. Additionally, she reported a several-year history of sobriety during her 30s, at which time she was doing well and denied psychiatric symptoms of depression or mania. After her current trauma, she has been depressed and tearful, with poor sleep. She has intrusive thoughts of the assault and nightmares.

Selma presents a dilemma in diagnosis. Her history of schizoaffective disorder, bipolar type, was questionable both because she was actively using cocaine and alcohol at that time and because her manic-like symptoms did not meet the duration criteria for mania or hypomania. Also, during her period of sobriety, she did not have psychiatric symptoms. Currently, Selma reports symptoms of ASD. In view of her significant past psychiatric history and her current symptomatology, it seemed appropriate to initiate pharmacological treatment with an antidepressant. Does Selma need a mood stabilizer as well? Her history of manic symptoms was very questionable since she had no manic symptoms during her period of sobriety. One might add a mood stabilizer prophylactically in case she truly experienced symptoms of schizoaffective disorder, bipolar type, but we were concerned that the more complex her medication regimen was, the less likely she would be to continue it as an outpatient. We started sertraline, educated her about manic symptoms, and referred her for substance use disorder treatment and outpatient psychotherapy at our outpatient trauma recovery center.

Chapter summary

Large-scale clinical trials are difficult to conduct in the population with ATSDs, so clear information about drug efficacy is often lacking. It is important to treat pain, withdrawal, and preexisting psychiatric disorders with appropriate medications. Pharmacological interventions may be of benefit in the sleep disturbances associated with ASD, and there is hope that medications, with further study, can relieve emotional distress and help prevent PTSD. Fig. 7.1 summarizes the psychopharmacological interventions discussed in this chapter.

References

Alexander, W. (2012). Pharmacotherapy for Post-traumatic Stress Disorder In Combat Veterans: Focus on Antidepressants and Atypical Antipsychotic Agents. *Pharmacy & Therapeutics, 37*(1), 32–38.

Barbee, J. G. (1993). Memory, benzodiazepines, and anxiety: integration of theoretical and clinical perspectives. *The Journal of Clinical Psychiatry, 54.*

Bertolini, F., Robertson, L., Bisson, J. I., Meader, N., Churchill, R., Ostuzzi, G., Stein, D. J., Williams, T., & Barbui, C. (2024). Early pharmacological interventions for prevention of post-traumatic stress disorder (PTSD) in individuals experiencing acute traumatic stress symptoms. *Cochrane Database of Systematic Reviews, 2024*(5). https://doi.org/10.1002/14651858.CD013613.pub2.

Brzezinski, A., Vangel, M. G., Wurtman, R. J., Norrie, G., Zhdanova, I., Ben-Shushan, A., & Ford, I. (2005). Effects of exogenous melatonin on sleep: A meta-analysis. *Sleep Medicine Reviews, 9*(1), 41–50. https://doi.org/10.1016/j.smrv.2004.06.004.

Davidson, J. R. T. (2006). Pharmacologic treatment of acute and chronic stress following trauma: 2006. *The Journal of Clinical Psychiatry, 67*(Suppl 2), 34–39.

Dewan, M. C., Rattani, A., Gupta, S., Baticulon, R. E., Hung, Y. C., Punchak, M., Agrawal, A., Adeleye, A. O., Shrime, M. G., Rubiano, A. M., Rosenfeld, J. V., & Park, K. B. (2019). Estimating the global incidence of traumatic brain injury. *Journal of Neurosurgery, 130*(4), 1080–1097. https://doi.org/10.3171/2017.10.JNS17352.

Difede, J., Cukor, J., Wyka, K., Olden, M., Hoffman, H., Lee, F. S., & Altemus, M. (2014). D-cycloserine augmentation of exposure therapy for post-traumatic stress disorder: A pilot randomized clinical trial. *Neuropsychopharmacology: Official Publication of the American College of Neuropsychopharmacology, 39*(5), 1052–1058. https://doi.org/10.1038/npp.2013.317.

Everitt, H., Baldwin, D. S., Stuart, B., Lipinska, G., Mayers, A., Malizia, A. L., Manson, C. C. F., & Wilson, S. (2018). Antidepressants for insomnia in adults. *Cochrane Database of Systematic Reviews, 2018*(5). https://doi.org/10.1002/14651858.CD010753.pub2.

Florido, A., Velasco, E. R., Monari, S., Cano, M., Cardoner, N., Sandi, C., Andero, R., & Perez-Caballero, L. (2023). Glucocorticoid-based pharmacotherapies preventing PTSD. *Neuropharmacology, 224.* https://doi.org/10.1016/j.neuropharm.2022.109344.

Freud, S. (1961). *Civilization and its discontents.* W.W. Norton & Company.

Giustino, T. F., Fitzgerald, P. J., & Maren, S. (2016). Revisiting propranolol and PTSD: Memory erasure or extinction enhancement? *Neurobiology of Learning and Memory, 130*, 26–33. https://doi.org/10.1016/j.nlm.2016.01.009.

Howlett, J. R., & Stein, M. B. (2016). Prevention of trauma and stressor-related disorders: A review. *Neuropsychopharmacology: Official Publication of the American College of Neuropsychopharmacology, 41*(1), 357–369. https://doi.org/10.1038/npp.2015.261.

Mahr, G., & Sweigart, J. (2020). Psychedelic drugs and Jungian therapy. *Journal of Jungian Scholarly Studies, 15*(1), 86–98. https://doi.org/10.29173/jjs127s.

McNally, G. P., & Westbrook, R. F. (2003). Opioid Receptors Regulate the Extinction of Pavlovian Fear Conditioning. *Behavioral Neuroscience, 117*(6), 1292–1301. https://doi.org/10.1037/0735-7044.117.6.1292.

Mintz,D. (2022). *Psychodynamic psychopharmacology: Caring for the treatment resistant patient.* American Psychiatric Association Publishing.

Mouthaan, J., Sijbrandij, M., Reitsma, J. B., Luitse, J. S. K., Goslings, J. C., Gersons, B. P. R., & Olff, M. (2015). The role of early pharmacotherapy in the development of posttraumatic stress disorder symptoms after traumatic injury: An observational cohort study in consecutive patients. *General Hospital Psychiatry, 37*(3), 230–235. https://doi.org/10.1016/j.genhosppsych.2015.02.010.

Plantier, D., & Luauté, J. (2016). SOFMER group, Drugs for behavior disorders after traumatic brain injury: Systematic review and expert consensus leading to French recommendations for good practice. *Annals of Physical and Rehabilitation Medicine, 59*(1), 42–57. https://doi.org/10.1016/j.rehab.2015.10.003.

Rahmani, E., Lemelle, T., Sharp, H., Smarbafzadeh, E., & Kablinger, A. (2022). A descriptive analysis of pharmacological management of aggression and/or agitation in patients with traumatic brain injury in a Southwest Virginia inpatient population. *Journal of Clinical Pharmacy and Therapeutics, 47*(12), 2083–2090. https://doi.org/10.1111/jcpt.13754.

Tani, J., Wen, Y. T., Hu, C. J., & Sung, J. Y. (2022). Current and potential pharmacologic therapies for traumatic brain injury. *Pharmaceuticals, 15*(7). https://doi.org/10.3390/ph15070838.

Taylor, C. P. (1997). Mechanisms of action of gabapentin. *Revue Neurologique, 153*(1), 1.

van der Kolk (2014). *The body keeps the score: Brain, mind and body in the healing of trauma.* Penguin.

Yi, X.-Y., Ni, S.-F., Ghadami, M. R., Meng, H.-Q., Chen, M.-Y., Kuang, L., Zhang, Y.-Q., Zhang, L., & Zhou, X.-Y. (2018). Trazodone for the treatment of insomnia: a meta-analysis of randomized placebo-controlled trials. *Sleep Medicine, 45*, 25–32. https://doi.org/10.1016/j.sleep.2018.01.010.

Żełabowski, K., Petrov, W., Wojtysiak, K., Ratka, Z., Biedka, K., Wesołowski, M., Fus, K., Ślebioda, D., Rusinek, M., Sterkowicz, M., Radzka, I., & Chłopaś-Konowałek, A. (2025). Targeting the Orexin System in the Pharmacological Management of Insomnia and Other Diseases: Suvorexant, Lemborexant, Daridorexant, and Novel Experimental Agents. *International Journal of Molecular Sciences, 26*(17). https://doi.org/10.3390/ijms26178700.

Zhdanova, I. V. (2005). Melatonin as a hypnotic: Pro. *Sleep Medicine Reviews, 9*(1), 51–65. https://doi.org/10.1016/j.smrv.2004.04.003.

Zohar, J., Yahalom, H., Kozlovsky, N., Cwikel-Hamzany, S., Matar, M. A., Kaplan, Z., Yehuda, R., & Cohen, H. (2011). High dose hydrocortisone immediately after trauma may alter the trajectory of PTSD: Interplay between clinical and animal studies. *Neuropsychopharmacology, 21*(11), 796–809. https://doi.org/10.1016/j.euroneuro.2011.06.001.

Chapter 8

Understanding and treating nightmares

James's Story

James was a 40-year-old man who received several serious stab wounds in an altercation with a coworker. His injuries required several surgical interventions. He described the following dream, which I paraphrase:

I am knocked out for surgery, lying on a hospital bed. I feel a presence watching me. He is just sitting there facing me with his arms and legs crossed. The environment I'm in is between the physical world and the next realm. He is watching me because he took my voice away. It is in this little zone, like a portal, like he's on a video call with me. I have the worst feeling of despair, death, no hope, and the absence of God and love. He is frustrated because he isn't getting what he wants. I looked at him with courage and no fear and said, "You have no power here." And when I said that it's like he ended, hanging up the call and receded and disappeared.

As James's dream shows, nightmares connect with powerful emotions. Sometimes, as in this dream, they seem to be meaningful and to convey an important message. Our modern psychological paradigms tend to discount the idea of dream as a message and view dream purely as a symptom. Current cognitive and behavioral models of nightmares and their treatment acknowledge that dreams are important as sources of distress and markers of pathology. As such, they are something to be controlled and treated, not understood. But when we return to the actual experience of the patient, a dream like this is experienced by the dreamer as deeply meaningful. That potential for meaning is important to explore as well.

The purpose of dreams: an overview of the physiology of the dream process

The typical sleep cycle consists of several phases. As the sleeper grows drowsy, slow rolling eye movements begin. This is phase 1 sleep. As sleep

The Psychology of Acute Trauma. DOI: https://doi.org/10.1016/B978-0-443-33212-8.00012-9

deepens, unique electroencephalogram (EEG) wave forms appear, called sleep spindles and K complexes. These are the defining features of phase 2 sleep. Slow wave sleep follows, then a unique phase of sleep called rapid eye movement (REM) sleep. In REM sleep, the EEG resembles an awake alert EEG, but the body is paralyzed. Dreams tend to occur during REM sleep. As the night progresses, the sleep cycle changes and REM sleep phases become longer. The most elaborate and vivid dreams and nightmares tend to occur in the early morning hours, just before awakening.

Although we all dream, the purpose of dreams remains a mystery. From an evolutionary perspective, REM sleep is present in higher animals like mammals, birds, and cephalopods. A unique feature of REM sleep is muscle atonia; we are paralyzed during REM sleep. REM must be important because muscle paralysis exposes an organism to predation and other environmental risks, yet higher organisms spend a significant amount of time in REM sleep every night. REM contributes to emotional memory and creative thinking. REM deprivation leads to "REM rebound" as the brain tries to "catch up" on lost REM. On a neuronal level, REM sleep is associated with selective suppression or reinforcement of dendritic spines in the neocortex (Mahr & Drake, 2022).

Of special relevance to the treatment of people who have experienced trauma, REM sleep seems to have a particularly important role in processing and integrating the negative aspects of a traumatic experience. The best current evidence suggests that REM may help consolidate emotional memories while attenuating the negative aspects of those emotional memories. The nightmares that occur so commonly after trauma may be the brain's attempt to consolidate and process the traumatic event.

Dreams are associated with REM sleep, but understanding the physiology of dream sleep does not necessarily clarify the meaning and purpose of dreams and their content. The purpose of dreams remains a mystery. Because they are emotionally charged, vivid, and often contain cryptic narratives, dreams have historically been viewed as a source of healing or prophecy. Asclepius, the Greek god of medicine whose staff is the symbol of medicine throughout the world, healed through dreams. Pilgrims flocked to healing temples, or Asclepieia, where they slept among the snakes. There they would sleep, hoping to incubate a dream that would be interpreted by a temple priest. The dream and its interpretation might stimulate a deeper understanding of the dreamer's distress and lead to healing. Hippocrates, the father of medicine, started his career in one of these Asclepieia (Edelstein & Edelstein, 1998).

A modern understanding of the healing aspects of dreams begins with Sigmund Freud. Freud viewed dream interpretation as a central component of psychotherapy and saw dreams as the "royal road" to the unconscious. Most modern clinicians have forgotten or neglected the art of dream interpretation. Some dreams are pleasant and invite exploration, but nightmares can be terrifying. Trauma profoundly affects dream life, and the nightmares that can follow trauma can be terrifying and interfere with sleep and trauma recovery. When nightmares are viewed purely as symptoms, the content of the nightmare tends to be ignored, but content is important and reflects the emotional processing of traumatic material.

What are nightmares?

Nightmares are distressing dreams that awaken the dreamer from sleep and tend to be elaborate and vividly remembered. They are distinguished from bad dreams, which are distressing dreams that do not cause awakenings. Nightmares tend to occur in REM sleep, or dream sleep, and usually occur in early morning hours when REM sleep phases are the longest. Night terrors, common in children, are distressing dreams that are not remembered and usually occur in deep sleep rather than REM sleep. They occur early in the night when deep sleep usually happens.

The Diagnostic and Statistical Manual of Mental Disorders, Fifth Edition, Text Revision (DSM-5-TR) describes nightmares as "extended, extremely dysphoric and well-remembered dreams that involve threats to survival or security of personal integrity" (American Psychiatric Association, 2022). As motor paralysis is present in REM sleep; the feeling of being unable to move or speak is often a particularly terrifying component of the nightmare experience when incorporated into dream content. In James's dream described above, the inability to speak may have been related to the REM paralysis.

Nightmares and trauma

Nightmares are closely associated with trauma and are important symptoms of both acute stress disorder and posttraumatic stress disorder (PTSD). Nightmares can be viewed negatively, as the reexperiencing of traumatic symptoms, or positively, as a form of emotional processing. Trauma researchers tend to have the former view, dream researchers the latter.

About half of those who have experienced trauma will report nightmares, with some of those nightmares being trauma-replicative. Trauma-replicative nightmares are those that reenact the trauma. Those reenactments can be vivid and realistic or more symbolic (Phelps et al., 2008). Dream content is important, and the continued presence of nightmares after trauma is a predictor of poor outcome (Casement & Swanson, 2012; Di et al., 2024; Germain et al., 2004; Khan et al., 2024; Krakow & Zadra, 2006; Lancee et al., 2008; Reffi et al., 2024; Schredl & Goeritz, 2019). In PTSD, nightmares that are more vivid, realistic, and threatening and that more closely resemble the trauma are associated with poorer prognosis. Such dreams may indicate a lack of emotional processing of the trauma (Possemato & Beliete, 2023). Trauma replicative dreams are rarely trauma replicative in every detail, and the differences between the dream and the trauma may indicate emotional processing. In one of our patients, for instance, his nightmare replicated the trauma except for the end. He had been shot at close range, but in his dream, he was able to wrestle the gun from his assailant before being shot.

Nightmares after acute trauma can have unique features, and a diagnostic entity of trauma-associated sleep disorder (TASD) has been proposed (Barone, 2020). Patients with TASD have symptoms that differ from those of typical nightmares, including a disruption of the usual paralysis that occurs in REM sleep. This disruption of REM paralysis can lead to symptoms like thrashing, yelling, or calling out during sleep. Disruption in the sleep-wake regions of the amygdala has also been noted.

Patients with nightmares after acute trauma are at higher risk for developing suicidal ideation, and the presence of nightmares after trauma, especially trauma-replicative nightmares, increases the risk of PTSD after trauma (Reffi et al., 2024). Certain kinds of trauma, like interpersonal violence, are more likely to cause nightmares than injury-related traumas like falls or motor vehicle crashes. Nightmares often lead to the experience of depression, anxiety, and PTSD, and treating nightmares can reduce those symptoms. Cognitive attitudes toward dreams and the manner in which the dreamer interprets their own dreams are very important. When dreamers believe that nightmares are a sign of poor recovery, they experience more nightmare distress.

Sometimes trauma survivors view nightmares as a sign that they are failing to recover. When nightmares are reframed as an aspect of trauma processing, they become less terrifying. If a nightmare is interpreted as a revisitation of the traumatic event, then every nightmare is a re-traumatization; when a nightmare is viewed as part of the healing-process it becomes a message to be honored and understood, instead of a terrifying new trauma.

Fear of sleep

Nightmares can also cause sleep disruption. Often, nightmares are so frightening that the dreamer avoids going back to sleep after the nightmare and sometimes even tries to avoid sleeping altogether. This fear of sleep can be an important complication of nightmares. The sleep disruption caused by nightmares might paradoxically interfere with the very trauma processing that dream sleep is meant to provide. Persistent nightmares, especially severe and trauma-replicative ones, may represent an attempt at emotional processing that has gone awry and become pathological in its own right. Nightmares might resemble autoimmune diseases, which are a distortion of the normal healing process.

The fear of sleep caused by nightmares became famous in the 1980s. At that time, the United States had an influx of Hmong immigrants from Southeast Asia. The Hmong are a traditional people who live in the mountains of Southeast Asia, including those in Laos and Cambodia. There, they allied themselves with American forces during the Vietnam Conflict, where they served as scouts and counterinsurgents. After the war, many Hmong were forced to flee because they had worked with U.S. forces. Many immigrated to the United States and settled in communities where they lacked the support of their traditional social structures.

At that time, there was an epidemic of 117 nighttime deaths among healthy, young Hmong men. Before their deaths, many of the Hmong described a series of terrible nightmares, and some tried to stay awake for days, afraid to fall asleep. The disorder was called sudden unexpected nocturnal death syndrome, or SUNDS. It was assumed to represent an ill-defined cardiac abnormality; some researchers even suggested all Hmong men should have pacemakers inserted to stop the spread of the "disease." By the 1990s, the epidemic had passed (Mahr & Drake, 2022).

Anthropologist Shelley Adler studied the SUNDS epidemic (Adler, 1995). She talked with the Hmong people in their language and came to understand their culture. According to Hmong tradition, ancestors must be honored annually in prescribed ceremonies. When these ancestors are not honored, they visit in nightmares. These nightmares are felt to be reminders of the prescribed rituals, which only men can perform. When these reminders are ignored, the ancestors become dark and dangerous and can kill. It was these beliefs about the nightmares, Adler felt, that made them eventually lethal. The death would occur after a series of nightmares and would occur almost exclusively among men.

The filmmaker Wes Craven read about the nightmares and nocturnal deaths of the Hmong and the fear that some of them had of falling asleep. He developed that concept into the Nightmare on Elm Street series of movies.

The sad story of the Hmong nightmares reminds us that what led to the deaths in the Hmong community was not just nightmares, but the way those nightmares were interpreted and understood. Because the nightmares were perceived as visitations from ancestors, the fear of sleep was heightened. The cognitive reframing of nightmares is always an important part of nightmare treatment.

Psychotherapy for nightmares

Image rehearsal therapy (IRT) and cognitive behavioral therapy for nightmares (CBT-N) have been shown to be effective in addressing nightmares, especially those associated with PTSD. IRT is a structured therapeutic intervention for nightmares involving educational and imagery components (Krakow & Zadra, 2006). Patients are taught that nightmares are a learned behavior that may have initially been adaptive in processing trauma, but are now maintained as a maladaptive habit. Using imagery skills, they are encouraged to change the nightmare and rehearse the new dream that they have developed to replace the original nightmare. IRT has strong empirical support and is among the treatments recommended by the American Academy of Sleep Medicine for nightmares (Morgenthaler et al., 2018). A recent metaanalysis showed improvement in nightmare frequency in about 50% to 80% of cases, with about 23% showing complete remission (Nappi et al., 2010).

CBT-N closely resembles IRT but encompasses a broader range of therapeutic interventions. Key features of CBT-N include sleep hygiene, relaxation training, exposure and desensitization, as well as rescripting strategies. Patients keep dream diaries and repeat their nightmares to the clinician in multisensory language and in the present tense to make the recalled dream more vivid. Nightmare content is also examined. CBT-N focuses on five nightmare themes involving loss of power, safety, intimacy, trust, and esteem. CBT-N has been shown to be as effective as IRT and has been used in a greater variety of settings and among different research groups (Lancee et al., 2008).

Rescripting in CBT-N involves reimagining a new ending for the terrifying dream that addresses one of the five themes. In James's dream about the demon and the portal, for instance, key themes include loss of power and safety. James, in this case, spontaneously takes charge of his own dream within the dream, as if rescripting it. He tells the demonic figure in the dream that he has no power, thus reasserting his own power. Rescripting involves mastery, and this increase in mastery is considered central to IRT's therapeutic effect.

Rescripting is similar to older psychoanalytic techniques, especially the Jungian technique of "dreaming the dream forward." A Jungian therapist might invite a patient to continue their dream in their imagination, imagining a different ending, and then, much like in CBT-N, contemplate that new dream and ending before going to bed. A friend of mine was in Jungian psychoanalysis. For several sessions, she discussed a terrifying, recurrent nightmare of being chased by a wolf. The therapist patiently explored the dream, then told my friend, "When are you going to feed that wolf?" She had the recurrent dream again, but with a new ending where she stopped, turned to face the wolf, and fed it. After that night, she never had the dream again. The analyst had reframed the figure of the wolf as an internal figure, a part of the dreamer that needed to be fed and cared for. The interpretation also created a sense of mastery over the dream content.

Besides formal rescripting techniques, thoughtful exploration of dream content can be extremely helpful. One patient, for instance, described a recurrent dream that he called a nightmare. He then described a dream of a family member sitting at his bedside, comforting him. "Why is that a nightmare?" I asked. He replied that this family member was deceased and was coming to call him to the next world. "Maybe she's there to comfort you," I suggested. He became tearful, suddenly realizing that what he had considered a nightmare was actually a gift.

Pharmacological treatments for nightmares

Prazosin remains the treatment of choice for nightmares. Although a recent study has raised some questions about the efficacy of prazosin in nightmares, many older trials have shown it to be effective. Other pharmacological agents with evidence of efficacy in nightmares include olanzapine, aripiprazole, fluvoxamine, gabapentin, nabilone, phenelzine, topiramate, trazodone and tricyclic antidepressants (Morgenthaler et al., 2018). Doxazocin has more recently shown efficacy in nightmares as well (Khan et al., 2024). Clonazepam and venlafaxine have been shown not to be effective in nightmares. Most of the research in pharmacological interventions in nightmares has been conducted in patients with PTSD, rather than those who are hospitalized in acute care settings.

The acute care setting

Patients in the acute care setting may experience distressing nightmares, and their nightmares contribute to poor sleep and, as we have described earlier, predict poor outcomes. Treating nightmares in the acute care setting can relieve distress and possibly improve clinical outcomes. But both CBT-N and IRT are structured therapies designed to be used to treat nightmares in outpatient settings. The structured formats of these therapies can make them challenging to apply in the acute care setting. Patients are injured, in pain, and often face surgery or other medical treatments. CBT-N and IRT involve tools and inventories, as well as homework exercises. Patients with acute trauma are often not able to complete detailed questionnaires or written assignments. The exposure aspect of CBT-N is unnecessary since the trauma and nightmare content is fresh and vivid. In our research and clinical work, we had been concerned that our patients with acute trauma would not want to talk about their nightmares; we were afraid of re-traumatization. To our surprise, patients were eager to share their nightmares and found it comforting rather than traumatizing to discuss them (Mahr & Drake, 2022).

Cognitive behavioral therapy for insomnia (CBT-I) and IRT in their ideal, protocol-based forms are also difficult to apply because hospital stays are usually short. But patients after acute trauma are in distress from nightmares, and it is important to relieve the distress as soon as possible. For these reasons, we have had to adapt these evidence-based nightmare therapies for use in the acute care setting.

Principles of nightmare therapy in the acute care setting

1. Ask about nightmares. Clinicians often feel uncomfortable discussing dreams, so they don't ask about nightmares. In our experience, patients are very comfortable talking about nightmares and appreciate being asked.
2. Engage in relaxation training and provide education related to sleep hygiene. Reducing the overall level of anxiety, especially at bedtime, can reduce nightmare severity.

3. Provide reassurance and psychoeducation. Describe nightmares as a part of healing and recovery. When nightmares are seen purely as symptoms, the patient becomes discouraged about having nightmares. To view them as part of the healing process is empowering.
4. Explore dream content and its relationship to the trauma. Even when nightmares are trauma-replicative, there are often important differences between the event and the dream. Those differences may be helpful in understanding the patient's perspective of their experience.
5. Discuss dream rescripting immediately. Imagining a new positive ending for a dream is empowering and increases the sense of control.
6. Reframe dreams internally. One patient, for instance, had frightening nightmares about protecting his children from attack. I explored the idea that his children in the dream were parts of his own psyche rather than his children. I suggested that perhaps they symbolized the inner potentials that he needed to protect. He was very comforted by the realization that the dream was about protecting parts of himself from the trauma he had been exposed to. The nightmare became much less terrifying, reframed in that way, and he could begin to focus on recovery and healing.
7. Nightmares can be an avenue to therapy. Sometimes patients who have experienced a traumatic injury can be disinclined to seek psychotherapy. Yet they are willing, because of the distress caused by their nightmares, to accept therapy for nightmares. Nightmare therapy can thus become a kind of Trojan Horse for other forms of trauma therapy; if therapy for nightmares is experienced as helpful, then other forms of trauma therapy become acceptable.

Our patient's dream

CBT-N involves techniques like dream rescripting, but sometimes patients rescript dreams on their own, spontaneously, as they recover. In the dream at the beginning of the chapter, James confronted a negative dream figure, and in that way performed a kind of rescripting of a terrifying nightmare by confronting the threatening "guardian of the portal" figure that was central to the dream. When James, in his dream, tells the figure, "You have no power here," he restores his own power, changes the dream, and banishes the demonic figure.

An important feature of the dream is the patient's loss of voice. This relates to one of the key dream themes identified in CBT-N: powerlessness. It may also represent the incorporation into dream content of the physiological experience of atonia. Being "knocked out" for surgery also reflects this theme. The dream has a spiritual dimension, with the demonic figure at the gate, or portal, and the absence of God. While fully respecting the spiritual aspects of the dream, it can also be interpreted internally. A negative aspect of the patient's own psyche wants to take him down to a portal of despair. When the patient bravely takes charge of the situation, this aspect of his psyche recedes.

A dream like this can be an important springboard for therapeutic discussions. The clinician might explore with James, for instance, what his portals of despair are and how he resists them. His courage in the dream can be reinforced and described as a sign that he has that same courage available to him in waking life. Because spiritual issues are important in James's dream, it may be important to discuss with James the spiritual aspects of recovery.

Chapter summary

Nightmares are an important aspect of trauma recovery and one that may become dysfunctional. Nightmares are important as symptoms and markers of trauma severity, but the content of nightmares may be important as well. The principles of psychotherapy for nightmares as applied to the acute care setting include talk therapy, relaxation training and sleep hygiene, reassurance and psychoeducation, exploring dream content, and rescripting and reframing dreams. Pharmacological interventions can be important in treating nightmares as well.

References

Adler, S. R. (1995). Terror in transition: Hmong folk belief in America. In B. S. Walker (Ed.). Out of the ordinary: Folklore and the supernatural (pp. 180–202). Utah State University Press. http://doi.org/10.2307/j.ctt46nwn8.

American Psychiatric Association (2022). Diagnostic and Statistical Manual of Mental Disorders (5th ed., text rev.). American Psychiatric Association Publishing. http://doi.org/10.1176/appi.books.9780890425787 .

Casement, M. D., & Swanson, L. M. (2012). A meta-analysis of imagery rehearsal for post-trauma nightmares: Effects on nightmare frequency, sleep quality, and posttraumatic stress. *Clinical Psychology Review, 32*(6), 566–574. https://doi.org/10.1016/j.cpr.2012.06.002.

Di, T., Zhang, L., Meng, S., Liu, W., Guo, Y., Zheng, E., Xie, C., Xiang, S., Jia, T., Lu, L., Sun, Y., & Shi, J. (2024). The impact of REM sleep loss on human brain connectivity. *Translational Psychiatry, 14*(1). https://doi.org/10.1038/s41398-024-02985-x.

Edelstein, E. J., & Edelstein, L. (1998). *Asclepius: Collection and interpretation of the testimonies*. Johns Hopkins University Press.

Germain, A., Krakow, B., Faucher, B., Zadra, A., Nielsen, T., Hollifield, M., Warner, T. D., & Koss, M. (2004). Increased mastery elements associated with imagery rehearsal treatment for nightmares in sexual assault survivors with PTSD. *Dreaming, 14*(4), 195–206. https://doi.org/10.1037/1053-0797.14.4.195.

Khan, D., Richardson, C., & Forsberg, M. (2024). Doxazocin immediate release as a novel treatment for nightmares in posttraumatic stress disorder. *Case Reports in Psychiatry, 26*. https://doi.org/10.1155/crps/6452923.

Krakow, B., & Zadra, A. (2006). Clinical management of chronic nightmares: Imagery rehearsal therapy. *Behavioral Sleep Medicine, 4*(1), 45–70. https://doi.org/10.1207/s15402010-bsm0401_4.

Lancee, J., Spoormaker, V. I., Krakow, B., & van den Bout, J. (2008). A systematic review of cognitive-behavioral treatment for nightmares: Toward a well-established treatment. *Journal of Clinical Sleep Medicine, 4*(5), 475–480. https://doi.org/10.5664/jcsm.27285.

Mahr, G., & Drake, C. (2022). *The wisdom of dreams: Science, synchronicity and the language of the soul.* Routledge. http://doi.org/10.4324/9781003223474.

Morgenthaler, T. I., Auerbach, S., Casey, K. R., Kristo, D., Maganti, R., Ramar, K., Zak, R., & Kartje, R. (2018). Position paper for the treatment of nightmare disorder in adults: An American academy of sleep medicine position paper. *Journal of Clinical Sleep Medicine, 14*(6), 1041–1055. https://doi.org/10.5664/jcsm.7178.

Nappi, C. M., Drummond, S. P. A., Thorp, S. R., & McQuaid, J. R. (2010). Effectiveness of imagery rehearsal therapy for the treatment of combat-related nightmares in veterans. *Behavior Therapy, 41*(2), 237–244. https://doi.org/10.1016/j.beth.2009.03.003.

Phelps, A. J., Forbes, D., & Creamer, M. (2008). Understanding posttraumatic nightmares: An empirical and conceptual review. *Clinical Psychology Review, 28*(2), 338–355. https://doi.org/10.1016/j.cpr.2007.06.001.

Possemato, K., & Beliete, S. N. (2023). Characteristics of posttraumatic nightmares and their relationship to PTSD severity among combat veterans with PTSD and hazardous alcohol use. *The Journal of Nervous and Mental Disease, 210*(3), 223–226. https://doi.org/10.1097/NMD.0000000000001422.

Reffi, A. N., Cheng, P., Kalmbach, D. A., Moore, D. A., Mahr, G. C., Seymour, G. M., Solway, M., & Drake, C. L. (2024). Understanding nightmares after traumatic events in Detroit (UNiTED): Prospective associations with interpersonal violence and posttraumatic stress disorder symptoms. *European Journal of Psychotraumatology, 15*(1). https://doi.org/10.1080/20008066.2024.2409561.

Schredl, M., & Goeritz, A. S. (2019). Nightmare frequency and nightmare distress: Socio-demographic and personality factors. *Sleep Science, 12*(3), 178–184. https://doi.org/10.5935/1984-0063.20190080.

Chapter 9

Somatic therapies and acute trauma

Chris's Story

Chris was an avid hiker and tennis player, and a complex trauma survivor. He was admitted to the hospital for prostatectomy after the discovery of prostate cancer. We were consulted because Chris had awakened during surgery because of an anesthesia issue. He experienced severe pain and overheard operating room conversations. The psychiatry consult team was consulted because Chris seemed angry and withdrawn. He acknowledged the apologies of the surgical team, said that he understood mistakes happen, but he was very guarded. He only showed interest and engagement when he talked about hiking.

Walking is an ancient form of therapy and can facilitate posttraumatic growth. Some great writers were dedicated walkers. Wordsworth is said to have walked 175,000 miles in his lifetime (Zurski, 2019), Dickens walked 30 miles a day, Virginia Woolf found great inspiration in her nightly walks in London (Solnit, 2000), and the painter Joseph Cornell walked the streets of New York for hours searching for discarded objects for his found art collages. The Appalachian Trail is an approximately 2190-mile trail that extends from Georgia to Maine, the longest continuous hiking footpath in the world. It was first "thru hiked" without interruption in 124 days by Earl Shaffer, a veteran of World War II, in 1948. When asked about his motivations for this long trek, he stated that he wanted to "walk the war out of my system."

Walking can be a form of healing, including healing from trauma. In 2013, Jen Schuringa was severely injured in a motor vehicle crash (J's Crew, n.d.). The crash left her partially paralyzed with locked-in syndrome that interferes with communication. Ten years later, as part of her journey of healing, she decided to travel, as best she could, on a specialized bicycle on the El Camino in Spain. Fr. Rob McChesney leads trauma survivors on that same walk in Spain, focusing on trauma recovery (McChesney, 2025).

The El Camino, also called St. Stephen's Way, has been a site of pilgrimage since the 9th century. This great spiritual journey culminates in a

The Psychology of Acute Trauma. DOI: https://doi.org/10.1016/B978-0-443-33212-8.00023-3

place associated with trauma, Santiago de Compostela. This church houses the relics of St. James, martyred in Jerusalem in the year 44. The Camino can be challenging; the most common route is nearly 500 miles, covered in about 30 days. Part of the power of the pilgrimage is the physical challenge, which forces one to be attuned to one's body. And the walk is spiritual. Rhian Sasseen, a writer for The Nation, nearly described his walk on the El Camino in spiritual terms. "One might deny an interest in belief, but on the Camino, belief has a way of finding you" (Sasseen, 2026).

Healing from trauma is often described as a journey. That term is typically used metaphorically, but it can be embodied, physically, as a literal journey, and some pilgrimage sites are in fact sites of trauma. Canterbury has been a popular pilgrimage site in England since the 1200s. Canterbury, like Santiago de Compostela, is a trauma site. Thomas Becket was murdered there in 1170, during a political dispute with Henry II. The pilgrimage to the site of his murder was the setting of Chaucer's great epic, The Canterbury Tales. This kind of trauma journey is memorialized in miniature form in every Catholic church in the world, in the form of the Stations of the Cross, where believers symbolically walk Christ's journey towards crucifixion on Good Friday.

Pilgrimage as a journey of spiritual healing is central to many faiths. One of the five pillars of Islam is the Hajj, or the pilgrimage to Mecca. Hinduism, Buddhism, Sikhism, and Baha'i, all have important sacred sites of pilgrimage. The idea of pilgrimage reminds us that healing is a physical, bodily act, not just a mental one. Healing comes through action, through the body. The four men who murdered Becket were eventually granted absolution by the Pope, but their penance was a bodily one: service in the Crusades.

The history of somatic therapies

This great truth of healing through the body has been rediscovered in recent decades with the development of somatic therapies. Somatic therapy honors the fact that, as we have discussed in earlier chapters, trauma is stored in the body, in a place in the psyche that is inaccessible by words. Somatic therapies involve a body-oriented approach to healing and recovery. Yoga and meditation are considered somatic therapies because they focus not on words and narrative, but on bodily and nonverbal experiences. Mindfulness exercises, described in Chapter 6, Psychological Interventions for Hospitalized Trauma Patients, have both a somatic and a verbal component.

Modern somatic therapy begins with the work of Pierre Janet in the early 20th century. Janet did pioneering work in trauma, memory processing, and dissociation. The idea that trauma is processed on a nonverbal, somatic level has its origin in Janet's work (van der Kolk & van der Hart, 1989). Wilhelm Reich, an analyst who was part of Freud's inner circle in the 1930's, felt that repression was enacted in the body and did pioneering somatic work such as breathing exercises to free the body from the effects of trauma (Reich, 1950).

In the 1950s, Alexander Lowen developed Bioenergetics, inspired by Reich's work. The term somatics was coined by Thomas Hanna, as he developed strategies for treating what he called "sensori-motor amnesia."

The common thread in these forms of body work was the idea that mind and body were a single entity and that the mind could be healed through work on the body. Somatic therapy had many adherents but was also controversial or even subversive because it ran against the grain of mainstream psychotherapeutic practice. The dominant psychotherapeutic modality since the 1980's has been CBT, and the mantra of CBT is that feelings follow thoughts. In other words, thoughts have primacy over feelings and the body. The core tenet of somatic therapy is that body must be the central focus of therapy. The body is, of course, at the center of acute trauma work as well. In contrast to issues like anxiety or depression, acute trauma involves the body and the trauma that befell the body.

Somatic treatment strategies

Common techniques in somatic therapy include grounding techniques, body scanning, mindful breathing, muscle relaxation, movement exercises, vocalization, boundary exercises, pendulation, resourcing, and mirror work. Grounding techniques involve focusing on the feeling of your feet on the ground, or if sitting or lying down, the feeling of the parts of body that are touching or resting on the bed or chair. Grounding sets a mental focus on the body and its relationship to the world. Body scanning involves paying attention to the sensations in the body, such as any feeling of tension or discomfort. Mindful breathing is the ancient meditative technique of paying attention to the inflow and outflow of breath from the body, to again reinforce the link between the body, the psyche, and the world. Progressive muscle relaxation involves systematically tightening and relaxing all the muscles of the body, usually beginning with the toes. Movement exercises can vary and can be yoga-like stretches or spontaneous movements in response to emotions or impulses. Vocalization involves using the voice to express or release tension. Boundary exercises involve the bodily enactment of emotional boundaries, such as pressing against a wall. Pendulation involves paying attention to areas of comfort, then areas of discomfort, and alternating between them to train awareness. Resourcing focuses on positive memories or feelings to create a sense of calm, like imagining yourself on a warm beach. Finally, mirroring refers to the observing of the body in a mirror as it responds to feelings and emotions, to validate the authenticity of bodily responses (Levine & Frederick, 1997; Levine, 2008).

The general focus of somatic therapy is the integration of mind and body. The false gap between the two constructs separates words from the lived experience. Acute trauma involves the body and is experienced in the body, and the experience of trauma by its nature is unspeakable. Trauma is experienced in the body and can be healed through the body.

Somatic therapies and acute trauma

The boundaries between somatic and traditional therapies are porous, and effective therapy is enriched by tools from both models. Grounding, body scanning, and relaxation techniques are readily applied to the acute care setting and easily combined with other types of psychotherapeutic interventions. Somatic therapy is generally flexible and unstructured, but a structured form has been developed and studied called Somatic Experiencing (Levine & Frederick, 1997). Preliminary evidence suggests that Somatic Experiencing may be effective for treating both affective and somatic symptoms of PTSD. Case reports have suggested potential benefits in acute trauma as well, but these effects have not been systematically studied (Kuhfuß et al., 2021).

Somatization and the body

Somatization, which can be a common defense mechanism and relational style in complex trauma, is best explored with somatic interventions. Somatization is associated with trauma (Elklit & Christiansen, 2009; van der Kolk et al., 1996), and it can be difficult to manage as it can lead to pharmacological and medical interventions and unnecessary workups. Somatizing patients can be challenging to work with in therapy because of their preoccupation with somatic concerns. They are described as having "abulia," which translates to "no words for feelings." Unnecessary evaluations and workups perpetuate the somatization cycle by maintaining a medicalized focus on the body. Instead, from a somatic therapy perspective, the clinician must attempt to explore what the body is trying to "say" in somatic language. I sometimes ask such patients, "If your body could speak, what would it say?"

Eye movement desensitization and reprocessing

Although eye movement desensitization and reprocessing (EMDR) is not traditionally thought of as a somatic therapy, it resembles somatic therapies in that it involves nonverbal and bodily processing of trauma. A cardinal feature of EMDR is the eye movement training. The trauma survivor follows the hand movements of the clinician while mentally concentrating on a traumatic memory. The eye movements cause bilateral stimulation of the brain and are felt by EMDR practitioners to mimic the eye movements during rapid eye movement (REM) sleep or the dreaming phase of sleep. The therapy is designed to mimic the trauma processing that occurs during REM sleep.

The unorthodox nature of EMDR invites skepticism. It feels like it shouldn't be helpful, but the best data suggests that it actually is helpful. van der Kolk recounts the story of a patient who, after an EMDR session, was very angry to have sat through such a silly treatment, but then reluctantly admitted that his trauma-related symptoms had significantly improved. EMDR has been used in the treatment of acute trauma and has been shown to be effective in clinical studies (Torres-Giménez et al., 2024).

The bilateral movements that appear to be crucial for the effectiveness of EMDR are also a natural part of walking. Van der Kolk, in The Body Keeps the Score, described the case of a woman who had relief of trauma symptoms while walking in the park, noticing things, with her eyes moving (van der Kolk, 2014). While this case inspired van der Kolk to consider the validity of EMDR, because she was moving her eyes as she noticed scenery, it is important to note that the woman was walking as well as moving her eyes. The healing that some patients feel in walking, as in the pilgrimages described earlier, may be related to the relief from trauma distress experienced in EMDR.

Focusing: listening to the body

Eugene Gendlin, a philosopher turned psychologist, was one of the pioneers of the somatic psychology movement. His clinical technique, which he called focusing, involves listening past the first automatic cognitive response of the conscious mind. When we calmly listen past this initial cognitive response, we can notice what the body is actually saying (Gendlin, 1978). Gendlin, from a philosophical point of view, became very interested in the process of thought formation and how a nonverbal or preverbal thought is expressed in verbal language. He felt that the initial quick response to a question in therapy was often based on an overlearned, defensive cognitive attitude. One needs to internally listen past this first response and let the body itself speak, from a deeper sense of somatic awareness, which Gendlin called the felt sense. This felt sense is the body speaking. Gendlin invites the subject to choose a handle, a word or image that carries the felt sense. The process of talking to the body can be summarized in six steps. The first is clearing a space, which involves listening past the first negatives or the first concerns and doubts, letting those float past. The second step is becoming aware of the felt sense, the third is identifying the handle. The fourth step is moving between the felt sense and the handle to clarify, listen, and test if the felt sense feels right. The final steps involve asking the body for its own insight, and the final step is receiving that insight.

Focusing is a technique that can be readily applied to the acute care setting and can be a way for a patient to connect more deeply with their inner experiences. Focusing can occur naturally when we create space to listen to our inner selves.

Chris and His Journey

Chris continued to be subdued and withdrawn. He denied being angry or sad, said that he understood that things happen sometimes in surgery. When a somatic intervention was attempted, Chris brightened. He was asked how his body felt

(Continued)

now, after his surgery. "I'm not sure," he said, but began to talk about how his body felt different overall, as if it were a stranger. This was the first surgery he had; ever had, he was worried about sexual functioning, and he wondered what his future would be like with his body. Mostly he had been thinking about hiking. He hadn't hiked in several years, he recalled how he enjoyed that his mind shut off from the everyday world when he hiked, how he had to pay attention, but in a different way, not to the noise of the world but to the feel of the trail and the feeling in his body as he connected to the trail. We talked about pilgrimages and the El Camino, and how it can take time to find a new path.

Chris apologized that he hadn't wanted to say much to people in the hospital; he simply didn't want to "cheapen" his experiences by talking about them before he was ready. He suggested talking again in 6 months, after he had recovered and done some hiking on the Appalachian Trail. We indeed met again 6 months later. Chris was solemn and thoughtful, and much more talkative. He talked about his prior feeling, after his surgical trauma, that his body had betrayed him by developing cancer, and that he had betrayed it by not protecting it during the surgery. That feeling was gone, Chris said; he had "walked it out." He talked of nature, of seeing the sun rise over the mountains every morning. He talked about gradually feeling peaceful again, and of realizing that he was a tiny creature in a vast universe, but that he still mattered.

Chapter summary

Somatic therapies, because they specifically address issues of the body, have an important role in the psychological treatment of acute trauma. The features of some of the major forms of somatic therapy, including EMDR, are reviewed with a focus on their role in the treatment of acute trauma. Somatic therapies can address more directly the somatizing behaviors that can occur after trauma. Walking and pilgrimage are discussed as an ancient form of somatic therapy and trauma recovery.

References

Elklit, A., & Christiansen, D. M. (2009). Predictive factors for somatization in a trauma sample. *Clinical Practice and Epidemiology in Mental Health, 5*. https://doi.org/10.1186/1745-0179-5-1.

Gendlin, E. (1978). *Focusing*. Bantam Books.

J's Crew, Jen's story. Available from: https://www.jenschuringa.com/jens-story.

Kuhfuß, M., Maldei, T., Hetmanek, A., & Baumann, N. (2021). Somatic experiencing–effectiveness and key factors of a body-oriented trauma therapy: a scoping literature review. *European Journal of Psychotraumatology, 12*(1). https://doi.org/10.1080/20008198.2021.1929023.

Levine, P. A. (2008). *Trauma healing. A pioneering program for restoring the wisdom of your body*. Sounds True.

Levine, P. A., & Frederick, A. (1997). *Waking the tiger: Healing trauma. The innate capacity to transform overwhelming experiences*. North Atlantic Books.

McChesney, R. W. (2025). *The soul also keeps the score: A trauma informed companion to the spiritual exercises of St. Ignatius*. Liturgical Press.

Reich, W. (1950). *Character analysis*. Vision Press.

Sasseen, R. (2026). *Walking the Camino in the shadow of belief*. The Nation.

Solnit, R. (2000). *Wanderlust: A history of walking*. Viking.

Torres-Giménez, A., Garcia-Gibert, C., Gelabert, E., Mallorquí, A., Segu, X., Roca-Lecumberri, A., Martínez, A., Giménez, Y., & Sureda, B. (2024). Efficacy of EMDR for early intervention after a traumatic event: A systematic review and meta-analysis. *Journal of Psychiatric Research, 174*, 73–83. https://doi.org/10.1016/j.jpsychires.2024.04.019.

van der Kolk, B. A. (2014). *The body keeps the score: Brain, mind and body in the healing of trauma*. Penguin.

van der Kolk, B. A., Pelcovitz, D., Roth, S., Mandel, F. S., McFarlane, A., & Herman, J. L. (1996). Dissociation, somatization, and affect dysregulation: The complexity of adaptation to trauma. *American Journal of Psychiatry, 153*(7), 83–93. https://doi.org/10.1176/ajp.153.7.83.

van der Kolk, B. A., & van der Hart, O. (1989). Pierre Janet and the breakdown of adaptation in psychological trauma. *American Journal of Psychiatry, 146*(12), 1530–1540. https://doi.org/10.1176/ajp.146.12.1530.

Zurski, K. (2019). The man who walked a lifetime. Unremembered: A History of the Famously Interesting and Mostly Forgotten, Available from: https://unrememberedhistory.com/2017/08/02/william-wordsworth-the-man-who-walked-a-lifetime/.

Chapter 10

Neurocognitive disorders and delirium

Jim's Story

Jim was a 75-year-old retired executive. He was happily married and had an active social life with a high level of functional independence at baseline. One day, as he was walking out of his health club on a snowy morning, he slipped and fell on the ice and struck his head on the curb. He was briefly unconscious and ultimately required emergency transport to the hospital. Upon presentation to the emergency department, he was observed to be experiencing persistent confusion and agitation, which ultimately led to his admission. On admission, he was oriented to person only and had no recollection of the events leading up to admission. Head imaging revealed that there was no skull fracture and no evidence of brain contusion or hemorrhage.

Acute trauma and cognitive functioning

Acute trauma can affect the brain and cognitive functioning. Sometimes, as in the case of delirium, the impairment in cognitive functioning is a result of medications or metabolic derangements that affect the body, including the brain, and may be time-limited. In other situations, the trauma can involve a specific brain injury. A traumatic brain injury (TBI) can be closed, where the brain is damaged by an impact to the skull strong enough to cause the brain to move within the cranium, or open, where an object penetrates the skull. Additionally, it is not uncommon for patients to present with novel traumatic injuries that have occurred in the context of an underlying preexisting neurocognitive disorder such as dementia. Extensive literature exists related to the experience of delirium, neurocognitive disorders, and TBI, as full consideration of these is beyond the scope of this book. But the problems can significantly affect the psychological management of the acute trauma patient and are important to acknowledge.

Delirium

Delirium is defined in the Diagnostic and Statistical Manual of Mental Disorders, Fifth Edition, Text Revision (DSM-5-TR) as a disturbance in

The Psychology of Acute Trauma. DOI: https://doi.org/10.1016/B978-0-443-33212-8.00021-X

attention and cognition that is acute and occurs as a result of another medical condition (American Psychiatric Association, 2022). The onset of delirium is often acute; typically, it resolves quickly but can become persistent and even chronic. Diagnostically, delirium is described as hyperactive, hypoactive, or with mixed levels of activity, and the etiology is also described if it is known.

When delirium is recognized, it should initiate an evaluation of potential causes, which can be metabolic, structural, or medication-related. Delirium is very common in inpatient medical settings, especially in the severely medically ill and those who require critical care. Between 70% to 87% of patients requiring mechanical ventilation will experience delirium, with rates of delirium as high as 53% in postoperative patients (Trivedi et al., 2024). Standard medical, psychiatric, and surgical textbooks provide excellent resources for the workup and treatment of delirium, but due to its prevalence in inpatient medical settings, an awareness of delirium is important for the psychological management of acute trauma patients. The presence of delirium affects the kinds of psychological interventions that are appropriate for use, as well as the degree of autonomy in decision-making that is appropriate. Delirium can be very frightening and can increase suspiciousness and feelings of loss of control. Delirious experiences are sometimes remembered and become an important source of medical trauma. Medical trauma itself is discussed in detail in Chapter 13, When treatment is traumatic: understanding and addressing medical trauma.

Recognizing delirium

The cardinal deficits in delirium involve attention and orientation. The presence of delirium is often apparent in the first minutes of clinical contact. The patient can appear confused or "wifty" and be distractible or inattentive. The patient experiencing delirium is typically disoriented and often requires frequent repetition of clinician's queries prior to providing a response. Although most cases of delirium can easily be recognized by an experienced clinician, delirium is easily missed in the hectic pace of acute patient care. Hyperactive delirium is the most obvious, because it causes agitation and other clinical management issues, such as pulling at lines or verbal and behavioral disinhibition requiring restraints or one-to-one observation. Hypoactive delirium, on the other hand, where the patient is calm and passively cooperative, although confused, is missed in about 60% of cases.

Because delirium is very common and easily missed, especially in its hypoactive form, screening for delirium should be a part of every clinical evaluation. In addition to the clinical interview, simple and readily available screening measures for delirium include the Mini-Mental State Exam (MMSE) (Folstein et al., 1975), the Confusion Assessment Method for the Intensive Care Unit (CAM-ICU) (Ely, Bernard, et al., 2001; Ely, Margolin, et al., 2001), or the Montreal Cognitive Assessment (MoCA) (Nasreddine et al., 2005). Once the presence or absence of delirium is established, screening does not need to be repeated at every interview; however when clinical status changes or behavioral changes are evident, delirium screening should be repeated.

An important aspect of delirium is its fluctuation. Delirious patients can be cognitively intact for periods of time but confused at other times as their clinical and metabolic situation varies or as medications wear off. Delirium also worsens in unfamiliar situations and environments and improves in the presence of familiar people like family. Delirium famously worsens at night when patients are more likely to be left alone, lights are dimmed, and orienting stimuli like family and visitors are gone. This nocturnal worsening of delirium is called sundowning.

While perceptual disturbances such as hallucinations are commonly experienced by patients impacted by delirium, it is important to note that their etiology is distinct from psychotic illnesses like schizophrenia spectrum disorders. Patients experiencing delirium are indeed psychotic in the technical sense; they have fixed beliefs or perceptions that are not in accordance with reality, but these beliefs and perceptions, like the delirium itself, are variable and tend to fluctuate. Delusions in delirium, in contrast to those in psychotic disorders like schizophrenia, will tend to be vague. Rather than describing a well-articulated delusional system, the patient experiencing delirium may say things like, "staff tried to kill me last night," but without being able to specify details or circumstances.

Understanding the experience of delirium

Because the patient experiencing delirium is "not all there," sometimes they are treated as if they were "not there at all." The patient is often "there" and hears and processes information, though that processing is altered and limited. The internal experience of delirium is often frightening; the world doesn't quite make sense, and insight into the cognitive changes they are experiencing may be highly unsettling. Rarely can this confusion be experienced in a pleasant way. I remember asking a patient once where he was, and he replied that he was on a sailboat in the Caribbean, while another reported that they were floating on a small raft in the middle of a river in Hell. Most commonly, delirium is experienced as frightening. The experience of confusion is frightening in itself, and in the hospital environment, things like needle sticks and tube insertions occur regularly, which can seem inexplicable and terrifying for the confused patient.

Standard milieu interventions can be helpful in managing delirium, but are sometimes neglected in acute trauma patients because of the urgency of medical and surgical interventions. These interventions include providing frequent reorientation, maintaining a clear and quiet environment, improving sleep hygiene, correcting circadian rhythm, encouraging early mobility and physical or occupational therapy, adequate pain management, reinforcing the importance of having positive social support system members present and increasing the presence of familiar objects in the room (e.g., the presence of photographs of family, objects from home like a familiar blanket or pillow).

In addition to such interventions, it is also important to avoid the use of restraints when possible, as well as limiting the use of benzodiazepines and anticholinergic medications when possible.

Clinicians sometimes use complex language and medical jargon when they speak to sick patients. The patient experiencing delirium is more likely to misinterpret complex language and medical terminology, which can lead to increased fear and confusion. Clinicians are also more likely to have medical discussions of treatment options and other academic considerations in the presence of a delirious or comatose patient as if they weren't there. But they are there, they hear bits and pieces, and draw conclusions that can be frightening and make them less likely to accept care. Teach-back strategies, where the clinician asks the patient to repeat back information that has just been shared, will increase the likelihood of adequate comprehension, giving the clinician the opportunity to correct misunderstandings in real time. Teach-back strategies also show empathy and demonstrate to the patient that the clinician truly cares if they understand the information that is being shared with them.

An empathy exercise might be helpful prior to talking to a patient experiencing delirium. For example, one can recall personal experiences of delirium, such as times when one was feverish or ill, and recall the feelings of disorientation and confusion, and how the world felt far away and strange. Such recollections can help the clinician approach the delirious patient with empathy and respect.

Delirium can also, paradoxically, be overdiagnosed. Once a patient is diagnosed with delirium, then everything they do can be interpreted to be the result of confusion. Once, I experienced a lengthy period of delirium in the hospital. When the delirium cleared, I realized that I was quite exposed, lying in a hospital gown without underwear. I saw my underwear on the chair next to me and reached over to grab them and put them on. Someone noticed me reaching over to my chair and assumed I was confused and trying to get up. I was barely able to convince an assembled group of staff that I didn't need restraints and that I wasn't trying to get up; I just wanted my underwear.

Delirium, and the interventions like restraints that are sometimes necessary to manage it can create a frightening sense of vulnerability and helplessness. In treating the acute trauma patient, who may already feel vulnerable and helpless because of their trauma, it is especially important to be sensitive to the psychological implications of milieu interventions.

Clinical tips for managing the patient experiencing delirium

1. Be aware that medical and surgical interventions can be experienced as re-traumatization. Explain all interventions as clearly and simply as possible and use teach-back strategies to ensure comprehension.
2. Use simple language and vocabulary, while emphasizing that your goal is to provide care, promote wellbeing, and increase safety.

3. Avoid harsh language or loud tones to avoid reawakening feelings of danger.
4. Monitor pain carefully. The confused patient may not be able to express pain clearly.
5. Monitor environmental issues that might contribute to delirium.
6. Attempt to maintain a normal sleep-wake cycle.
7. While the reality testing of the patient may be impaired, the experience to them is very real. Validating the emotional content of the patient's experience, even if it is rooted in an inaccurate interpretation of reality, will increase the sense of safety and often improve the therapeutic alliance in the resolution of the altered mental status.

Traumatic brain injury

TBI is a common form of traumatic injury. Although accurate data about TBIs are difficult to come by, the best estimates suggest that there are 27 million new cases of TBI annually, worldwide, and about 1.5 million Americans suffer a TBI every year. Permanent brain injury-related disability affects more than 5 million Americans. Brain injury disproportionately affects the young, and its incidence is increasing. The most common causes of TBI are falls and motor vehicle crashes (Berwick et al., 2022). TBI is an important cause of delirium, and concerns about decision-making capacity commonly arise in dealing with patients impacted by TBIs because of the cognitive impairments often associated with acute TBI. The general strategies we have described for dealing with acute trauma apply to the TBI, but with important special issues regarding recognition and treatment. Penetrating TBI's are obvious, but closed head injuries can be difficult to diagnose. The mechanisms of closed TBIs include diffuse axonal injury, concussion, contusion, and hematoma.

Symptoms of traumatic brain injury

Symptoms of a closed TBI include headache, dizziness, confusion, nausea, photosensitivity, and fatigue. Irritability can occur as well, but usually develops later in the recovery process. Later onset symptoms also include emotional symptoms such as depression and anxiety (NIH, National Institute of Neurological Disorders and Stroke). The symptoms of a closed TBI can be masked by the adjustment and coping processes that can be associated with acute trauma. Because TBIs are associated with falls, TBIs are very common in older adults. Because of the nonspecific nature of TBI symptoms, it is also very easy to miss TBIs in older adults. Additionally, older adults are also often on anticoagulants, so a lower energy bump to the head is more likely to cause contusions, hematoma, and significant brain injury.

With acute trauma, especially falls in older adults, it is important to be aware of the possibility of TBI. Headaches and dizziness can be especially important screening symptoms for TBI in the acute trauma survivor.

The clinical tips listed earlier for the patient experiencing delirium apply to the cognitively impaired TBI patient as well. Additionally, the presence of TBI also increases the risk for the presence of delirium, oftentimes leading to diagnostic confusion as the etiology of cognitive impairment may be difficult to discern. This is especially the case for individuals experiencing hyperactive delirium with behavioral disturbance, as they may require increased sedation, which in turn may interfere with the observation of the natural recovery from TBI while increasing risk for delirium. While delirium is most commonly a short-term issue, recovery from moderate to severe TBI can take several years (Brett et al., 2023). Treatment planning with the patient impacted by TBI should always have a long-term focus, including a referral for inpatient rehabilitation with a TBI focus and an outpatient neuropsychological assessment with subsequent cognitive rehabilitation if eligible. While the slow pace of TBI recovery can be frustrating, patients and caregivers can have some reassurance that improvement remains possible and even likely months and years after initial injury.

Traumatic brain injury and mood

After a closed TBI trauma, survivors are at significant risk for depression and suicidality. One third of patients will develop depression after a TBI, not only because of issues related to adjustment and loss, but also because of poorly understood factors related to the neurophysiology of brain injury itself (Jorge et al., 2004). Suicide risk in these patients more than doubles as well (De Luca et al., 2025). This increase in suicidality may be related not only to depression but also possibly to issues involving higher cortical processing. TBI patients, especially those with injuries to their frontal lobes, tend to experience impulsivity and show deficits in impulse control and affect management.

Decision-making capacity

Acute trauma is often unexpected, and trauma survivors have often not planned for illness that may lead to incapacitation, including making arrangements for surrogate decision makers. Cognitively impaired, the patient experiencing delirium may not be able to make the complex decisions that may be needed for the management of acute trauma. Emergent, life-threatening situations must be managed safely, but sometimes trauma involves urgent but nonemergent issues like limb amputation. Additionally, questions often arise related to the patient's ability to make decisions related to disposition, code status, and even naming a surrogate decision maker. Can the sick and confused patient participate in such decisions? How can patient safety and autonomy be balanced? Is it possible to conduct the assessment of decision-making capacity in such a way that it also carries therapeutic benefit?

Assessment of decision-making capacity is among the most common consult questions in the inpatient setting, especially in the context of the patient with delirium, traumatic brain injury, or preexisting neurocognitive disorders such as dementia. In such consults, the primary goal is assessing the patient's understanding of specific issues related to their plan of care. Such assessments are often conversational in nature but can be formalized by integrating a structured approach, such as the aid to capacity evaluation (Etchells et al., 1999). Capacity assessments, when necessary, are an important aspect of good care and should be understood and described to the patient, not as an attempt to take away rights but as a means of formalizing help and support. The existential, humanistic, and solution-focused approaches discussed in Chapter 6: Psychological Interventions for hospitalized trauma patients may be integrated into the capacity assessment to increase the likelihood of a therapeutic outcome. The assessment of decision-making capacity requires the balancing of the goal of honoring autonomy against the principles of beneficence and nonmaleficence.

The decision-making capacity assessment can potentially lead to a revocation of personal autonomy and the assignment of a surrogate decision-maker. Because of this, we must consider the potential counter-therapeutic effects that violating the right to autonomy may have on an individual. Ideally, the capacity assessment can be a catalyst for posttraumatic growth and can lead to the acknowledgment of current deficits, the potential for improvement, and the involvement of the support system in the assignment of a surrogate decision maker.

If the patient's cognitive functioning allows, helpful approaches incorporate open-ended questions with validation of the patient experience, and should they have insight into their cognitive impairment. Additionally, pairing psychoeducational information related to the effects of delirium, traumatic brain injury, or neurocognitive disorders may destigmatize changes in cognition and increase the likelihood of strengthening the therapeutic alliance and avoiding a rupture in the relationship should autonomy be revoked. Asking simple questions such as, "Have you found it hard to understand some of the information that doctors are sharing with you?" or "Would it be helpful if someone you trusted was able to assist you with decision-making?" can open the door to shared decision-making processes and increase confidence and trust in their health care teams.

The general principles of assessing decision-making capacity include (a) communicating a choice, (b) understanding the meaning of medical information, (c) appreciating the significance of the medical information, and (d) reasoning logically through treatment options (Appelbaum & Grisso, 1988). Concerns have been expressed that the traditional model for capacity assessment is hierarchical and assumes that the clinical team has the best understanding of clinical options. A nonhierarchical narrative-based model of capacity assessment has been suggested to address the same clinical constructs in a nonhierarchical manner (Mahr, 2015).

Jim's Recovery

Over the first few days after admission, Jim showed improvements in cognitive functioning. He became more depressed, however, and voiced active suicidal ideation with plans. He was transferred to the psychiatry unit for safety and was started on an antidepressant. He showed very little improvement with either mood or cognition after two weeks of hospitalization, although his acute suicidality seemed to resolve; his memory was still very poor, and he was impulsive and often disoriented. On mental status testing, he was typically able to recall only 1 of 3 words. The clinical team decided that longer-term rehab treatment would be more appropriate than acute hospitalization. Long-term placement options were explored. On the day of the planned transfer, I approached the unit with sadness that Jim had shown such minimal improvement. I found him, to my amazement, playing pinochle with peers on the unit. His mood was bright, and he was cognitively intact. "I'm back, doc, this is me!" he told me.

Chapter summary

The cognitively impaired acute trauma patient presents special issues. Psychological interventions and therapeutic strategies must be modified for the patient experiencing cognitive impairment, and decision-making capacity can be an important concern. Delirium is highly prevalent in medical settings, especially for patients requiring mechanical ventilation or who have recently undergone operative intervention. Traumatic brain injury is a major public health problem worldwide, and in addition to cognitive impairment, can lead to the development of depression and suicidality.

References

American Psychiatric Association (2022). *Diagnostic and Statistical Manual of Mental Disorders* (5th ed., text rev.). American Psychiatric Association Publishing. https://doi.org/10.1176/appi.books.9780890425787.

Appelbaum, P. S., & Grisso, T. (1988). Assessing Patients' Capacities to Consent to Treatment. *New England Journal of Medicine, 319*(25), 1635–1638. https://doi.org/10.1056/NEJM198812223192504.

Berwick, D., Bowman, K., & Matney, C. (2022). *Traumatic Brain Injury: A Roadmap for Accelerating Progress (2022) Traumatic Brain Injury*. National Academies Press, 1–228. https://doi.org/10.17226/25394.

Brett, B. L., Temkin, N., Barber, J. K., Okonkwo, D. O., Stein, M., Bodien, Y. G., Corrigan, J., Diaz-Arrastia, R., Giacino, J. T., Mccrea, M. A., Manley, G. T., & Nelson, L. D. (2023). Long-term Multidomain Patterns of Change After Traumatic Brain Injury: A TRACK-TBI LONG Study. *Neurology, 101*(7). https://doi.org/10.1212/WNL.0000000000207501.

De Luca, R., Calderone, A., Maggio, M. G., Gangemi, A., Corallo, F., Pandolfo, G., Mento, C., Muscatello, M. R. A., Bonanno, M., Quartarone, A., & Calabrò, R. S. (2025). The Relationship Between Traumatic Brain Injury and Suicide: A Systematic Review of Risk Factors. *Clinical Neuropsychiatry, 22*(1), 66–86. https://doi.org/10.36131/cnfioritieditore20250106.

Ely, E. W., Bernard, G. R., Speroff, T., Gautam, S., Dittus, R., May, L., Truman, B., Gordon, S., Margolin, R., Inouye, S. K., Francis, J., & Hart, R. P. (2001). Delirium in mechanically ventilated patients: Validity and reliability of the Confusion Assessment Method for the intensive care unit (CAM-ICU). *Journal of the American Medical Association, 286*(21), 2703–2710. https://doi.org/10.1001/jama.286.21.2703.

Ely, E. W., Margolin, R., Francis, J., May, L., Truman, B., Dittus, R., Speroff, T., Gautam, S., Bernard, G. R., & Inouye, S. K. (2001). Evaluation of delirium in critically ill patients: Validation of the Confusion Assessment Method for the intensive care unit (CAM-ICU). *Critical Care Medicine, 29*(7), 1370–1379. https://doi.org/10.1097/00003246-200107000-00012.

Etchells, E., Darzins, P., Silberfeld, M., Singer, P. A., McKenny, J., Naglie, G., Katz, M., Gordon H, G., Molloy, D. W., & Strang, D. (1999). Assessment of patient capacity to consent to treatment. *Journal of General Internal Medicine, 14*(1), 27–34. https://doi.org/10.1046/j.1525-1497.1999.00277.x.

Folstein, M. F., Folstein, S. E., & McHugh, P. R. (1975). "Mini-mental state". A practical method for grading the cognitive state of patients for the clinician. *Journal of Psychiatric Research, 12*(3), 189–198. https://doi.org/10.1016/0022-3956(75)90026-6.

Jorge, R. E., Robinson, R. G., Moser, D., Tateno, A., Crespo-Facorro, B., & Arndt, S. (2004). Major Depression Following Traumatic Brain Injury. *Archives of General Psychiatry, 61*(1), 42–50. https://doi.org/10.1001/archpsyc.61.1.42.

Mahr, G. (2015). Narrative medicine and decision-making capacity. *Journal of Evaluation in Clinical Practice, 21*(3), 503–507. https://doi.org/10.1111/jep.12357.

Nasreddine, Z. S., Phillips, N. A., Bédirian, V., Charbonneau, S., Whitehead, V., Collin, I., Cummings, J. L., & Chertkow, H. (2005). The Montreal Cognitive Assessment, MoCA: A brief screening tool for mild cognitive impairment. *Journal of the American Geriatrics Society, 53*(4), 695–699. https://doi.org/10.1111/j.1532-5415.2005.53221.x.

Trivedi, N., Sarangi, A., Boriwala, H., Bhatt, V., & Rohatgi, S. (2024). Prevalence and management of ICU delirium—Time to think outside the box. *Discover Medicine, 1*(1). https://doi.org/10.1007/s44337-024-00139-y.

Chapter 11

Substance use and misuse

Thomas's Story

Thomas, a 34-year-old construction worker, had just reached the end of a long work week. He had been a heavy drinker for about 15 years, typically consuming between 12 and 18 cans of beer per day, and more on the weekends. This Saturday started like most, with Thomas finishing a 12-pack of his favorite beer by the afternoon. He then remembered that his chimney needed caulking. He grabbed his ladder and positioned it haphazardly against the gutter, then shakily climbed the ladder, lifting himself onto the roof. As he approached the chimney, he stumbled and fell off the roof onto his driveway. He suffered significant orthopedic injuries, including a fractured femur.

Alcohol, licit and illicit substances, and acute trauma

The relationship between substance use and acute trauma is complex and bidirectional. Alcohol use and licit and illicit substance misuse increase the risk of falls and are also associated with increased risk of sustaining an assault and other kinds of traumatic injuries. Half of all violent crimes involve alcohol use by either the perpetrator, the victim, or both (Collins & Messerschmidt, 1993). Most sexual assaults are perpetrated by men who have been drinking, and often both the perpetrator and victim have been consuming alcohol (Abbey et al., 2001). In this way, alcohol and substance use can lead to acute trauma exposure. Because of this relationship between substance use and trauma exposure, the American College of Surgeons requires the development and implementation of screening, brief intervention, and referral to treatment (SBIRT) programs for alcohol misuse (American College of Surgeons, 2025).

The experience of posttraumatic stress disorder (PTSD) and complex trauma is associated with an increased rate of alcohol and substance use and misuse. In these populations, substance misuse seems to develop as a maladaptive avoidance-based coping mechanism for the insomnia, intrusive reexperiencing symptoms, and dysphoric affect associated with PTSD and complex trauma. So, in this regard, substance misuse can also be a result of acute trauma.

Inpatient admissions for the management of acute traumatic injuries can also represent an opportunity for intervention in the patient presenting with comorbid substance use concerns. The crisis that acute trauma represents can be a turning

The Psychology of Acute Trauma. DOI: https://doi.org/10.1016/B978-0-443-33212-8.00029-4

point that may lead to insight and recovery, a "teachable moment" if you will. In this sense, the traumatic event leading to admission may serve as a sentinel event that is associated with a need to engage in both short- and long-term behavior change to reduce the likelihood of future negative health events (Boudreaux et al., 2012). In this chapter, we will explore several aspects of the complex relationship between acute trauma, complex trauma, and substance use.

Substance use, misuse, and use disorders

Both the use and misuse of substances are important to understand in the context of acute trauma. Substance use is common worldwide and constitutes the nonproblematic, socially acceptable use of substances that does not lead to functional impairment. Conversely, substance use disorders involve a pattern of recurrent use characterized by functional impairment, increased tolerance, a loss of control, and continued use despite adverse consequences, and can include dependence and withdrawal. Substance use behaviors exist on a spectrum, with socially acceptable substance use and substance use disorders on the far ends of the spectrum, and substance misuse in between. Substance misuse refers to the use of a substance in a way that causes adverse consequences, like a traumatic injury, but does not meet the full criteria for a substance use disorder.

Differentiating between use and misuse in inpatient settings can pose some challenges due to its reliance on contextual information regarding the events surrounding the index trauma, though it is important in any case involving substances to avoid unnecessary stigmatization. For instance, operating a vehicle while intoxicated with a blood alcohol content (BAC) of 0.10, in a moment of poor judgment, can occur in someone who is not impacted by an alcohol use disorder but can still result in a significant traumatic injury. Thus, in this instance, the alcohol consumption would be classified as substance misuse. Using this same scenario, but imagining the patient to be the passenger, not the driver, with a designated driver who isn't intoxicated, the same alcohol consumption behavior would now be classified as substance use rather than substance misuse and likely will not require intervention. Information sources such as emergency medical services (EMS) run sheets or law enforcement reports, as well as information documented in emergency department medical records, may assist in understanding the underlying factors contributing to the index trauma. This information can both corroborate or highlight inconsistencies in the patient's self-reports related to the events surrounding their index trauma or assist in understanding the underlying factors contributing to injury if they are unable to communicate or are experiencing impaired memory. Both use disorders and misuse are important to explore in the acute trauma patient, and each may benefit from interventions to reduce the potential likelihood of future injury.

Assessment of substance use

Assessment of substance use is an important part of every psychological and psychosocial evaluation conducted within the trauma center for several important reasons. First of all, substance misuse is an important risk factor for exposure to trauma, especially falls, motor vehicle crashes, and assaults. Additionally, substance withdrawal can increase patient distress and cause significant morbidity and mortality, with the potential to complicate delirium in intensive care settings. Withdrawal is also a common reason for patients to request to leave the hospital against medical advice. When withdrawal is missed or underappreciated it can be more difficult to manage and require more intensive medical interventions. Finally, awareness of substance use provides an important opportunity for secondary prevention.

Due to social stigma surrounding substance use, patients are sometimes not forthright about their use histories, especially if their use constitutes misuse or meets criteria for a use disorder. Denial, shame, and guilt are part of the illness and are very common components of substance use disorders, and other sources of history, like medical records and collateral history, are especially important to consider. Labs, including urine drug screening (UDS) and BAC testing, can have a role in identifying recent substance use when history is not available or in supporting patient reports during the clinical interview, and can be embedded in our order sets for all admitted trauma patients. When interpreting the results of the UDS, it is important to consider if the patient had received any medications prior to arrival at the hospital during emergency medical transport, such as opioids for pain or benzodiazepines for agitation, to avoid inadvertently interpreting positive results as a sign of illicit substance use. For patients with negative BACs who are exhibiting signs of alcohol withdrawal but are denying or are unable to confirm the presence of alcohol use, a phosphatidyl ethanol (PEth) test may provide insight into the patient's recent use patterns. PEth is a whole blood alcohol biomarker and can typically be detected for two to four weeks following last alcohol use, with interpretation typically stratified into three use levels: Light use or abstinence (< 20 ng/mL), moderate use (20 ng/mL to 200 ng/mL), and heavy or chronic use (> 200 ng/mL). Substance use disorders involve continued use in the face of adverse consequences, but sometimes patients do not consider falls or assaults as adverse consequences of their substance use. Psychoeducation is particularly useful in this context.

Meeting trauma center reverification criteria

While SBIRT interventions may be provided by team members such as residents, social workers, or nurses, any team member may be asked to assist the Trauma and Acute Care Surgery team in meeting the American College of Surgeons (2025) reverification criteria for alcohol misuse screening and intervention. To do so, 80% or more of all trauma patients must receive screening via a validated tool such as the Alcohol Use Disorders Identification Test (AUDIT-C) (Bush et al., 1998), the Cutting down, Annoyed by criticism, Guilty feeling and Eye-openers (CAGE) questionnaire (Mayfield et al., 1974) or routine assessment of BAC. Of those that score positive, 80% or more must have documentation supporting the provision of a brief intervention to address alcohol misuse, or a referral for alcohol use intervention if not able to receive treatment during their hospital stay. Examples of interventions include: Trauma and Acute Care Surgical Psychology (TACS Psych) consults for motivational interviewing sessions, addiction medicine consults for psychopharmacologic intervention or management of withdrawal, and the provision of educational materials containing information related to the connection between alcohol misuse and exposure to trauma.

Alcohol and falls

As Thomas's story illustrates, there is a strong correlation between falls and alcohol use. Alcohol causes impaired judgment, gait instability and poor coordination during the period of intoxication. In addition, chronic heavy alcohol users often develop cerebellar degeneration and peripheral neuropathy, which cause impaired gait. When falls occur in the context of alcohol use, they are more likely to cause traumatic brain injuries (Johnston & McGovern, 2004). Even "usual" or nonhabitual use of alcohol causes an increase in falls (Chen & Yoon, 2017); in fact, there is a linear relationship between alcohol use and the likelihood of falls (Cherpitel et al., 2015). Alcohol misuse plays a significant but often underrecognized role in falls in older adults (Bye et al., 2022). In short, alcohol use should be explored in all cases of acute trauma related to falls. Alcohol misuse is a treatable and preventable cause of acute traumatic injuries.

Alcohol and sexual assault

Sexual assault often occurs in contexts where both the perpetrator and victim have been consuming alcohol. Alcohol use often contributes to the shame that victims of sexual assault sometimes feel; they may feel the assault was somehow their fault because they were intoxicated. It is important to actively address this potential source of shame. The victim of sexual assault needs to understand that the assault was not their fault, even if they were intoxicated. Safety concerns do need to be discussed, but without blaming the victim; intoxication does create increased vulnerability to assault and should be avoided in any context where personal safety may be an issue.

Cannabis

Cannabis use has increased dramatically over the past decade. In 2023, nearly 23% of American adults reported using cannabis. Cannabis is often viewed as safer than alcohol or opiates, with monthly rates of use in college-age adults increasing from 16.1% in 1988 to 39.5% in 2023. Additionally, 24% of teen drivers who use cannabis report driving under the influence of cannabis. Cannabis is the most detected substance in drivers involved in motor vehicle collisions, and cannabis is a present finding in 21% of motor vehicle crash-related fatalities. Twenty-four states have legalized recreational cannabis use, and 40 states have legalized cannabis for medical use (National Center for Drug Abuse Statistics, n.d.). Cannabis use does cause impulsive behavior and poor judgment and may, like alcohol, increase the risk of motor vehicle crashes and assaults. Unlike alcohol, the presence of cannabis on screening assessments in patients admitted for acute trauma is not associated with increased mortality, morbidity, or length of stay (Fujii et al., 2020). Cannabis use is also associated with increased falls in older adults (Workman et al., 2021). Heavy cannabis users may also experience cannabinoid hyperemesis syndrome, which has the potential to complicate surgical recoveries due to the presence of intractable nausea, severe vomiting, and abdominal pain. This cyclical pattern of vomiting often reduces oral intake and may lead to protein-calorie deficiencies that slow or impede healing of wounds and surgical sites.

Other substances of misuse

While alcohol is the substance that has been most studied in relation to acute trauma, hallucinogens, opiates, and stimulants such as cocaine and methamphetamine can also cause impaired judgment that leads to acute trauma. Hallucinogens can cause frightening hallucinations, which can lead to efforts to escape hallucinated dangers by fleeing in unsafe ways, like jumping out of windows or impulsively entering roadways with active traffic. Sometimes even pleasant hallucinations can lead to poor judgment, feelings of omnipotence, and risky behavior (Darke et al., 2024). Cocaine, other stimulants, and opiates can cause similar judgment issues and can increase the risk of acute traumatic falls and injuries (Marzuk et al., 1995; Tardiff et al., 1995). Patients with preexisting opioid use or misuse often experience difficulties related to pain control following surgical intervention due to increased tolerance and may require special management via anesthesia pain teams or palliative medicine. Withdrawal in such cases may be delayed due to the use of opioid pain medication in surgical settings. Stimulants such as cocaine and methamphetamine pose unique challenges due to the rapid onset of withdrawal. With those agents there are no specific pharmacological interventions to reduce withdrawal severity, although supportive measures can provide some symptom relief. We have observed high rates of requests for discharge against medical advice (AMA) in this population. With patients who are intoxicated or in withdrawal, an assessment for decision-making capacity may be useful prior to authorizing an AMA discharge.

Withdrawal syndromes

The general management of substance withdrawal is well described in standard texts in internal medicine, surgery, and psychiatry. Important issues specific to acute trauma care are recognition and prevention. In the complex care of the acute trauma patient, it is easy to forget basic issues like monitoring for the possibility of substance withdrawal. Alcohol withdrawal poses significant medical risks and is usually preventable. Opiate withdrawal causes less medical risk but causes significant patient distress and is also preventable and readily treatable. In acute trauma, there is significant distress related to the trauma itself that cannot be "treated," so it is especially important to treat what can be treated and relieve distress that can be relieved so that the trauma survivor feels, in a tangible way, that their medical or surgical team is concerned about them and focused on their well-being.

Cultural considerations related to substance use

Cultural factors can be relevant in substance use assessment. Alcohol use is more stigmatized in Muslim and Hindu populations, so it is less likely to be reported by patients, and families may be less aware of alcohol use in their family members. Inhalant misuse is uncommon in adults but is much more common in younger teens. Certain substances or mood-altering products are associated with certain cultural subgroups. Khat, for instance, is commonly used and occasionally misused, but its use is often limited to Middle Eastern populations, especially those of Yemeni origin. Additionally, some cultures may utilize substances as part of ritualistic practices. Clinicians should take extra care to address use under these circumstances, especially if use is consistent with generally accepted subcultural beliefs.

Complex trauma, posttraumatic stress disorder, and alcohol misuse

Complex trauma, as discussed in Chapter 4, Appreciating the Impact of Complex Trauma, often begins with abuse and neglect in childhood. Parental alcohol misuse can be a causal factor related to child abuse, although the relationship is difficult to quantify. In this way, the cycle of complex trauma can begin with the presence of a parental alcohol use disorder, which also highlights the genetic vulnerability of the patient. Complex trauma survivors, as well as individuals with PTSD, are at high risk for developing problematic patterns of substance use, including alcohol use disorders. Abuse and trauma, especially in childhood, can interfere with the development of healthy coping strategies. Victims of abuse often feel alone, abandoned, and unloved. Internal mechanisms for self-soothing fail to develop properly, and alcohol can become a substitute coping mechanism and survival strategy. In these scenarios, alcohol often becomes a tool to avoid unpleasant intrusive re-experiencing symptoms or to increase somnolence prior to sleep to reduce hyperarousal. Additionally, alcohol use prior to bed may provide sedation and suppress rapid eye movement (REM) sleep and nightmares early in the night. While patients may seek this sedation and suppression of nightmares, such REM suppression may lead to REM rebound and a subsequent increase in nightmares. When complex trauma survivors are retraumatized by an acutely traumatic event, they can turn to familiar but maladaptive strategies like alcohol or other substance use. Preventative and psychoeducational interventions can help avoid such relapses into maladaptive patterns of substance use. Patients can be educated about the risks of relapse, and psychotherapeutic interventions that increase affect tolerance can be initiated. The nonspecific elements of therapy, like empathy and caring, can mitigate the feeling of isolation and abandonment that can occur in the complex trauma patient who suffers from acute trauma. Oftentimes, patients report that the nonjudgmental interactions with the TACS Psych team allow for open and honest conversations related to underlying substance use. That may not be true if clinicians convey, either intentionally or unintentionally, a sense of disapproval related to substance use behavior. Specific therapeutic modalities to address substance use, such as motivational interviewing, are well-suited for use in inpatient medical settings and are further discussed in Chapter 6, Psychological Interventions for Hospitalized Trauma Patients.

Substance misuse, especially in the complex trauma patient, can be a component of an overall pattern of maladaptive, avoidant coping. As mentioned above, substance misuse can become part of an overall strategy of avoidant coping; patients with substance use disorders are accustomed to managing emotional distress and dysphoric affect with substances and have not developed coping mechanisms to manage the emotional distress associated with their novel acute trauma. They may require higher levels of emotional support from the trauma team.

Denial, shame, and guilt

Shame and guilt have a prominent role in the maintenance of substance use disorders. Substance users are frequently ashamed of the illness and their powerlessness over it, embarrassed about their relapses and difficulties maintaining a state of sobriety. For these individuals, shame and guilt can lead to denial. To acknowledge the illness of substance use causes shame and guilt, so the individual tends to deny and minimize their illness, which paradoxically perpetuates the illness itself. The dysphoria related to shame and guilt persists and further increases the risk of relapse, but the denial makes it difficult for the individual to seek and accept help.

When substance use has a causal role in an acute traumatic injury, the shame and guilt can be even stronger. We have previously discussed self-blame after an acute traumatic event as a defense against the existential meaninglessness and horror of the traumatic event. In those cases, the self-reproach is maladaptive, and psychoeducation and the exploration of the existential meaning of the trauma can be very helpful. When an individual's choices are, in fact, the cause of the trauma, issues of self-blame and self-reproach are more complicated to deal with. Sometimes the distinction between blame and responsibility is a useful one. Through therapeutic interventions, the patient with a substance use disorder can acknowledge and accept their role in their traumatic injury and work towards acceptance and behavioral change, rather than blaming themselves. Self-blame can lead to another cycle of denial, passivity, and relapse, but acceptance and responsibility can lead to true recovery.

Phases of recovery

The Transtheoretical Model of change represents a useful conceptualization for the stages of substance misuse recovery (Prochaska et al., 1992). In this model, the state before change begins is called precontemplation. Precontemplation involves lack of motivation, lack of insight, and denial. The next stage, contemplation, involves awareness of the problem and the beginnings of change. The stage of preparation follows, which involves a commitment to change. In the preparation stage, individuals begin to explore change-related options. The final stages, action and maintenance, then occur. Following this, relapse is considered, which then may lead to the initiation of another cycle of change.

Sometimes, the most difficult phase of recovery is the transition from precontemplation to contemplation. The powerful impact of acute trauma can rapidly move patients from precontemplation to contemplation, preparation, and change.

Hitting "rock bottom"

A clinical maxim in substance use treatment is that the individual sometimes must "hit rock bottom" to finally quit drinking or using substances. Clinical literature bears out this maxim. Different kinds of events can be the "rock bottom." Job loss can be one such event, or a spouse or family member severing ties. Alcohol related illnesses like pancreatitis can be the rock bottom, and are often treated by Trauma and Acute Care Surgery teams. A serious injury related to a fall or assault can also represent rock bottom.

It is important to remember that an acute trauma like Thomas's serious fall might serve as a catalyst for recovery, the sentinel event for behavior change. Confrontation and education, without blame and criticism, can sometimes lead to an awareness of the negative life impacts of alcohol misuse. A fall like Thomas's can be a form of hitting rock bottom and can lead to abstinence, recovery, and posttraumatic growth.

The spiritual aspects of recovery

Spirituality has long been associated with substance use recovery. Alcoholics Anonymous (AA), founded in 1935 by Bill Wilson, has long been an effective mainstay of alcohol use disorder treatment. Wilson was a patient of Carl Jung, whose depth psychology emphasized the spiritual dimension of personal growth and recovery. It is said that the best stories of conversion are not heard from church pulpits but in church basements, where the AA meetings are held.

For a variety of reasons beyond the scope of this chapter, modern psychology and psychiatry have re-medicalized substance use disorder treatment and de-emphasized its spiritual dimensions. But as we will discuss in Chapter 17, Spiritual Aspects of Recovery, the recovery from acute trauma can itself have a spiritual dimension. If spiritual issues have been stirred in a trauma patient with substance misuse concerns, those two aspects of recovery might meaningfully be linked.

Addressing Thomas's Alcohol Use

When Thomas presented to the hospital, he was visibly intoxicated, with a BAC of 0.33 supporting clinical observations. Following stabilization, he completed the AUDIT-C as part of his trauma tertiary examination, with results indicating the need for a brief intervention to address his alcohol misuse. Alcohol was an obvious cause of Thomas's fall, and even Thomas was able to recognize that, despite his initial feelings that he could control his drinking and that it was not a problem. Thomas's recovery was complicated, and his fractured femur required several revisions of his initial surgical intervention. Although Thomas initially insisted that this alcohol use was "no big deal" and he was annoyed by our focus on alcohol related issues, he gradually came to accept, through his hospital course, that his alcohol use was "a big deal."

Throughout his course of care, motivational interviewing interventions were integrated into his regular follow-up visits, with a focus on "rolling with resistance" to break down barriers to change. He moved quickly through the stages of change, and eventually, he began to express that he wanted to do anything he could to quit drinking. We engaged regularly in discussions related to options for maintenance of remission and prevention of relapse, and ultimately, he was able to accept referrals for outpatient substance use disorder treatment and AA. While he was initially uncomfortable that AA was, in his view, too religious, when the difference between religion and spirituality was explored, he accepted the potential importance of spiritual issues in his recovery.

Chapter summary

Acute trauma and substance misuse can be strongly linked, and substance misuse can be both a cause and result of acute trauma. Especially in the case of alcohol, the strong association between trauma and alcohol use disorders is well documented. Because of this, the American College of Surgeons (2025) requires that all verified trauma centers have protocols to screen for alcohol misuse, with the provision of an alcohol misuse intervention or referral for outpatient care. Effective therapeutic interventions, such as motivational interviewing, can address both substance use disorder recovery and trauma recovery in an integrated approach.

References

Abbey, A., Zawacki, T., Buck, P. O., Clinton, A. M., & McAuslan, P. (2001). Alcohol and sexual assault. *Alcohol Research & Health, 25*(1), 43–51.

American College of Surgeons (2025). *Resources for optimal care of the injured patient 2022 standards, revised July 2025* (7th ed.). American College of Surgeons, https://www.facs.org/quality-programs/trauma/quality/verification-review-and-consultation-program/standards/.

Boudreaux, E. D., Bock, B., & O'Hea, E. (2012). When an event sparks behavior change: An introduction to the sentinel event method of dynamic model building and its application to emergency medicine. *Academic Emergency Medicine, 19*(3), 329–335. https://doi.org/10.1111/j.1553-2712.2012.01291.x.

Bush, K., Kivlahan, D. R., McDonell, M. B., & Fihn, S. D. (1998). Katharine A. Bradley, The AUDIT alcohol consumption questions (AUDIT-C): An effective brief screening test for problem drinking. *Archives of Internal Medicine, 158*(16), 1789–1795. https://doi.org/10.1001/archinte.158.16.1789.

Bye, E. K., Bogstrand, S. T., & Rossow, I. (2022). The importance of alcohol in elderly's hospital admissions for fall injuries: a population case-control study. *NAD Nordic Studies on Alcohol and Drugs, 39*(1), 38–49. https://doi.org/10.1177/14550725211015836.

Chen, C. M., & Yoon, Y.-H. (2017). Usual Alcohol Consumption and Risks for Nonfatal Fall Injuries in the United States: Results From the 2004–2013 National Health Interview Survey. *Substance Use and Misuse, 52*(9), 1120–1132. https://doi.org/10.1080/10826084.2017.1293101.

Cherpitel, C. J., Ye, Y., Bond, J., Borges, G., & Monteiro, M. (2015). Relative risk of injury from acute alcohol consumption: Modeling the dose-response relationship in emergency department data from 18 countries. *Addiction (Abingdon, England), 110*(2), 279–288. https://doi.org/10.1111/add.12755.

Collins, J. J., & Messerschmidt, P. M. (1993). Epidemiology of alcohol-related violence. *Alcohol Health & Research, 17*(2).

Darke, S., Duflou, J., Peacock, A., Farrell, M., Hall, W., & Lappin, J. (2024). A retrospective study of the characteristics and toxicology of cases of lysergic acid diethylamide (LSD)- and psilocybin-related death in Australia. *Addiction (Abingdon, England), 119*(9), 1564–1571. https://doi.org/10.1111/add.16518.

Fujii, Q., Olsen, I., & Mccague, A. (2020). Marijuana screening and trauma outcomes. *Journal of Emergencies, Trauma and Shock, 13*(1), 35–38. https://doi.org/10.4103/JETS.JETS_6_19.

Johnston, J. J. E., & McGovern, S. J. (2004). Alcohol related falls: An interesting pattern of injuries. *Emergency Medicine Journal, 21*(2), 185–188. https://doi.org/10.1136/emj.2003.006130.

Marzuk, P. M., Tardiff, K., Leon, A. C., Hirsch, C. S., Stajic, M., Portera, L., Hartwell, N., & Iqbal, M. I. (1995). Fatal injuries after cocaine use as a leading cause of death among young adults in new york city. *New England Journal of Medicine, 332*(26), 1753–1757. https://doi.org/10.1056/NEJM199506293322606.

Mayfield, D., McLeod, G., & Hall, P. (1974). The CAGE Questionnaire: Validation of a New Alcoholism Screening Instrument. *American Journal of Psychiatry, 131*(10), 1121–1123. https://doi.org/10.1176/ajp.131.10.1121.

National Center for Drug Abuse Statistics, Drug abuse statistics. (n.d.). https://drugabusestatistics.org/.

Prochaska, J. O., DiClemente, C. C., & Norcross, J. C. (1992). In search of how people change: Applications to addictive behaviors. *American Psychologist, 47*(9), 1102–1114. https://doi.org/10.1037//0003-066x.47.9.1102.

Tardiff, K., Marzuk, P. M., Leon, A. C., Hirsch, C. S., Stajić, M., Portera, L., & Hartwell, N. (1995). Cocaine, opiates, and ethanol in homicides in New York City: 1990 and 1991. *Journal of Forensic Sciences, 40*(3), 387–390.

Workman, C. D., Fietsam, A. C., Sosnoff, J., & Rudroff, T. (2021). Increased likelihood of falling in older cannabis users vs. Non-users. *Brain Sciences, 11*(2), 1–12. https://doi.org/10.3390/brainsci11020134.

Chapter 12

Severe and persistent mental illness

Henry's Story

Henry was admitted to the hospital for multiple contusions and rib fractures after he was assaulted with a pool cue. The assailant was the manager of a gas station and convenience store that Henry regularly visited. Henry had frequently taken small items without paying, especially food, from the convenience store. The manager had been tolerant of Henry visiting the all-night store to warm up, but had become frustrated by the repeated thefts. The prior week, the manager physically escorted him out of the store; this time, there was a scuffle, which resulted in the assault.

Henry has been unhoused for many years. He frequently wanders the streets near the store and solicits donations on the freeway ramp nearby. Henry often talks to himself, sometimes loudly. He has been psychiatrically hospitalized on three occasions but has never had follow-up care. Henry misuses alcohol and cocaine on occasion. He describes his use as "whenever I can get it." The consult was requested to "prevent future high-risk behavior that might lead to another assault."

The patient experiencing symptoms of psychosis

Those who experience psychiatric illnesses like schizophrenia and bipolar disorder are at higher risk for exposure to acute trauma. They are more likely to engage in risky behaviors. As we see in Henry's case, psychosis and mania can also cause impaired social judgment and increase the risk of being assaulted by another person. Individuals experiencing symptoms of psychosis can be difficult to manage in the milieu. They may experience paranoia, perceiving medical interventions like blood draws and dressing changes as assaults, and become resistant to care. They are also at high risk for comorbid substance use and misuse, and the symptoms of psychosis may cause the treatment team to overlook symptoms of intoxication and withdrawal.

The Psychology of Acute Trauma. DOI: https://doi.org/10.1016/B978-0-443-33212-8.00018-X

The experience of psychosis

Those affected by symptoms of psychosis can experience hallucinations or delusions, which can be frightening. They can also experience what might be described as an excess of meaning-making. They can have ideas of reference, meaning that neutral stimuli like a television commercial or a voice on the radio apply specifically to them. Acute trauma creates special issues for patients experiencing symptoms of psychosis, whereas many trauma survivors struggle with issues of meaning. Trauma patients experiencing severe mental illness may ascribe inappropriate or excessive meaning to the traumatic event. The trauma had to mean something; it is incorporated into a delusional or paranoid worldview. The motor vehicle crash occurred because someone was trying to get me. In this delusional state of mind, medical interventions become terrifying assaults and might be desperately resisted.

Special treatment considerations for the patient experiencing symptoms of psychosis

Antipsychotic medications are the mainstay of treatment for the patient experiencing symptoms of psychosis. Whether psychosis is caused by schizophrenia or mania, antipsychotic medications are effective. Furthermore, such medications are effective very quickly. Standard clinical teaching has been that antipsychotic medications don't begin to relieve psychotic symptoms for days or even weeks. The readily observable calming effects of medications like haloperidol were felt to be related to nonspecific sedation rather than an actual antipsychotic effect. Recent evidence suggests that they begin to work very quickly, even on the first day, and provide specific benefit for psychotic symptoms (Agid et al., 2006). Sedating agents like benzodiazepines can augment the effects of antipsychotics.

Milieu management is also very important for patients experiencing symptoms of psychosis. In treating them, it is important to remember that the poorly controlled behavior often reflects an internal feeling of being out of control. A clinical environment that provides firm boundaries and structure will often lead to an increased sense of safety and security. "I feel like I'm losing control inside, but the staff is able to be in control for me and keep me safe" may be what the patient experiencing symptoms of psychosis will feel, though they may not be able to articulate that feeling. A calm environment, a private room, and minimal commotion are helpful, especially in patients experiencing mania who are keenly responsive to the environment around them. Interventions like blood draws and procedures should be minimized if possible, but if required, the necessity should be presented firmly and clearly, with the clear expression that all interventions are being done to serve the purpose of the patient's rapid recovery, health, and safety. If restraint becomes necessary because of symptoms of acute psychosis, the need for restraints to protect safety should be reinforced. Restraints should be avoided if at all possible, as they can worsen agitation, though it is also important to note it may also paradoxically make a patient feel safer to know that external control is possible when internal control is lacking.

Some patients with psychotic symptoms have poor follow-up with medical and psychiatric care. They are sometimes suspicious of caregivers, and the poverty associated with chronic mental illness can cause a "social drift" to underserved urban areas where access to care is poor. The index trauma, if a supportive relationship with the trauma team can be developed, may provide an opportunity to facilitate care for both psychiatric and medical problems.

Aftercare

The admission for acute trauma may be related to a significant relapse of symptoms of psychosis. Further psychiatric treatment may be required after the acute medical and surgical stabilization related to the acute trauma are resolved. This may include outpatient or even inpatient psychiatric care. Psychiatric patients, especially those experiencing symptoms of psychosis, may lack insight into their illness and may require involuntary treatment. Specific standards for involuntary care vary by state and country, but usually require that a patient be a danger to themself or others, or unable to take care of basic needs. In the United States, the law tends to err on the side of protecting patient autonomy; the presence of psychosis in and of itself is usually not sufficient to justify involuntary treatment. This can be frustrating for the medical and surgical teams, who want something to be done to help the patient. It can be sad and frustrating for the treatment team when a patient like Henry is released to an uncertain fate and an uncaring environment.

Mental health and social resources are often limited for those experiencing mental illness. Mental illness itself sometimes makes it difficult for a patient to utilize the resources that might be available. Patients might be suspicious or paranoid about getting help, and often lack the patience and tolerance to negotiate the bureaucratic machinery that makes resources available.

Also, patients sometimes simply don't want the resources that might be available. Henry, for instance, had been offered housing resources many times. He found shelters to be dirty and unsafe, and he didn't like the rules and restrictions about having to be in the shelter at a certain time to be allowed to stay the night. He preferred to, as he put it, "Make do on my own."

Henry's decision to remain unhoused is directly related to the quality of the resources that are available. If housing resources were available that met Henry's needs more effectively, he might be inclined to avail himself of them. In other words, there is a cultural and political aspect to Henry's care refusal. Patients with psychotic symptoms can be very rational when making decisions, even decisions we might not agree with. The autonomy narrative that we craft as caregivers may sometimes serve to rationalize and justify an important socio-political issue of resource misallocation.

Severe and persistent mental illness

The term severe and persistent mental illness (SPMI) has been used in psychiatry for the past three decades to describe a subpopulation of those experiencing mental illness who face special issues and have special needs. Patients experiencing SPMI, diagnostically, often experience serious mental illnesses, such as schizophrenia spectrum disorders or bipolar disorders. Their problems are chronic and disabling, and sometimes they are chronically unhoused. Traditional mental health interventions, such as inpatient psychiatric hospitalization and psychotropic medications, are of little benefit. They tend to be treated overly aggressively, despite the marginal benefits of treatment, or they tend to be neglected out of therapeutic nihilism. The term SPMI is associated with the concept of palliative psychiatry; this population is probably treated best with a palliative approach of relieving distress rather than attempting to treat illness (Zumstein & Riese, 2020).

The SPMI population is at high risk of assault and other types of trauma (Lu et al., 2013). They tend to display deficits in social insight and judgment. The impaired judgment can sometimes create barriers to empathy. In Henry's case, for instance, some staff would wonder, "Why does he keep stealing from the same place?"

Patient-centered care and language

The term patient-centered care refers to a model of health care delivery focused on the patient's needs and goals. As Abid and colleagues put it, the central patient question in patient-centered care is not "What's the matter with you?" but rather "What matters to you?" (Abid et al., 2024).

Patient-centered care is often symptom-based rather than illness-based. In Henry's case, in an illness-based care model, we would consider aggressive use of antipsychotics and possibly inpatient psychiatric care. Henry would refuse treatment but might be a candidate for involuntary psychiatric treatment. Commitment laws vary by state, and Henry might meet the criteria for involuntary treatment based on his inability to care for himself. Interventions like guardianship might even be considered, followed by placement in a supervised living environment.

Patient-centered care would have as its goal the relief of distress. Involuntary interventions might still be considered patient-centered, as long as they could be seen to forward the goals of the patient if they were not experiencing symptoms of psychosis. In Henry's case, because he was at his psychiatric baseline before sustaining his traumatic injuries, involuntary interventions were not deemed appropriate.

Palliative care is, by its nature, patient-centered, with a focus on distress and safety, as well as strategies for relieving distress. Antipsychotic medications would have a potential role, if Henry agreed that they might help.

Patient-centered care interventions must balance autonomy and "paternalism." Paternalism involves making active interventions on a patient's behalf, even when the patient is unwilling. Long-acting injectable medications for psychotic symptoms, for instance, represent a paternalistic intervention to address medication nonadherence, but one that sometimes improves patient outcomes. Paternalistic interventions can only be used with proper legal authority.

Finally, person-centered language should be used in tandem with person-centered care. Person-centered language aims to destigmatize those who experience serious mental illness and can rehumanize those with whom we work. Stigmatizing language related to the description of the experience of mental health concerns is prevalent in medical documentation and often focuses on describing the illness rather than the experience. For example, descriptions of patients as "a schizophrenic" or "a psychotic" may dehumanize the individual experiencing the illness, distancing clinicians from empathy and leading to therapeutic nihilism. Person-centered language, like that used in this chapter, emphasizes the individual first within the context of their experience. Examples of person-centered language include "an individual experiencing symptoms of psychosis" or "a person experiencing symptoms of mania." Using person-centered language in clinical conversations with members of the surgical team often leads to a better understanding of the patient's lived experience and ultimately better outcomes.

Social skills training

Psychoeducational interventions, like social skills training, are specifically designed for the social impairments seen in individuals experiencing SPMI (Kopelowicz, 2006). What led to Henry's difficulties with a community member were poor social skills and boundaries. While there is obviously no justification for the assault, Henry misread a social situation and engaged in behavior that was likely to result in adverse consequences. With better social skills, he might have maintained an informal community resource. While social skills training is not typically conducted within the context of an inpatient admission for trauma care, the psychosocial needs assessment may shed light on patient needs, such as ongoing social skills training after leaving the hospital, which ultimately may inform the treatment plan and discharge planning process to include appropriate outpatient referrals. If social impairments are present during the hospital stay and lead to an inability to appropriately engage in care, behavior plans may be utilized to provide clear and objective expectations related to both patient behavior and staff responses.

Multidisciplinary care

Engaging the patient experiencing symptoms of psychosis in care, especially in follow-up care, can be challenging. Building a therapeutic alliance can be especially important in the context of acute trauma because medical and surgical follow-up may be necessary when the acute trauma has necessitated surgical intervention. Remember that the patient's goals of care might be different from what you would consider to be optimal goals. Your job is not to set the goals, but to facilitate and inform the goal-setting process based on the patient's value system. Collaboration is based on the development of shared goals. For instance, a patient may not accept antipsychotic medication as a treatment for delusions because they deny the presence of delusions, but will accept it for the side effect of improved sleep. Social work involvement is often crucial to offer, which may assist with the implementation and the utilization of available resources.

Treatment principles

General principles for the management of patients experiencing symptoms of psychosis include the following:

1. Early use of antipsychotic medication, with patient consent.
2. Supportive but firm and structured milieu with clear limits and boundaries.
3. Awareness and exploration of the meaning of the acute trauma within the patient's personal narrative.
4. Frame treatment according to the patient-centered care model, using patient-centered language.
5. Develop, as best as possible, shared goals.
6. Frame all interventions and plans from the perspective of being for the patient, and for the successful attainment of shared goals.
7. Comprehensive and multidisciplinary aftercare planning was developed in collaboration with the patient.

Henry's Medical Care

Henry's hospital course was generally smooth. He was quite distressed by his assault and complained of poor sleep. He did not want antipsychotic medications for the treatment of his symptoms of psychosis, but recalled that quetiapine had been helpful to him in the past with sleep. He did agree to low-dose quetiapine. After a discussion related to optimizing his health to maintain his independence, he became amenable to aftercare for his fractured ribs and agreed to a temporary stay at a shelter because it was near a primary care clinic where he could receive follow-up. He was cooperative throughout his hospital stay and appreciative of the comparative comforts of the surgical team.

Summary

The special issues related to the treatment of patients experiencing symptoms of psychosis after acute trauma are important to consider, including the use of antipsychotic medications and milieu management. Collaborative goal setting is critical to include in the treatment plan and increases the likelihood of positive patient outcomes, especially as it relates to aftercare and discharge planning. Patient-centered care and the use of patient-centered language may work towards destigmatizing the experience of serious mental illness while rehumanizing some of the most vulnerable individuals with whom we work.

References

Abid, M. H., Kumah, A., Newera, A., & Hafez, P. (2024). Patient-centered healthcare: From patient experience to human experience. *Global Journal on Quality and Safety in Healthcare, 7*(4), 144–148. https://doi.org/10.36401/JQSH-24-X2.

Agid, O., Seeman, P., & Kapur, S. (2006). The "delayed onset" of antipsychotic action–an idea whose time has come and gone. *Journal of psychiatry & neuroscience: JPN, 31*(2), 93–100.

Kopelowicz, A. (2006). Robert Paul Liberman, Roberto Zarate, Recent advances in social skills training for schizophrenia. *Schizophrenia Bulletin, 32*(SUPPL.1). https://doi.org/10.1093/schbul/sbl023.

Lu, W., Yanos, P. T., Silverstein, S. M., Mueser, K. T., Rosenberg, S. D., Gottlieb, J. D., Duva, S. M., Kularatne, T., Dove-Williams, S., Paterno, D., Hawthorne, D., & Giacobbe, G. (2013). Public mental health clients with severe mental illness and probable posttraumatic stress disorder: Trauma exposure and correlates of symptom severity. *Journal of Traumatic Stress, 26*(2), 266–273. https://doi.org/10.1002/jts.21791.

Zumstein, N., & Riese, F. (2020). Defining Severe and Persistent Mental Illness—A Pragmatic Utility Concept Analysis. *Frontiers in Psychiatry, 11*. https://doi.org/10.3389/fpsyt.2020.00648.

Chapter 13

When treatment is traumatic: understanding and addressing medical trauma

In Shock

Dr. Rana Awdish is an intensive care specialist in a large health care system. A few years ago, while she was 7 months pregnant, she developed severe abdominal pain. In her best-selling memoir In Shock: My Journey from Death to Recovery and the Redemptive Power of Hope (Awdish, 2017). Dr. Awdish described her harrowing journey, a confrontation with life-threatening illness, and then through the labyrinthine, indifferent, and casually traumatizing world of health care. Her experience takes her from perfect health and the anticipation of a child, through a nearly fatal abdominal bleed, medical errors, empathic failures, and finally to recovery and posttraumatic growth.

Besides the trauma of her catastrophic illness, Dr. Awdish experienced medical trauma. The care that ultimately saved her life was also traumatic, and some of that trauma was due to medical errors and flaws in the care system. Besides necessary but traumatic procedures like surgery and mechanical ventilation, Dr. Awdish, although she is an "insider," experienced errors and mistreatment in a large and highly regarded academic health care system that was sometimes too impersonal and too rigidly adherent to policy and protocol. The net result is a complex mixture of the sudden horror of the medical event, followed by the trauma of medical care. Sometimes it is the errors and system failures that we remember most; we remember nightmares more vividly than we remember pleasant dreams.

We will use Dr. Awdish's experiences in more detail when we describe the internal experiences of the medical trauma survivor.

What is medical trauma?

The term medical trauma refers to the psychological and physiological responses we may have in response to the painful, life-threatening, fear-inducing and dehumanizing aspects of medical care (Kazak et al., 2006). Medical and surgical care, from a phenomenological perspective, resembles

The Psychology of Acute Trauma. DOI: https://doi.org/10.1016/B978-0-443-33212-8.00027-0

assault. The integrity of the body is violated, and there is pain. Medical interventions are necessary and performed in the service of healing and recovery for the body. Consciously, we know this, but in the deeper levels of the mind, they may be experienced as assaults. A medical procedure like a cardiac catheterization involves a violation and threat to the bodily integrity that would be horrific in a nonmedical context. We consciously accept it and agree to it for our health and well-being, but inwardly it retains some aspects of the experience of trauma.

The term medical trauma can refer to several different kinds of events. One is receiving a terminal or life-altering diagnosis. Another is the distress caused by unexpected and painful medical procedures, like intubation or emergency surgery. These kinds of medical trauma are related to the misfortune of medical illness and the interventions required for treatment, and are very common for patients receiving care in trauma centers.

Another, and an especially important category of distress is that caused by medical errors, inappropriate care, and insensitive care. Dr. Awdish's story illustrates several aspects of this kind of medical trauma. In her case, the medical error of ineffective anesthesia exposed her to some of the most inappropriate aspects of her care, and her medical knowledge made her aware of medical errors that would not have been apparent to a lay patient. If not understood and addressed from a sensitive and conscientious perspective, patients are likely to experience errors and poor care as a betrayal and violation of trust.

Medical errors are sometimes difficult to distinguish from unavoidable complications, especially for patients who, unlike Dr. Awdish, may have a limited understanding of the nuances of critical care. For many patients, complications are seen as errors, and even normal disease progression is sometimes perceived as a medical error or failure. They may have difficulty understanding on a visceral level that appropriate and necessary interventions sometimes have adverse consequences. This is partially a cultural issue. Western medicine has oversold the idea of cure, and views health as an expectation rather than a gift.

On the other hand, true errors occur frequently in medicine and are sometimes concealed and denied. According to the Institute of Medicine (Committee on Quality of Health Care in America, 2000), about one in every three patients admitted to a hospital is exposed to a medical error. For clinicians, the process of assigning and concealing blame distracts from truly taking responsibility. Adopting an approach that overly focuses on defending oneself and saying that you are not to blame can divert us from the deeper and more challenging journey of acceptance and growth. For patients, it is important to understand what happened and why so that acceptance and emotional healing can begin.

Diagnostic issues

Diagnostic criteria for medical trauma must be framed very carefully in the official nomenclature to maintain the selectivity and specificity necessary to identify psychopathology. Unless we die suddenly, we all have faced life-threatening illness or will face life-threatening illness in the future. The Diagnostic and Statistical Manual of Mental Disorders, Fifth Edition, Text Revision (DSM-5-TR) specifies that life-threatening and debilitating illnesses or conditions are not necessarily traumatic (American Psychiatric Association, 2022). Examples of traumatic events cited in the DSM-5-TR include awakening during surgery and anaphylactic shock.

Diagnostic schemas like those presented in the DSM-5-TR are designed to describe pathology, not validate distress and suffering. Learning that one has a diagnosis of a serious illness like cancer or cardiac disease may cause appropriate and serious distress and suffering, though it would not automatically meet the formal criteria of a traumatic event. The suffering that patients endure because of medical illness and medical treatment can be as severe as the suffering caused by other kinds of trauma, and can induce the same patterns of social withdrawal, flashbacks, intrusive thoughts, and nightmares that are seen in posttraumatic stress disorder (PTSD) and acute stress disorder, even though those diagnoses are sometimes not permissible under the DSM-5-TR. In treating such patients, diagnoses like adjustment disorders or mood and anxiety disorders must be used, although those diagnoses often do not capture the severity of the stress response of such clinical presentations.

Key features of medical trauma

How does medical trauma happen? Why do the institutions that are meant to heal end up causing harm? Some aspects of medical trauma cannot be prevented, but other traumatic medical experiences are things that should have never happened. Institutions have rules and policies, and those policies can be the best way of providing safe care to patients in a large system, but can sometimes be applied too rigidly and without sensitivity to the needs and wishes of an individual patient. Patients are entitled to empathic care, but empathy has limitations and must sometimes be suspended when accurate, urgent decisions must be made. Some mistakes are made because caregivers are human, but some mistakes are made because caregivers are tired, ignorant, lazy or upset and need help and care themselves. Finally, sometimes things happen because the universe is chaotic and unpredictable. That chaos sometimes brings wonder and magic, but sometimes brings horror and suffering. As discussed in Chapter 2, The Next Day: Beginning the Process of Recovery, this experience is in line with the shattering of the just world hypothesis that so often accompanies the experience of trauma.

We have tried to tease apart some of the key elements of the emotional response to medical trauma, using Dr. Awdish's words as guideposts. These different elements are all interrelated and are really different aspects of the same traumatic experience.

Powerlessness

Powerless marks Dr. Awdish's first entry to the health care system. When she presented to the emergency department with acute abdominal pain, she knew from her training and clinical experience that she would require care from the Trauma and Acute Care Surgery team. Instead, institutional protocol required, because she was 7 months pregnant, that she be admitted to the care of the obstetrical team. Dr. Awdish knew that this was a wrong decision and would delay the urgent surgical care that she required. Yet despite her status as an intensive care unit (ICU) physician and her important clinical role in the hospital, she could not circumvent it. Triage staff suddenly "outranked" her, and the decision was theirs, not hers.

Many common interventions deployed in acute care medical settings limit independence. Medical and surgical interventions such as endotracheal and nasotracheal intubation, mechanical ventilation, tracheostomy, percutaneous endoscopic gastrostomy (PEG) tube for feeding, total parenteral nutrition (TPN) dependency, restraints and sedation are described by patients as particularly distressing. These challenges to autonomy are cumulative and often lead to intense feelings of helplessness and hopelessness. If left unaddressed, disturbances of conduct such as refusal of care, verbal and physical aggression, as well as requests for discharge against medical advice may develop as the patient attempts to reassert power in the face of overwhelming feelings of powerlessness.

Proactively integrating psychological and behavioral interventions that foster a sense of control prior to the development of maladaptive coping skills can be important. When that is not possible, early intervention following the development of maladaptive coping behaviors is crucial. Such approaches often combine components of interventions from different psychotherapeutic modalities, many of which are discussed in Chapter 6, Psychological Interventions for Hospitalized Trauma Patients (e.g., motivational interviewing, acceptance and commitment therapy, communication skills training). High yield interventions provide patients with the opportunity to develop a sense of control in creative and collaborative ways. For instance, if a patient has begun to exhibit behaviors related to a refusal of care, such as declining to participate in physical and occupational therapy sessions or refusing certain medications, the clinician may begin their approach via an inquisitive assessment utilizing motivational interviewing that ties in a discussion of the patient's underlying values.

After determining that the root of refusal is related to a sense of powerlessness or helplessness, a plan may be formulated either directly with the patient, with the patient's primary health care team or collaboratively with both. To continue the example of declining specific aspects of care, developing treatment plans that emphasize patient autonomy via increasing flexibility in the delivery of care is often recommended as a first step. Such interventions may include statements to the patient, from the health care team member that lead with a values-based reflection such as "I remember you mentioning that regaining your ability to walk is incredibly important to you, and also how hard it is with all of the pain you are experiencing." followed by a choice based response such as "Would you like to engage in your physical therapy session now or in 30 minutes after your pain medicine has started to work?" In our experience, responses emphasizing the ability to choose an element of care tend to lead to higher rates of participation as compared to typical approaches to engaging patients, which are often along the lines of "Would you like to do your physical therapy session now?" These direct statements, while not inherently countertherapeutic, may offer an easy "out" for patients who are attempting to regain a sense of control.

Dehumanization

The term dehumanization refers to the powerful experience patients describe of not being real anymore. They feel like they are not people, they don't exist, they have become objects whose physical forms exist solely to be manipulated by the will of others. Their status as humans is violated. This experience was described several times in Dr. Awdish's memoir. When she was in surgery, and when she was in the ICU and appeared to be comatose, she overheard her colleagues say things she was not meant to hear. On the operating table, she heard members of the surgical team say, "We're losing her," and, even more coldly, "She's circling the drain" (Awdish, 2017, p. 29–30). We don't talk to people in that way; that is how we talk about people when they stop being people and become bodies.

This experience of dehumanization is one that patients commonly report, both in intensive care contexts as well as the surgical general practice (i.e., step-down) units. They describe that they don't feel heard or that their concerns aren't taken seriously. Even mundane and seemingly innocuous experiences that we as clinicians consider part of the daily workflow may cause notable distress and feelings of disconnection in the patient. For instance, many patients describe that during morning rounds, they are often startled awake, hours earlier than they normally would rouse, and are provided critical information related to their care before being fully awake. Afterwards, they feel they don't fully understand their plan of care because they weren't fully awake. Patients often describe long wait times after requesting assistance via their call bell, sometimes having to wait while soiled for prolonged periods of time because they can't go to the bathroom without help. Many share concerns related to a lack of adequate pain control or difficulties related to long wait times for placement in rehabilitation facilities following completion of their acute surgical care. While some of these interactions are out of the control of the clinician, interventions aimed at rehumanizing those with whom we work can have a profound impact.

These approaches aim to strip away the sterility of the clinical setting, emphasizing the humanness of both providing and receiving health care, and, like the interventions to reduce patients' sense of powerlessness described above, generally don't fall under the umbrella of one specific therapeutic modality. As the experience of dehumanization requires an interaction between the patient and their environment, we have found that interventions supporting both the team and the patient themselves are optimal for reducing the experience of dehumanization. In effect, the medical care environment must be "rehumanized."

After learning of the patient's concerns, asking for their consent to collaborate directly with their primary medical or surgical team to sensitively address their needs is the best first step. This shows an appreciation of the patient's voice and concerns, while simultaneously opening the door to educate the care team members. Oftentimes, teams may be naive to the impact that their interactions have had, and a simple conversation is enough to correct behavior. Sometimes we encourage team members to engage in nonclinical conversations with their patients, to understand their values and the things that make them who they are as individuals.

Personhood not policy

Policies are typically well-intentioned and designed to protect patients and standardize good, high-quality care, but sometimes there is tension between a policy and how to apply it in a particular situation. For Dr. Awdish, this policy versus patient tension was experienced in a very poignant way. Dr. Awdish was pregnant when her surgical crisis occurred, and her fetus, which weighed less than a pound, had lost signs of life and had to be evacuated from her uterus. Soon after her surgery, a nurse from the perinatal loss program appeared in Dr. Awdish's room asking, "Did you want to see the baby?" When Dr. Awdish replied no, the nurse said, "That's very sad." She added, "A baby deserves to be held by her mother at least once," and, "You won't get another chance" (Awdish, 2017, pp.48–49).

This scene was on the surface, at least, well-intentioned, but it was offered at the wrong time to the wrong person. A few decades ago, fetuses after a fetal demise were considered biological waste, and mothers were given no opportunity to see or hold their lost babies. Honoring maternal grief after fetal demise has been a major positive cultural shift in medicine, enshrined in hospital procedures and care protocols. In Dr. Awdish's case, the protocol took precedence over the patient, and the protocol itself became traumatizing because it was delivered insensitively in a situation where it was not appropriate.

If you notice a policy or protocol-related concern consistently arising, there are several options available to the clinician to begin to address the change. Many policies are "owned" by a specific individual or department, and often institutions require policy reviews and revisions at set intervals to ensure their applicability and efficacy. Beginning conversations with the "owner" of the policy may introduce an opportunity to shape policy change or to contribute to the process of revising the policy when it comes time. Additionally, for protocols not driven by formal health system policies, discussions with members of the unit leadership team (e.g., nursing unit manager, medical director) may provide an opportunity for exemptions from typical unit rules. For instance, allowing a younger child to visit a dying loved one in the intensive care unit or for a family member to spend the night in a patient's room to assist with reorientation and calming efforts should the patient be experiencing recurrent distressing nightmares. Spending time getting to know leadership teams in advance is an investment well worth making and likely will provide mutual benefit to both parties.

Betrayal, anger, and medical errors

Medical errors can occur for a variety of reasons. Sometimes an error is a personal failure, sometimes it is a system failure. Bad outcomes are sometimes experienced as errors, and as care becomes more complex errors, are more likely. But medical errors, whatever their cause, can have a serious impact on the individual. A patient entrusts their body and life to the caregiving team, and when that trust is compromised by a real or perceived medical error, it can feel like a betrayal. Among the many unfortunate events surrounding Dr. Awdish's care, one was a frank error; she was given a potent diuretic when her kidneys were failing, and the diuretic, predictably, worsened the kidney failure. Dr. Awdish, as well as the resident who wrote the order, knew it was a mistake. Both were powerless to prevent the error: Dr. Awdish because she was now a patient, and the resident because he felt he had to honor the hierarchical structure of hospital care and do what his staff supervisor told him to do. Both felt powerless, and Dr. Awdish felt betrayed and angry, to the point where she angrily threw a small plastic piece of equipment at the resident. As she recovered, her anger passed, and she understood his predicament and developed a good relationship with him. But sometimes the anger and sense of betrayal never pass, and interfere with recovery and the development of posttraumatic growth.

Hidden sometimes, among the multiple macro- and micro-betrayals by the care team, is a deeper kind of betrayal, a betrayal by our own body. This body that we have effortlessly inhabited, and which has served us with vigor and joy, is suddenly no longer a friend. That may make us angry and make us feel betrayed. We must acknowledge those authentic feelings and give them space in our hearts. But we can't hold grudges, our body cannot be blamed for disease, and we must reconnect with it on different terms, on its own terms. Interventions adapted from acceptance and commitment therapy are particularly well-suited to address this phenomenon.

Blaming and isolation

Clinicians often don't like to feel powerless; powerlessness is a feeling that runs counter to the core of their professional mission. Clinicians like to take action, and they like to pretend that they are in control of outcomes. When patients don't get better, they sometimes instinctively blame themselves. Early in Dr. Awdish's recovery, when she was still at risk of death, and she overheard a member of her surgical team saying, "She's been trying to die on us." In other words, "We are doing everything right, the patient is choosing to die." That implied blame was hurtful to hear, but Dr. Awdish realized she had used that same turn of phrase many times herself. In the stress of providing medical care, the relationship can almost become adversarial; the patient becomes an imaginary impediment to heroic and omnipotent rescue fantasies.

Sometimes, instead of blaming patients, clinicians avoid patients who have had a bad outcome. The patient may then complain that their clinician "disappeared." Clinicians don't want to face the patient's anger, or they don't know what to say, or they are afraid to admit fault because of malpractice concerns. This avoidance oftentimes worsens a patient's feelings of anger and betrayal. Clinicians may also disappear internally and try to avoid that part of themselves that grieves and feels guilty about the bad outcome, possibly leading to the experience of second victim syndrome, which will be discussed later in this chapter. Disappearing delays healing and recovery for both the patient and the clinician.

If a clinician notices internal shifts in terms of the assignment of blame or the feeling that the relationship has become adversarial, self-reflection and peer consultation are recommended. In terms of the dynamic of the clinical team, an indicator of this shift in another is often evident in the language used to describe the patient. Should concern arise related to the development of these beliefs in one of our partners on the care team, thoughtful reflection and utilization of the skills described above related to addressing experiences of dehumanization are recommended.

Minimizing medical trauma: recommendations for survivors

The following recommendations may be shared with patients to assist them in navigating the impact of medical errors, whether your own or another clinician's. Realize that anything can happen at any time. Medical errors are common. That does not mean they are acceptable; everything possible should be done to prevent them, but they do happen.

1. Advocate for yourself as much as possible. Express your needs and wishes clearly, ask for information and clarification, but also accept that you cannot always change a system. Even Dr. Awdish, despite her insider status as a physician at the institution where she was receiving care, could only influence her care to a certain degree. Part of being a patient is to realize that others have knowledge or power that you don't have.
2. Accept help from family and friends in advocating for yourself. Sometimes, because of your medical situation, you will have to depend on others for advocacy and support. Realize that they also will have limited power over what goes on in the hospital. Engaging with supervisory staff, such as attending physicians or unit managers, and patient advocates may also prove fruitful if a higher level of support is required.
3. Expect to be treated as a person. Share your needs and wishes, even emotional ones, ask questions, and share concerns. Treat others as people, too, and try to understand their reasoning.
4. Rebuild your relationship with your body. Dr. Awdish's recovery began when she started physical therapy and learned to put her socks on again. This was a turning point in her relationship to her body. She realized:

> *I had to learn to soften; I had to learn to accept my body's limitations .... I was defeated, I couldn't stand, much less walk, but I still had agency ... I could inhabit my broken body with a reverence for what it was capable of in the past and what it was able to do in this moment .... I felt oddly grateful. (Awdish, 2017, p.81).*

She decides to reinhabit, with gratitude, her damaged body, which she felt had betrayed her. What was at first physical therapy in essence became somatic therapy and created a moment of insight and a path forward to acceptance and posttraumatic growth.

Minimizing medical trauma: recommendations for clinicians

As previously mentioned, we have found that the most effective interventions for addressing medical trauma involves supporting both the patient and the members of their healthcare team. Thus, the below recommendations may assist clinicians in navigating conversations with their patients related to unexpected outcomes and medical errors.

1. Responsibility versus blame. Accept responsibility for your actions. Dr. Awdish ended up having a productive conversation with the resident who had made the prescribing error involving the diuretic medication. He successfully dodged the plastic object that Dr. Awdish threw at him, accepted her anger, took responsibility, apologized, and explained his

actions. He accepted responsibility, not blame. Sometimes self-blame has a hollow, insincere quality and can become an assertion of victimhood. Such self-blame can be detrimental to a patient's emotional well-being. The patient hears, "Don't be mad at me, I am already blaming myself!" and may feel as if their right to express their own anger or frustration is taken away from them. Sometimes blaming, oneself is easier than accepting the chaotic randomness of life. Like the trauma survivor who must face the fact that anything can happen at any time, the clinician must accept that bad outcomes happen, and good, caring people make mistakes. You can express regret thoughtfully and with kindness, without taking blame.

2. Appraise your actions and behavior. Part of recovery is accepting responsibility for whatever role you had in the unwanted outcome. Be honest with yourself, be willing to change. If you made a mistake, you need to understand why so you can avoid making the same mistake again. Don't blame yourself; blame fosters passivity and makes true change less likely. Remember, the root of acceptance isn't liking that something has happened, merely acknowledging that it has, which will allow more space for healing. You are not a bad clinician; you are a good clinician who made an unfortunate and unexpected mistake.
3. Assume your patient is listening. Don't say things out loud that you wouldn't want your patient to hear. Several of the examples of Dr. Awdish's medical trauma involved her overhearing things that were said when people thought she was unconscious. Your team conversations should never be dehumanizing; if they are, that needs to be a matter for thoughtful reflection by the team and the team leadership. Even your personal thoughts and internal dialogue about your patient should not be dehumanizing. Remember that the opportunity to care for others is a gift and a privilege, even though it can be frustrating at times. And, as Dr. Awdish reminds us, even when patients are angry and frustrated, they are doing their best.
4. Don't disappear. Clinicians have a duty to care for their patients even if the outcome is unsuccessful. It is especially important not to disappear when the outcome is unwanted. Most importantly, don't disappear from yourself. While it is important not to disappear in a clinical sense from the care for your patient, it is also important not to disappear to your own self. Pretending that your feelings about what happened are "no big deal" makes things worse in the long run. Accept the pain and the shame, grow from it.

Second victim syndrome

Second victim syndrome refers to the trauma- and stressor-related disorder–like symptoms that can occur in health care providers after adverse medical outcomes. Second victim syndrome includes classic trauma symptoms like poor sleep, intrusive thoughts, guilt, and anxiety, as well as loss of confidence in one's work. The term second victim syndrome was coined by Albert Wu. In Wu's conceptualization, the first victim of an adverse outcome is, of course, the patient, but the second is the clinician (Wu, 2000). While Wu provides a valuable framework for discussion of this important issue, he does not imply some kind of equivalence between the patient's medical trauma and the clinician's struggle to cope with having committed a medical error. To use Dr. Awdish's case as an example, causing renal failure in a patient is very different than being in renal failure yourself.

Nonetheless, second victim syndrome is real, common, and long-lasting (Vanhaecht et al., 2019). It affects about half of all medical providers at some point in their careers (Edrees et al., 2011). It is a problem not only for clinicians, but for patients too. Clinicians suffering from second victim syndrome are less likely to provide good empathic care because of anxiety, guilt, and emotional withdrawal. Indeed, in Dr. Awdish's case, one of the residents who treated her confided, with regret, that caring for her was made especially difficult by an unexpected patient death the prior night. Evidence shows that patient mortality is the unwanted outcome most likely to cause second victim syndrome (Vanhaecht et al., 2019).

Besides second victim syndrome, medical staff in emergency departments and trauma centers are vulnerable to PTSD itself through repeated exposure to traumatic situations. Emergency department nurses are at the highest risk, followed by emergency department physicians (DeLucia et al., 2019). Health care workers in those settings are exposed to both vicarious trauma and second victim syndrome when outcomes are poor.,

The language Wu uses for recovery from second victim syndrome is very spiritual. He talks of confession, restitution, and absolution. Health care providers often deny and minimize the impacts of traumatic events; sometimes, the most important first step in recovery from trauma is to acknowledge its impact.

Hope and Recovery

Dr. Awdish's memoir was widely read, within the medical community and also by the general public. It became a best seller not only because of her ability to thoughtfully articulate her inner experience, but because it resonated with an aspect of trauma that is common and important, but often neglected. When Dr. Awdish first saw some of her colleagues when she left the ICU, they were startled and said, "I thought you were dead!" Although such tactless remarks continued after recovery, Dr. Awdish is very much alive. Her story provides a very personal memoir of trauma, hope, recovery, and posttraumatic growth.

Dr. Awdish notes that one of the important steps in processing her medical trauma was acknowledging and accepting it, but simultaneously letting go of it, and her memoir was a means of doing that. She described a conversation she had with her traumatized self. The internal dialogue went as follows: "This thing happened at this time, and this is what it felt like; now it's over, and here, you can

(Continued)

hold it. We can both look at it together" (Awdish, 2017, p.98). We are not all great writers like Dr. Awdish is, but we all craft an inner personal narrative out of what we experience in our lives. Crafting the narrative is part of the healing process. The narrative lets us hold and honor our trauma by looking at it tenderly, as Dr. Awdish does, but then realizing that it is over.

Chapter summary

Medical trauma is an important and common type of trauma that can affect any of us when we need and seek medical care. It also complicates other types of acute trauma, and can retraumatize the trauma survivor themself. Strategies for recovery from medical trauma are reviewed, as well as recommendations for members of health care teams who may have contributed to a health care error or have developed second victim syndrome.

References

American Psychiatric Association. (2022). Diagnostic and statistical manual of mental disorders (5th ed., text rev.). American Psychiatric Association Publishing. https://doi.org/10.1176/appi.books.9780890425787.

Awdish, R. (2017). *In shock: My journey from death to recovery and the redemptive power of hope*. St. Martin's Press.

DeLucia, J. A., Bitter, C., Fitzgerald, J., Greenberg, M., Dalwari, P., & Buchanan, P. (2019). Prevalence of post-traumatic stress disorder in emergency physicians in the United States. *Western Journal of Emergency Medicine, 20*(5), 740–746. https://doi.org/10.5811/westjem.2019.7.42671.

Edrees, H. H., Paine, L. A., Feroli, E. R., & Wu, A. W. (2011). Health care workers as second victims of medical errors. *Polskie Archiwum Medycyny Wewnetrznej, 121*(4), 101 8.

Committee on Quality of Health Care in America. (2000). To err is human: Building a safer health system (L. T. Kohn, J. M. Corrigan, & M. S. Donaldson, Eds.). Institute of Medicine. National Academies Press.

Kazak, A. E., Kassam-Adams, N., Schneider, S., Zelikovsky, N., Alderfer, M. A., & Rourke, M. (2006). An integrative model of pediatric medical traumatic stress. *Journal of Pediatric Psychology, 31*(4), 343–355. https://doi.org/10.1093/jpepsy/jsj054.

Vanhaecht, K., Seys, D., Schouten, L., Bruyneel, L., Coeckelberghs, E., Panella, M., & Zeeman, G. (2019). Duration of second victim symptoms in the aftermath of a patient safety incident and association with the level of patient harm: A cross-sectional study in the Netherlands. *BMJ Open, 9*(7). https://doi.org/10.1136/bmjopen-2019-029923.

Wu, A. W. (2000). Medical error: The second victim. *Western Journal of Medicine, 172*(6), 358–359. https://doi.org/10.1136/ewjm.172.6.358.

Chapter 14

The support network

Diane and James's Story

Diane and Steve were a married couple in their 60 s. One of their favorite activities was riding their motorcycle on the open road. One night a distracted driver ran a red light at an intersection as Steve and Diane passed, T-boning their motorcycle. Steve was killed instantly, and Diane sustained severe injuries, including a traumatic brain injury (TBI). Diane's 25-year-old son James was suddenly, and unexpectedly, a caregiver. He spent every day at the hospital holding Diane's hand as she began her very slow recovery.

As a result of her TBI, Diane had difficulty encoding and recalling new memories. Initially, she had no recollection of the crash or even her marriage, but slowly she began to recover cognitively, and she started to ask about Steve. James asked the intensive care team, "What should I tell Mom about Steve? Is she ready to hear it?"

What is a caregiver?

According to the Family Caregiver Alliance, a family caregiver, in contrast to a professional caregiver, is "any relative, partner, friend or neighbor who has a significant personal relationship with, and provides a broad range of assistance for, an older person or an adult with a chronic or disabling condition" (Family Caregiver Alliance, n.d.). Operational definitions of caregiving for research purposes can be very complex and can specify the number of hours spent daily in caregiving (Kent et al., 2016). Caregiving has become an important social role, with about 21% of the U.S. population serving as caregivers (Lam, 2025). Sometimes the caregiving role is assumed gradually, as in cases of dementia, but sometimes it must be adopted suddenly, as in instances of acute trauma. Diverse forms of the family in modern society require broader definitions of the caregiver that may include nonkin caregivers such as friends and neighbors (Patterson et al., 2025).

Because the largest group of individuals requiring care is older adults, much of the literature on caregiving has focused on this population. But much of the data applies conceptually and practically to the broader range of

The Psychology of Acute Trauma. DOI: https://doi.org/10.1016/B978-0-443-33212-8.00020-8

caregiving, including caring for trauma survivors. Caregiving creates important social, financial, and occupational stresses, but it can also be a significant source of gratification and meaning (Neller et al., 2024).

The emotional impact of caregiving

It is important to remember that caregivers, especially those who are family members, may meet criteria for acute stress disorder (ASD). A life-threatening event that happens to a family member or close friend is, according to the Diagnostic and Statistical Manual of Mental Disorders, Fifth Edition, Text Revision (DSM-5-TR), a severe enough stressor to qualify for ASD, an additional complication to the other costs and burdens that caregivers encounter (American Psychiatric Association, 2022).

In James's case, as in the case of many caregivers, his own emotional difficulties were overshadowed by those of his mother. He tended not to feel entitled to acknowledge his own emotional burdens because, in his own mind, he was not entitled to complain because his mother's suffering was so much worse.

Caregivers face some of the same kinds of emotional issues as trauma survivors, including a sense of helplessness and denial. The term caregiver burden describes the negative aspects of caregiving, such as stress, financial losses, time burdens, and impacts on other members of the family (Liu et al., 2020). The positive aspects of caregiving tend to be underrecognized and include meaningfulness, sense of belonging, personal growth, and empathetic understanding (Cohen et al., 2002; Mishra et al., 2023). Caregiving growth, the opposite of caregiver burden, might be considered a term analogous to posttraumatic growth.

The emotional responses of caregivers

The sudden and unexpected nature of acute trauma creates special issues for the loved ones of the trauma survivor. They must suddenly adjust to a new reality, and the responses to this change are complex and change over time. Some individual responses to trauma, like denial and helplessness, are echoed in the responses of the family system.

Caregiving in the setting of acute trauma has not been extensively studied. A recent review described the efficacy of interventions for caregivers in acute trauma. Most interventions in this review focused on survivors of TBI or patients with posttraumatic stress disorder (PTSD), and most were brief educational interventions (Shepherd-Banigan et al., 2018). For those with TBIs, such interventions had no impact on functional status, quality of life, or psychological symptoms in either the patients or their caregivers. In the TBI population, effects consistently trended in the positive direction but were not statistically significant because of sample size and other statistical factors. These interventions were beneficial, however, for those affected by PTSD.

The pain and grief that support networks suffer can cause defensive responses. Avoidant coping, denial, and what has been called "gaze aversion" all describe a pattern of coping by pretending problems don't exist. The term gaze aversion refers both to looking away from emotional distress as well as literally to having poor eye contact (Coll et al., 2022). Overprotectiveness and poor communication have been found to be maladaptive in chronic illness, as well. Families that are not controlling but rather encourage autonomy and provide support are associated with better coping in chronic illness (Kotchick et al., 1996).

The impacts of caregiving on the caregiver have been extensively described. While caregiving is difficult and causes significant psychological distress, it can have benefits as well, such as greater appreciation of life, greater closeness with loved ones, and enhanced self-efficacy and self-esteem. The family system as a whole is deeply affected by acute trauma. The initial distress of acute trauma for the caregiving system can lead to a kind of posttraumatic growth: Many caregivers have described how deeply meaningful the experience of caregiving has been for them.

Love and caring

Our many years of working with trauma patients and their loved ones have taught us a great deal about the power and sanctity of human love. People who have survived trauma are often surprised by the depth of the love and concern that they experience from those who care about them. Survivors of traumatic suicide attempts, for instance, often believed that no one loved them but discovered that they are, in fact, deeply loved in ways they did not realize.

Altruism has been well described as a human emotion, but the love and caring shown by members of the support network can be remarkable. Caregivers sometimes must radically change their lives to help their loved one, but they typically do so without regret. While caregiving can be very stressful, to be able to care for someone is also a great gift. Trauma survivors sometimes feel very guilty about "burdening" their caregivers. We remind them that they are giving their caregivers a gift, as well, the gift of the opportunity to love and care for another.

Regression

Regression refers to the tendency to return, psychologically, to an earlier stage of development. Regression can occur in response to a stressor. For example, a child who is fully toilet-trained can regress to soiling themselves when a sibling is born. Sigmund Freud used a military metaphor and described that a person, advancing developmentally like an army, might be forced to retreat in the face of a stressor, and that retreat will tend to be to a level of previous conflict where, according to the metaphor, the army has left more troops behind to control a restive population. Under stress, members of the support network can react in maladaptive ways, based on their own past histories and traumas, but with time and coaching, they can become more effective in their role as caregivers.

Helplessness

Important to normal maturation is the gradual development of a sense of agency. Agency is the power to take charge and make changes for oneself. Acute trauma can cause a loss of agency and a feeling of helplessness, both in the patient and in caregivers and families. "What can I do?" "What can I say?" "How can I help?" "Nothing I can say or do will make a difference!" Helplessness is a very deep, primitive fear. When we feel helpless, we feel the way we felt as young children, when we actually were helpless. Caregivers can respond to feelings of helplessness with withdrawal, despair, or rage. As we will discuss below, helplessness can be effectively addressed through the use of communication tools.

Displacement

When feelings appropriate to a person or situation are transferred to another, they are "displaced." When family members, instead of being angry at a situation or the unknown perpetrator of a crime, become angry at the surgeon caring for their loved one, they are displacing their anger. The surgeon must examine whether the anger directed at them is, in fact, appropriate. Justifiable anger at a mistake or a miscommunication should never be dismissed as displacement. Displacement is best addressed by accepting and honoring legitimate feelings through the use of validating statements and reflective listening.

Denial

To deny something is to pretend to yourself that something that has happened did not happen. While denial of the traumatic event itself is rare, the denial of aspects of a trauma is very common and can be adaptive, especially initially. Family members might deny aspects of the trauma, such as its emotional impacts and long-term effects. This denial can help family members adjust to the initial horror of the trauma, but can lead to a maladaptive communication pattern that denies the authentic experience of the trauma survivor. Speaking from denial, they might tell a severely injured loved one, for instance, "You'll be back at work in no time!" This comment, apparently well-intentioned in its positivity, denies the authentic lived experience of the trauma survivor and makes them feel more isolated in their suffering. The trauma survivor hears this comment as, "Your suffering is no big deal." The gaze aversion and avoidant coping described above are forms of denial.

Family pathology

Sometimes trauma can illuminate deep family pathology that goes beyond simple regression. The communication strategies that help families cope with trauma are ineffective, and trauma survivors must realize and accept the limitations of their caregivers.

Jerry's Story

One of our trauma survivors, Jerry, aged 50, had an amicable but codependent relationship with his mother. He spent a great deal of time and energy taking care of her emotional needs. She had been emotionally neglectful when he was a child, and I think he hoped to "get back by giving," although he never really got much back. As we worked with Jerry after his injury, he recalled a conversation he had with his mother when he first awakened from his coma. She told him, "I'm so glad you are alive. It would have been so hard, as a mother, to bury my son." Jerry realized how profoundly self-centered his mother was. She would never change; he would never "get back" from her emotionally. He realized that he had never really been mothered and began to effectively "mother" himself emotionally.

Social support and trauma recovery

Social support mitigates the impacts of trauma and facilitates recovery from traumatic events (Friedman et al., 2007). Friends, family members, and intimate partners can all provide effective social support (Calhoun et al., 2022). Besides direct day to day assistance, social support networks can provide validation, encouragement, and acceptance.

The Integrated Biopsychosocial Model for Posttraumatic Stress Recovery (IBM-PSR) considers intrapersonal and interpersonal factors that assist in trauma recovery (Calhoun et al., 2022). The impacts of trauma on the social support network are bidirectional; support reduces the impacts of trauma, but trauma also strains the support network by causing emotional and financial distress and the pressures of time required by caregiving. Trauma can weaken an existing support network, but networks that are flexible and healthy can sometimes summon additional caregiving resources. Because of the important role of the social support network in trauma recovery, monitoring and supporting the social support network is an important aspect of good trauma care.

How to facilitate effective social support

The focus of treatment for members of the medical or surgical team is always the trauma survivor, but it can include the support network to the extent that it is an important part of trauma care. The treatment relationship is always with the trauma survivor, and no treatment relationship, actual or implied, exists with any caregiver. But supportive work with caregivers is appropriate when it facilitates the treatment of the trauma survivor. Some tips for working with caregivers include the following:

- Explore prior family communication patterns and work within those hierarchies and channels. If grandfather has traditionally been the center of the family communication network, then grandfather should be used to deliver updates and information if he is amenable.
- Support honest communication. Sometimes families try to protect the trauma survivor by not delivering bad news about the details of the traumatic event. In traumatic events where a fatality is involved, families are sometimes tempted to deliver false information to "protect" the trauma survivor. James might, for instance, be tempted to pretend that Steve was still alive when Diane asked. Such strategies can be motivated by genuine altruism but also by fear of facing the pain of the loved one's grief. Families can be reminded that the truth will eventually emerge and that when trauma survivors are given false information, they feel betrayed and less likely to trust other information given by family members.
- Monitor avoidant coping. Avoidant coping is a maladaptive response to trauma that involves the denial and suppression of feelings. Validate feelings, even feelings of helplessness, distress, and despair, and encourage their expression.
- Acknowledge and give voice to caregiver distress. Caregivers are entitled to their own pain, even though they are not the identified trauma survivor. They have been traumatized as well, even though they may minimize the impacts of the trauma on themselves in their attempt to be as supportive as possible to the trauma survivor.

Coping tips for caregivers

Part of the mission of the Trauma and Acute Care Surgical Psychology (TACS Psych) team is to support the caregiver. The following guidelines can help caregivers negotiate the process of caring for both themselves and the trauma survivor.

Accept your limitations

First, we all have limitations based on who we are as humans. We can't undo what happened, we can't reverse time, and we can't make the suffering of our loved one disappear, as much as we wish we could. We must also accept that there is nothing magical that we can say that can make the pain go away. We may also face limitations due to our time and financial and emotional resources. When we fail to accept our limitations, we may feel helpless and withdraw. Because there is nothing to say that "fixes things" or makes the pain just "go away," we say nothing or pretend everything is normal. Sometimes all we can do is be there, and sometimes being there is exactly enough.

Use direct communication

It is natural to try to protect our loved ones from the pain of trauma. The suffering becomes the elephant in the room that no one will speak of. The trauma survivor doesn't want to burden their family, and the family doesn't want to upset the trauma survivor. The result is silence and emotional distance when there might be healing.

Validate the distress of the trauma survivor

When a caregiver accepts their own limitations, it is easier to accept and validate the distress of the trauma survivor. To validate does not mean to fix. As Woodcock pointed out, pain is not pathology (Woodcock, 2022). Space must be allowed for loss and grief.

Accept suffering as part of recovery

Sometimes, caregivers and trauma survivors will use avoidance-based coping. They try to look away from the horror of the traumatic experience and deny its emotional impacts. There are cultural aspects to this avoidance. We isolate the suffering and the dying in hospitals, and we pretend that suffering is not a normal part of human existence. We medicalize suffering and treat it as though it were illness, and we pretend that pills like antidepressants will entirely relieve the suffering of trauma. For the trauma survivor, to begin the quest narrative that leads to true recovery, we must accept the suffering that comes with trauma. The caregiver can only encourage and participate in this journey by accepting suffering, as well.

Observe and clarify

Often, families simply have no experience in dealing with difficult emotional issues and lack of communication skills. This lack of skill can make them feel helpless. A technique called "observe and clarify" gives families a safe way to initiate communication. For instance, a caregiver might say, "I notice you looked sad after you talked to the surgeon. What happened?" The observation helps create an emotional connection, and the question invites clarification and the potential exploration of emotional issues. Trauma survivors may not be willing to talk about emotional issues, especially early in recovery, and any such hesitancy should always be respected; nonetheless, good communication builds a loving connection that is available as a source of support when such support is needed.

Encourage belonging

The trauma survivor needs to continue to be a valued part of the family. The family can be a place where the universal need for esteem and self-validation is supported and encouraged (Woodcock, 2022). Wherever possible, the trauma survivor should be encouraged to be an active member of the family, not a burden. When possible, the family should try to alleviate the guilt that is often involved in accepting care. Remind the trauma survivor of your love for them and the joy and purpose that you receive from caregiving.

Practice self-care

As a caregiver, your health and well-being are important for the caregiving system. Take care of yourself physically and emotionally. Just as you help the trauma survivor, allow yourself to be helped and supported. Heroism and martyrdom are not good long-term strategies; self-care is.

Professional caregivers

The social support network has two components: The informal network of family and friends that provide care, and the formal network of professional caregivers. Professional caregivers are always an important part of the support network. Providing care for Diane was a difficult experience emotionally for the caregiving team. The culture of medicine reinforces stoicism. We are expected to be professional and not let a patient's suffering "get to us."

In a practical sense, professional caregivers must set boundaries for empathy. A professional caregiver may be simultaneously caring for multiple patients in severe distress. They might also, for the good of a patient, be forced to conduct procedures that cause pain and suffering, such as dressing changes, surgeries, and central line insertions. On the one hand, empathy is needed, but on the other hand, practical boundaries for empathy must be set and maintained for the professional caregiver to be effective in their work. This is a delicate line to walk.

Different members of the care team experience the difficulties of caregiving in different ways. Nursing staff, because of the extensive time spent in direct care, face issues of empathy and its boundaries most acutely. Surgical and intensive care unit staff spend less time at the patient's bedside but face special issues related to delivering difficult news and poor outcomes, and deciding between care options in urgent and challenging situations.

Mental health providers are expected to always know how to handle painful emotions, not only of the patient and their family members but of the care team as well. In the case described at the beginning of the chapter, both James and the surgical staff wanted the trauma psychologist to give Diane the news that Steve had died, as if the psychologist would have some way of delivering that news that would not cause distress. He did not; he could only model tolerating distress and providing support to an individual in distress.

Supporting the treatment team

As the trauma psychologist, I regularly check in with team members while rounding on patients, especially emotionally challenging ones like Diane. I acknowledge the feelings of vulnerability and sadness that come up in dealing with such cases by saying things like, "I feel so sad for this family." My acceptance of my own feelings gives team members permission to accept their feelings. Interventions with team members are part of a dynamic process that involves more than a one-time discussion. Rather, it is an ongoing, intentional process of regular support and availability. Trauma psychologists have increased credibility with other members of the trauma team when they are "in the trenches" dealing with emotional issues and distress that the trauma survivor faces. They must not be perceived as being insulated in some separate "ivory tower."

Delivering difficult news

Who should tell Diane about Steve's death? And when? James raises a poignant question. A substantial literature does exist about how to deliver difficult news in the context of medical diagnoses, and some of these principles are relevant to the context of acute trauma, but with modifications.

First, with regard to when to deliver news about a fatality or serious injury in the context of trauma, a good rule of thumb is that when the trauma survivor begins to ask, they are, barring some special circumstance, ready to be told.

In terms of who should deliver the news, we typically offer families an array of options:

1. Family members can deliver the news, with behind-the-scenes support and guidance from the treatment team.
2. Family members can deliver the news with the TACS Psych team or other team members in the room.
3. The treatment team, usually the TACS Psych team members, can deliver the news with the family inside or outside of the trauma survivor's room.

There is no right or wrong or best way, though we encourage all teams to begin with a family meeting where family communication preferences may be discussed prior to disclosure.

In this case, James wanted the trauma psychologist to deliver the news while he waited outside the room. Diane had suspected the truth, but her acute grief was difficult to bear, as such pain always is. After we delivered the news, James joined us in his mother's room. The two hugged and cried for a long time, sharing a pain that, though unbearable, had to be borne. As caregivers, we feel grief in such moments but also awe in the face of the power of human resilience and love.

A Happy Ending

Diane had a 3-month hospitalization because of her multiple orthopedic and other injuries. Her memory and cognitive processing gradually improved. Sadly, the news of Steve's death had to be delivered several times because she would forget and begin to ask again, "How is Steve?" Eventually, she was able to remember her loss consistently and begin to process it. Her retrograde amnesia had caused her to forget her 7-year marriage entirely, but as she began to remember her life with Steve, she felt that she was rediscovering part of a life narrative that was happy and meaningful. She came to appreciate how deeply she had been loved by Steve. She also realized her son James loved her, and that was a great solace. After her long hospital stay, she was transferred to a specialized TBI treatment program where she continued to recover, both cognitively and emotionally. James would visit his mother frequently at the rehabilitation facility, but he would also stop by at the hospital on occasion to say hello to the staff he had come to know so well. There is no easy resolution in such situations, but there can be growth, healing, and love. That can be enough.

Chapter summary

This chapter explored the impacts of trauma on the caregiver network. Acute trauma can cause psychological responses in caregivers and interfere with social support. Besides the financial burden of caregiving, caring for the acute trauma patient can be costly for the support network in terms of time and energy. Simple interventions to facilitate the healthy functioning of the support network are described. Acceptance is important for caregivers, just as it is for patients.

References

American Psychiatric Association (2022). *Diagnostic and statistical manual of mental disorders* (5th ed., text rev.). American Psychiatric Association Publishing. https://doi.org/10.1176/appi.books.9780890425787.

Calhoun, C. D., Stone, K. J., Cobb, A. R., Patterson, M. W., Danielson, C. K., & Bendezú, J. J. (2022). The Role of Social Support in Coping with Psychological Trauma: An Integrated Biopsychosocial Model for Posttraumatic Stress Recovery. *Psychiatric Quarterly, 93*(4), 949–970. https://doi.org/10.1007/s11126-022-10003-w.

Cohen, C. A., Colantonio, A., & Vernich, L. (2002). Positive aspects of caregiving: Rounding out the caregiver experience. *International Journal of Geriatric Psychiatry, 17*(2), 184–188. https://doi.org/10.1002/gps.561.

Coll, S. Y., Eustache, F., Doidy, F., Fraisse, F., Peschanski, D., Dayan, J., Gagnepain, P., & Laisney, M. (2022). Avoidance behaviour generalizes to eye processing in posttraumatic stress disorder. *European Journal of Psychotraumatology, 13*(1). https://doi.org/10.1080/20008198.2022.2044661.

Family Caregiver Alliance. (n.d.) Defiinitions: What do we mean by.... Available from: https://www.caregiver.org/resource/definitions-0/.

Friedman, M. J., Keane, T. M., & Resick, P. A. (2007). In M. J. Friedman, T. M. Keane, & P. A. Resick (Eds.). *Handbook of PTSD: Science and Practice*. Guilford Press.

Kent, E. E., Rowland, J. H., Northouse, L., Litzelman, K., Chou, W. Y. S., Shelburne, N., Timura, C., O'Mara, A., & Huss, K. (2016). Caring for caregivers and patients: Research and clinical priorities for informal cancer caregiving. Cancer, *122*(13), 1987–1995. https://doi.org/10.1002/cncr.29939.

Kotchick, B. A., Forehand, R., Armistead, L., Klein, K., & Wierson, M. (1996). Coping with illness: Interrelationships across family members and predictors of psychological adjustment. *Journal of Family Psychology, 10*(3), 358–370. https://doi.org/10.1037/0893-3200.10.3.358.

Lam, L. T. (2025). Caregiving and mental well-being: the role of caregivers' age and insomnia. *Frontiers in Psychiatry, 16*. https://doi.org/10.3389/fpsyt.2025.1482890.

Liu, Z., Heffernan, C., & Tan, J. (2020). Caregiver burden: A concept analysis. *International Journal of Nursing Sciences, 7*(4), 438–445. https://doi.org/10.1016/j.ijnss.2020.07.012.

Mishra, N., Datti, R. S., Tewari, A., & Sirisety, M. (2023). Exploring the positive aspects of caregiving among family caregivers of the older adults in India. *Frontiers in Public Health, 11*. https://doi.org/10.3389/fpubh.2023.1059459.

Neller, S. A., Hebdon, M. T., Wickens, E., Scammon, D. L., Utz, R. L., Dassel, K. B., Terrill, A. L., Ellington, L., & Kirby, A. V. (2024). Family caregiver experiences and needs across health conditions, relationships, and the lifespan: a Qualitative analysis. *International Journal of Qualitative Studies on Health and Well-being, 19*(1). https://doi.org/10.1080/17482631.2023.2296694.

Patterson, S. E., Caywood, K., Pantelic, S. M., & Morreale, O. (2025). Traditional and Non-traditional Caregivers Define "Family" and Caregiving Obligations. *American journal of Alzheimer's disease and other dementias, 40*, 15333175251357328. https://doi.org/10.1177/15333175251357328.

Shepherd-Banigan, M. E., Shapiro, A., McDuffie, J. R., Brancu, M., Sperber, N. R., Van Houtven, C. H., Kosinski, A. S., Mehta, N. N., Nagi, A., & Williams, J. W. (2018). Interventions That Support or Involve Caregivers or Families of Patients with Traumatic Injury: a Systematic Review. *Journal of General Internal Medicine, 33*(7), 1177–1186. https://doi.org/10.1007/s11606-018-4417-7.

Woodcock, J. (2022). *Families and individuals living with trauma: A guide for therapists, relatives, and friends*. Palgrave Macmillan.

Chapter 15

Breaking down barriers: addressing social determinants of health

Luis's Story

Luis woke up to the faint sound of scratching and whining outside his bedroom door. "I forgot to feed the animals again last night," he thought. It had been hard to keep up with his chores since mamá moved into the nursing home. Both he and Juan, developmentally delayed brothers in their mid- to late-60s, had relied on mamá so much. When she got sick 6 months ago, everything changed, but they had managed as best they could. Luis searched for his clothes, sifting through piles of unpaid bills, tax forms, and fast-food wrappers on the floor, eventually finding the shirt and pants he had been wearing this week. As he rose and made his way to the door, the floor of the old home creaked beneath his weight. The doorknob hung uselessly from the broken door.

It happened too quickly; Luis had no time to react. One of the stray dogs that he and Juan had let into the home just last week pushed the door open and lunged forward with a snarl, sinking its teeth into his forearm. Luis stumbled out of his bedroom, tripping on discarded objects as he attempted to make his way downstairs to the front door. He had to fend off repeated attacks from the dog. He was covered in blood. Just as he was about to reach the stairs, he suddenly felt himself falling, and heard a shrill shriek from the dog, felt several thuds, and then a sharp pain in his shoulder and pelvis as he tumbled down the stairs. He noticed the lifeless body of the dog beneath him and heard Juan frantically calling his name.

Trauma care is whole person care

As seen throughout this text, the definition of trauma care is changing, with the American College of Surgeons describing that the goals of recovering from traumatic injuries should now include addressing the psychological well-being of the survivor as well as optimizing their ability to reintegrate into society. No longer is it acceptable to view the inevitable psychosocial impact of trauma exposure as an unavoidable consequence. Trauma centers are now empowered

The Psychology of Acute Trauma. DOI: https://doi.org/10.1016/B978-0-443-33212-8.00017-8

to pioneer novel approaches to the holistic care of the traumatically injured patient. Additionally, the conceptualization of traumatic injuries themselves is changing, with many clinicians adopting the mindset that traumatic injuries are first and foremost the result of a social disorder. This is highlighted by the literature surrounding factors impacting exposure to trauma and our ability to recover from it.

Successful treatment outcomes are determined not only by biological and psychological factors but by the social context in which people live. Five key social determinants of health have been identified by the (Office of Disease Prevention and Health Promotion U.S. Department of Health and Human Services Healthy people, 2030). They include:

1. Economic stability
2. Education access and quality
3. Health care access and quality
4. Neighborhood and built environment
5. Social and community context

Social determinants of health are especially important when conceptualizing the lived experience of individuals impacted by acute trauma. Trauma survivors who sustained an assault may be returning to economically disadvantaged communities where violence is endemic; older adults who have experienced a fall may be returning to unsafe living environments where falls are more likely and social support is limited. Trauma survivors may be unhoused and have limited access to health care, including difficulty accessing follow-up care for their injuries. Clinical outcomes should be broadly defined and include not just the state of health at time of hospital discharge, but long-term recovery and reintegration into the community.

Factors often associated with an increased risk of exposure to trauma include lack of employment, lack of housing stability, and involvement with the justice system, such as incarceration, especially if experienced prior to adulthood (Bender et al., 2014; Deck & Platt, 2015; Dierkhising et al., 2013; Hartwell et al., 2014; Wolff & Shi, 2009). While factors associated with trauma exposure are generally well studied, less is known about the social determinants of health that may be associated with peri- and posttrauma outcomes. Results of a recent systematic review suggest that while race was not associated with mortality and morbidity during the peritraumatic period, Black individuals were significantly less likely to transition to physical rehabilitation centers following discharge (Tremont et al., 2025). Additionally, uninsured individuals demonstrated a greater risk for mortality, and, similar to Black individuals, were significantly less likely to be placed in a physical rehabilitation center following discharge. Trauma survivors also reported higher levels of dissatisfaction related to the financial aspects of their care during their inpatient stay as compared to patients receiving care on a general hospitalist service (Moore et al., 2016).

Assessing social determinants of health during the inpatient stay

Due to the complex needs of our patients, we have developed a three-tiered model for assessing and addressing the psychosocial aspects of recovery during their inpatient stay. While our model will be discussed in detail in Chapter 20, Building an Effective Trauma and Acute Care Surgical Psychology Program, it's important to review the relevant aspects of the assessment of social determinants of health at this time. Every individual admitted to the Trauma and Acute Care Surgery service receives a psychological vulnerability risk screening by the resident surgeon or advanced practice provider during the completion of their trauma tertiary exam, which is the complete assessment following stabilization that aims to ensure that no injuries are missed and all relevant areas of recovery need are addressed. Those who screen positive are referred for a comprehensive psychosocial needs assessment with a licensed master social worker (trauma social worker) who is a dedicated member of the Trauma and Acute Care Surgical Psychology (TACS Psych) service, an individual who will follow the patient for the duration of their inpatient stay and beyond. The trauma social worker's role is distinctly different from that of a traditional inpatient hospital case manager or social worker. The trauma social worker focuses solely on comprehensively addressing the survivor's psychosocial needs both in the hospital and following discharge rather than just facilitating medical discharge, planning or providing counseling support. During this assessment, social determinants of health are reviewed, and the patient is given the ability to share any concerns related to their housing status, financial stability, insurance status, community and home safety, barriers to accessing care, need for legal assistance, social support systems, transportation difficulties, as well as mental health history and need for formal psychological or psychiatric intervention during the hospital stay.

I Need Help

Luis struggled to reopen his eyes as the bright lights flooded the room. He was no longer on the floor by the stairs, he thought, but where was he? As the fog of anesthesia continued to clear, he saw a figure carrying a small white tote bag. "Hi, Luis, I'm Allison O'Sullivan. You're in the hospital. You had an accident, you're safe, now and we are working to get you better. I'm the trauma social worker who will be helping you during this hospital stay. When you're feeling up to it I'd love to have a conversation about how we can help." "That's right," Luis whispered, "That dog attacked me!"

Luis had sustained multiple serious lacerations to both of his upper and lower extremities as a result of the attack, as well as a pelvic ring and clavicle fracture from his fall down the stairs. Luis's physical recovery was just beginning, but that didn't mean that the stressors that had been weighing on him prior to his admission were gone. At the end of her first visit, Allison had left a trauma recovery tote bag with Luis, which included her contact information as well as a brief educational

(Continued)

brochure on what to expect during his admission. She had promised to follow up regularly during this hospital stay, and promptly presented for another conversation the next day.

Luis began sharing more about his life and how hard things had gotten after mamá got sick. He shared his concerns for his brother, Juan, who had difficulties living independently and was still in the home alone. Luis expanded, describing that they had run out of food and were surviving on one peanut butter sandwich per day, and to make matters worse, someone from the county kept leaving papers on the porch saying they were going to take the house away! Neither Luis nor Juan could drive, and without mamá there to help, they couldn't get to any of their medical appointments. He was worried that they couldn't take care of the animals that they had let into the home after mamá moved to the nursing home. Their social support was limited, though Luis shared that a kind older woman, Ms. Maria lived next to them, and she used to bring food over during the winter. Mrs. O'Sullivan talked with Luis about options for support and shared that Dr. Preeya, a trauma psychologist on the team, would be meeting with him while she started to work on helping him deal with some of his practical needs.

Luis thought to himself, "Maybe things will be OK."

Practical psychosocial interventions

After the comprehensive psychosocial needs assessment, psychosocial interventions begin with the goal of initiating assistance as soon as possible in the survivor's hospital stay. The needs of individuals seeking care for the management of traumatic injuries are often complex, especially in urban and underserved communities. By working with the survivor to identify a hierarchy of personal needs, the trauma social work team quickly builds trust in the TACS Psych service and also frees up space for the survivor to actively engage in the therapeutic process with the treating TACS Psych clinician. While not all obstacles are surmountable within the timeframe of an inpatient hospital stay, honestly sharing options for beginning to address needs, no matter how small they may be perceived, is critical. In addition to preexisting needs, the experience of a new trauma almost always introduces a new set of concerns. Using the Office of Disease Prevention and Health Promotion, U.S. Department of Health and Human Services (n.d.) five key social determinants of health as a guide, let's discuss some examples of practical psychosocial interventions.

Economic stability

Economic stability is often shared as one of the most salient concerns for survivors of trauma, especially during the acute phase of recovery. By their very nature, it is nearly impossible to prepare for a traumatic injury. We hear stories daily about individuals going about their normal routines in life, which are suddenly upended by the unpredictability of injury. As such, especially in underserved environments, most individuals receiving care may be either under- or uninsured. Beginning with the process of applying for Medicare and Medicaid during their hospital stay can provide a tangible and productive option for immediately addressing the financial stressors associated with injury. For survivors who have been the victims of violent crime, investigating and beginning to complete (if available) your state's crime victim compensation application can also provide an additional option for decompressing financial stress. Knowledge of community-based programs in your region will also assist in identifying specific resources that may assist with reducing the financial burden of trauma recovery.

Education access and quality

Health literacy concerns, as well as access to education related to recovery resources, are both critical areas to address as soon as possible in the survivor's hospital stay. Practical interventions may be as simple as moderating multidisciplinary meetings with the members of the patient's family and their surgical teams, which can increase lines of communication and directly address potential misunderstandings related to care, or engaging in teach-back discussions where the survivor is asked to share their understanding of the plan of care to provide an opportunity to ensure adequate comprehension. Some communities may also have access to special programs to allow survivors of trauma to gain access to more traditional educational experiences following the resolution of their acute injuries, which may assist survivors in attaining traditional education or job training. Examples of statewide programs that we may access include multiple free tuition programs such as the Michigan Reconnect program, the Michigan Community College Guarantee, and the Go Blue Guarantee; each of which supports different groups of learners. Self-edification related to your own state or country's educational support resources will prove useful in assisting your program in reducing trauma recidivism and improving the overall quality of life of the community members you serve.

Health care access and quality

Unburdened health care access following discharge is critically important to ensure an uncomplicated recovery Understanding preexisting barriers to access will ultimately allow for the development of a robust discharge plan that reduces the likelihood of missed appointments. One major area of concern related to access centers on limited transportation options, especially if public transportation options are lacking. To directly address this need, we developed a philanthropic fund that allows our team to sponsor a rideshare program that patients may access, at no cost to them, to assist with transportation to and from medical, surgical, mental health, or rehabilitation appointments. Holding annual fundraisers has allowed for the ongoing replenishment of funds, ensuring future generations of survivors will have access to transportation for care-related appointments whenever they may need. Additionally, incorporating an assessment of primary care engagement at the onset of admission can lead to a seamless continuity of care and the involvement of a trusted preexisting clinician, or a referral to a primary care provider if one is needed.

Neighborhood and built environment

Especially in urban environments, community safety following discharge is a primary concern. Assisting the patient in identifying a safe discharge plan includes screening for safety risks in their home environment, including the potential for risks within the home itself. These risks may relate to the lived environment, for instance, in a case of hoarding disorder, or safety related to their presence in the community itself. In the community surrounding our health system, violence is quite prevalent, with 75% of survivors receiving care on our service reporting that they have heard gunshots from their home within the past 90 days (Reffi et al., 2026). Assisting the patient in working with law enforcement officials may increase the likelihood of safe retrieval of the survivor's personal possessions if relocation is required. Engaging community-based agencies that assist with relocation to either different communities or states oftentimes proves beneficial for high-risk groups, such as individuals who are the victims of human trafficking or domestic violence. For in-home safety concerns, home physical and occupational therapy safety evaluations may reduce the risk for recurrent fall-related injuries in the home. Additionally, should the living environment be lacking basic necessities such as heat, power, water, or protection from the elements, utilizing community contacts, such as county representatives, to assist with the mitigation of these stressors may prove beneficial. Ensuring discharge plans take the patient's functional capabilities into consideration is critical, and working with case management teams to make sure durable medical equipment is available is essential.

Social and community context

Assisting with reintegration into the community is one of the key goals of trauma recovery, and understanding the survivor's social and community stressors may assist in proactively addressing them to reduce complications related to their recovery trajectory. For individuals whose injuries will lead to legal involvement, creating a repository of legal resources that are available at little or no cost to the survivor will prove beneficial. Begin by seeking out contacts in local or regional universities with law schools to inquire about any potential programs, as well as community organizations that can assist victims of crime. Additionally, referrals for community support groups and behavioral activation programs may increase quality social support and promote prosocial reintegration into the community. For vulnerable adults or children who have been the victims of neglect or abuse, special protective services programs may assist with additional resources to ensure the safety and well-being of those involved.

The transition to outpatient care

Because the initial phases of care for the management of serious acute trauma occur in inpatient medical settings, we have focused predominantly on the inpatient aspects of care in this text. For many survivors, this will be sufficient, though some will require ongoing follow-up care in outpatient settings after discharge from the hospital. For these individuals, the crucial final phase of inpatient treatment is planning for the transition to outpatient care. This phase is often initiated by the treating TACS Psych clinician, and then led by the trauma social worker assigned to the case both in the hospital and following discharge via regular telephone check-ins. If dedicated trauma social work and case management services are not available in your setting, becoming familiar with local and regional outpatient resources is critical.

Besides setting, outpatient care differs from inpatient care in several important ways. Clinical issues are typically less urgent, resources are less accessible, multidisciplinary collaboration is more challenging, and issues like transportation, accessibility of care, and cost of care become more prominent. In the outpatient environment, trauma recidivism becomes an important issue, and the targets of care usually focus on addressing the presence of clinically significant psychological distress rather than the prevention of the development of distress. Additionally, many individuals transitioning from acute care settings have a range of competing medical and surgical follow-up appointments, which offer both unique challenges and opportunities for collaborative care.

The ideal outpatient setting

Many models of care exist for the provision of general outpatient mental health care, though few address the complex needs of trauma survivors. The ideal outpatient setting would be in direct communication with the inpatient TACS Psych service, and housed within the trauma center or department of surgery. Clinicians would have specialized training and expertise in the conceptualization and provision of care for individuals seeking assistance for the management of distress related to both acute and chronic trauma, would be able to schedule trauma patients very quickly if necessary, and would be able to see all trauma patients regardless of funding, insurance, or resources. The ideal trauma outpatient program might even share staff with the inpatient TACS

Psych service so that the inpatient clinician who had established a relationship with the trauma survivor could continue to see them on an outpatient basis. The program would be multidisciplinary and include psychiatry, psychology, and social work. To increase collaboration and reduce the burden of time associated with multiple appointments on different days, the ideal clinic might be housed in an outpatient surgical setting where necessary trauma surgery care and follow-up could opportunely be provided in the same setting, making surgical and mental health follow-up convenient for the patient.

Of course, in practice, such ideals are rarely attained. Typical factors that might impact the transition to optimal outpatient care include the following:

1. Access. Typical obstacles to access are both internal and external. External obstacles include transportation, funding, and insurance coverage. Internal obstacles include wait lists and a lack of clinician expertise related to the complex needs of trauma survivors. In urban settings, there may be many options for general outpatient services, but few clinicians are trained in the evidence-based treatment of posttraumatic psychological distress. In rural or underdeveloped settings, access to basic mental health care, let alone specialty care, may be extremely limited.
2. Transportation. In both rural and urban settings, the availability of transportation can be a notable obstacle to attaining care. Mass transit or buses may not be available or may not be able to readily accommodate the physically impaired. Cabs and other formal transport systems may be limited or costly, and family and caregiver resources for transportation may be unavailable, especially for chronic and ongoing care.
3. Insurance and Funding. Insurance issues can be very complex, and approval for mental health coverage is often different than coverage for medical and surgical issues. Copays can be high for mental health visits. If the acute trauma is the result of a crime or a motor vehicle crash, sometimes other types of funding might be available, such as crime victim compensation or auto insurance funds.
4. Waitlists. The waitlist is the bane of every clinician who attempts to make a referral for outpatient mental health services. Waitlists for mental health services are significantly longer than waitlists for other kinds of medical appointments, and waitlists in public clinics for the poorly insured are even longer. Sometimes besides, the official waitlist for the initial evaluation, there may be a second wait for actual treatment.
5. Acute Trauma Expertise. Some aspects of good psychological care for the trauma survivor are common to all psychotherapies, like empathy and support. Others, like cognitive behavioral therapy for nightmares or prolonged exposure, are very specific interventions that may be less familiar to the general psychotherapist. Community mental health clinics, which are sometimes the only referral option for underinsured patients, were originally developed to provide aftercare for the psychiatric patient

after discharge from the psychiatric hospital. They tend to focus on issues like medication compliance, support, and social skills training and, are less oriented toward trauma-related psychotherapy and existential issues of purpose and meaning.

The handoff to outpatient care

The ideal transition to outpatient care would include a warm handoff in person to a clinician skilled in the management of acute trauma, with an appointment set up at the time of handoff. The worst-case scenario is to hand the trauma survivor a "1–800" number to a mental health clinic that has limited access, long wait times, and impersonal care. What usually happens is something in between, but whatever resources and organizational opportunities can be mustered, the more effective the aftercare will be for the trauma survivor.

Trauma recidivism

An important goal of acute trauma aftercare is the prevention of trauma recidivism. Trauma recidivism is defined as new and recurrent injuries that occur in a survivor of acute trauma (Strong et al., 2017). Reported recidivism rates in cases of urban violence are described as high as 44%. Substantial recidivism also occurs in cases of falls in older adults. Trauma recidivists are likely to have a recurrent event in an average time of 18.4 months.

Readmission and nonadherence

Readmission refers not to the recurrence of trauma, but instead to readmission for complications associated with the original traumatic event. Readmission can be related to a lack of outpatient follow-up or poor medication adherence. When trauma survivors are not able to follow up with routine aftercare, medical or surgical complications are often not identified or treated, and may become severe enough to require readmission; or if they do not adhere to medication regimens, infections can develop that require inpatient care.

Medical and surgical follow-up

Part of the role of outpatient trauma treatment should be to work in tandem with medical and surgical care to prevent readmission. The clinic should support and facilitate medical and surgical interventions and assist with the psychological issues that might interfere with medical adherence. Strategies to foster adherence can include education, mobilization of resources both in caregivers and community members, and treating psychological concerns like psychosis or denial that might interfere with medical and surgical follow-up.

The mission of a specialized trauma psychology clinic

If a specialized outpatient trauma psychology clinic can be developed, it will become important to clarify the mission of that clinic. Examples of established models include the Trauma Recovery Center (TRC) model at the University of California, San Francisco, and the Bullet Related Injury Clinic (BRIC) in St. Louis, Missouri. Because of the lack of community mental health resources and the high prevalence of comorbid mental health disorders in many trauma survivors, there may be pressure to provide a full range of mental health services, such as management of underlying psychotic, mood, or personality disorders. While the wish to provide comprehensive services is laudable, a trauma clinic can quickly lose its specialized identity as a trauma program if it attempts to provide long-term treatment for chronic underlying mental health concerns. Certainly, while a survivor is in trauma treatment, it is clinically appropriate to provide whatever mental health treatment is beneficial and feasible to provide, but such treatment needs to be short-term and focused.

Similarly, psychotherapeutic interventions should be trauma-focused, and avoid attempting to treat, say, an underlying panic disorder, attention deficit disorder, depressive disorder, or obsessive compulsive disorder; except to the extent that it interferes with the trauma treatment program, including the medical and surgical aspects of that program. Psychological treatment for acute trauma is typically time-limited, and the duration is between 10 and 20 sessions on average, depending on the clinical context.

Substance use disorder treatment typically requires specialized care and usually falls outside the purview of the trauma psychology clinic. Psychological interventions for trauma-related concerns may be appropriate for survivors with substance misuse issues, as long as misuse and intoxication do not interfere with meaningful utilization of psychotherapy. In individuals with substance misuse concerns, trauma care can provide ongoing opportunities for motivational interviewing and for ongoing education about the potential connections between substance misuse and risk for future exposure to trauma.

The Road Home

Following her initial conversation with Luis, Allison knew that he would require multiple regular visits during this admission, with likely regularl follow-up phone contact after his return home to ensure continued progress and increase his ability to make follow-up appointments. She created a stepped plan for providing support based on Luis's needs, with an initial call to adult protective services to ensure the safety of Juan, who was still fending for himself at the home. With permission from Luis, she contacted their only support person, Ms. Maria, to discuss a plan for a grocery delivery for Juan which would be paid for by discretionary funds attained through the trauma center.

(Continued)

Throughout the hospitalization, Luis continued to open up to Allison, gradually sharing more concerns related to the impending foreclosure on the home, as well as his and Juan's sadness that their mother would likely never return home. Allison began to engage county officials on their behalf, and within a matter of months, was notified that the back taxes had been forgiven and that Luis and Juan wouldn't lose the family home. Additionally, Luis and Juan requested help with the feral animals in their home, which were causing unsanitary conditions. Allison coordinated with a local chapter of the American Society for the Prevention of Cruelty to Animals to ensure that the animals could be safely rehomed prior to Luis's return. Finally, as Luis was preparing for discharge from his physical rehabilitation facility, Allison assisted him in scheduling follow-up outpatient mental health care services and developed a plan to utilize our rideshare program to ensure that barriers related to transportation were proactively addressed.

Months after discharge, Luis was back home, safely with his brother. He called Allison one last time, "Thank you so much, Mrs. O'Sullivan," he started, "I don't know what we would have done without you, I would be homeless right now and probably starving. God bless you."

Chapter summary

Trauma care is whole person care. The American College of Surgeons has challenged the perspective of traditional trauma care to now include the incorporation of efforts to support the psychological well-being of trauma survivors, as well as acknowledgment of the importance of addressing the social factors associated with exposure to trauma. Social determinants of health are essential to consider when evaluating the pre-hospital needs of the patient, as well as the types of support services offered following discharge. Complex needs require creative solutions, and incorporating specialized team members into your program, such as trauma social workers, will enhance the quality of patient care, leading to a truly holistic recovery plan. For programs where specialized support is unavailable, treating clinicians may build a repository of available community resources to begin to address their patients' social determinants of health needs while streamlining the discharge planning process.

References

Bender, K. A., Thompson, S. J., Ferguson, K. M., Yoder, J. R., & Kern, L. (2014). Trauma Among Street-Involved Youth. *Journal of Emotional and Behavioral Disorders, 22*(1), 53–64. https://doi.org/10.1177/1063426613476093.

Deck, S. M., & Platt, P. A. (2015). Homelessness Is Traumatic: Abuse, Victimization, and Trauma Histories of Homeless Men. *Journal of Aggression, Maltreatment and Trauma, 24*(9), 1022–1043. https://doi.org/10.1080/10926771.2015.1074134.

Dierkhising, C. B., Ko, S. J., Woods-Jaeger, B., Briggs, E. C., Lee, R., & Pynoos, R. S. (2013). Trauma histories among justice-involved youth: Findings from the National Child Traumatic

Stress Network. *European Journal of Psychotraumatology, 4*(SUPPL.). https://doi.org/10.3402/ejpt.v4i0.20274.

Hartwell, S. W., James, A., Chen, J., Pinals, D. A., Marin, M. C., & Smelson, D. (2014). Trauma among justice-involved veterans. *Professional Psychology: Research and Practice, 45*(6), 425–432. https://doi.org/10.1037/a0037725.

Moore, D.A., McMahon, C.E., Gilrain, K., Capano-Wehrle, L., Chovanes, J., Hazelton, J., & Lodge, L. (2016). *Biopsychosocial correlates of patient satisfaction and adherence to general medical advice across multiple medical settings.* [Poster presentation]. 43rd Annual Camden Scholars' Forum Poster Contest, Camden, NJ, United States.

Office of Disease Prevention and Health Promotion U.S. Department of Health and Human Services. (n.d.). *Healthy People 2030.* https://odphp.health.gov/healthypeople/priority-areas/social-determinants-health.

Reffi, A. N., Jovanovic, T., Kalmbach, D. A., Pruiksma, K. E., Moore, D. A., Jankowiak, L., Hsieh, H.-F., Cheng, P., Basarkod, S., & Drake, C. L. (2026). Fear of Sleep in the Acute Aftermath of Trauma Predicts Future Posttraumatic Stress Disorder: The Moderating Role of Community Violence Exposure. *Behavioral Sciences, 16*(3), 443. https://doi.org/10.3390/bs16030443.

Strong, B. L., Greene, C. R., & Smith, G. S. (2017). Trauma Recidivism Predicts Long-term Mortality. *Annals of Surgery, 265*(5), 847–853. https://doi.org/10.1097/SLA.0000000000001823.

Tremont, J. N. P., Ander, E. H., Lim, S.-I., Gallaher, J. R., & Reid, T. (2025). The effect of social determinants of health on patient outcomes in acute trauma: A systematic review. *American Journal of Surgery, 243.* https://doi.org/10.1016/j.amjsurg.2025.116284.

Wolff, N., & Shi, J. (2009). Contextualization of physical and sexual assault in male prisons: Incidents and their aftermath. *Journal of Correctional Health Care, 15*(1), 58–77. https://doi.org/10.1177/1078345808326622.

Chapter 16

Considering cultural context

Rosa's Story

Rosa is a 70-year-old female living with her daughter and son-in-law in South Florida. Rosa is of Haitian descent and immigrated to Florida when she was 30. The current admission was precipitated by a fall on a stairway in the home, which resulted in a fractured rib and clavicle. In describing her fall, Rosa insisted that a ghost pushed her down the stairs. She also insisted that staff sprinkle salt across the entrance to her room to protect her from evil spirits. Psychological consultation was requested to rule out psychosis.

Rosa's Hospital Course

As previously mentioned, we were able to confirm that Rosa was not psychotic. We were able to explain to Rosa, with family support, that we could not put salt at the entrance to her room because it would violate hospital policy, while acknowledging the great personal significance that it held for her. We reassured her that we want to always keep her safe and asked her what we might do to make her feel secure in the hospital. She described some amulets and charms that she kept at home to ward off negative spirits. We encouraged her family to bring those to the hospital. Though she still talked of ghosts pushing her, she was able to acknowledge that gait and strength issues contributed to her fall and worked with physical therapy. Additionally, our interactions with Rosa opened a window of opportunity to provide culturally sensitive education to her primary surgical team, decreasing stigma surrounding her belief system. She was discharged in good condition with home physical therapy after a four-day hospital stay.

Western medicine and the culture of surgical teams

Trauma is a worldwide phenomenon, and responses to trauma vary by culture. Despite this, most cross-cultural research has focused on the experience of posttraumatic stress disorder (PTSD). The aspects of PTSD that appear to be stable across cultures include distress, emotional arousal, and the reexperiencing of the traumatic event. Avoidance and affective numbing are less common in other cultures, while somatic responses are much more common in some (Hinton & Lewis-Fernández, 2011; Patel & Hall, 2021).

The Psychology of Acute Trauma. DOI: https://doi.org/10.1016/B978-0-443-33212-8.00001-4

Western medicine tends to approach distress from a symptom-based, biomedical orientation. A broader multicultural approach includes the concept of idioms of distress. Different cultures and different subgroups within cultures conceptualize and express distress in different ways. These different forms and expressions of distress have a social context and may be seen as strategies for seeking help and support from other members of their culture (Desai and Chaturvedi, 2017). Somatic symptoms, for instance, in Western medicine are medicalized and then conceptualized as functional neurological symptom disorder (previously known as conversion disorder), somatic symptom disorder, or on the factitious to malingering disorder spectrum; while in other cultures, they may be acceptable idioms of distress that elicit help from others without being medicalized. Cross-cultural assessment of emotional distress can benefit from culturally sensitive approaches modified for the cultural context, rather than a blind adaptation of assessment tools developed and validated according to Western conceptualizations of distress (Bolton & Tang, 2002).

The Western medicalization of distress is rooted in a naïve belief that trauma and distress are not intrinsic to the human experience; they tend not be viewed as an aspect of life that must be integrated and accepted. According to this belief, psychological responses to trauma and associated distress are aberrations to be cured and eliminated with a pill or a treatment. As we have seen at length, acute trauma is not exactly a medical disorder, but a reaction of distress after an acute insult to the integrity of the body and the mind. Trauma- and stressor-related disorders are responses to external events, so they are more apt to be influenced by culture-related idioms of expression.

Cross-cultural understanding can, in fact, enrich the Western conceptualization of the experience and expression of trauma. Western practitioners often internalize Western biomedical views of illness and consider their Western metanarrative as the only possible way of conceptualizing human distress. Arthur Kleinman, in the 1980s, began an important critique of this culture-bound view that continues to this day as we attempt to understand inclusive approaches to healing in a multicultural world (Kleinman, 1988).

Western medical narratives tend to emphasize the biological aspects of healing and neglect issues of meaning. I once heard a story shared by an American clinician working in Africa. He saw a patient of his who he had cured of malaria waiting outside the hut of the local faith healer. He asked his former patient why he was going to the faith healer. His patient said, "You cured me of the malaria that I got from the mosquito, and I am very grateful for that. But I need to see the faith healer because I want to know why the mosquito bit me." Particularly in recovery from acute trauma, those questions of meaning are left unspoken and unanswered by Western medicine.

Surgical services are in some ways the epitome of the "find it and fix it" Western model of medicine. Of course, surgeons frequently treat chronic illness, but the Western "culture of cure" attitude can persist. As discussed extensively throughout this text, Trauma and Acute Care Surgical Psychology

(TACS Psych) services tend to be directly embedded within surgical teams with, their focus on acute interventions, symptom relief, and short-term care. While the surgical focus is to identify problems and try to fix them, the psychological care of the acute trauma patient is more focused on acceptance and coping with distress and life change. The two treatment subcultures can sometimes be in tension, but they can also enrich each other through mutual interaction and understanding. Thus, it is important to understand both the culture of the institution as well as the specific culture of the surgical team to optimize patient outcomes and the working relationship with the surgical team itself. To most effectively do this, clinicians are encouraged to be as physically present as possible on surgical units, with a willingness to shadow or observe the surgical and nursing teams as they complete routine tasks. High yield points of contact include observing new surgical consults or trauma activations, attending case conferences and sign-out meetings, and observing an overnight call shift if possible. Such involvements help the TACS Psych clinician understand the surgical micro-culture.

Ataque de nervios: an example of a culture-bound trauma response

Different cultural groups, including our own, can exhibit unique responses to trauma. There is no "normative" trauma response; all responses to trauma have a cultural component. While it is not within the scope of this text to provide a comprehensive overview of all potential cultural concepts of distress, it is important to acknowledge the presence of such a phenomenon. In order to aid in the conceptualization of culture-bound trauma responses, let's review an example of one such response. Ataque de nervios is a psychological distress syndrome seen in Hispanic and Caribbean communities, which involves tremulousness, crying, shivering, and a feeling of warmth going from the head to the chest to the head. It can include auditory hallucinations, fainting, and seizure-like spells. Ataque de nervios literally means "attack of the nerves" and often occurs as a result of a traumatic event. Attacks can vary in duration, and the sufferer will often have no recollection of the attack itself. The feeling of being out of control is an important aspect of ataque de nervios (Guarnaccia et al., 2010). This aspect of the disorder may relate to the essential nature of trauma, as we have described in previous chapters, as that which cannot be processed by the conscious mind.

In the typical categories of Western psychology, ataque de nervios might be categorized as a panic attack, or, because it can resemble a nonepileptic seizure, as a factitious or functional neurological symptom disorder. But such a categorization would not be faithful to the internal personal and cultural experience of the sufferer and would be giving a Western conceptualization primacy over the lived cultural experience.

Expressions of distress, like ataque de nervios, had formerly been described as culture-bound syndromes. The broader current conceptualization is that of cultural concepts of distress. Cultural concepts of distress include cultural syndromes, which are clusters of symptoms that occur and are recognizable in cultural contexts; cultural idioms of distress, which are shared ways of experiencing and talking about distress; and cultural explanations, which are causal attributions of a cultural meaning for symptoms or distress. Ataque de nervios would be categorized as a cultural syndrome, a term like bad nerves, which is common in many cultural groups and subgroups, but doesn't map well onto a discrete disorder, is a cultural idiom of distress, and the attribution of a traumatic event as punishment from God would be a cultural explanation (American Psychiatric Association, 2022).

Underrepresented communities

In the United States, some underrepresented groups, especially individuals identifying as Black or African American, are disproportionately exposed to violence and trauma in socioeconomically deprived urban communities (Roberts et al., 2011). Racial discrimination also creates a background of race-based stress and microaggressions. The terms historical trauma or multigenerational trauma refer to the social trauma that occurs across the lifespan and across generations in populations exposed to massive group trauma. The term historical trauma was originally applied to the Indigenous American community, but it is appropriate to the Black community as well (Avalos, 2021). Historical trauma adds to the impacts of acute trauma. Black patients, because of past discrimination and abuse by the health care system, are more likely to mistrust doctors and hospitals and be resistant to seeking medical care or mental health care (Ranjbar et al., 2020).

Underrepresented communities vary considerably in size, socioeconomic status, and the degree and character of the stigma they may face. In Rosa's case, because of the large Caribbean population in South Florida, her beliefs and practices were immediately recognizable as typical of Santeria. In another part of the country where the Caribbean population is smaller, her beliefs might not have been recognized as culturally normative.

The psychological consultation in Rosa's case was still made, because at times, delusional beliefs masquerade as religious practices. Patients experiencing psychosis do sometimes describe their own beliefs as religious and normative to a denomination or religious subgroup, but further exploration may reveal that the patient is considered to be experiencing aberrant behavior within their own identified religious subgroup. Only by exploring the beliefs in a cultural context can we confirm that they are indeed culturally normative. Religious beliefs particular to a specific subgroup can often affect medical care. Many practicing Jehovah's Witnesses, for instance, consider blood transfusions contrary to their faith and will typically refuse them.

Rural trauma

While acute trauma tends to often be thought of as a problem primarily impacting urban areas, in fact, rural trauma is an important public health issue as well. Mortality rates from traumatic injuries sustained in rural areas are almost twice as high as in urban areas, probably because medical and surgical care is less available. While intentional firearm injuries are less common in rural areas, unintentional firearm injury rates are higher per capita, likely because of high rates of firearm ownership. Motor vehicle crash fatalities are also much higher in rural areas. There are fewer traffic control devices, more two-lane roads, and higher traffic speeds. Rural drivers are also less likely to use seatbelts and are more likely to drink alcohol prior to driving. Agricultural work and mining are high-risk occupations that are unique to rural areas (Peek-Asa et al., 2004).

Serious injuries in rural communities sometimes require treatment in urban trauma centers, where more medical resources are available. These rural trauma survivors are then geographically separated from natural support systems and feel more socially isolated. Additionally, many injuries occur in the context of self-employed work, such as farming, and may pose unique challenges to the patient's recovery due to prolonged loss of income or an inability to manage livestock or crop harvesting schedules.

Urban trauma

Cultural and institutional racism can affect care for the trauma patient. Implicit racial biases are a long-standing issue in health care, and trauma survivors are sometimes judged implicitly by members of their health care team. Assaults, for instance, are sometimes viewed as being related to organized crime activity or volitional risk-taking behaviors. I have been told, "jokingly," that "nothing good happens when you are out at 2 AM." While clinicians know, consciously, that all patients are entitled to the same level of care, they may make implicit judgments about the patient's behavior or lifestyle and feel that the patient is to blame for the trauma that happened to them (McCuistian et al., 2022). Implicit biases are sometimes not strictly racial but cultural. Generational poverty and historical trauma can lead to lifestyle choices that are considered unacceptable to the clinician. Implicit bias can extend to pain management issues, with Black patients tending to receive fewer opiate pain medications than White patients, probably because they are assumed to be substance misusers (Haq et al., 2021). Additionally, urban areas have higher population densities, which are typically comprised of more culturally diverse communities.

Gender, sexual orientation, and trauma

Violence directed against women is a global public health issue. According to the World Health Organization, 840 million women, or one in three women worldwide, have experienced partner or sexual violence during their lifetime. Assaults against women tend to be underreported. Unfortunately, women are sometimes blamed when they are assaulted, as if they had somehow provoked the assault. We see this ancient tendency even in mythology. Medusa was transformed into a horrible monster in punishment for being raped by the god Poseidon. Her rape desecrated a sacred temple, but she was the one punished, not her assailant, Poseidon. This important myth and others are discussed in greater length in Chapter 23, Trauma Narratives: Historical and Literary Examples. Patriarchal cultures sometimes view a woman as the property of her male partner. Marital and intimate partner assaults are then trivialized, as if the male had the right to treat his property as he wished. Echoes of these patriarchal roots are present in many cultures and sometimes reveal themselves in Western health care settings when individuals who have recently immigrated or who have a strong cultural identity tied to their country of origin present for care.

Gender-based violence can occur in other contexts as well. Men can be the victims of sexual assaults, and members of sexual and gender minority communities are often victimized because of their orientation and gender. Additionally, people who identify as lesbian, gay, bisexual, transgender, or questioning (LGBTQ+) are five times more likely to be victims of violent crime than nonLGBTQ+ people (Meyer & Flores, 2025). Furthermore, LGBTQ+ people carry a substantially higher risk related to the development of PTSD, with prevalence rate estimates as high as 48%, as compared to 4.7% in the general population (Goldstein et al., 2016; Livingston et al., 2020). As such, it is imperative that clinicians take the utmost care in ensuring that these high-risk groups are given access to high-quality emotional recovery services like those provided by TACS Psych teams. Inclusion of TACS Psych teams may also reduce the likelihood of interpersonal discrimination while the patient is admitted through the modeling of appropriate social interactions and direct education to the medical and surgical teams.

Stereotypes and cultural mismatches

Cultural assumptions and stereotypes can affect medical care. Just as implicit biases and racism can impact how reports regarding pain and related behaviors are perceived, so can cultural biases. Hispanic females, for instance, might be viewed through the lens of both cultural and gender stereotypes and be described by medical and surgical teams as "dramatic" when they report distress, leading to those reports of distress being dismissed.

Cultural mismatches can also occur, based on implicit cultural assumptions and stereotypes. A clinician from a culture where stoicism is overvalued and the expression of the pain or sadness is seen as a weakness can misinterpret the experience of a patient who comes from a culture where the expression of affect is highly valued and encouraged. This issue may be amplified even further when some somatic responses to trauma, common in many nonwestern cultures, are part of the trauma response. It is important to be aware of one's own cultural biases and assumptions to protect the empathic aspects of the therapeutic relationship.

Know the place where you live and work

Communities are complex tapestries of cultural groups and subgroups. In our city, for instance, the population is mostly black, but there are large subgroups of Asian, European, Hispanic, and Middle Eastern residents. The Asian communities include Bengali and Indian subgroups. The Middle Eastern communities include Palestinians, Yemenis, Chaldeans, and Lebanese. European immigrants include Poles, Lithuanians and Irish; the Hispanic communities include Mexicans, Venezuelans, and other individuals from Central and South America. Each group has its own history and culture, its own stereotypes, its own views of medical care, and its own ways of constructing meaning from traumatic events. While the large Middle Eastern and Bengali populations are distinct from the metro Detroit region, it's important to acknowledge that every area will have its own unique cultural tapestry and history that needs to be understood and celebrated.

Cultural humility

In cultures other than our own, we are always visitors and guests. To be allowed to share the cultural experiences of another is a privilege. As suggested by (Kleinman, 1988) and others, we should never aspire to "cultural competence." Such a goal is culturally presumptuous and implies that one can understand the internal experience of another culture by reading about or hearing a brief cultural analysis. Rather than cultural competency, we should seek cultural humility, which is an openness to learn while striving to understand the cultural experiences of another. Cultural humility also avoids the dangers of cultural stereotyping.

It is impossible for any one person to possess knowledge related to all of the different cultural and subcultural beliefs that exist within the world, though we should always strive to understand each patient's unique perspective. Approaching cultural issues with an attitude of cultural humility leads to a lifelong pursuit of self-reflection and self-critique regarding the appreciation of our own cultural experiences and how they interact with others (Tervalon & Murray-García, 1998). As such, we also recognize the pervasiveness of unavoidable cultural biases in this book. We are writing as males in the Western culture. We realize that our historical and literary examples are mainly from the Western tradition, and we acknowledge that covert biases may affect our work. Exploring and acknowledging our own biases helps us be open to the varied experiences of other cultures and cultural subgroups, to truly embrace and understand the unique experiences of the individuals and communities that we serve.

In Rosa's case, from the beginning of this chapter, we were able to explore with Rosa and her family the nature of her religious beliefs and understood from her family that they were culturally normative. Rosa's children no longer practiced Santeria, but many of Rosa's generation and subculture did. Rosa was definitely not psychotic. If we did not have family to consult, and Rosa's beliefs and practices were less common in the South Florida community, we would have sought community experts to clarify such cultural issues.

Kleinman (1988) suggested some questions that may be useful in beginning to understand the cultural experience of a medical patient. The Diagnostic and Statistical Manual of Mental Disorders, Fifth Edition, Text Revision (DSM-5-TR) includes a 16-item Cultural Formulation Interview, which explores, in a systematic way, the four domains of cultural assessment, which include the cultural definition of a problem, cultural perception of cause and context, cultural factors affecting coping and past help-seeking, and cultural factors affecting current help-seeking (American Psychiatric Association, 2022).

We have modified those questions for the acute care setting to guide the process of co-creating a meaningful cultural narrative with our trauma patients. These types of questions may not be useful in every scenario, but are important to remember when cultural issues may be impacting care. In Rosa's case, these questions were a useful way of addressing issues related to coping from within her own cultural narrative.

- What do you think caused your trauma?
- What has trauma done to your body?
- How has it affected your mind or your nerves?
- How severe is it? Will it get better soon or take longer?
- What do you fear most about what happened to you?
- What are the major problems your trauma has caused for you (personally, family, work, etc.)?
- What kind of treatment do you think you should receive? What are the most important results you hope to receive from the treatment?
- What types of things normally help you deal with stress?

Chapter summary

We are all part of a culture and subculture that influences our experience of trauma and medical care. Cultural humility is an important aspect of trauma care, one that all clinicians should strive towards. Cultural factors affect both the type of trauma one is at risk of sustaining and the emotional response to the traumatic experience itself. Practical strategies for exploring the cultural aspects of the trauma response are described.

References

American Psychiatric Association (2022). *Diagnostic and statistical manual of mental disorders* (5th ed., text rev.). American Psychiatric Association Publishing. https://doi.org/10.1176/appi.books.9780890425787.

Avalos, N. (2021). What does it mean to heal from historical trauma? *AMA Journal of Ethics, 23*(6). https://doi.org/10.1001/amajethics.2021.494.

Bolton, P., & Tang, A. M. (2002). An alternative approach to cross-cultural function assessment. *Social Psychiatry and Psychiatric Epidemiology, 37*(11), 537–543. https://doi.org/10.1007/s00127-002-0580-5.

Desai, G., & Chaturvedi, S. (2017). Idioms of distress. *Journal of Neurosciences in Rural Practice, 8*(5), 94–97. https://doi.org/10.4103/jnrp.jnrp_235_17.

Goldstein, R. B., Smith, S. M., Chou, S. P., Saha, T. D., Jung, J., Zhang, H., Pickering, R. P., Ruan, W. J., Huang, B., & Grant, B. F. (2016). The epidemiology of DSM-5 posttraumatic stress disorder in the United States: results from the National Epidemiologic Survey on Alcohol and Related Conditions-III. *Social Psychiatry and Psychiatric Epidemiology, 51*(8), 1137–1148. https://doi.org/10.1007/s00127-016-1208-5.

Guarnaccia, P. J., Lewis-Fernandez, R., Martinez Pincay, I., Shrout, P., Guo, J., Torres, M., Canino, G., & Alegria, M. (2010). Ataque de nervios as a marker of social and psychiatric vulnerability: Results from the NLAAS. *International Journal of Social Psychiatry, 56*(3), 298–309. https://doi.org/10.1177/0020764008101636.

Haq, N., McMahan, V. M., Torres, A., Santos, G.-M., Knight, K., Kushel, M., & Coffin, P. O. (2021). Race, pain, and opioids among patients with chronic pain in a safety-net health system. *Drug and Alcohol Dependence, 222*. https://doi.org/10.1016/j.drugalcdep.2021.108671.

Hinton, D. E., & Lewis-Fernández, R. (2011). The cross-cultural validity of posttraumatic stress disorder: Implications for DSM-5. *Depression and Anxiety, 28*(9), 783–801. https://doi.org/10.1002/da.20753.

Kleinman, A. (1988). *Rethinking psychiatry: From cultural category to personal experience*. Free Press.

Livingston, N. A., Berke, D., Scholl, J., Ruben, M., & Shipherd, J. C. (2020). Addressing diversity in PTSD treatment: Clinical considerations and guidance for the treatment of PTSD in LGBTQ populations. *Current Treatment Options in Psychiatry, 7*(2), 53–69. https://doi.org/10.1007/s40501-020-00204-0.

McCuistian, C., Kimball, S. L., Buitron de la Vega, P., Godfrey, L. B., Fortuna, L. R., & Valentine, S. E. (2022). Consideration of racism experiences in the implementation of trauma-focused therapy in primary care. *Health Services Research, 57*(S2), 235–248. https://doi.org/10.1111/1475-6773.13998.

Meyer, I.H., & Flores, A.R. (2025). *Anti-LGBT victimization in the United States: Results from the National Crime Victimization Survey (2022–2023)*. The Williams Institute, UCLA School of Law. https://williamsinstitute.law.ucla.edu/publications/anti-lgbt-victimization-us/.

Patel, A. R., & Hall, B. J. (2021). Diagnoses: A cross-cultural approach to assessing trauma reactions. *Focus (American Psychiatric Publishing), 19*(2), 197–203. https://doi.org/10.1176/appi.focus.20200049.

Peek-Asa, C., Zwerling, C., & Stallones, L. (2004). Acute traumatic injuries in rural populations. *American Journal of Public Health, 94*(10), 1689–1693. https://doi.org/10.2105/ajph.94.10.1689.

Ranjbar, N., Erb, M., Mohammad, O., & Moreno, F. A. (2020). Trauma-informed care and cultural humility in the mental health care of people from minoritized communities. *Focus (American Psychiatric Publishing), 18*(1), 8–15. https://doi.org/10.1176/appi.focus.20190027.

Roberts, A. L., Gilman, S. E., Breslau, J., Breslau, N., & Koenen, K. C. (2011). Race/ethnic differences in exposure to traumatic events, development of post-traumatic stress disorder, and treatment-seeking for post-traumatic stress disorder in the United States. *Psychological Medicine, 41*(1), 71–83. https://doi.org/10.1017/S0033291710000401.

Tervalon, M., & Murray-García, J. (1998). Cultural humility versus cultural competence: A critical distinction in defining physician training outcomes in multicultural education. *Journal of Health Care for the Poor and Underserved, 9*(2), 117–125. https://doi.org/10.1353/hpu.2010.0233.

Chapter 17

Spiritual aspects of recovery

There is only one truly serious philosophical problem, and that is suicide. Judging whether life is or is not worth living amounts to answering the fundamental question of philosophy.

—Albert Camus, The Myth of Sisyphus

Lisa's Story

When I met Lisa in the hospital after a suicide attempt, she was 18. She had faced some difficulties culminating in the termination of the relationship with her boyfriend. She was upset and angry, deciding that life without Jason wasn't worth living. When her parents went out for the evening, she got drunk, grabbed her father's rifle, went to the garage, leaned it against her chin, and fired.

When individuals flinch right before pulling the trigger, the bullet sometimes fires through the upper jaw and then out near the nasal cavity. Lisa suffered massive facial injuries, but no fatal wounds, and no brain injury. She had a lengthy hospital stay with multiple reconstructive surgeries. She faced a lifetime of pain and disfigurement. She had been suicidal before her acute trauma; I wondered how she felt about life now. I was afraid to ask that question, but it needed to be asked. I feared what the answer might be, and how I would deal with it.

At that time, I was a new faculty member, just out of residency. New faculty get assigned the toughest cases, but I liked Lisa, although I felt helpless in the face of the horror she was facing. I imagined how she must feel and knew that my usual armamentarium of pills and kind words was no match for her pain. What solace could I offer? I wondered about the injustice and cruelty of her terrible injury. I struggled with the meaninglessness of what happened to her and knew that any solace had to have a spiritual dimension.

When I asked her how she made sense of her life now, I was surprised by her answer. "I'm just so glad I'm alive," she replied. "I know they will have to rebuild my jaw and that I will probably always eat through a straw. I know that when these bandages come off, I will look like a monster, but I'm so glad I'm alive." Despite the horror she faced, Lisa was at peace. Her survival meant to her that life must have a purpose and that she was here for a reason. She trusted that whatever pain she faced, it would be worth it; she mattered. When the bandages came off, we made sure the family was there. Lisa studied herself in the mirror, shuddered, and cried. "I can handle this," she finally said. "It's OK."

The Psychology of Acute Trauma. DOI: https://doi.org/10.1016/B978-0-443-33212-8.00015-4

(Continued)

What happened? What changed? Why was Lisa no longer suicidal? How did she find that sense of meaning? Lisa had been suicidal before, and now her life, by any logical standards, was going to be much harder. But instead of being even more suicidal, she felt that life was worth living.

"What do you see in the mirror?" I asked.

"It'll never be the same. I have no religious experience or background; my family didn't believe in God," Lisa explained, "but I know that my life means something to some higher power, and I trust that. That feeling is unshakeable."

Without using traditional religious imagery, Lisa was describing a conversion experience. The term conversion is often used to describe a religious conversion to a particular faith or sect, but it can have a broader meaning as well. Lisa's trauma resulted in a genuine conversion, not to a set of dogmas but to a spiritual perspective, giving her life a meaning that transcended her suffering.

Trauma and suffering

The terms trauma and suffering come from different traditions. Trauma is a psychological term; suffering is a religious and spiritual term. When we deal with patients with acute trauma like Lisa, we must attempt to merge or harmonize those two perspectives.

In their book Post-Traumatic Public Theology, Stephanie Arel and Shelly Rambo (Arel & Rambo, 2016) offer strategies to harmonize those two perspectives. Using the view that trauma is that which cannot be processed by the psyche, they described trauma as "suffering that remains." Suffering is human pain that is incorporated into a meaning system or narrative and thus has the potential to be healed. Trauma is that which is left over in human pain, that which cannot be incorporated into a system of meaning.

Suffering refers to the internal human response, while trauma points outward at the external event because it remains outside any system of meaning. Lisa's trauma became suffering because she was able to miraculously accept it as meaningful and to see her survival as a divine gift. Suffering carries embedded within it the ancient idea that pain and sorrow area necessary part of the human condition; trauma carries embedded within it the modernist assumption that a life might be lived without sorrow, that illness and injury impinge on the normal human state, that life can be lived without pain.

Why me?

Trauma, suffering, and spirituality are inextricably linked. When Siddhartha leaves the palace, he bears witness to the suffering in the world, and his journey to enlightenment begins. In Islam, one response to suffering is a spiritual one, called tawakkul—a turning toward or reliance on Allah. In Christianity, the central symbol of the faith, the cross, represents the suffering of the crucified Jesus. In Hinduism, suffering is ignorance, and the trials and trauma of life are teachers.

Acute trauma raises one of the great theological and philosophical dilemmas; namely, why does suffering exist in a world where God is both good and all powerful. Theodicy is the attempt to answer this question. In our everyday lives, before trauma, we assume the world is governed by the hypothesis of a just world, that good things happen to good people and vice versa. Trauma, with a single stroke, nullifies the just world hypothesis. For Lisa, it was the rifle shot that changed her life. True, her suicide attempt was a rash and impulsive act, but she is a good person. For her single rash act to lead to a lifetime of pain and disfigurement is unjust.

Theodicy is the philosophical endeavor to restore the just world hypothesis, to explain why suffering and trauma exist in a world created by a just and all-powerful God. The trauma survivor asks us, "Why me?" There is no easy answer to that question. The question cannot be answered by reason and logic; the trauma survivor must "live into" the answer with trust and courage and choose acceptance over despair.

Job

The Book of Job in the Christian and Hebrew Bible is an exploration of the issue of theodicy issue in narrative form. Job is a good and just man. He is wealthy and successful. God puts Job through a series of traumas and trials. He loses both his wealth and health; his children all die. Much of the text of the book is a lengthy dialog between Job and his less-than-helpful friends. Job asks over and over, "Why me?" His friends answer, "You must be guilty of something; admit your sins!" Finally, God himself appears to resolve the dilemmas. He chides Job's friends; "They have not spoken of me rightly as my servant Job has." (The Holy Bible, New King James Version, 1982) (Job 42:7) He does not explain His actions to Job but simply asserts His power with questions like, "Where were you when I laid the foundations of the earth?" (Job 38:4) He then restores to Job all that Job has lost. Job's story is explored in more detail in Chapter 23, Trauma Narratives: Historical and Literary Examples.

Spirituality and religion

The terms spirituality and religion refer to different aspects of the spiritual experience. Spirituality refers to the belief that life has purpose or meaning and that a Higher Power has a presence in our lives. Religion includes the idea of spirituality, but places it in the context of a particular religious structure and dogma. Christianity, Islam, and Hinduism are religions; Alcoholics Anonymous is a spiritual group. Both spiritual and religious beliefs can affect or be affected by the experience of acute trauma. Lisa, for instance, became more spiritual after her trauma but not more religious.

More and more people are uncomfortable with religious dogmas, but still have deep spiritual yearnings. According to the 2023 report from the PEW Research Center, Spirituality Among Americans, although belief in traditional religions has declined in the United States, 22% of U.S. adults describe themselves in a newer category of "spiritual but not religious" (SBNR) (Pew Research Center, 2023). People who are not traditional churchgoers may be deeply spiritual.

Spiritual and religious responses to trauma

As we have previously described, trauma can suddenly change how we view the world and its relationship with us. For Frida Kahlo, the world became "a painful planet, transparent as ice" (Kahlo, 2007).

Potential religious or spiritual responses to trauma fall into four patterns:

1. For those with religious faith, that faith can provide a meaning and context for traumatic experiences. One of the founders of Christianity, Saint Paul, was an example of someone whose faith allowed him to survive trauma. In his many missionary journeys, Paul was flogged, stoned, and shipwrecked. Paul accepted his trauma: "That is why, for Christ's sake, I delight in weaknesses, in insults, in hardships, in persecutions, in difficulties. For when I am weak, then I am strong" (The Holy Bible, New King James Version, 1982) (2 Corinthians 12:8-10). His religious beliefs helped him accept trauma and view it as meaningful suffering.
2. Alternatively, a religious perspective can lead to a negative response to trauma. In these scenarios, religiously oriented individuals may develop the idea that the survivor of trauma is to blame for what happened to them. God is good, so what happened to me must be my fault, a result of my sin. This is the perspective taken by Job's friends when they admonished him for the ills that befell him, saying he must be deserving of divine punishment.
3. A spiritual response can occur because of trauma. Lisa's story illustrates this pattern. Prior to her trauma, she was not religious or spiritual; after her trauma, she developed strong spiritual beliefs. Trauma can lead to a conversion experience and subsequent posttraumatic growth.
4. Trauma can lead to the abandonment of religious or spiritual beliefs. One often sees this pattern early in the response to trauma. The person who experienced trauma may feel that if this terrible thing happened, then the world must make no sense and have no purpose. A good God would not have allowed this to happen; therefore, there must be no God. As Frida Kahlo put it, this is a "painful planet." The abandonment of religious or spiritual beliefs can be a temporary response that leads to a deeper exploration of spiritual issues and posttraumatic growth, as it did in Kahlo's case, or a long-lasting sense of despair.

Empirical studies

Empirical data on the relationship between traumatic stress and religion have been limited, especially for acute trauma. Most studies related to trauma recovery make no mention of religious or spiritual issues (Park et al., 2016). Available empirical data are of limited utility. Issues of terminology are complex, assessments of religiosity and spirituality are not standardized, and the underlying theoretical constructs related to spiritual issues are poorly understood. The narrow 1-month time window for the diagnosis of acute stress disorder further restricts research. Most empirical research on spirituality and trauma has focused on posttraumatic stress disorder (PTSD), and those studies have had mixed results. In general, religious and spiritual beliefs appear to be associated with improved coping after trauma.

Clinical experience suggests that acute trauma often leads to a rejection of religious or spiritual approaches to coping early in recovery. Often trauma survivors feel overwhelmed early in recovery, and religious solutions are sometimes offered too glibly by family and friends. Trauma survivors may experience religious platitudes like, "It must be God's will," as minimizing their experience of suffering. To say, "It must be God's will," comforts the comforter, not the trauma survivor. Only when the impact of the trauma is genuinely experienced and recognized can genuine recovery, including spiritual acceptance, begin.

Prayer

In the Western Christian tradition, William James called prayer "the very soul and essence of religion" (James, 1902), but prayer is not a unitary phenomenon. In the Christian tradition, Saint Paul described four types of prayer: (1) supplication, which is an entreaty, or asking for something; (2) pouring out, or the expression of all that one needs and wishes and all of one's hurts; (3) intercession, a plea to God as an all-powerful superior; and (4) thanksgiving, a giving of thanks not only for answered prayers but for God himself and his true nature (The Holy Bible, New King James Version, 1982) (1 Timothy 2:1).

Prayers of supplication are sometimes dismissed as being purely transactional. Singer-songwriter Janis Joplin offered a comical example of a prayer of supplication in her song "Mercedes Benz": "Oh Lord, won't you buy me a Mercedes Benz/My friends all drive Porsches, I must make amends." Yet prayers of supplication can be very heartfelt and tragic, like "Please God, let my paralysis be cured," or "Please help me pay the bills since I cannot work." Prayers of supplication can sometimes be misused as tests of God's love. When the prayer is not answered, then the supplicant can feel that God does not exist or that God does not love them. The truest forms of supplication acknowledge that God hears and answers in His own way and in His own time.

The "pouring out" form of prayer is an important expression of faith, awe, and acceptance. We pour out to God because sometimes only God can bear the pain that even loved ones cannot hear. Prayers of thanksgiving can include gratitude for both happiness and suffering.

The most common response to acute trauma is not seeking psychotherapy, but prayer. Around 44% of Americans pray daily (Smith et al., 2025); in times of crisis, especially medical crises, about a quarter of those who never pray begin to pray. Although the effects of prayer in acute trauma have not been studied, research has shown that religion and prayer help individuals cope with adverse life events (Pargament et al., 2005). Coping with stress has been described as one of the primary functions of prayer, although such transactional language is misguided. The function of religion is to nurture and experience a relationship with God; whatever benefits may arise from that relationship are secondary. To offer an analogy, marriage may help increase life span, but you don't marry someone to live longer; you marry someone because you love them.

Gottlieb argued that prayer may be helpful in a very specific way, by assisting individuals in coping with events that cannot be altered, avoided, or easily resolved (Gottlieb, 1997). Prayer, according to Gottlieb (1997), promotes "peaceful acceptance" (p. 28). Prayer of supplication can be problematic in the response to acute trauma if one believes, as some do, that God answers prayers right away and gives exactly what is asked for. Such prayer beliefs in the face of acute trauma that cannot be altered can lead to despair. Others believe that God answers prayers in His own time and in His own way (Krause, 2004). This kind of trusting attitude is more likely to lead to peaceful acceptance (Krause, 2009).

Intercessory prayer

Many studies have examined the benefits of intercessory prayer, or praying for another. Initial studies in the 1990s appeared to suggest that intercessory prayer could be of benefit in a variety of medical conditions. These studies received a significant media attention, but more carefully controlled studies could not replicate these findings (Fosarelli, 2011). Current studies suggest that intercessory prayer has not been shown to be of benefit. Prayer in its highest forms is not about asking for or getting something. Even the comfort that comes from prayer is not its goal, but a secondary benefit that can come from a deepened relationship with God. As Job learned, God acts in His own time and in His own way.

Incorporating spiritual care into treatment

The National Center for PTSD has identified a four-part continuum of spiritual integration into therapy, which applies to acute trauma, as well. In spiritually avoidant care, clinicians avoid spiritual concerns and issues altogether. Spiritually conscious care involves assessing spirituality and religion and being open to their importance. Spiritually integrated care incorporates spiritual issues into treatment based upon patient goals, and spiritually directive care uses spiritual practices, such as prayer. Care for the patient with acute trauma should be spiritually conscious or spiritually integrated. Spiritually directive care should be reserved for clergy or pastoral care providers (Larsen et al., 2025).

The guidelines from the National Center for PTSD include useful questions for assessing spirituality and religiosity (Larsen et al., 2025). Some of these questions include the following:

1. Do you see yourself as a religious or spiritual person? In what way?
2. Are you affiliated with a religious or spiritual community?
3. What are your ultimate values? Or what do you think your life is about?
4. Has the traumatic event affected your religiousness or spirituality? If so, how?
5. Has your religion or spirituality affected the way you have coped with this event?

Such open-ended questions invite genuine exploration, while conventional religious responses described in the prior section tend to shut down conversation. Spiritually conscious or spiritually integrated care allows the clinician and trauma survivor to explore deeper issues of meaning and purpose. In Lisa's case, when she saw herself in the mirror for the first time, she began talking about who she is now and what her new life will be like. I talked with her about realistic goals and options, but she was less comfortable with spiritual issues. True spiritually conscious care would have allowed her to more deeply explore the meaning of her new life.

Spiritual work can be painful and forces us, as the clinician, to confront our own spiritual doubts and the issues of meaning that we sometimes avoid. To invite spiritual exploration is to accept the pain that such exploration brings, but only by accepting pain can we truly join with the ones we love or care for who have experienced acute trauma.

Posttraumatic growth

Posttraumatic growth will be discussed in more detail in the next chapter, but it is important to note that the relationship between spirituality and posttraumatic growth is complex. A number of studies in a variety of different populations have demonstrated a correlation between religious faith and posttraumatic growth (Joseph et al., 2005; Linley & Joseph, 2005). Especially interesting is that religious distress early in recovery from trauma can be a predictor of posttraumatic growth. Those who struggle with religious doubts and the existential questions we have described, such as the theodicy question (why does suffering exist in a world where God is both good and all-powerful), are more likely to experience posttraumatic growth. Prayer has been shown to facilitate posttraumatic growth, as well, especially prayer for calm and focus. This type of prayer is difficult to distinguish from other mind-body practices, such as medtation.

The dangers of antireligious bias

Psychologists tend to be much less religious than their patients (Delaney et al., 2007), and only 30% of psychologists discuss spiritual issues with their patients (Vieten et al., 2013). Most patients are religious or spiritual, and especially after trauma, we have seen that spiritual seeking, as expressed in prayer, increases significantly. It can be natural for clinicians to consider religious beliefs in psychological terms, as cognitive distortions, ways of denying suffering, or as avoidance-based coping. In Lisa's case, for instance, it would be easy to dismiss her newly discovered spirituality as a defense against the horror of what had happened to her. Defenses, however, are maladaptive. Lisa's spirituality led to personal growth and acceptance.

Culture, spirituality, and religion

Culture and religion have been closely linked through much of human history. The idea of the separation of church and state is a relatively modern one, associated with Jefferson. The idea of spirituality as an internal experience not associated with a group religious practice is an even more modern idea. Atheism and agnosticism are dominant trends in Western culture, especially in academic culture. The lack of religious belief is a cultural belief and attitude that deeply affects how we understand and view trauma. The culture in which we live creates an internal matrix that affects our thoughts, feelings, and the way we respond to traumatic events. We live in a multicultural world where spirituality plays a less important role than it has in past decades. The matrix of meaning in which a traumatic event can be experienced is lost. As mental health providers, we are embedded in a cultural role that psychologizes distress. Philip Reiff (1966) in his classic sociological study, The Triumph of the Therapeutic, argues that in Western cultures religious, and spiritual values have been replaced by concepts based in psychotherapy, like self-esteem, comfort, and personal satisfaction. Trauma challenges this paradigm, but we as clinicians in the Western tradition are trained in a therapeutic rather than a spiritual paradigm (Reiff, 1966).

Attitudes toward caregiving are also affected by cultural and spiritual beliefs. Western cultures tend to be individualistic in nature, emphasizing the importance of the individual over the collective group. For that reason, spirituality is more naturally experienced in the West in an individual context, rather than the social context of an organized religion. Trauma recovery work focuses on individual care, with the central, culture-bound goal of autonomy.

From an individualistic perspective, caregiving can be viewed as a burden, rather than as a natural and spiritually meaningful aspect of group life. Many nonwestern cultures tend to emphasize collectivism and are more oriented towards family and society; caregiving is more likely to be seen as a natural expectation with spiritual meaning and significance.

How to approach discussions related to spirituality and religion

First, explore your own feelings about spirituality and religion. It is challenging to become comfortable talking about these important beliefs with your patients unless you are comfortable contemplating your own beliefs. If your response would simply be "I have no religious or spiritual beliefs," or "Culture doesn't impact my care, I treat everyone the same," think deeply about issues of meaning in your life. Are you simply avoiding such issues? Why? As we work with trauma survivors, we are forced to face the potential horror and unpredictability of life. If this work is part of your path, accept this part of the journey as well.

Second, realize that these issues are probably important to most of your patients. If none of your patients talk to you about these matters, you are probably tacitly conveying discomfort about discussing such topics.

Include some of the questions described from the section on incorporating cultural beliefs and spiritual care into treatment part of your regular clinical interviews. They will remind you that these topics are important and should be a standard part of treatment.

Don't expect yourself to have answers to questions that have no answers. Your goal is not to have answers, but to accompany your patient on the journey. To accompany them on that journey is a gift and a privilege.

Chapter summary

A comprehensive approach to trauma care encompasses the spiritual and cultural aspects of recovery. Acute trauma raises spiritual and religious issues, and their responses to those issues may include prayer. Empirical studies demonstrate the psychological benefits of prayer in the recovery from acute trauma and in increasing posttraumatic growth. Effective strategies for approaching the religious and cultural aspects of trauma with patients are described.

References

Arel, S. N., & Rambo, S. (2016). Post-traumatic public theology Post-Traumatic Public Theology. United States: Springer International Publishing. http://doi.org/10.1007/978-3-319–40660-2.

Delaney, H. D., Miller, W. R., & Bisonó, A. M. (2007). Religiosity and Spirituality Among Psychologists: A Survey of Clinician Members of the American Psychological Association.

Professional Psychology: Research and Practice, 38(5), 538–546. https://doi.org/10.1037/0735-7028.38.5.538.

Fosarelli, P. (2011). Outcomes of intercessory prayer for those who are ill: Scientific and pastoral perspectives. *Linacre Quarterly, 78*(2), 125–137. http://doi.org/10.1179/002436311803888384.

Gottlieb, B. H. (1997). Coping with chronic stressProminent modes of coping with chronic stress. In B. H. Gottlieb (Ed.). *Coping with chronic stress*. Plenum.

James, W. (1902). The varieties of religious experience: A study in human nature. Longmans, Green and Co. https://doi.org/10.1037/10004-000.

Joseph, S., Andrews, L., Harris, G., Howle, B., Linley, P. A., Woodward, C., & Shevlin, M. (2005). Assessing positive and negative changes in the aftermath of adversity: Psychometric evaluation of the changes in outlook questionnaire. *Psychological Assessment, 17*(1), 70–80. https://doi.org/10.1037/1040-3590.17.1.70.

Kahlo, F. (2007). Frida by Frida. *Editorial RM*.

Krause, N. (2004). Assessing the Relationships Among Prayer Expectancies, Race, and Self-Esteem in Late Life. *Journal for the Scientific Study of Religion, 43*(3), 395–408. https://doi.org/10.1111/j.1468-5906.2004.00242.x.

Krause, N. (2009). Lifetime Trauma, Prayer, and Psychological Distress in Late Life. *International Journal for the Psychology of Religion, 19*(1), 55–72. https://doi.org/10.1080/10508610802471112.

Larsen, S. E., Hopkins, S., & Harris, I. (2025). *Addressing religious or spiritual dimensions of trauma and PTSD*. National Center for PTSD. Veterans Administration.

Linley, P. A., & Joseph, S. (2005). The human capacity for growth through adversity. *American Psychologist, 60*(3), 262–264. https://doi.org/10.1037/0003-066X.60.3.262b.

Pargament, K. I., Magyar-Russell, G. M., & Murray-Swank, N. A. (2005). The sacred and the search for significance: Religion as a unique process. *Journal of Social Issues, 61*(4), 665–687. https://doi.org/10.1111/j.1540-4560.2005.00426.x.

Park, C. L., Currier, J. M., Harris, I., & Slattery, J. M. (2016). *Trauma, meaning and spirituality: Translating research into clinical practice*. American Psychological Association Press.

Pew Research Center (2023). *Spirituality among Americans*. https://www.pewresearch.org/religion/2023/12/07/spirituality-among-americans/.

Reiff, P. (1966). *The Triumph of the Therapeutic*. New York: Harper.

Smith, G. A., Cooperman, A., Alper, B. A., Mohamed, B., Rotolo, C., Tevington, P., Nortey, J., Kallo, A., Diamant, J., & Fahmy, D. (2025). *Decline of Christianity in the U.S. has slowed, may have leveled off*. Pew Research Center.

The Holy Bible, New King James Version. (1982). Thomas Nelson.

Vieten, C., Scammell, S., Pilato, R., Ammondson, I., Pargament, K. I., & Lukoff, D. (2013). Spiritual and religious competencies for psychologists. *Psychology of Religion and Spirituality, 5*(3), 129–144. https://doi.org/10.1037/a0032699.

Chapter 18

Posttraumatic growth and survivorship

Jamie's story

Jamie was a 22-year-old premed student. One Sunday afternoon, she studied outside on a lawn in a secluded part of campus. Students came and went, and a man with a backpack sat among the students. At dusk, Jamie started to walk home, chatting on her cell phone with a friend. Suddenly, a voice said, "Put the phone down!" and she felt a knife at her throat. "Do what I tell you, or I'll kill you," he told her as he pulled her into an abandoned church.

Jamie described the assault in a piece she published in The Washington Post: *This is it, I thought. I might as well say goodbye to my family, my friends, my life. Hopefully someone will find me back here, even though I'll probably be dead. In that moment, I said goodbye to myself, too. I knew I'd never be the same, even if I made it out alive. I'd accepted my fate. Then I felt a moment of absolute clarity. "Why are you doing this to me?" I asked "Did someone do this to you?" (Sweigart, 2018).*

Jamie's story, continued

Abruptly, the man stepped away from me. Big tears started rolling down his face. Sobbing, he slowly lowered himself until he was sitting next to me. He looked at me through a stream of tears.

"You must be an angel," he said. To my bewilderment, he continued to weep, muttering, "I'm so sorry," over and over (Sweigart, 2018).

Jamie has been a good friend of mine for more than 10 years. Her story is horrific, but what followed was miraculous.

The man released Jamie. Soon, campus police arrived, and eventually the man was arrested. He had assaulted several women over the last few years. Jamie met several of them during the subsequent court proceedings. One of whom had a long scar on her neck from a knife gash. Jamie's long and painful emotional recovery is a story of posttraumatic growth (PTG). We will follow her recovery in her own words, as eloquently described in her Post article.

History of the concept of posttraumatic growth

PTG is a relatively recent term that refers to the positive psychological changes that often occur after a traumatic event. The concept of PTG should not in any

The Psychology of Acute Trauma. DOI: https://doi.org/10.1016/B978-0-443-33212-8.00028-2

way discount the suffering associated with exposure to trauma. Psychological responses to trauma are multidimensional in nature, meaning that PTG can exist simultaneously with posttraumatic distress, and the presence of PTG does not mean that clinically significant distress should not be addressed. In fact, the same mechanisms that cause acute stress disorder (ASD) and posttraumatic stress disorder (PTSD) are hypothesized to initiate PTG (Tedeschi et al., 1998). PTG is common; more than half of trauma survivors report positive psychological changes following exposure to trauma (Wu et al., 2019). Because of this, PTG is important to recognize and acknowledge. Strategies aimed at facilitating and encouraging PTG are an important part of the treatment of acute trauma. As discussed in Chapter 6 (Psychological interventions for hospitalized trauma patients) the goals of treatment should not solely be the relief of suffering, but also the promotion of personal growth and improved overall well-being. The idea of PTG helps us view distress not exclusively as pathology, but as an aspect of recovery.

The concept of PTG is an ancient one, rediscovered in modern times. In the Epic of Gilgamesh, Gilgamesh seeks immortality after the traumatic death of his best friend Enkidu. Instead of immortality, he discovers his true purpose in life. In Egyptian mythology, the body of Osiris, dismembered through trauma, is put back together and healed by love. In the Iliad, Achilles is enraged when his friend Patroclus is killed in battle. This trauma also transforms him, as he weeps and comes to realize the common humanity he shares with even the hated Trojans. In the Arthurian legends, a central figure is the Fisher King, the guardian of the Grail. The Fisher King nurses an eternal wound suffered in battle while protecting the Grail. In his woundedness, he is the guardian of the greatest of treasures. The Fisher King story is described in more detail in Chapter 23 (Trauma narratives: historical and literary examples).

In modern psychological literature, the term PTG was first used in 1979 (Antonovsky, 2008). The modern scientific study of PTG begins with the work of Tedeschi and Calhoun in the 1990s. They identified and studied five key psychological improvements that occur in PTG: (a) enhanced appreciation of life, (b) improved relationships with others, (c) awareness of new possibilities in life, (d) enhanced personal strength, and (e) a deepened sense of spirituality (Tedeschi et al., 1998). They also developed an inventory to measure PTG in a quantifiable way, the Posttraumatic Growth Inventory (Tedeschi & Calhoun, 1996). PTG has a complex relationship with posttraumatic distress and PTSD. A degree of distress is necessary for PTG to develop, but severe distress can interfere with its development(Wu et al., 2019).

PTG also has a complex relationship with hope and optimism. PTG has been described as Janus-faced, with positive and negative aspects, like the two-faced Greek deity Janus. One face is PTG and acceptance, the other face is an optimism colored by denial (Maercker & Zoellner, 2004). The actor Christopher Reeve is an excellent example. After his traumatic spinal cord injury and paralysis, he became an important spokesman and sponsor of spinal cord recovery research, suggesting PTG; but on the other side, he spoke of cures for spinal cord injury as if they were imminent, when in fact they were not. His story is discussed in more detail in Chapter 23 (Trauma narratives: historical and literary examples).

Resilience

PTG and resilience are sometimes used synonymously, but they represent very different concepts. Resilience, as discussed in Chapter 5 (The psychology of acute trauma: assessment and case conceptualization), refers to the capacity to respond effectively to adversity. Resilience differs from PTG in that resilience suggests a capacity to return to baseline after trauma, whereas PTG implies actual psychological improvement. Resilient trauma survivors can accept traumatic events and return to baseline. Survivors who develop PTG after trauma are, in a sense, less resilient. They suffer distress after trauma and ruminate on the effects and impacts of their trauma, but that distress and cognitive exploration drive the PTG process (Schubert et al., 2016). PTG and resilience might be viewed as complementary aspects of trauma recovery; they are distinct but not mutually exclusive aspects of trauma recovery. An ideal trauma recovery program would encourage both.

Posttraumatic growth, distress, and suffering

Suffering is a distress contextualized. Suffering is distress that has found a home in a context of purpose, spirituality or ritual. PTG might be described as a way to transform distress into suffering. Jamie certainly faced a lengthy period of emotional turmoil, but she came to accept the injustice of her trauma and contextualized the trauma she endured into her life narrative. Politically, the acceptance of suffering has been used as a religiously sanctioned tool to justify oppression. Yet such misuse of the idea of suffering should not blind us to the fact that distress after trauma is a form of human suffering and that part of recovery can be contextualizing that distress in a spiritual manner as an aspect of the human condition. The goal of clinical care, and the goal of political systems, should be to maximize justice and minimize suffering, but suffering will remain and must be accepted and processed.

Jamie's posttrauma experience, in her words

For me, the months and years that followed were a journey of change and growth. At first, I couldn't accept that I would never be myself again. I turned to unhealthy distractions and gave up my dream of med school.

I could never be a doctor, as damaged as I now am, I thought. I spent most of my energy trying to block out my feelings of disappointment, grief, and shame over being violated. I distanced myself from others to avoid the intensity of intimate relationships. I was quick to anger and easily hurt.

(Continued)

The initial two years were the toughest: I oscillated between paralyzing fear, anxiety, and despair. When I felt overwhelmed, flooded with emotions that were too intense, I'd regress to feeling completely detached—"numbing out," as my therapist called it (Sweigart, 2018).

Factors that predict posttraumatic growth

An understanding of the factors that predict PTG may enhance the clinical assessment and treatment planning process. PTG after acute trauma is more common in adults rather than children, in women, in personality styles that tend toward extraversion, and in those with the personality trait of openness to new experiences. Intimate relationships and romantic partners can play an important role in facilitating PTG (Purol & Chopik, 2024). Social support and psychotherapy can nurture PTG, although currently no empirical data are available as to what specific types of therapy may prove more effective in fostering PTG. Since PTG involves the acceptance of the impacts of trauma on the trauma survivor, one might suppose that therapeutic interventions that explicitly encourage such acceptance, such as acceptance and commitment therapy and existential therapy, might more effectively encourage PTG. Important theoretical issues remain about the goals of therapy in relation to PTG. Therapies focused exclusively on symptom reduction might relieve distress but might, paradoxically, make PTG less likely. The best way to facilitate PTG is to provide informed and compassionate care, which includes awareness and acceptance of the pain and grief associated with trauma.

Sean's story

Sean was a 23-year-old gang member who was involved in a shooting, sustaining a gunshot wound to the head. Because of the assault, Sean was left permanently blind. As we worked with Sean, we learned that he actually felt some relief at his blindness. He had been contemplating a safe way to exit the gang. Blindness served that purpose. As a blind man, he would no longer be welcome in the gang. The trauma offered Sean a tragic way to escape from a lifestyle he no longer wanted.

Special cultural and methodological issues in posttraumatic growth

Let us consider another clinical case.

Is Sean's case an example of PTG? From the perspective of the dominant culture, and from Sean's perspective, exiting the gang is a good outcome. Although Sean felt that his new lifestyle would be better than his old lifestyle, besides his self report, we have no objective measure of improvement. To confirm improvement, from a research perspective, one would have had to have some objective measures of mood or adjustment pre-trauma. Such data are very rarely available in acute care settings, so we are left not knowing with objective certainty if his self-reported improvement is genuine or a retrospective rationalization and acceptance of a tragic fate.

Cultural critics have further suggested that the general concept of PTG is, infact a culture-bound narrative. The dominant culture strongly values narratives about overcoming obstacles because such narratives support collective economic myths about competition and success. This cultural narrative marginalizes distress and suffering as failure and encourages the idea of PTG as a way of avoiding the reality of human suffering. The idea of PTG can be exploited to serve this kind of malignant narrative. Also, PTG is facilitated by personal and cultural support. Poverty and stigma can make PTG more difficult (Infurna et al., 2024).

Although PTG can be used to support a false narrative, PTG is a very real phenomenon. Many trauma survivors like Jamie experience PTG, and as clinicians, we must honor that lived experience. Furthermore, the concept of growth and transformation through suffering is a universal and timeless cultural motif, not just a culture-bound one. Joseph Campbell described the nearly universal myths of the hero's journey (Campbell, 2008). Suffering and descent to the underworld are part of that universal, human journey.

The internal experience of posttraumatic growth

Again, we will use Jamie's words to describe how PTG feels to the trauma survivor.

Jamie's experience of posttraumatic growth

Gradually, I was able to regain my bearings and rebuild my sense of who I am, integrating my former hopes, dreams, and idealism with my new understanding of the world around me.

Before, I'd been unwilling to acknowledge the existence of evil. Now, I had to examine the dark side of life, if only to see the light more clearly. I discovered that, as humans, we've all suffered varying levels of trauma, and many of us spend our lives trying to avoid feeling the resulting pain. When I was able to let myself feel the full spectrum of my painful emotions, especially through art and writing, a ray of hope began to emerge.

I underwent a radical transformation, from victim to survivor. I began to see myself as someone who could be healed—and perhaps even bring healing to others (Sweigart, 2018).

Jamie did finish medical school. Partially because of her traumatic experiences, she chose psychiatry as a career. She had the financial and intellectual resources to make that dream attainable. Her memory of her powerful, intuitive intervention with her assailant gave her hope that she might have a talent for connecting with others. Her experience of recovery helped her understand and connect with the suffering of others. Her story of trauma recovery helps us understand more deeply the process of PTG.

Towards survivorship

Survivorship refers to a focus on long-term recovery and growth following discharge from the acute care setting. According to the American College of Surgeons, trauma survivorship encompasses four domains of care: (a) physical health and pain, (b) behavioral health, (c) cognitive health, and (d) caregiver support (Gore, 2025). PTG is an important component of survivorship; disposition recommendations and discharge planning should optimize PTG and survivorship. The inpatient treatment team can provide input to maximize opportunities for survivorship. Because PTG is a long-term goal, maximizing opportunities for PTG is a component of survivorship.

Historically, trauma has been viewed as an acute event, with the treatment goal of survival and acute recovery. The concept of survivorship recognizes the long-term issues facing the trauma survivor and the importance of longitudinal support (Herrera-Escobar & Schneider, 2022). Long-term issues include the prevention and treatment of PTSD, if it occurs, and the facilitation of PTG. Many trauma survivors, like Jamie, have a split life narrative. They describe their life in two parts: life before the trauma and life after the trauma. Jamie certainly describes her life in that way. Trauma changes us forever, but recovery can surprise us, fill us with wonder, and take our lives on a path we never expected.

Chapter summary

Trauma survivors sometimes experience personal growth and integration after trauma. PTG is a spontaneous part of the healing process, but it is important for the treatment team to understand and recognize PTG and to facilitate it as much as possible with empathic care that recognizes and accepts the pain of trauma. The idea of PTG has a complex relationship with both cultural and spiritual issues. While PTG is spontaneous and often surprising, the opportunities for PTG should be facilitated as much as possible.

References

Antonovsky, A. (1979). Health, stress and coping. Jossey-Bass.

Campbell, J. (2008). *The hero with a thousand faces* (3rd ed.). New World Library.

Gore, A. (2025). Surgical palliative care: A surgeon's guideModule: Survivorship. In S. Siegel, A. Berlin, & A. Gore (Eds.). *Surgical palliative care: A surgeon's guide*. American College of Surgeons.

Herrera, J. P., Escobar, J. C., & Schneider (2022). From survival to survivorship—Framing traumatic injury as a chronic condition. *New England Journal of Medicine, 387*(7), 581–583. https://doi.org/10.1056/NEJMp2205162.

Infurna, F. J., Jayawickreme, E., Woods-Jaeger, B., & Zalta, A. K. (2024). Understanding adaptive responses to adversity: Introduction to the special issue on rethinking resilience and posttraumatic growth. *American Psychologist, 79*(8), 989–998. https://doi.org/10.1037/amp0001442.

Maercker, A., & Zoellner, T. (2004). The Janus face of self-perceived growth: Toward a two-component model of posttraumatic growth. *Psychological Inquiry, 15*(1), 41–48.

Purol, M. F., & Chopik, W. J. (2024). Do many hands make light work? The role of romantic partners and close relationships in posttraumatic growth. *American Psychologist, 79*(8), 1214–1226. https://doi.org/10.1037/amp0001331.

Schubert, C. F., Schmidt, U., & Rosner, R. (2016). Posttraumatic growth in populations with posttraumatic stress disorder—A systematic review on growth-related psychological constructs and biological variables. *Clinical Psychology and Psychotherapy, 23*(6), 469–486. https://doi.org/10.1002/cpp.1985.

Sweigart, J. (2018). *After sexual assault, I knew I'd never be the same*. The Washington Post.

Tedeschi, R. G., & Calhoun, L. G. (1996). The posttraumatic growth inventory: Measuring the positive legacy of trauma. *Journal of Traumatic Stress, 9*(3), 455–471. https://doi.org/10.1002/jts.2490090305.

Tedeschi, R. G., Park, C. L., & Calhoun, L. G. (1998). *Posttraumatic growth: Positive changes in the aftermath of crisis*. Lawrence Erlbaum Associates Publishers.

Wu, X., Kaminga, A. C., Dai, W., Deng, J., Wang, Z., Pan, X., & Liu, A. (2019). The prevalence of moderate-to-high posttraumatic growth: A systematic review and meta-analysis. *Journal of Affective Disorders, 243*, 408–415. https://doi.org/10.1016/j.jad.2018.09.023.

Chapter 19

Teaching the next generation of clinicians

Integrating Education: Morning Triage

During the morning triage discussion, Kim, a junior psychiatry resident, Jonas, a health psychology intern, and Matt, a senior staff psychiatrist who is supervising the team meet to review a new case.

Matt: Kim, can you and Jonas see that new trauma consult together? It sounds like the patient had recently experienced a pretty severe accident and is reporting some changes in mood and difficulties with sleep now that they have been extubated. Jonas just started his rotation with us, so I want him to watch you interview at first, Kim.

Kim: Ok, but I have a hard time with those cases. I never know what to say. I can never tell if they need medicine or not. It's always so sad.

Matt: Thanks so much for sharing that. I agree these cases can be challenging when there isn't one clear "right answer" on how to proceed. It's really important to self-reflect on our own experiences prior to seeing the patient, too, as they might influence how we go about the interview. Great job. What are your thoughts on how you might want to approach the assessment?

Kim: Well, we know that one of our primary goals is to assess the patient's adjustment following his accident, and the team specifically mentioned changes in mood and sleep. After introducing our services and consenting him for treatment, I think I would like to start by asking what his current understanding of his medical status is, and if he's noticed any changes in how he has been thinking or feeling.

Matt: Excellent idea! Take it one step at a time; you are on the right track. As you said, we know that the team is concerned about both changes in mood and sleep following his accident. I agree it's a good idea for you to start there after consenting the patient and building rapport. If sleep is a problem, Jonas can also show you some cognitive behavioral strategies for addressing insomnia. Remember you don't have to "fix" our patient after one visit; sometimes, the right thing to do is to be with them in their distress. You ok with that plan, Jonas?

Jonas: Sure, that sounds great.

Matt: Excellent, I'm looking forward to hearing how it goes. You are both going to do great!

The Psychology of Acute Trauma. DOI: https://doi.org/10.1016/B978-0-443-33212-8.00007-5

Teaching as an aspect of clinical work

Teaching is often an important part of running a Trauma and Acute Care Surgical Psychology (TACS Psych) service. TACS Psych services are often housed in tertiary academic centers, where teaching is part of the core institutional mission. Teaching facilitates learning, for both the educator and the student, and can be gratifying for both. Teaching junior clinicians in fast-paced medical settings can present special challenges. Due to the multidisciplinary nature of trauma care, oftentimes our TACS Psych team is tasked with educating a wide range of trainees from different professional backgrounds. Different trainees with different backgrounds will have unique needs when learning to work with trauma survivors.

Facing the existential aspects of care

Almost every area of medicine touches on issues of mortality, death, and dying, and sudden unexpected life change. Trauma work is slightly different because it involves an external event rather than an illness; the intrusion of an external event increases the poignancy and contingency of the traumatic event. The word contingency is meant in its philosophical sense, as something not necessary, that didn't have to happen. Health care providers sometimes have a conflicted relationship with painful issues related to death, dying, and sudden illness. On one hand, they are drawn to helping, comforting, and healing, but on the other hand, they can have rescue fantasies and struggle to face situations where human suffering is inescapable and must be endured. As discussed in Chapter 2 (The next day: beginning the process of recovery), this may cause one to experience a challenge to their belief in the just world, that good begets good, and that "bad things happen to bad people."

Teaching empathy

Because the experience of acute trauma powerfully raises issues of mortality and suffering, empathy is a critical skill to develop when working with trauma survivors. Empathy is often defined in contrast to sympathy; empathy is feeling with, whereas sympathy is feeling for (McWilliams, 2004). Empathy is a necessity in good clinical work; sympathy tends to interfere with good clinical work, it is akin to pity.

Empathy has cognitive, emotional, and behavioral components. Four types of empathy in therapy have been described (Buie, 1981). The first is conceptual empathy, based on the clinician's conceptual experiences of the case and their recollection of personal experiences of the type described by the patient. The second is self-experiential empathy, where the treatment itself stirs a spontaneous memory of a feeling in the clinician, independent of a conceptual understanding. The third is imaginative imitation empathy, where the clinician actively places themselves in the patient's situation in the imagination, and thus stirs empathetic feelings. The fourth is resonant empathy, where the clinician experiences the emotion the patient feels, spontaneously, as if by contagion. Unlike self-experiential empathy, which stirs a feeling or memory, resonant empathy is a direct experiencing of the patient's feeling (Buie, 1981).

Trainees and novice clinicians sometimes imagine that all empathy is of the resonant type, which is a highly intuitive experience that cannot easily be taught. Resonant empathy is uncommon. The most common type of empathy, conceptual empathy, is teachable, as is imaginative imitation empathy.

As educators, we have met trainees who have naturally and intuitively conveyed empathy and a sense of caring, and others who seemed to struggle with experiencing and conveying empathy. Medical and doctoral training is very competitive; the undergraduate grade point average of a student admitted to medical school is now 3.84. It tends to go up by 0.01 point every year. Doctoral psychology programs are just as, if not more competitive, than medical schools. Students who have focused on grades throughout their academic careers may not have had the kind of life experiences that foster the development of rich empathic skills. Grades and exam scores are easily measured; empathic skills are not. Training programs often include measures of extracurricular activities, such as volunteer work, into the admission process, but such experiences are easily contrived. Medical schools and psychology doctoral programs are full of soup kitchen volunteers.

Medical school, instead of increasing empathy, may actually reduce it, especially in the third year of medical school (Hojat et al., 2009). The third year of medical school is usually when clinical experiences begin; perhaps the intensity of these experiences and the new clinical workloads and responsibilities causes stress that reduces the self-reflection that is known to build empathy. Additionally, it is during this transition from learning medicine to practicing medicine that one is often confronted with the harsh realities of the world. In the United States, access to care is particularly complex, and just because a specific treatment or diagnostic test is available doesn't mean that it is equally available to all individuals regardless of their payor status. One might hope that clinical experience, when conducted thoughtfully and under mentorship well, could build empathy.

Specific techniques and strategies can build empathic skills (DasGupta & Charon, 2004; Taigman, 1996). These include the following, adapted for the acute care setting:

- Reflective practices: Self-reflection when interacting with acutely injured trauma survivors can increase self-awareness and empathy. Being aware of one's own feelings allows one to experience empathy for another.
- Active and reflective listening: Listening skills are teachable, including simple strategies like sitting down rather than standing when talking.

Sitting conveys an active, unhurried presence. Active listening in the acute care setting can involve the powerful human experience of being with someone in their pain and suffering, without the need to "fix" their distress. Reflective listening involves active attention to the patient's words coupled with mirroring for clarification and feedback. Reflective listening allows the clinician to demonstrate genuine interest in the patient's lived experience using the patient's own language. Mirroring provides the patient with the opportunity to correct the clinician if a reflection doesn't accurately characterize their experience.

- Self-compassion: We all make mistakes. To err is human, especially in emotionally challenging situations. Giving oneself permission not to be perfect allows awareness of flaws and mistakes and provides the clinician with the opportunity for honest self-reflection.
- Using mentoring: Role models are helpful, as is observing skilled clinicians interacting with patients. Trainees often wonder "What do I say?" when faced with navigating challenging clinical situations. Watching a skilled clinician conduct an interview with a trauma survivor can help model what to say and how to say it. Supervision in real time by observing a trainee performing a clinical interview can provide excellent opportunities for coaching, feedback, and modeling. Chapter 22 (Talking trauma: selected dialogs for challenging situations), presents a selection of clinical dialogs aimed at providing examples of how one may navigate commonly encountered challenging clinical conversations.
- Cultural education: Reading Shakespeare or Chaucer is a great way to build empathic skills. The competitive nature of health care education often makes it difficult for trainees to have a broad educational base and experience the depth and wisdom of our shared cultural tradition. Trauma and trauma recovery, as we will see in Chapter 23 (Trauma narratives: historical and literary examples), are common themes in literature, art, and music, so cultural education is especially important in trauma work. In addition to building a more well-rounded knowledge base, cultural education also increases relatability and opens up opportunities for the clinician to confidently discuss relatable media with their patients. This may serve the purpose of quickly building rapport and strengthening the therapeutic alliance.

The emotional pain and distress experienced by the trauma survivor during the acute phase of recovery can make empathy difficult. Kim's reluctance to see her acute trauma patient is common among trainees. Like all clinicians, trainees want to help, and sometimes feel that the trauma has already happened and "nothing can be done." That helpless feeling interferes with empathy and is a defense against the pain of authentic presence with the patient. Self-reflection, mentoring, and coaching can help avoid feelings of helplessness and maintain empathy.

Essential competencies

The National Collaborative on Trauma-Informed Health Care Education and Research (TIHCER) developed a validated set of trauma-informed care competencies for undergraduate medical education (Berman et al., 2023). Although these competencies are designed for medical school education and address trauma in general rather than acute trauma, they nonetheless are useful goals to incorporate into trauma-informed educational plans for trainees in a wide range of health care-related fields. Some competencies are knowledge-based and include the meaning of terms like trauma and resilience. Others are care-based and include principles like safety, respect, and autonomy. Interpersonal and communication skills are also care competencies, and include empathy, acceptance, and validation. Interprofessional collaboration is also a core competency, as is professional development, systems-based practice, and professionalism, including awareness of bias.

Specific issues related to trainees of different disciplines in the acute care setting

While it is important not to stereotype or typecast trainees, we have encounter similar themes and issues in different types of trainees, and it may be helpful to describe those typical issues.

Psychology practicum students, interns, and fellows

Training in most psychology graduate programs is focused almost exclusively on the provision of evidence based treatments in traditional outpatient settings. Evidence-based treatments are those that can be "manualized," operationalized, and tested in large cohorts via clinical trials. While these skills are critical to develop, they often leave the trainee unprepared for practice in fast-paced medical settings. Other interventions or ways of conceptualizing psychopathology and the experience of human suffering are often not prioritized. Additionally, few programs offer formal coursework or training experiences related to the conduct of clinical services, such as those provided by consultation liaison teams, which are common in acute care medical settings. As we have discussed, clinical work conducted in trauma centers, given the setting and acuity, does not lend itself to the kind of double-blind trials that are possible in other, more traditional ambulatory settings. Psychology trainees often approach acute trauma work gingerly because they lack clear operationalized interventions. Especially for trainees, manualized treatments can create an emotional distance; the focus for the trainee is often on being faithful to the manual, not on the human aspects of the intervention. It is important to educate the psychology trainee that practicing in the acute care setting is different than in clinic settings and the needs of the trauma survivor in the acute phase of recovery are unique. Interventions like process-based or existential therapies that the trainee may not be as comfortable and familiar with can sometimes be the optimal treatments. Similarly, in dealing with nightmares, they may be familiar with cognitive behavioral therapy for nightmares (CBT-N) but may have trouble modifying those concepts and applying them in an acute care setting. Also, many psychology trainees have never been exposed to some of the clinical syndromes that are common in medical settings, especially substance intoxication and withdrawal, delirium, functional neurological disorder, and the acute effects of traumatic brain injury. Many also have a limited understanding of anatomy, physiology, and the neurobiological underpinnings of behavior change in medical settings. Additionally, they often possess only a superficial understanding of psychopharmacological interventions, especially those used in inpatient medical settings.

Psychology trainees greatly benefit from multidisciplinary training experiences, including shadowing members of the surgical and psychiatric teams and attending educational offerings such as grand rounds, morbidity and mortality rounds, team case conferences, and bioethics committee meetings. Encouraging the early incorporation of biomedical knowledge, such as interpreting labs and imaging studies, is critical as trainees learn comprehensive case conceptualization skills.

Psychiatry residents

Psychiatric trainees often choose a psychiatric residency because they want to spend more time with patients and wish to experience meaningful interactions with them, but they sometimes become more oriented towards the provision of psychopharmacologic interventions as a result of their training and mentoring. Because of their medical training, they are inclined to focus on taking concrete action on behalf of their patients. While the psychology trainee might avoid the empathic pain of interacting with the trauma survivor by clinging to manualized treatments, the psychiatry resident may try to avoid that pain by clinging to their virtual prescription pad. Psychiatric residents tend to have little experience with psychotherapy, especially early in their training, and they welcome coaching and modeling related to psychotherapeutic interventions. Additionally, they may receive less training related to the understanding of the etiologic underpinnings of psychopathology and often benefit from discussions related to case conceptualization.

Senior psychiatry residents sometimes come to the TACS Psych service in a junior faculty role. These residents are near graduation and have a strong knowledge base, as well as substantial clinical experience, and are often well-suited to provide mentorship to more junior trainees.

Surgical residents and fellows

Surgery residents and fellows sometimes choose to spend time shadowing the TACS Psych team. They are often seeking to improve their bedside manner and interpersonal skills, while refining their understanding of the psychopathology that often afflicts their patients. They tend to initially feel "out of place" on the TACS Psych team but welcome the chance to learn about and observe psychological interventions. Often their presence invites shared learning opportunities; the psychology team trainees gain a deeper understanding of surgical interventions and the patient's surgical pathology, while the surgical resident gains comfort with psychological interventions and psychodiagnostics. Such experiences tend to create mutual understanding and respect, truly embodying the spirit of the multidisciplinary work that is core to this subspecialty. In addition to clinical training, surgical trainees often benefit greatly from mentorship related to the design and conduct of high-quality research.

Medical students

Medical students sometimes spend time on the TACS Psych service as part of their required psychiatry clerkship or as an elective rotation. We have created a special elective TACS Psych clerkship rotation, which medical students may apply for while completing their surgery clerkship. Medical students vary greatly in the level of interest they have in psychological interventions. Some enter medical school bringing with them significant clinical experience from other disciplines, and some have never been in a hospital before starting medical school. Often, they tend to struggle with their role and identity; they want to try out the role of "doctor" and actively participate in care, but they also feel unskilled, especially on rotations that include a significant mental health care component. Because of this heterogeneity of backgrounds, collaborative goal setting at the onset of the rotation is critical. Many may want to be observers, which offers the opportunity for staff to model trauma-informed interviewing approaches. Others may want to have a more active clinical role and can benefit from direct observation and mentoring. When possible, clinical duties can be assigned according to comfort level.

Medical students, like many trainees, tend to be thorough to a fault. Typically, they are criticized in other medical rotations for not having gathered adequate information, so they tend to try to gather complete information even when it is unnecessary or when it interferes with developing the therapeutic alliance with the patient. They tend to focus on details rather than the big picture. Most are eager to learn, but a few are dismissive of psychological interventions. Education, exposure to high-quality clinical interactions, and experience are the best approaches to inspire the dismissive student. Sometimes the dismissive attitude is a defense against helplessness or other negative emotions. Awareness of one's own feelings about clinical work can be an important goal of the clerkship student, and facing negative feelings can be an important learning opportunity.

Social work trainees

In addition to clinical training programs, training experiences for allied support staff are critical to develop as well. Social work interns can greatly benefit from training as part of a TACS Psych team. Social determinants of health impact the experience of trauma and increase risk for further exposure to future traumatic events, and social work trainees tend to be very attuned to such issues. Integrating social work trainees facilitates the development of skills related to navigating the complex social systems in which our patients live. Social work training is often more pragmatic than psychology or medical training, with less of a focus on diagnosing psychological disorders and manualized treatments. They are more comfortable navigating the world of limited resources and can accept the incomplete information and uncertainty that limit clinical decision-making for psychologists and psychiatrists. They appreciate exploring intrapsychic issues and can help other trainees become aware of the contingencies of real-world access to resources.

Learning to work in multidisciplinary teams

One important aspect of the psychological care of the trauma survivor is the involvement of a multidisciplinary team. Interprofessional collaboration is, as we have seen, one of the TIHCER core competencies. Psychiatry, TACS Psych, social work, and acute care surgery must collaborate closely to effectively manage these complex patients. Such team collaboration is an important teaching opportunity. In some settings, psychiatry and psychology teams work competitively rather than collaboratively, but psychology, psychiatry, and social work trainees can learn a great deal from each other since they tend to have different interactive styles and often employ different kinds of interventions. Psychology and social work trainees can learn basic psychopharmacology from the psychiatry residents, while psychiatry residents can learn important skills like mindfulness training and relaxation techniques from the psychology trainees and basic case management skills from the social work trainees. As demonstrated by Vygotsky in the 1970s, mixing learners of different skill sets and levels of experience can be beneficial for all (Vygotsky, 1978). Mutual learning opportunities can facilitate respect and a deeper understanding of the skill sets of the other mental health disciplines and prepare future health care leaders who truly value the importance of multi-disciplinary teamwork.

Incorporating evidence-based educational approaches

Additionally, utilizing evidence-based educational strategies can enhance the efficacy of clinical teaching while simultaneously improving patient care. Teaching in academic medical centers oftentimes focuses on the identification of deficits, with corrective criticism or feedback being provided as the primary mechanism for change. While this tradition is longstanding, emphasizing evidence-based approaches rooted in learning theory may enhance clinical teaching and the sense of psychological safety felt by our trainees. As is shown in the case example dialog in this chapter, intentionally reinforcing the trainee when target behaviors are exhibited (in this case, an accurate understanding of the consult request and self-reflection) enhances the likelihood of those behaviors occurring again in the future. Should corrective feedback be required, it is recommended that it be provided in a manner that contains validation of the trainee's effort while correcting behavior or providing education in a nonpunitive or critical fashion. Additionally, asking learners about their preferred methods for delivery of feedback may increase psychological safety in the learning environment, leading to greater trust in the supervisor when discussing clinical errors or near misses. Utilizing the Socratic method and scaffolding approaches based on Vygotsky's (1978) concept of the zone of proximal development, where the educator supports the learner as they navigate from being unable to complete a task at all to becoming functionally independent, empowers trainees while creating lasting and deeply integrated learning experiences.

Cultural education: training the well-rounded clinician

Obviously, decades of cultural neglect cannot be undone by a brief clinical rotation, but it can be helpful to include a brief taste of trauma-related literature, art, or music to deepen the understanding of the human response to trauma with the goal of increasing empathy. To illustrate this and provide a foundation for discussion with peers and trainees, a number of brief stories from trauma survivors, both from history and from mythology, are included in Chapter 23 (Trauma narratives: historical and literary). Such cultural material deepens our understanding of the human experience of trauma and helps the trainee realize that the experience of trauma is not a singular event outside of normal human experience, but part of the rich tapestry of human culture through all of history. The trainee comes to realize that the trauma survivor is not alone and that caring for the trauma survivor can reintegrate them into the human family. Literary works like I Know Why the Caged Bird Sings by Maya Angelou (Angelou, 1969), "Bullet in the Brain"by Tobias Wolff (Wolff, 1995), or any of the short works of Kafka and Dostoevsky can provide rich insights into the internal experience of trauma and can become a springboard for discussion with interested trainees. "The Lottery in Babylon" by Jorge Luis

Borges is a beautiful depiction of the randomness of life, which is an important issue that trauma survivors often struggle with (Borges, 1962). The poem "Musée des Beaux Arts" by W. H. Auden (1979) portrays beautifully the indifference and isolation that the person affected by trauma can feel. The poem is ekphrastic, meaning that it describes a painting. In this case, the painting is Pieter Bruegel the Elder's (c. 1560) Landscape with the fall of Icarus (Fig. 19.1).

Icarus is the mythological character who tragically crashes into the sea and dies when he flies too high on wings made of wax and feathers, leading them to melt as he draws closer to the Sun. The painting is shown in Fig. 19.1, an excerpt from the poem follows:

"Musée des Beaux Arts" by W. H. Auden
About suffering they were never wrong,
The Old Masters: how well they understood
Its human position;...
In Brueghel's Icarus, for instance: how everything turns away
Quite leisurely from the disaster; the ploughman may
Have heard the splash, the forsaken cry,
But for him it was not an important failure; the sun shone
As it had to on the white legs disappearing into the green
Water; and the expensive delicate ship that must have seen
Something amazing, a boy falling out of the sky,
Had somewhere to get to and sailed calmly on. (Auden, 1979)

FIGURE 19.1 Landscape with the fall of Icarus by Pieter Bruegel the Elder c. 1560. Oil on canvas. From the Old Masters Museum, Royal Museums of Fine Arts of Belgium.

The painting and poem convey a depth of wisdom and understanding of the experience of trauma that hours of didactic lectures could never convey. Such tools can enrich the trainee's experience without taking too much time from clinical duties. Cultural education enhances self-reflection and deepens understanding of the internal experience of trauma.

Integrating Education: End-of-Day Staffing

As the day progressed, the team reconvened to discuss the outcome of their new consult.

Matt: So how did it go?

Kim: It wasn't as bad as I thought. We had a good conversation with our patient. It felt better for me to listen instead of trying to make his sadness go away. He talked a lot about how unfair his accident was; he's got no money, very little family, and he won't be able to work for a long time. Overall, it seemed like his emotional changes fell within normal limits, as there wasn't any functional impairment. I know you always say we don't want to pathologize normal human responses to trauma, so I think that's what we are seeing here. He also said that he normally copes with stress by reading, and that his favorite book is The Great Gatsby. Interestingly, he described that he identifies with the main character, especially since he never gives up on his dream, but that he was having a hard time concentrating when trying to read after his accident.

Matt: Great work, it sounds like he really felt comfortable discussing his experience with you! I agree with your conceptualization of his distress, too. We should definitely keep an eye on it during this admission, though. What do you make of his description of his joy for reading, especially since he referenced a specific book?

Kim: I agree, we will follow him closely to monitor his mood as he moves through this admission. I was glad to hear he did have an identified activity to use for behavioral activation, and I was also a bit concerned when he shared his new changes in concentration. To be honest, I was also a little embarrassed, too, as even though I know that's a classic work, I haven't read that book. I used to like reading too, but it's something I haven't done since I started medical school due to all of our required readings. Jonas and I were discussing it more on the walk back. I really wish we knew a bit more about the book when he shared that, so we could have had a richer conversation with him about his connection to the character. I really think that could have strengthened the therapeutic alliance.

Matt: I really appreciate your self-reflection, as well as your desire to find ways to connect deeply with your patients. Having a wide breadth of knowledge, including that of the arts and humanities, helps us to better appreciate the human condition and to connect with those we work with, whether they be our patients or peers. Unfortunately, that's often lost once we progress in our training. I would encourage you to try reconnecting with that interest while also seeing how it augments your efficacy as a clinician. Before we wrap up and head to see him on rounds, how was his sleep?

(Continued)

Kim: Not good. He has a history of bipolar disorder, and has done well in the past on olanzapine, though he's been off it for months. I wanted to put him back on it.

Matt: I think that makes sense, though we don't want to rely just on medications alone. Were you and Jonas able to help with behavioral interventions for sleep?

Kim: Jonas was a big help. He taught the patient some mindfulness meditation skills, including relaxation training and guided imagery. The patient is going to trial them before bed tonight and will track his response to the intervention.

Matt: Thanks, Jonas. Excellent work all around.

Jonas: I learned a lot too, Kim was really helpful when I had some questions about the patient's medications. The patient did mention some nightmares, but I wasn't sure what to do with that.

Matt: That's a great question. Have you heard about any nightmare treatments in outpatient settings before?

Jonas: A little. I know dream rescripting can be helpful, but I'm not sure how to adapt it to an inpatient setting where the patient is still in the hospital.

Matt: You're correct, and adapting interventions can definitely be tough at first. I'd be happy to demonstrate how to deliver the treatment when we visit the patient later today on rounds.

Building a teaching service

TACS Psych faculty will have the responsibility for promoting and building a teaching program. Relationship building is crucial, especially with the existing teaching programs in various disciplines. Teaching will involve extra effort by faculty in terms of developing goals and objectives and scheduling supervision sessions while prioritizing clinical teaching. Some of these time investments will be offset by the assistance with clinical services that trainees can provide. Psychology and psychiatry trainees can see patients under supervision and can assist with note writing and other documentation. Elective rotations can be a good first step in building a teaching service.

Integrating education: a review of the vignette

As seen in the interaction between Matt, Kim, and Jonas, the process of providing high-quality education may be both subtle and direct. After reviewing the initial consultation question, Matt sees an opportunity for a multidisciplinary learningess of providin experience. Specifically, in this scenario where the patient has multiple levels of need, both Kim and Jonas have a chance to provide each other with peer-level support as they conduct the evaluation, each drawing upon their own strengths to complete the consult. Additionally, Matt enhances the psychological safety of the learning experience by validating Kim's initial concern related to her ability to satisfactorily complete the consult, as well as reinforcing her self-reflection. As they are preparing for the consult, Matt also prompts Kim with an open-ended question to provide her with the opportunity to develop her own plan to approach the evaluation, while also following up with a more specific suggestion related to the patient's reported sleep disturbance. While her response was not technically comprehensive, Matt understands that to be an effective educator, one must create an environment where the learner feels comfortable asking questions. Providing a corrective response with a tone echoing that of criticism may distance the learner and decrease the likelihood that they will both integrate the educator's feedback and feel comfortable answering or asking questions in the future.

Following the consultation, Matt continues with his supportive interactional style, allowing Kim to freely describe the encounter. Again, we see him reinforcing her introspection and vulnerability as she honestly describes reflections on her experience during the consult, while finding an opportunity to provide more direct education about the importance of integrating education related to the arts and humanities into her training. Finally, he provides Jonas with equal attention and an opportunity to discuss his experience observing the consult. Matt closes by extending an offer for the trainees to observe him providing direct clinical care to the patient so that they may learn more about adapting evidence-based treatments into evidence-supported interventions.

Chapter summary

Both faculty and students learn from the experience of teaching. The TACS Psych service can offer great opportunities to explore the empathic and existential aspects of care. Different kinds of trainees have different needs and skill sets, which impact their experience on the TACS Psych service. The TACS Psych service provides a great opportunity to develop empathy and self-reflection, and integrating evidence-based educational approaches into a multidisciplinary learning environment often leads to optimal outcomes.

References

Angelou, M. (1969). *I know why the caged bird sings*. Random House.

Auden, W. H. (1979). In E. Mendelson (Ed.). *Selected poems*. Vintage Books.

Borges, J. L. (1962). The lottery in Babylon. In D. A. Yates, & J. E. Irby (Eds.). Labyrinths: Selected stories & other writingsNew Directions .

Berman, S., Brown, T., Mizelle, C., Diep, T., Gerber, M. R., Jelley, M., Potter, L. A., Rush, P., Sciolla, A., Stillerman, A., Trennepohl, C., Weil, A., & Potter, J. (2023). Roadmap for trauma-informed medical education: Introducing an essential competency set. *Academic Medicine, 98*(8), 882–888. https://doi.org/10.1097/ACM.0000000000005196.

Buie, D. H. (1981). Empathy: Its nature and limitations. *Journal of the American Psychoanalytic Association, 29*(2), 281–307. https://doi.org/10.1177/000306518102900201.

DasGupta, S., & Charon, R. (2004). Personal illness narratives: Using reflective writing to teach empathy. *Academic Medicine, 79*(4), 351–356. https://doi.org/10.1097/00001888-200404000-00013.

Hojat, M., Vergare, M. J., Maxwell, K., Brainard, G., Herrine, S. K., Isenberg, G. A., Veloski, J., & Gonnella, J. S. (2009). The devil is in the third year: A longitudinal study of erosion of empathy in medical school. *Academic Medicine, 84*(9), 1182–1191. https://doi.org/10.1097/ACM.0b013e3181b17e55.

McWilliams, N. (2004). *Psychoanalytic psychotherapy: A practitioner's guide*. The Guilford Press.

Taigman, M. (1996). Can empathy and compassion be taught? *JEMS: A Journal of Emergency Medical Services, 21*(6).

Vygotsky, L. S. (1978). Mind in society: The development of higher psychological processes. In M. Cole, V. John-Steiner, S. Scribner, & E. Souberman (Eds.). Harvard University Press.

Wolff, T. (1995). Bullet in the brain. *The New Yorker, 71*(29).

Chapter 20

Building an effective trauma and acute care surgical psychology program

Developing the program

Our trauma psychology program began in 2012 with the dream of establishing an integrated mental health team to provide high-quality preventive psychological care for patients admitted to the Trauma and Acute Care Surgery (TACS) service. The goal was to identify individuals who had recently sustained a high-risk traumatic injury and provide them with evidence supported psychological intervention. The program began as a grant-funded training initiative aimed at showing efficacy and feasibility of implementation. In 2017, I was recruited to be the first dedicated clinical health psychologist for the team and was tasked with running the Trauma and Acute Care Surgical Psychology (TACS Psych) services. My goals were not only to carry on the tradition of high-quality preventive care but to further develop screening protocols and the service line. I wanted our team to provide truly comprehensive trauma-informed psychosocial recovery services. In 2024, our team implemented a new screening protocol and expanded it to include two licensed master's level social workers, an additional clinical health psychologist and a clinical research psychologist. We currently have the capability to provide mental health risk screening to nearly all admitted trauma patients, touching thousands of lives yearly. Throughout this chapter, I will utilize examples from our own program development experiences to illustrate how to navigate your own program development process.

A new standard for trauma care

As mentioned in Chapter 2, The Next Day: Beginning the Process of Recovery, new standards for psychologically centered trauma care have been mandated by the American College of Surgeons (ACS). The seventh edition of the Resources for Optimal Care of the Injured Patient 2022 Standards, Revised July 2025, contains new recommendations and requirements focused on the incorporation of mental health screening and referral

The Psychology of Acute Trauma. DOI: https://doi.org/10.1016/B978-0-443-33212-8.00011-7

processes (American College of Surgeons 2025). Throughout this chapter, you will see variations of the word “verified” (e.g., reverified, verification, reverification, etc.), which is a term used by the ACS to describe programs that have met the standards to be classified as a Level I, II, or III trauma center. In essence, it is a term that is analogous to accreditation in other fields.

An additional verification requirement that also supports the development of a TACS Psych program includes the alcohol misuse and intervention requirement, which mandates the development and implementation of a Screening, Brief Intervention and Referral to Treatment (SBIRT) protocol (ACS, 2025). In this chapter, I will discuss the key elements related to program development and sustainability so that a program may not only meet reverification requirements but also become an effective service line that addresses the unique needs of both the trauma center and the communities alike. While this chapter is written from the perspective of a clinical health psychologist and psychiatrist, it is designed for use by other mental health specialists, physicians, and hospital administrators as well.

Identifying key stakeholders

The successful development of TACS Psych services is a team initiative, and prior to beginning to plan the overall program structure and the clinical services offered, key stakeholders must first be identified. Implementing programs within the context of a trauma center requires an understanding of the organizational structure within the hospital where it is to be implemented, as well as the other departments and divisions that may be involved in this area of practice.

As a mental health specialist, it is important to identify an ally within the surgical team, whether that be a surgeon, administrator, or other team member who is passionate about integrating psychosocial recovery services. Both trauma medical directors and trauma program managers are directly responsible for developing and implementing trauma quality improvement program initiatives, as well as ensuring that their trauma center meets all the ACS verification requirements. Additional leadership members within the surgical team that oftentimes have an interest in the development and implementation of TACS Psych teams include division heads and department chairs. Without invested key stakeholders from within the trauma team, it will be difficult to successfully implement a TACS Psych program. In addition to the champion from within the surgical team, it is also important to identify key allies within hospital administration to ensure seamless integration into the hospital structure and to assist with the development of a business plan. This may include directors of surgical service lines, members from nursing leadership teams, and hospital leadership teams.

For members of the surgical team or administrators who are looking to implement TACS Psych programs, the list of key stakeholders above also applies, although the additional identification of key stakeholders who are experts in mental health service delivery is required. First, explore the service line organizational structures of any available behavioral health programs. Common programs include consultation liaison psychiatry and psychology programs, behavioral medicine programs, as well as outpatient behavioral health service lines that provide clinical care to trauma survivors. If no trauma psychology experts exist within your system, consultation with external experts will be invaluable not only for developing a strong program structure but also for assisting with developing job descriptions and screening applicants so that you may recruit high-quality candidates to staff your program.

Needs assessment

Once key stakeholders are identified, the needs assessment phase of program development can begin. Conducting a needs assessment is critical to understanding the unique gaps that your service can fill. Needs assessments should include a wide range of input from all of your identified key stakeholders. Your stakeholders may guide you to individual team members with specialized expertise or experience who may further illuminate the needs to be serviced.

It is advantageous to collect both qualitative and quantitative data in multiple ways, starting with individual discussions with your key stakeholders and broadening out to include potential formats such as focus groups. Team members who can help assess needs should include individuals providing bedside patient care. Connecting with a wide range of team members, including nursing assistants, registered nurses, unit educators, advanced practice providers, resident physicians, residency/fellowship program directors, and unit medical directors, will provide invaluable information related to the areas that you may directly need to address with your program. In addition to developing plans to meet reverification requirements, it is important to identify other high-priority areas of need, such as the provision of specific types of clinical services (e.g., decision making capacity assessments and psychopharmacological evaluations), specific high need subgroups (e.g., patients over the age of 65 who have fallen), the development of research and program evaluation infrastructures, as well as educational needs for any teams or trainees you will be interacting with. Needs assessments can be ongoing and integrated into program evaluation processes and should be updated to include or remove any services that are no longer required or have become obsolete.

Conducting individual interviews or focus groups with community members who have received care at the institution can be beneficial. As our services are ultimately designed to improve the well-being of our community members, it is important to integrate them into the needs assessment process if possible. Community members may provide unique perspectives related to the experiences of individuals receiving care, as well as the unique barriers that they may face as they navigate hospital stays and postdischarge reintegration into the community itself.

Important objective data include estimated clinical volumes, average lengths of stay, and the distribution of mechanisms of injury leading to admission. Identification of this information early in the process will guide decision-making related to planning the program structure and what levels of staff are required (e.g., clinical psychologist, psychiatrist, licensed social worker) and how many positions will be necessary to meet the demands of the department. After conducting your needs assessment, developing an action plan will help guide your process of program development. The ACS Best Practices Guidelines Screening and Intervention for Mental Health Disorders and Substance Use and Misuse in the Acute Trauma Patient provides sample action plans that may be used when developing TACS Psych services (American College of Surgeons, 2022).

Conducting our needs assessment

As our program was developed before the publication of the ACS (2025) verification requirements, the needs assessment focused solely on identifying high-priority gaps that existed in the psychosocial recovery services available to patients treated by the TACS teams. A hospital-wide psychiatry consultation liaison service existed, although no trauma-oriented specialty mental health services were available to trauma patients. The available clinical services focused on providing reactive interventions related to patients currently experiencing distress, rather than preventive interventions aimed at mitigating the risk of developing distress in the future.

As suggested by the literature, individuals with high-risk mechanisms of injury, such as gunshot wounds, assaults, and high-speed motor vehicle crashes, experienced elevated levels of psychological distress compared to individuals with lower-risk mechanisms. We chose that high-risk population to initially offer preventive psychological services to. Additionally, data related to overall trauma center volume indicated that approximately 50% of patients admitted to the TACS teams were individuals who were over the age of 65 who had experienced a mechanical fall. This provided a unique opportunity to develop a highly sustainable specialty service line that was able to be integrated into the system's "senior fall initiative," which allowed for the provision of high-yield specialty evaluations assessing for potential cognitive impairment that may limit an individual's ability to safely return to independent living following discharge.

Since joining the team in 2017, I have assessed the needs of our teams every 6 months, discussing potential areas of growth as well as underutilized service line items. Through this process, as well as conducting a community member focus group, we were able to work as a team to identify significant needs related to ongoing case management for psychosocial recovery services, as well as increased overall consult volume. The identification of these needs led to the creation of three new positions and the expansion of service line offerings, including screening for social determinants of health and ongoing case management services

(Continued)

that may be utilized following discharge. Additionally, academic output and education were identified as high-priority needs for the TACS team, which led to the integration of a clinical research psychologist and the expansion of our research infrastructure. Research productivity also assists with meeting the academic productivity requirements related to ACS reverification.

Different consultation models

After the needs assessment, the next step is choosing the type of consultation model. The two general consultation-liaison models are (a) the integrated consultant who is directly embedded within the TACS team, and (b) the external consultant practicing from an on-call model. Each model has unique advantages and disadvantages, and the selection of a model will depend on the needs of your program as well as financial factors.

Integrated consultants are directly embedded within the surgical team and function as a consistent element of the care team. This destigmatizes the provision of psychological services to trauma patients. For both the patient and the treatment team, psychological services become part of the holistic recovery of the patient. The integrated model also facilitates a high level of communication within the team and the ability to develop streamlined pathways for screening and referrals. Integrated consultants can have an important liaison role and can liaise with the surgical teams and attend case conferences and program development meetings. This liaison component may further enhance the integration of psychological services. The team learns how to use psychology services, and the psychology consultation service learns the needs of the primary surgical service. Furthermore, as integrated consultants, the TACS Psych service is more fully dedicated to the Department of Surgery, so they will not be as readily called away for the provision of other kinds of psychological services outside of the department. One challenge of integrated consultants is the financial aspect of staffing the TACS Psych service, as these positions often must be fully or partially funded by the trauma center or the Department of Surgery. The revenue associated with psychology services may not fully offset their cost, but such services offer benefits in terms of clinical care, patient satisfaction, reduced lengths of stay, increased efficiency of surgical providers, and the fulfillment of clinical guidelines and requirements.

External consultants fall into two main categories: those who are hospital-based within the health system and those who are community-based and provide consultation via a private practice or consulting agency. One major benefit of external consultants is that they are often more cost-effective than their integrated counterparts. Hospital-based consultants can sometimes be supported through their home department or the hospital as a whole, which may require them to provide consultation services to all hospital-based specialties. Community-based consultants may also prove more cost-effective as services may be directly billed through the patient's insurance or paid for by the department on a per-consult basis. External consultant options have some limitations, including a lack of immediate availability should an urgent need for services arise. External consultants are typically generalists in hospital psychiatry and psychology. They often do not have the same level of understanding of service needs as their integrated counterparts, and usually do not provide liaison services. External consultants are sometimes less inclined to provide follow-up care after the initial consultation, as the reimbursement for the initial consultation is much better than the reimbursement for follow-up services. External consultant models are good options to show clinical utility and feasibility of implementation of TACS Psych services, which may then lead to funding internal positions.

The Evolution of our Consultation-Liaison Model

In 2012, our program was initially implemented by an external clinical psychologist consultant Jennifer Peltzer-Jones, PsyD, RN who primarily provided services for the Department of Emergency Medicine after being awarded a training grant that allowed for expansion of services for the TACS team. After showing feasibility and data related to both the preventive aspects of early intervention and sustainability, the full-time integrated consultant position was funded in 2017. Currently, our team is fully integrated and provides dedicated clinical services, education, and research support to all specialties, providing care under the umbrella of our Level I trauma center.

Planning the program

After gathering stakeholders, conducting a needs assessment, and choosing a consultation model, the next step is planning the specifics of the program implementation process. Planning your program first requires consideration of staffing structures. Determining the reporting structure for each of the different team roles and creating an understandable organizational chart is essential to program success. Roles should be clearly defined, and expectations related to each role's job duties should be documented in concise job descriptions and conveyed during the interview and hiring processes. Reporting hierarchies and structures should provide clear guidance to team members regarding who they directly report to and how to obtain supervisory support should it be needed. In addition to developing the organizational structure, the core elements of care that your team members will be able to provide must be defined. This includes developing screening protocols and deciding upon referral pathways and documentation processes to ensure consultation requests are completed in a timely fashion. Additionally, this stage will allow the development of protocols that align with trauma center verification requirements for both mental health screening and SBIRT interventions, which allow for some flexibility regarding structure (ACS, 2025).

While trauma centers have some leeway related to the development and implementation of these screening protocols, the guidelines must be met. It is strongly recommended that these approaches integrate objective screening measures aimed at identifying psychological risk into the screening process. The ACS (2022) Best Practices Guidelines Screening and Intervention for Mental Health Disorders and Substance Use and Misuse in the Acute Trauma Patient provides some recommendations related to commonly used screening approaches and tools for both mental health risk screening and SBIRT screening and intervention. At their core, screening protocols should be able to differentiate patients with a high level of sensitivity, aiming to identify those who may benefit from preventive psychological intervention. While a major focus of this section is on meeting the verification standards, it is important to note that additional specialty services that provide care to acute trauma patients should also have discrete consult triggers included in the screening process. For instance, senior fall evaluations may have a consult trigger that includes a psychological evaluation for all patients over the age of 65 whose mechanism of injury is a mechanical fall.

After you decide upon a screening approach, you must then determine your referral pathway. Referral pathways are determined based on the organizational structure and preferences for communication between teams. In the era of electronic medical records, a vast majority of referral pathways include placing a consult order directly through the medical record. Some programs prefer communication of consults through secure messaging systems, paging systems, or even direct phone calls. One significant benefit of integrating consult orders directly into medical record systems includes the ease of data collection, which may then be used for reverification reviews and program evaluation purposes. Developing referral pathways also includes designating specific team members who will both place consult requests and monitor service communications so that TACS Psych consults may be seen in a timely fashion. All consults should typically be completed within 24 hours. It is critical that the program plan is feasible in relation to implementation and that expected workloads align with the staffing model. A visual representation of service pathways and decision points may assist with optimizing the flow of care and eliminating the potential for the provision of duplicite services. See Fig. 20.1 for our TACS Psych service consultation decision tree.

In addition to planning the service-related structure of your program, it is also important to consider tangible factors related to program development, such as physical space in the practice environment. It is strongly encouraged that internally based teams colocate their surgical and psychological staff in administrative areas with close physical proximity. Colocation enables high-quality collaboration and the potential to strengthen the integration of psychological services into the surgical teams. With an external consultation

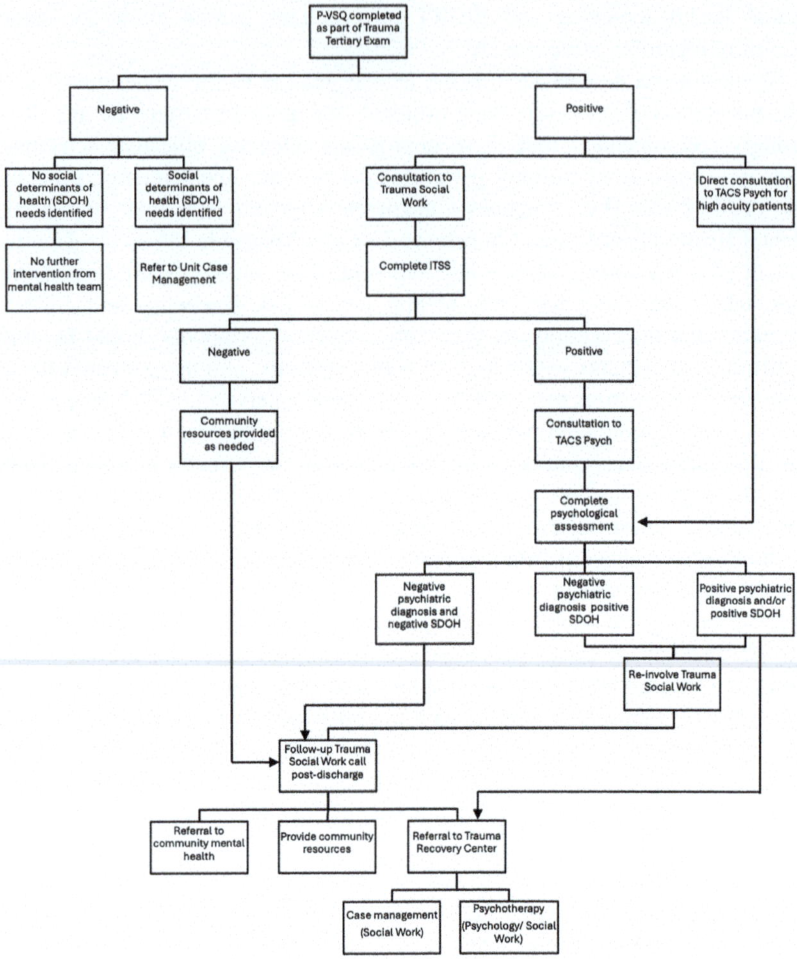

FIGURE 20.1 **Trauma and acute care surgical psychology (TACS Psych) service consultation decision tree.** A visual representation of service pathways and decision points in the authors' TACS Psych program.

Reprinted with permission from Taormina, S. P., Jankowiak, L., Vinyard, A., O'Sullivan, A., Reffi, A., & Moore, D. A. (2025, November). The evolution of a multidisciplinary team: Mental health continuum of care from admission to postdischarge follow-up [Poster presentation]. American College of Surgeons Trauma Quality Improvement Program Annual Conference, Chicago, IL.

model, identifying a dedicated workspace that the consultant can use and that is easily accessible to surgical team members providing care on surgical floors and units is strongly advised. Physical visibility will increase the likelihood of "curbside consults," leading to more effective integration and the potential for bidirectional learning between teams.

Our screening model

Based on our clinical experiences, we have created a new three-tier screening model with referral decision points at each tier to ensure that patients gain access to the most appropriate levels of service. Our team believes that it is everyone's responsibility to provide psychologically minded care. The first tier of the screening process begins with the surgical team during the trauma tertiary survey. Because it is important to identify patients at risk for developing distress in the future, not just those experiencing distress in the moment, we developed a novel approach to risk factor–based screening that may be quickly and easily completed by the surgical resident or advanced practice provider shortly following admission (Moore et al., 2025). This tool, the Psychological Vulnerability Screening Questionnaire (P-VSQ; see Fig. 20.2), is directly integrated into the trauma tertiary survey. If the patient screens positive, they are then referred to tier two, our trauma social work team, for a psychosocial needs assessment. The P-VSQ may be freely used for noncommercial purposes.

As part of the social work team's psychosocial needs assessment, the patient's social determinants of health are assessed, as well as and any barriers that they may be facing related to accessing resources in the community. Additionally, to assist with appropriately identifying the level of risk for the development of specific psychological disorders such as posttraumatic stress disorder or major depressive disorder, the social workers complete the Injured Trauma Survivor Screen (ITSS) (Hunt et al., 2017) as part of their psychosocial needs assessment. Should the patient score positive on the ITSS, a referral to tier three for a full psychological assessment via the integrated clinical health psychologist covering the TACS Psych service is made. Additionally, all patients are contacted by the trauma social work team via phone at 2 and 4 weeks postdischarge to identify ongoing recovery needs as well as to screen for the development of psychological distress following

Psychological Vulnerability Screening Questionnaire (P-VSQ)

Ask the patient each of these questions during the trauma tertiary survey or complete via chart review/observation if the patient is unable to fully participate	No = 0	Yes = 1
1. Would the patient like to speak to a mental health specialist?	0	1
2. Did the injury include any of the following: Gunshot wound, assaultive violence, motor vehicle accident, amputation, spinal cord injury, sexual violence?	0	1
3. Is significant distress present (e.g., tearfulness, nightmares, angry outbursts, decreased participation in care, social withdrawal), self-reported or observed?	0	1
4. Has there been any prior exposure to trauma (e.g., Assault, sexual or physical abuse, seeing community violence), including in childhood?	0	1
5. Is there a prior history of mental health concerns?	0	1
6. Is there a lack of social or family support, self-reported or observed?	0	1
Sum (max of 6) =		

****If sum ≥ 2 or item 1 = yes, and patient is being admitted to the hospital, patient requires a referral to a mental health provider****

FIGURE 20.2 Psychological vulnerability screening questionnaire (P-VSQ).
Reprinted with permission from Moore, D. A., Reffi, A. N., Jankowiak, L., Mahr, G., Drake, C. L. & Johnson, J. (2025). Predicting mental health referrals following acute trauma: Preliminary evidence for a novel risk factor based screening tool (Paper Presentation). 41st Annual Meeting of the International Society for Traumatic Stress Studies, Baltimore, MD.

(Continued)

discharge, so that referrals to outpatient behavioral health providers may be provided. Patients may continue engaging the trauma social work team for trauma recovery-related case management assistance for as long as it is helpful, with no set end date.

We have also included some override criteria to appropriately escalate individuals directly to tier three for a full psychological evaluation if needed. These criteria include suicide attempt as a mechanism of injury, active suicidal or homicidal ideation, concern for mania or psychosis, new cognitive impairment, or the presence of significant psychological distress. Additionally, some consult requests, such as decision-making capacity assessments, are automatically escalated for full psychological evaluation. In these scenarios, the trauma social work team may complete the psychosocial needs assessment once the patient is stabilized and the level of risk has been reduced. Finally, during either the psychological evaluation or psychosocial needs assessment, if the need for psychopharmacologic intervention arises, we directly consult with our consultation liaison psychiatry and addiction medicine teams.

Pathways for funding

It is difficult to sustain a properly staffed TACS Psych service using only revenue from clinical services. Trauma patients are often uninsured or underinsured, and psychological services are time-intensive and poorly reimbursed. Cost offsets like reduced length of stay, better surgical outcomes, and improved patient satisfaction can be difficult to measure and quantify. Pathways for funding should be strategically developed to ensure the ability to support ongoing program development and maintenance of established specialty services. Funding streams may change due to sociopolitical factors or internal leadership transitions within the organization. Diversifying funding streams that support the service line will ensure, as much as possible, the financial stability of the service. There are three main approaches to supporting service lines from a financial perspective: (a) internal funding, (b) external funding and (c) hybrid funding.

When initially developing programs, external grant funding is helpful as it reduces the risk assumed by the organization when developing a novel service. Grant funding may come through typical pathways at the federal level, such as the National Institutes of Health, National Institute of Mental Health, or the Health Resources and Services Administration, the state or city level, or via private foundations. Creative utilization of grant funds may allow for the expansion of already existing services into your area of practice via pilot programs to demonstrate feasibility. Additional external funding opportunities include private donors, who may have an interest in ensuring the development and delivery of high-quality psychosocial recovery programs to trauma survivors. Engaging in local and statewide community-facing outreach efforts, as well as engagement with government officials at the city and state level, may also assist with identifying creative pathways to funding, especially if it aligns with politically supported missions. Victims of Crime Act (VOCA) funding is sometimes available for clinical services that are needed as a result of criminal acts.

Internal funding is often more straightforward and typically provided via the home department in which the program resides. As trauma centers are oftentimes viewed as hospital-wide services, funding may be acquired directly through the hospital itself rather than through the Department of Surgery. Specialty services may also be developed and implemented utilizing financial support from additional clinical services, for instance, the integration of a neuropsychological assessment service for the neurosurgery team or the development of a proactive behavioral pain management service for the plastic surgery team. Internal funding can be more stable than grant-related support, although it regularly requires the provision of data to continue ongoing funding. Internal funding can sometimes be justified with cost offsets related to length of stay and increased efficiency of surgical services.

Hybrid funding incorporates both internal and external approaches to the financial support of TACS Psych programs and may be the optimal way to build a financially sustainable program. Creative utilization of funds may allow for the incorporation of internal funding to provide salary coverage for faculty positions, with external funding providing support for additional materials or expansion to new departments. Engaging with your department's administrative business partner may uncover unexpected pathways for support, which in, tandem with collaboration with institutional government affairs teams, may provide a unique competitive edge when vying for publicly available funds.

Finally, if your program is embedded in a teaching hospital, you may consider the use of trainees to increase your service footprint. Some trainees, such as psychology practicum students, require minimal funding and can efficiently augment clinical services. Utilizing psychology internship and fellowship training programs, as well as psychiatry residency and fellowship programs embedded within your health system, may also provide a pathway for training trusted clinicians who can seamlessly integrate into a faculty role following graduation. The use of trainees requires that TACS Psych staff spend substantial time in teaching and supervision, and away from clinical duties.

Program evaluation and sustainability

After the funding pathways are identified, plans for program evaluation and sustainability should follow. The funding pathway will impact program evaluation and sustainability plans in multiple ways, related to which agencies or funding sources you are accountable to. Granting agencies may require reports at regular time intervals, and internal funding sources may rely on outcome measures unique to your health system. Because of this, it is important to define what success means for your program. Success should be driven not only by your funding source but by the underlying values of your institution and the needs assessment that was conducted earlier in the process of program development. Program evaluation plans should incorporate a range of objective and subjective measures that may be used to support the ongoing maintenance and expansion of the program. After defining what success means for your program, the development of metrics to measure success is required. Ideally, program evaluation should be efficient and not unduly burdensome.

Quantitative metrics are essential to incorporate into your program evaluation plan and oftentimes include items such as the number of patients served, reductions in readmissions, impact on length of stay, patient satisfaction scores and decreases in scores related to psychological distress both during and following discharge. Measures should be easy to administer, and data should be readily accessible for analysis. Data should be stored in accordance with your institution's health information protection policies and regularly checked for accuracy. An additional quantitative metric that is often included in program evaluation discussions relates to billing and revenue streams. Some programs, like those that are grant-funded, may not require billing, whereas those that are internally funded often rely on billing to partially support sustainability. Working with billing and coding teams is essential to ensure the maximization of billing processes. If practicing within the United States, the ACS (2022) Best Practices Guidelines Screening and Intervention for Mental Health Disorders and Substance Use and Misuse in the Acute Trauma Patient provides examples of frequently used billing codes as well as documentation requirements related to each Current Procedural Terminology (CPT) code. To maximize billing and minimize the potential for error, we incorporate all required billing information, including billing codes, at the end of each consultation and progress note. Creating a billing code matrix in collaboration with your billing and coding team may simplify your process should your service frequently utilize multiple codes.

While quantitative metrics often drive the determination of whether a program is successful from the an objective perspective, qualitative metrics provide a richer context for measuring success. Providing trauma survivors with the opportunity to freely describe their experiences with your services via anonymous surveys or focus groups may illuminate intangible aspects of care that go beyond numerical data. I utilize an approach that involves the power of objective data combined with qualitative descriptors to develop the narrative of the program's success. Of course, providing good care is the best way to be successful; good therapeutic relationships with patients foster immediate feedback and communication of problems more effectively than surveys.

Navigating barriers

Inherent to the process of developing a new program is navigating barriers that may unexpectedly arise as you move through the stages of program development. Programs must be resilient and prepared proactively for a wide range of potential problems. Resilience and persistence will help not only in developing a new program but in sustaining it for the future. An important strategy when navigating barriers is utilizing the key stakeholders and the solid administrative structure that you have developed throughout the program planning process. Often, attempts to expand service lines, attain additional funding, or incorporate new team members may be faced with barriers outside of the control of the clinical team. Creative problem-solving and consulting with internal and external experts will increase the likelihood of success. The process of program development frequently takes years, and programs will sometimes grow suddenly after years of preparation when a new source of funding is attained. Proactively preparing for those moments of growth will ensure success when the opportunity arises. As I often remind audiences when I'm presenting on program development, Rome wasn't built in a day. The full quote, from the English playwright John Heywood, is even more instructive: "Rome wasn't built in a day, but they were laying bricks every hour" (Clear n.d.). Persistence and patience are close allies of success.

Chapter summary

Based on their practical experiences, the authors describe the process of developing an effective Trauma and Acute Care Surgical Psychology program. Early planning decisions can have important long-term ramifications, and thoughtful attention to issues such as models of care and financial support can pay great dividends later. Committed stakeholders must model patience and perseverance as they manage the obstacles a new program may face.

References

American College of Surgeons, (2022). *Best practices guidelines: Screening and intervention for mental health disorders and substance use and misuse in the acute trauma patient.* https://www.facs.org/media/nrcj31ku/mental-health-guidelines.pdf.

American College of Surgeons (2025). *Resources for Optimal Care of the Injured Patient 2022 Standards, Revised July 2025* (7th ed.). American College of Surgeons. https://www.facs.org/quality-programs/trauma/quality/verification-review-and-consultation-program/standards/.

Clear, J. (n.d.), Rome wasn't built in a day, but they were laying bricks every hour. Available from: https://jamesclear.com/lay-a-brick.

Hunt, J. C., Sapp, M., Walker, C., Warren, A. M., Brasel, K., & De Roon-Cassini, T. A. (2017). Utility of the injured trauma survivor screen to predict PTSD and depression during hospital admission. *Journal of Trauma and Acute Care Surgery, 82*(1), 93–100. https://doi.org/10.1097/TA.0000000000001306.

Moore, D. A., Reffi, A. N., Jankowiak, L., Mahr, G., Drake, C. L., & Johnson J. (2025, September).*Predicting mental health referrals following acute trauma: Preliminary evidence for a novel risk factor based screening tool.* Cutting Edge Paper Presentation 41st Annual Meeting of the International Society for Traumatic Stress Studies. Baltimore, MD.

Chapter 21

Future directions

Greg's Story

The year is 2060. Greg fell down his basement stairs, seriously injuring his hip. He was transported from his home by the self-driving ambulance team to the local mini-hospital. Since the amazing and unexpected political and economic reforms of the 2040s, traumatic injuries have become a rarity. Firearm related injuries are as uncommon as measles had become in the early 2000s, and driverless vehicles have made motor vehicle–related injuries a rarity as well. Nonetheless, the kind of thing that happened to Greg still happens to others, and the local mini-hospital had a fine Trauma and Acute Care Surgery program. Soon after admission, Greg saw David, the trauma psychologist. Through work with David, Greg realized that at 130, it was probably time for him to move out of independent living to the senior living center down the street from the mini-hospital. After his hip surgery, Greg would continue to see David as he reimagined the next phase of his life.

Certainly, Greg's story is a fantasy, but perhaps a fantasy that can guide us in our thinking and planning.

Primary prevention

In the United States, the most common causes of traumatic injuries are falls, motor vehicle crashes, assaults, and firearm injuries. Most of these causes are, in theory, preventable. Falls can have a clear medical component and association with dizziness and balance issues, but assaults, motor vehicle crashes, and firearm injuries all have significant behavioral components and can predominantly be considered social problems rather than medical ones. Injuries related to assaults are more common in the United States than in other developed countries, which suggests a social and cultural component to such injuries (Kessler, 2000). Public health measures, like seatbelts and airbags, have significantly reduced injuries related to motor vehicle crashes. Firearm violence might lend itself to similar types of mandated reforms and behavioral restrictions. Weapons like knives and fists must be used at close quarters, so time passes between the impulse to harm and the actual event, allowing for reflection on the part of the assailant and defense or escape on the part of the

The Psychology of Acute Trauma. DOI: https://doi.org/10.1016/B978-0-443-33212-8.00014-2

potential victim. Firearms injure or kill instantly and at a distance, precluding regret or reflection when they are used.

There are nearly 100,000 firearm injuries in the United States annually, a much higher rate per capita than other developed countries (NIHCM Foundation, 2024). Firearm violence–related deaths in the United States are five times the rates of all other wealthy nations, and in 2019, firearm injuries became the leading cause of death in individuals aged 1 to 19 (Goldstick et al., 2022). Trauma programs, because they are at the forefront of confronting the impacts of firearm violence, should strive to support and study primary prevention measures for highly preventable mechanisms of injury, such as assaults and firearm violence. This mission is in accord with the American College of Surgeons' Committee on Trauma's initiatives related to supporting the development of hospital-based violence intervention programs.

Secondary prevention

We have discussed repeatedly how the effective treatment of acute stress disorder and other trauma- and stressor-related disorders can potentially prevent posttraumatic stress disorder (PTSD). Unfortunately, as has been shown throughout this text, there is a dearth of high-quality research rigorously testing the development and deployment of preventive treatments in inpatient settings. The preventive effects of structured approaches to treatment need to be further documented and studied. Additionally, increased focus on identifying and treating prodromal symptoms such as sleep disturbances and nightmares would prove highly beneficial as it would give clinicians practicing in acute care settings clear targets for preventive treatments.

Secondary prevention efforts can only be carried out if there are clinicians to deliver them. As the subspecialty of Trauma and Acute Care Surgical Psychology (TACS Psych) is still in its infancy, it is critical for existing programs to attempt to integrate training experiences into their structure so that future generations of clinicians may be trained. Additionally, efforts should focus heavily on advocating for policymaking that supports funding the development and maintenance of high-quality educational programs serving trauma survivors in acute care settings. Advocacy within professional societies such as the American College of Surgeons will also help to increase the integration of emotional recovery resources into trauma centers, with the ultimate goal of re-verification requirements including the need for embedded and fully integrated mental health services.

Translating clinical wisdom into research data

Due to the nature of acute stress disorder and adjustment disorders, ideal research methodology like double-blind clinical trials are more difficult to conduct. Acute trauma is unpredictable and the disorders associated with it, such as adjustment disorders and acute stress disorder, are time limited. Also, acute trauma patients are often ill and require medical and surgical interventions, so informed consent and even structured and formalized psychological interventions are difficult to implement in chaotic inpatient settings. Often in acute care settings we are treating specific symptoms of distress rather than an illness, so interventions are more difficult to conceptualize. Short-term interventions focused on symptom reduction are often clinically beneficial and deserve systematic study.

Because of the difficulty in obtaining ideal research data, clinical wisdom and qualitative data are important in the psychological treatment of acute trauma. Special attention must be paid to avoiding bias in such data, so self-reflection and collaboration are especially important. We have included substantial case material in this book to show the importance of such clinical, qualitative data. Such data are an incredibly powerful way of understanding the internal experience of the trauma patient. Publication of case studies related to the utilization of evidence-supported approaches may help to broaden the literature base and inspire other clinicians to develop approaches to adapt additional evidence-supported treatments. In future translational research qualitative data will become more certain and reliable.

Incorporating technology

New technological advances applied to the treatment of trauma- and stressor-related disorders have shown considerable promise in outpatient settings and would benefit from studies evaluating their efficacy in acute care settings. For example, new phone-based apps for sleep hygiene have been shown to be effective in mitigating insomnia (Armitage et al., 2024), which is a significant concern for individuals receiving care in hospital settings. Additional apps that assist with the utilization of relaxation training skills or meditation interventions provide opportunities for supporting clinical practice outside of the treatment session. Pairing relaxation training and meditation skills with biofeedback, especially for patients in intensive care settings whose heart rate and blood pressures are almost always continuously monitored, may provide unique opportunities to accelerate learning and increase the incorporation of skills into daily life. Virtual reality–assisted therapies have shown efficacy in outpatient settings and may hold potential promise for utilization in inpatient settings for the treatment of specific symptoms of distress, such as re-scripting of the traumatic experience to reduce the frequency and intensity of nightmares. Such treatments have not been attempted in acute trauma–related disorders and deserve further study in that population.

As poor social support has been widely recognized as a significant risk factor for the development of future distress, novel approaches using technology to increase social support need further exploration. Specifically, the development of virtual support groups and encouraging the use of video conferencing with new and existing support networks may prove beneficial. Chat programs driven by artificial intelligence (AI) may hold promise for increasing access to on-demand social support, especially for patients who have limited or poor-quality social support networks. Complex ethical issues remain about virtual support and whether it encourages of discourages participation in the "real" world and whether it facilitates long term personal growth beyond symptom relief. A danger of AI is that patients, especially when they are isolated and lonely, can use AI relationships to substitute for human love.

AI has an ever increasing role in clinical and academic medicine. AI currently provides ready access to valuable information and clinical protocols in complex medical and surgical situations. AI can listen to therapy sessions and write notes. The future challenge will be how to incorporate AI into clinical care in a meaningful way that does not not conflict with the essential human aspect of relationships.

Prioritizing posttraumatic growth

Psychology and psychiatry have focused on treating illness. With trauma we are forced to deal with the impacts of an external event. The concept of posttraumatic growth challenges the illness model that is fundamental to current psychiatric and psychological treatment programs. Encouraging posttraumatic growth is not treating illness but facilitating survivorship. Posttraumatic growth forces us to reconsider what psychology is all about. A wise supervisor once told me that we never solve psychological problems, we "grow" past them. Facilitating growth suggests a reinvention of psychology away from symptom management and illness treatment to issues of transformation, growth and meaning. Tools to systematically study positive psychology need to be developed and evaluated in inpatient settings. A deeper understanding of the spiritual dimensions of therapy and recovery needs to be integrated into a broader and richer view of trauma and its complex impacts and meaning.

Empowering caregivers

Caregiver stress and growth need further study, but in both professional and nonprofessional caregivers. How can caregivers be more effectively involved in care for their loved ones while preserving their own well-being? The unique stresses faced by professional caregivers in acute care settings need to be more thoughtfully considered with a view to mitigating those stresses. Beyond mitigating caregiver stress, we might imagine a social and economic structure where caregivers are supported both emotionally and financially, so that a loved one's injury does not lead to financial distress for the whole caregiving system. Currently caregivers can be provided with support and information but not clinical services as they have not consented to those services. Perhaps care can be conceptualized more broadly in the future to include care for the whole support system.

Enhancing service delivery models

What does the ideal TACS Psych program look like? How is it structured? Those questions remain unanswered. It seems that ideal clinical models would focus on integration between different clinical disciplines and between inpatient and outpatient programs; but what are the best strategies for achieving such integration? The goal is patient-centered trauma-informed care, and an ideal model would provide continuity of care across different treatment settings and programs. Existing programs should strive to publish outcomes data while sharing insights into the unique aspects of their models.

Maximizing community involvement

Especially in urban areas, a wide cultural and socioeconomic gap separates the local community and care providers. Patients from underrepresented groups in urban centers often distrust medical institutions. As we re-envision trauma care in terms of survivorship and long-term treatment, that gap of culture and trust must be bridged. The ongoing integration of trauma-informed recovery programs within the community is an important goal of effective trauma care. Natural partnerships may form with community-based violence interrupting organizations, whose goal is to decrease violence via a combination of mediation efforts, mentorship programs and assertively connecting at-risk individuals with programs to address combined emotional and social determinants of health needs. Additionally, strengthening partnerships with programs providing assistance to the survivors of human trafficking and domestic violence is critical to increase the likelihood of successfully engaging these incredibly at risk subgroups. These programs may serve as cultural brokers, allowing for trust to be built within the community, increasing comfort related to engagement with clinical services.

Conversely, trauma patients are sometimes stigmatized by the medical community. Certain mechanisms of injuries, like firearm injuries and stabbings, are often assumed to be a consequence of involvement in illicit activities. Sometimes, sadly, there is the unspoken assumption that the injuries were somehow "deserved." That kind of stigma is always unethical and can certainly interfere with empathetic care. Effective community integration can address that kind of stigma. The Bullet Related Injury Clinic (BRIC) Institute, a wraparound clinic inSt. Louis, for instance, seeks to rehumanize the survivor while simultaneously reducing the stigma associated with firearm injuries. With education and activism such stigma might finally disappear. Hopefully the future will show more progress in the destigmatization of trauma care.

Acknowledging and addressing global health disparities

As discussed in Chapter 1, What is Trauma?, exposure to trauma is a global concern, with more than 40 million people worldwide suffering permanent injuries as a result of trauma each year (Miclau et al., 2025). Many countries lack sophisticated mental health service infrastructures, and low- and middle-income countries have a lack of qualified mental health providers. Nearly 50% of the world's population live in countries with an average of 1 psychiatrist for every 200,000 or more individuals (World Health Organization, 2021). Thus, secondary prevention programs such as integrated TACS Psych services may play a vital role in not only addressing the unmet mental health needs of the global community but in reducing the strain on existing mental health delivery systems by effectively preventing disorders that would require treatment in outpatient settings. We should strive to establish global partnerships, working together to collectively address the avoidable burden of post-injury mental health concerns.

A personal message of hope

Over the past 10 years we have traveled to many different conferences and academic medical centers to discuss program development and the delivery of acute trauma care. We have been inspired by the dedication and effort of our colleagues around the country who are building integrated TACS Psych programs and implementing thoughtful approaches to trauma-informed care. Caring for acute trauma patients is a calling. Answering a true call brings challenges and difficulties, but also great rewards.

One of the most common concerns we hear is, "We want to have an integrated mental health program, but we don't have...." Typical obstacles that are listed include time, resources, administrative support and staff. Here, the wish for perfection interferes with the goal of progress. We don't expect our patients to change right away, so we shouldn't expect that of ourselves, our staff, or our programs. The first changes are within. When we accept the call, we are duty bound to honor it. Like our patients, we must begin with acceptance and a realistic appraisal of our current situation, then move incrementally toward growth and change. We must avoid being discouraged. We don't need a fully functioning TACS Psych service to acknowledge the suffering that our patients face and to deliver sensitive care. Start with what you have, teach others, inspire others. The most important resources are within you.

Early in my career I cared for a young man recovering from severe trauma. The case ended sadly, with the death of the patient. I couldn't help but feel I, along with the whole team, had failed the patient and let the family down. A day or two after his death, his wife called me. Struggling with the self-centered anxieties that most of us have early in our careers, I assumed she was calling to berate me. Her voice was kind. "Thanks," she said. "You helped make his last days a little easier." I'm still not sure exactly what it was that I did, but I am grateful that I did it. When you answer the call, you won't always be sure when or if you have made a difference, or how. That doesn't matter. Getting credit doesn't matter. Doing the right thing in the best way you can is all that matters.

Flying cars

We sometimes imagine a future using a lens of present-day solutions. Entranced by technology, we are inclined to envision a future populated by more and more advanced technology and more and more sophisticated AI. Using this kind of thinking people in the 60 s imagined the world of the 2000s would be full of flying cars, as if more and more of what we have would make things better and better. There are no flying cars. Perhaps the future could be envisioned as something different altogether; perhaps the future might be marked by a deeper inward turn. Perhaps instead of more technology and more forms of psychotherapy we could attain inner wisdom, recognize our own traumas and woundedness and the centrality of spiritual and existential issues within all of us, and in that way take better care of our patients. Work with acute trauma invites such a vision of inner progress. Though not as glamorous as a flying car, an inward turn may be a different and more meaningful path to the future.

Chapter summary

This chapter envisions future models of ideal trauma care. Care in the future is ideally more strongly evidence-based, yet with more attention to the relational and personal aspects of care. Technology may augment and facilitate the therapeutic relationship. Posttraumatic growth is encouraged, and community and caregivers are a more integral part of care.

References

Armitage, B. T., Potts, H. W. W., Irwin, M. R., & Fisher, A. (2024). Exploring the impact of a sleep app on sleep quality in a general population sample: Pilot randomized controlled trial. *JMIR Formative Research, 8*. https://doi.org/10.2196/39554.

Goldstick, J. E., Cunningham, R. M., & Carter, P. M. (2022). Current Causes of Death in Children and Adolescents in the United States. *New England Journal of Medicine, 386*(20), 1955–1956. https://doi.org/10.1056/NEJMc2201761.

Kessler, R. C. (2000). Psychiatric epidemiology: Selected recent advances and future directions. *Bulletin of the World Health Organization, 78*(4), 464–474.

Miclau, T., Balogh, Z. J., Miclau, K. R., Bernstein, B., Kojima, K. E., Kurozumi, T., Leighton, R. K., Lundy, D. W., Putzeys, G., Schipper, I. B., Vandesande, W., de Camargo Leonhardt, M., Miranda Goncalves, M. A., Pelosini Gaiarsa, G., & Pape, H.-C. (2025). Trauma systems: a global comparison. *OTA International, 8*(3). https://doi.org/10.1097/OI9.0000000000000376.

NIHCM Foundation. (2024). *Gun violence: The impact on society*. https://nihcm.org/publications/gun-violence-the-impact-on-society#:~:text=Published%20on:%20January%2016%2C%

202024,on:%20December%2017%2C%202024.&text=This%20infographic%20explores %20the%20rapidly,leading%20cause%20of%20premature%20death.&text=rates%20remain %20higher%20than%20pre%2Dpandemic%20levels.&text=died%20from%20a%20gun %2Drelated,3.4%20injuries%20per%20100%2C000%20people.&text=gun%20injuries %2C%20134.3%20injuries%20per%20100%2C000%20people.

World Health Organization. (2021). *Comprehensive Mental Health Action Plan 2013–2030*. Geneva: World Health Organization.

Chapter 22

Talking trauma: selected dialogs for challenging situations

Often, we are approached by peers or trainees and asked about what to say when approaching different types of clinical interactions. The following brief scenarios illustrate common but challenging clinical situations. The scenarios are presented as dialogues to provide examples of the words that might be used in a particular clinical situation. Of course, such interventions and dialogues reflect personal therapeutic style. They are our words, intended to illustrate a clinical point. You need to find your words. We do not mean to imply that the words we have chosen are the only possible words, or even the best words. There are no easy ways to handle difficult situations. The words you choose must be the right words for you.

In the following dialogues, the text in (parentheses) is an attempt to show what the clinician was thinking and why they made the verbal choices they did. When possible, a connection is made between the intervention and the relevant school or type of therapeutic modality to which that intervention might belong. Some interventions are simply human reactions that cannot be reduced to a particular therapeutic school. Maintaining and supporting that human connection is often more important than applying a specific therapeutic label.

Initial patient contact

The initial contact between the patient and the Trauma and Acute Care Surgical Psychology (TACS Psych) service is crucial. Oftentimes, trauma patients are not expecting to be offered mental health services during their hospitalization for physical health concerns, and there may be stigma associated with receiving mental health care. If not approached with great intentionality and care, individuals may respond in a guarded or disinterested manner. The following "script" for the initial patient contact with the TACS Psych team has evolved over many years and rarely results in surprise or rejection.

The Psychology of Acute Trauma. DOI: https://doi.org/10.1016/B978-0-443-33212-8.00013-0

Charlotte is a recent trauma survivor. This is her initial meeting with the TACS Psych service.

Introductions

Clinician: Hi, Charlotte, my name is Dr. Moore, and I'm one of the psychologists on the surgery team. We meet with everyone who comes to the hospital after experiencing an accident or injury, as we know it's very common to experience changes in our thoughts and emotions when these things happen to us. Would you feel up to having a conversation about how things have been going to see how we can best help you as you move through your recovery process? (Dr. Moore has introduced himself, provided immediate psychoeducation related to adjustment processes, and normalized the interaction so that Charlotte does not interpret that she is viewed as experiencing mental illness.)

Charlotte: OK, thanks. It's nice to meet you.

Clinician: It's a pleasure to meet you as well. Thanks so much for taking the time to speak with me today. Would you mind if I take a seat? I hate to stand over folks while we talk. (Through the use of early permission-related questions, such as asking to sit immediately after asking for permission to engage in a discussion, the clinician sets the foundation for the relationship, indicating a high level of respect for the patient's autonomy and genuine care about their input. This often promotes a sense of control over the encounter and serves to strengthen rapport, indicating that the interaction "isn't just another checkbox:" and that the clinician is truly there to improve the well-being of the patient. Additionally, a wealth of research exists indicating that clinicians sitting bedside during clinical encounters may improve the overall quality of the encounter by increasing the patient's understanding of medical information, as well as the patient's perception related to the amount of time the clinician has spent in the clinical encounter) (Golden et al., 2022; Swayden et al., 2012).

Charlotte: Absolutely, you can sit in that chair over there.

Clinician: Thanks so much. Before we begin, I wanted to share that I'm glad that you have someone from your support system here with you today. Who's joined you here?

Charlotte: This is my sister Jean.

Clinician: Nice to meet you, Jean. Charlotte, would you like Jean to stay while we talk?

Charlotte: Yes, I'd rather my sister stays.

Clinician: Fantastic, we know that it's so important to have our support people with us as we navigate our recoveries. I'm glad Jean will be able to join us. If you change your mind at any point, please let me know, and we can continue our discussion in private. (The clinician acknowledges the presence of the visitor and provides education related to the important role social support plays in the recovery process. Prior to progressing to the evaluation, the clinician also reinforces that private conversations may occur if the patient chooses.)

Charlotte: OK, I'll let you know if I change my mind.

Clinician: I'd love to tell you a little bit more about my role on the team and how we assist individuals when they are here. As I mentioned when we first met,

(Continued)

my name is Dr. Moore, and I am one of the psychologists on your surgery team. We know that the emotional part of your recovery is just as important as your physical recovery, which is why I meet with folks as soon as possible once they are admitted. I am one of the senior doctors on your team, and I can follow you for this entire hospital stay. One of my main roles is to meet with you regularly, usually at least once per week, to discuss the emotional aspects of your recovery so that we can help you get better as a whole person. Another very important role that I have is to act as an advocate for you, helping everyone else on your surgical team understand your goals and what's important to you. With your permission, I can share with the surgical team some of your thoughts and feelings to help them do the best job possible in taking care of you. Otherwise, I will only share medically necessary information with them. Most importantly, I also want you to know that our time together is under your control. If it's not a good time to talk for any reason, like if you are feeling sick or are too tired, we can decide to meet at a different time. I know that was a lot of information, so I just wanted to check in to see what questions you might have for me. (The clinician reminds the patient of their name and role, explaining the aspects of care that they assist with during the hospital stay. Expectations related to average follow-up schedules are provided, as well as the limitations of confidentiality related to sharing information with their surgical teams. The clinician closes by reinforcing the importance of patient choice, empowering them to express if they are not feeling well enough to engage in the full evaluation, finally ending with a check-in prompt asking for any questions.)

Charlotte: I don't think I have any questions right now. You explained everything pretty well. I'm looking forward to talking.

Clinician: OK, great. I've had a chance to review your medical records and have discussed what brought you to the hospital with your surgical team, though I like to give everyone I meet with the opportunity to tell me in their own words what happened and how you have been feeling, so I don't make any assumptions. How are you feeling today?

(Sometimes patients don't like to repeat their stories. It can make them feel like they are not valued, important, or frustrated, as if the clinician working with them hasn't read the documentation related to prior encounters where those questions have already been answered. Preemptively sharing that you have read the records shows respect and the detail-oriented nature of your preparation for the evaluation, while offering an opportunity for the patient to provide their own experience of the traumatic event and validating the importance of their perspective.)

Complex Trauma

Susan is a 45-year-old patient with a history of complex trauma admitted after a motor vehicle crash. She has a prior history of childhood sexual abuse and an incident of date rape at age 30. She appears very anxious and tearful, stating that she feels overwhelmed. She has minimal family support.

Complex Trauma

Susan: Please tell them I can't be alone at night. I have to have staff with me at all times.

Clinician: We want to do everything we can to help you feel safe. Tell me what's going on? (Clinician tries to avoid a direct response to the request for 24-hour staff presence, knowing that such a request is a "trap." The clinician knows that they cannot promise 24-hour staff presence, but realizes that to say "no" would be experienced by Susan as a confirmation that "no one really cares about her.")

Susan: I just don't feel safe when no one is around. I have to have someone with me.

Clinician: Sounds like the crash stirred up a lot of feelings.

Susan: I can't believe this happened to me. I have so much going on. I can't deal with another thing.

Clinician: It is very unfair. You've had to deal with so many difficult things so many times in your life, and now you find yourself having to rise to face another challenge again. (Validates the patient's experience then, reframes via expressing admiration for the patient's resilience as a strength in order to support those strengths.)

Susan: I am a survivor.

Clinician: You certainly are, and we know you need extra help right now. We'll be sure to check in on you as often as we can. If you are having a particularly tough day and we haven't been by yet, please feel free to let your nurse or surgical team know, and they can page us to see you as soon as possible. (The demand for 24-hour staff presence was really an expression of concern and fear on Susan's part that no one cares about her. Exploring this fear and acknowledging Susan's strengths has made the demand recede to the background. Reinforcing that active and regular follow-up will occur during this hospital stay strengthens rapport and sets appropriate expectations for follow-up timing to avoid fears of abandonment.)

Susan: Thanks. I'll be ok.

Facing despair

John is a gunshot wound survivor, facing permanent bilateral lower extremity paralysis.

Despair

John: What's the point? I can't go on like this. What kind of a life can I really expect?

Clinician: That's a very important feeling. Tell me more. (Validation and exploration.)

John: I just can't imagine what I am going to do for the rest of my life. I won't be able to work, and I'll need help all the time. I just can't see a way forward.

Clinician: You are hurting a lot now. This has been a huge change in who you are, your life, and your future. You are asking big, important questions about

(Continued)

meaning and purpose, and it will take time to find your "new normal." Those questions can't be answered quickly. You will have to live into the answers. (More validation, taking the first steps in existentially oriented therapy, with the clinician resisting the impulse to offer some facile pseudo-solution to make themself feel better, not trying to take responsibility for John's journey.)

John: What if I can't find a purpose? What if I have to be dependent on others for the rest of my life?

Clinician: You seem to really struggle with needing help from others. I know that asking for help is so challenging and losing your independence, so suddenly has turned your world upside down, so you probably assume other people hate giving help as much as you hate getting it, but that may not be true. (This is a cognitive behavioral therapy–style intervention for confronting a cognitive distortion, but it is also beginning to address a core self-concept of independence at all costs.)

From here, this conversation could go in several directions, including the use of the value sorting exercise or the offer of psychoeducation about receiving help and the joy others may experience in providing it.

Addressing survivor's guilt and bearing the death of another

Junjie was severely injured in a motor vehicle crash in which his wife Xinyi, was killed. Junjie was driving while intoxicated at the time of the crash. He has been in a coma for several days. His delirium is resolving, and he is asking how his wife is doing. The family has asked that the TACS Psych team share the information with him that his wife did not survive the crash.

Survivor Guilt

Clinician: We wanted to talk to you this morning about something very important. (Sets an agenda of gravity and importance, so Junjie is prepared for a difficult conversation.) We know your head has been clearer and that you have been asking about Xinyi. I am sorry to give you the terrible news, but Xinyi didn't survive the crash. (Clear, direct, and unambiguous information.)

Junjie: (Sobbing softly) I knew something terrible had happened. I just knew it. How did she die?

Clinician: Unfortunately, the crash was very severe, and she had multiple injuries. We've been told that she had already passed away by the time the paramedics arrived. I'm so sorry. (Factual yet sensitive responses based on information that had been provided to us by the family. Simple and direct expression of sympathy.)

Junjie: Did she suffer?

Clinician: From the best we can tell, she likely didn't.

Junjie: (Still crying) At least she didn't suffer.

(Continued)

Clinician: (Touches Junjie's shoulder) I'm so sorry. (Simple human contact felt authentic to the clinician as they repeated condolences without attempting to minimize grief.) What would be helpful now? Your family is just outside the door. I can invite them in or sit with you for a while.

Junjie: Please sit with me. I need a few minutes; I'm not ready to face family yet. Was it my fault? I had a couple of drinks. Was I drunk? How could this have happened?

Clinician: Terrible things happen. At this point, it's hard to truly say what happened. There is no point in assigning guilt or blame. (Existential intervention of acknowledging loss without seeking or finding blame. The clinician makes a subtle but important distinction, but indirectly. He does not try to absolve Junjie of responsibility, which would be dishonest and false. Responsibility is different from blame, and self-blame can be a way of avoiding grief. Now is the time for grief, not blame.)

Junjie: Please send my family in. I want to be with them now.

Clinician: I'm here if you need me. I'll stop by later to see how you are doing. (The clinician reminds Junjie of their ongoing presence and availability. This is especially important at this moment because Junjie may expect rejection since he is probably realizing that the crash was likely influenced by his alcohol use. He needs to know that he is cared for as a person in spite of what happened or what his role may have been.)

The patient experiencing suicidal ideation in the context of acute trauma

Regulatory agencies have prioritized the screening and assessment of suicidality in inpatient settings. Much time and energy has been devoted to screening, but much less to actual treatment. When a patient voices suicidal plans or even ideation, a cascade of events occurs, including loss of privacy with the presence of one-to-one observation and loss of privileges like phone use. Patients, therefore, learn not to share suicidal feelings. As a result, regulations in some situations have the unwitting effect of reducing reporting. Nonetheless, acute trauma is a significant risk factor for suicide, and the assessment of suicidality is an important component of clinical assessment.

Albert had significant traumatic injuries after a motorcycle crash in which he struck a parked car. He was sad and regretful. He was a member of a local motorcycle club and had multiple club tattoos. He had a history of alcohol use, but no history of suicidal ideation, intent, plan, or prior attempts.

Suicidality

Clinician: Albert, you've been through a lot these last few days. Sometimes, when people have been through a lot, especially when they have been experiencing significant pain, they can get very discouraged. In these situations, it's not

(Continued)

uncommon to have thoughts about death and dying, or even wanting to hurt ourselves. Have you ever had any thoughts like that? (The clinician guessed, based on the patient's background and the fact that he was in a motorcycle club, that he might be embarrassed to discuss suicidality, so he normalized suicidality as a potential part of the trauma response.)

Albert: Doc, I've been so mad at myself. How could I have crashed my bike? I'm grateful I survived, but, yeah, I wish I had died in the crash, and I keep thinking I should just end it.

Clinician: Tell me about the thoughts you get. (Deeper exploration to assess suicide risk.)

Albert: This is just too much to bear. What am I going to do? How am I going to deal with the pain, the surgeries? I'm not ready for all this. It seems like the only way out sometimes.

Clinician: Would you hurt yourself in here? (The clinician realizes that they were a source of comfort and refuge, and that trying to eliminate the fantasy of escape would only increase the despair. So, the clinician explored safety concerns during the hospital stay.)

Albert: I'd never do anything here. Not at home, either. I'm too much of a chicken to kill myself. I know I have to face this.

Clinician: It takes a lot of courage to face what you are dealing with. That's real courage. It sounds like you experience the thoughts related to wanting to no longer be alive when you get overwhelmed or feel an increase in pain. Let's talk about some skills that we can use to give you a sense of control and physical comfort in those moments. (The clinician has assessed that there is no acute risk and that suicide precautions are not necessary. They realize that courage is an important value for Albert and reframe facing the trauma as being brave. They subtly also suggest that suicide is not brave. They decide not to say so explicitly because it might make Albert feel he is cowardly for having suicidal thoughts. The clinician wants to normalize the suicidal thoughts and give Albert permission to have them. To reject and try to push away those thoughts will only make them more powerful, whereas to accept them will allow them to pass. Suggesting the incorporation of skills to actively manage thoughts related to death will likely foster a sense of control, leading to a reduction in the frequency, intensity, and duration of suicidal ideation. Potential options include a range of behavioral pain management, acceptance-based, distress tolerance-focused, mindfulness meditation, and relaxation training interventions. Safety planning should also be conducted following resolution of acute distress.)

Dealing with thoughts of wanting to harm another

Emily was injured during an altercation with her cousin, Suzanne, after an argument about infidelity related to her boyfriend. Emily is very angry at Suzanne, and the staff has overheard her saying she is going to kill her.

Homicidality

Clinician: So, Emily, I wanted to talk to you about safety. Safety includes not only your safety, which is really important to us, but also Suzanne's safety. The staff has heard you saying you are going to kill Suzanne. Tell me about that. (The clinician initiates the discussion of Emily's homicidal ideation, but in a supportive way, which also includes an awareness of Emily's genuine concerns and issues.)

Emily: I am going to kill that bitch, and no one is going to stop me! Wouldn't you kill her?

Clinician: I understand how angry you must be toward her, but killing someone in revenge is a different issue altogether. We can't let that happen, both for Suzanne's sake and to protect you from doing something that might have severe consequences for you. (The clinician sets firm limits, but expresses them in a way that includes legitimate concerns about Emily and her welfare. Ignores the attempt to personalize the conversation and does not say what they would do.)

Emily: Oh, I know, I'm just really mad. I'm not going to do anything to her.

Clinician: So, when you see her again, what will you do? (Trying to confirm the absence of homicidality and level of safety.)

Emily: Oh, nothing. I'm just going to try to ignore her if I have to see her again. (No need for initiation of safety precautions, legal action, or warning of intended victim.)

Dreamwork

Working with dreams is usually seen as a long-term process, suitable for outpatient work only. We have found that many patients have significant distress from nightmares in the acute phase of recovery, and that brief interventions based on reframing nightmare content and addressing the central affect in the dream may be helpful. The dream, in effect, guides us to address key effects in supportive interventions that include aspects of rescripting.

Cognitive behavioral therapy for nightmares is most readily applied to trauma-replicative nightmares, but the following dialog illustrates the acute affective reframing of a nontrauma replicative nightmare.

Nontrauma replicative nightmares

Barry was assaulted by a crowd of strangers in a melee after a college basketball game. He was punched and trampled and sustained several fractures that required surgical repair. Barry had developed very troubling nightmares shortly after he was admitted to the hospital.

Nightmares

Barry: I had a really bad nightmare again last night. I woke up really upset and couldn't go back to sleep. My heart was racing, I couldn't move, and I felt like I couldn't catch my breath. It was terrifying.

(Continued)

Clinician: Tell me about what happened in the nightmare. (Eliciting dream content.)

Barry: I was running through hallways and tunnels. I was trying to get out, but all the doors were locked. People were chasing me. I was running and running, and I couldn't get out.

Clinician: Dreams can be very important, even nightmares. They can be the mind's way of trying to process the trauma. (Psychoeducation, reframing the nightmare as part of the healing process and placing it in a realm of potential meaning and as an aspect of healing. This in itself makes the dream less terrifying.) Does that dream remind you of your assault? (Exploring whether the dream is trauma-replicative.)

Barry: Not really. I mean, the attack happened in the parking lot. But it sort of felt the same.

Clinician: What do you mean? Can you tell me more about that?

Barry: Well, there was the same feeling of being so alone, so outnumbered, so helpless.

Clinician: That's a very important observation. (Support and empowerment by validating and recognizing his insight.) Sometimes the mind tries to process the feelings and not the exact event. (More psychoeducation and empowerment, demystifying the dream.)

Barry: What can I do? It's not like I can control my dreams.

Clinician: I think your mind is showing you the most important feelings to work on. We know that there are ways to potentially reduce the number of nightmares people experience and the intensity of the dreams themselves. When you are going to sleep tonight, remind yourself that you are safe now in the hospital—you are not alone, people are with you, and you are protected. (Providing psychoeducation related to the treatment, which may foster hope. The clinician focuses on the key effects and on reassuring and encouraging Barry to utilize reorientation skills on waking, which may help him remember that he is safe.) If you could reimagine that dream, how could it go differently so that you would feel safe? (Working toward a rapid, acute rescripting of dream affects.)

Barry: Well, maybe friends would be with me, or a door would open.

Clinician: Great ideas. So when you are getting ready to go to sleep, after you remind yourself that you are safe now and that people who care about you are always nearby, tell yourself that if a dream like that comes back and you feel trapped, a door will open. (Rapid, mini rescripting. The suggestion of the door opening has a dual message. The clinician means, of course, the door in the dream, but they also mean that a metaphorical inner door, to an inner recovery and acceptance of safety, needs to open. Also, just having a plan is empowering and reinforces that effects can be modified and that emotional recovery is possible.) Does that feel comfortable to try?

Barry: Yes, definitely, I'll try tonight.

Trauma-replicative nightmares

Rahim owned a convenience store in Detroit. One night, he was working with his nephew when three masked individuals wielding handguns entered the store, quickly demanding the money from the cash register. Rahim attempted to protect his nephew and sustained three gunshot wounds in the abdomen. He faced a lengthy hospitalization and was troubled by trauma-replicative nightmares.

Rescripting

Rahim: The nightmares were really bad again last night. I was up all night.

Clinician: Tell me about the nightmare.

Rahim: It's just like what happened. Three men came in with guns. I was behind the counter with my nephew. We were giving them the money, but they started shooting. I pulled my nephew behind the counter, but they reached over the counter and shot me.

Clinician: Is that exactly like what happened when you were shot? (Further exploration. Traumatic replicative nightmares are rarely exactly replicative.)

Rahim: Yes, exactly. Except, well, the store in the dream is back home, in Yemen. It's weird.

Clinician: Tell me about Yemen. (Focuses on the point of difference, which may be important.)

Here, Rahim tells a story of life in his country of origin, which included instability, unrest, poverty, and political turmoil. His brother was his main source of support, and they moved to Detroit together. Additionally, they run the store together. They thought life in the United States would be safer and easier, but it hasn't been.

Clinician: It could have been different. It should have been different. No one should ever have to experience what you have. I think it's important that the dream takes place in Yemen. Perhaps the dream is reminding you that, in your mind, the trauma here and the traumas in Yemen are connected. (Further exploration of the dream content with the search for a key theme, especially one that would connect the two settings in terms of rescripting.)

Rahim: It's so different here. In some ways, it's better; in some ways, it's worse. It was worse in Yemen because there were money problems and more violence, but I didn't feel so alone there. I knew everyone. Back home, this wouldn't have happened like this. There would have been people around, friends and family. Someone would have protected me.

Clinician: So, one of the scariest parts of the nightmare is how alone you felt. (Key theme identified.) It can be helpful sometimes to reimagine a nightmare, change the story, and give it a different ending. (Rescripting is introduced. In the actual therapeutic interaction, a longer discussion of rescripting followed, which is not reproduced in this vignette.)

Rahim: If I could redo the dream, I'd have it take place here, but all my friends and family would be living here. People I knew would be nearby, out in the street. When the trouble started, they would hear the commotion. They would come in

(Continued)

and protect me. (Rahim rescripts the dream in a beautiful and creative way, with a focus on the fears of being alone but incorporating the cultural aspects of life in Detroit versus life in Yemen. The difference between the actual event and the nightmare becomes a key element of the rescripting.)

Clinician: That's a nice way of rescripting your dream. Remember that people you love can always be with you, inside you, even if they are far away. Now think about the new dream when you are going to bed. (The clinician gently encourages the utilization of internal resources and a reminder to Rahim that he is loved as a subtle way of addressing the existential issues of abandonment that are an aspect of both the dream and the traumatic event. Further rescripting information followed.)

Rahim reported substantial symptomatic relief in general distress and nightmare severity. The recurrent nightmare did not happen again during the hospital stay.

Assessing decision-making capacity

William is a retired business owner with a history of severe alcohol use disorder that is currently in remission. His family lives in the area but is minimally involved in his care. His wife died three years ago, and he has had increasing difficulty with self-care. He has had several hospital admissions in the past three months for falls. He is currently admitted to the Trauma and Acute Care Surgery service after a fall at home that resulted in multiple rib fractures and a mild traumatic brain injury (subdural hematoma not requiring neurosurgical intervention). Cognitive testing reveals moderate cognitive impairment. He has previously met with the TACS Psych team for an initial evaluation during this hospital stay.

As discussed in Chapter 10 (Neurocognitive disorders and delirium), decision-making capacity is related to a discrete decision and does not directly correlate with a specific score but rather is related to the individual's understanding specifically from the point of view of the four criteria for decision-making capacity, namely (a) communicating a choice, (b) understanding relevant information, (c) appreciating the consequences and (d) reasoning about treatment options. William has been demanding to go home, but the team has recommended inpatient rehabilitation or a long-term care facility. In this case, the question is related to safe placement in view of repeated falls. We were asked to assess his dispositional or welfare decision-making capacity. In other words, can William independently make decisions related to his discharge planning?

Note that the level of clinician who is permitted by law to conduct capacity assessments varies by country and from state to state within the United States.

Decision-Making Capacity

Clinician: Hi William, it's great to see you. Have we met before? (Despite previously meeting with William, the clinician begins the conversation with a question aimed at gauging whether he recalls the previous interaction with the TACS Psych team. If the consultation request was not for a capacity assessment, the salutation "it's great to see you again" would be used to cue the patient to recall the previous clinical interaction).

William: Ya, we have, you are the doctor who fixed my ribs, right?

Clinician: Close, I am one of the doctors on your team. My name is Dr. Moore, and I'm the psychologist for your surgery team. We had a chance to meet last week. I help with the emotional and cognitive recovery after someone has to come here for help. (The clinician validates the patient's statement and provides general reorientation to the clinician's role. The use of generalities is important so as not to inadvertently taint the validity of the examination results, as the goal of these assessments is to ascertain the patient's ability to provide responses to the queries solely from memory with as little cueing as possible. This includes erasing the date from orientation boards located within the hospital room prior to commencing the evaluation.)

William: Oh ya, that's right.

Clinician: It's good to see you again. How have you been feeling?

William: Great, I can barely feel the pain in my ribs anymore.

Clinician: That's really good to hear. I'm happy you are feeling better. Can you remind me, did you have any other injuries besides your rib fractures? (The clinician is attempting to see if the patient recalls being provided information related to the traumatic brain injury.)

William: Nope, that's it.

Clinician: What brought you in to get help? (The clinician is attempting to understand the accuracy of the patient's narrative related to his admission, again using some generalities to avoid invalidating the assessment of orientation that will occur at the close of the evaluation.)

William: Oh, I just tripped carrying something up to my bedroom. It was no big deal.

Clinician: Have you had a chance to talk to the surgical team about what the plan is from here? (The clinician is again attempting to ascertain the patient's understanding of the current plan of care and disposition recommendations with as little cueing as possible).

William: They said that I am totally fine, and they want to send me home today.

Clinician: That's great to hear that they feel you are doing well and are ready to leave the hospital. Did they discuss any other options of potential places you could be discharged to in addition to home? (The clinician is beginning to take a more directive approach now to specifically assess William's understanding of the discharge options).

William: Naw, they just said I should go home.

Clinician: Earlier in our conversation, you mentioned that you had fallen at home prior to coming to get help here. Are there any concerns that might happen

(Continued)

again? (Directly assessing the patient's understanding of the risks related to a direct discharge home to an unsupervised living environment.)

William: They didn't say they were concerned when they talked to me; they just said I should go home.

Clinician: Let's talk about future planning for a moment. The surgical team mentioned to me that you have had to come here several times within the last few months after falling at home. We really care about you and are worried about how many times you've fallen. Do you think it might be unsafe currently for you to be at home without support? (Trying to assess Williams's grasp of the severity and implications of the discharge issues.)

William: I'm fine, doc. I'll just be more careful. It's no big deal.

Clinician: They are very concerned about your safety. You've had three serious falls requiring medical attention within the past three months. (Trying to assess whether William appreciates the significance of the placement issue.)

William: Look, man! I told you, I'm fine! I've been living on my own for years now and doing just fine. I think we are done talking now. (In combination with his inability to accurately report his discharge options without cueing, William's continued refusal to acknowledge the significance of the clinical placement issue suggests a lack of dispositional decision-making capacity based on criteria b, c, and d. To demonstrate decision-making capacity to return home to an unsupervised living environment, William would need to understand the concern about falls, not just minimize it, and have some plan for addressing his multiple falls.)

Exploring substance misuse associated with acute trauma

Thomas is the patient described in Chapter 11 (Substance use and misuse). He has had multiple falls, the most recent being off his roof while intoxicated, resulting in a fractured femur and his current admission.

Substance Misuse

Clinician: I know you've had a long, tough hospital stay. I'd like to talk about how we may be able to prevent falls like this from happening again. (The clinician begins with support and empathy, setting the stage for a conversation that is about caring, not about creating shame and guilt.)

Thomas: Yeah, I'm really going to have to be a lot more careful. It's so easy to stumble on a roof.

Clinician: I know you do a lot of roofing work. What do you think made this time different? (The clinician is trying to gauge insight and encourage self-reflection. Additionally, the patient's response will help to identify which stage of change he is in.)

Thomas: I think I was just tired. (Response indicates limited insight and that the patient is likely precontemplative related to a desire to change.)

(Continued)

Clinician: It seems like in this fall and in the prior falls, alcohol was involved. How much did you drink before going up on the roof? (Gentle confrontation, with a focus on objective facts.)

Thomas: I guess it was more than a six-pack. But I wasn't drunk or anything. (Beginnings of contemplation.)

Clinician: It's been found that any amount of alcohol increases the risk of falls. The more you drink, the bigger the risk. (Psychoeducation related to the impact of alcohol on falls is provided). But besides that, this is the third time you've fallen after you were drinking. How do you feel that alcohol has impacted your life? (Supportive confrontation, initiating motivational interviewing.)

Thomas: Nah, it's no big deal. I'll just be more careful. Alcohol hasn't really impacted my life much. I don't even get drunk often.

Clinician: It sounds like you feel that alcohol hasn't had too much of an impact on your life. It's hard to think about these things sometimes. People get embarrassed and ashamed about it. For some, it's easier sometimes to just think it's not an issue. (Addressing shame and denial in a supportive way. Incorporating some motivational interviewing strategies.)

Thomas: I guess lots of people tell me I drink too much. I just don't know. (The clinician is listening for DARN [desire, ability, reasons, and need] statements, which would indicate a desire to change. The patient's perspective is continuing to evidence contemplation.)

Clinician: It sounds like others have noticed the impact alcohol has had on your life. It sounds like they must really care about you if they are willing to share how concerned they are. We care about you, too, and want to help you get better as a whole person. Our goal isn't just to treat your physical injuries, but to help you get back to a life with value and meaning. (Reframing being controlled to being cared about.)

Thomas: I know, I know. I really do need to quit. I've tried, I've really tried. I really think I should stop drinking after I leave the hospital, I mean, I haven't had anything to drink here. I think I can do it. (The presence of DARN statements indicates a desire to change, the ability to change, and a need to change.)

Dealing with "drug-seeking" behavior

The term "drug-seeking" behavior is intrinsically pejorative. It refers to the staff perception of a patient who reports false or exaggerated complaints of pain or other distress, like anxiety or insomnia, as a way of obtaining medication, especially controlled substances such as opiates or benzodiazepines. It is a form of malingering; that is, falsely reporting symptoms for the purpose of secondary gain. Sometimes, malingering is obvious and can be confirmed by medical records or collateral sources. Often, malingering is not obvious. Furthermore, pain is, by its very nature, a subjective experience. What can appear to be drug-seeking behavior can, in fact, represent untreated or undertreated pain. In fact, patients with a history of substance misuse often have a higher tolerance for pain medications and are commonly undertreated for pain. Yet patients commonly do misuse pain medications. How can we "talk through" such challenging issues without blame or judgment?

Frank is a 40-year-old male with a history of opiate addiction who was stabbed in the abdomen during a substance-related assault. On day 5 of his hospital admission, his IV opiates have been tapered, and he is frequently reporting pain. Some staff have noted that complaints of pain sometimes appear to be inconsistent with observed behavior. He has been reported to voice complaints of pain when staff enter the room, although he had been soundly sleeping just moments before. For this dialog, the staff member is a physician. Because physicians are typically the prescribers of pain medication, they are the staff members who typically make the final decisions about pain medication and other controlled substances. We have kept the conversation generic and avoided specific details of medications and dosing.

Pain and Malingering

Physician: How have you been doing?

Frank: Not so good, doc. The pain is has been really bad since yesterday.

Physician: What is the pain like? (Malingered reports of pain are usually vague, diffuse, constantly present, and unresponsive to interventions.)

Frank: It's really bad all the time. The oral meds just don't help.

Physician: It's hard. I know you have a lot of pain with the injury. But we need to stay on the path of tapering the opiates and switching to a medicine you can take by mouth. (Support and empathy, coupled with firm limits.)

Frank: No, doc, you don't get it. Those meds don't work. I need the IV meds.

Physician: We'll have to stick with the dosing schedule. We can add some other nonnarcotic medications to help with some of the pain and distress. (Still reinforcing limits with some adjustment of nonaddictive adjunctive medications.)

The trauma patient experiencing severe and persistent .mental illness

Henry is the patient described in Chapter 12 (Severe and persistent mental illness). Henry is unhoused and often experiences symptoms of psychosis. The dialog describes a follow-up session near the time of discharge.

Patients Experiencing Psychotic Symptoms

Clinician: So, Henry, how are you feeling today?

Henry: I'm still hurting a lot, but I want to leave the hospital.

Clinician: I know you haven't had a place to stay recently. Any ideas about where you might go? (Attempting to explore placement options in a nonstigmatizing, nonjudgmental way but being direct about housing concerns.)

Henry: I'm doing fine.

(Continued)

Clinician: Now, we do have some resources for housing and shelters. I know you told our social worker that you didn't want resources, but I wasn't sure why.

Henry: Oh, I've tried all those places. I don't want that stuff. I like to come and go, don't want anyone telling me what to do.

Clinician: I know those places aren't perfect by any means. But they could be helpful now because you're still recovering. (Respects the patient's autonomy, expresses genuine understanding for the patient's concerns, but suggests a short-term placement in view of medical follow-up related to the acute trauma.)

Henry: I really just want to go. I'll figure it out.

Clinician: OK, that's up to you. (Previous assessment had established that Henry has decision-making capacity, so the clinician accepts that and decides nothing is to be gained by pressing for shelter placement. They want to preserve the therapeutic relationship they have with Henry.) I wanted to talk to you about how you ended up in the hospital and what happened.

Henry: He hit me! I thought he was my friend. I didn't do anything wrong.

Clinician: He shouldn't have hit you, and the police are investigating that, but what could you do to be sure you don't get hit again? (Clinician validates the traumatic assault but recognizes poor insight and the delusional themes in Henry's thinking. Decides to focus on developing shared goals with Henry that both they and Henry could accept as being helpful.)

Henry: Nothing. It wasn't my fault.

Clinician: He had no right to hit you; that was a terrible thing. But you also have to keep yourself safe, avoid him, and not take things without paying from anybody. That makes people mad. (More validation, coupled with social skills training.)

Henry: I know, I get it. I wasn't really thinking. I'll be more careful about stuff like that.

Delivering difficult news: "You killed me!"

Sometimes cases end sadly despite initial successes and the best efforts of the treatment team.

Lane was a 68-year-old male admitted after sustaining multiple injuries in a fall from a roof, including some deep lacerations on his buttocks from metal on the roof. These lacerations became infected, and he developed necrotizing fasciitis. Lane suffered from complex trauma, including severe physical abuse as a child. Initially, during his hospital stay, he was withdrawn and resistant to of help. His social isolation was amplified by the fact that his injury occurred during the COVID pandemic. The hospital was in lockdown, and no visitors were allowed.

Gentle, persistent efforts from staff were very helpful, and eventually Lane developed a good relationship with the psychologist on the TACS Psych service. It turns out that Lane was an excellent drummer and did some studio work for prominent country music performers. When Lane shared this personal information, he was able to develop a more trusting relationship with the treatment team, and they were able to see him more easily as a person.

Lane improved, and he was looking forward to transferring to an inpatient physical rehabilitation program. He developed symptoms of severe pneumonia, however, and workup confirmed that he had developed COVID during his hospital stay, contracted from hospital staff. Because of the good relationship Lane had with the TACS Psych team, the psychologist was asked to inform Lane of his hospital-acquired COVID, which was severe and likely would be fatal.

Delivering Difficult News

Clinician: Lane, I wanted to tell you that the treatment team was reviewing the latest labs. The pneumonia you have is from COVID, and as you know, that is very serious.

Lane: I've been in the hospital for 3 weeks. How did I catch COVID?

Clinician: COVID is everywhere now, even in the hospital. I'm really sorry. (Expresses genuine regret, acknowledges that infection was hospital-acquired, indirectly also reminding Lane that such events were outside of staff control.)

Lane: So, I caught it from someone here?

Clinician: Sadly, yes. Despite the lockdown and our best efforts, it happened. (Accepts responsibility, expresses regret, and reminds that efforts at prevention were made.)

Lane: Lane was enraged. He lifted his head from the bed, shakily raised his hand, and pointed his finger directly at the clinician shouting,"You bastards! You killed me!"

Clinician: I'm so very sorry. I want to help as much as I can in this difficult situation. What can I do for you now?

Lane: Nothing, just leave me alone. (Lane turned away)

Clinician: I understand, and I will respect your wishes. Despite what has happened, we care about you very much. If you change your mind, I will always be here for you. (The clinician validated the patient's emotional state, honoring his autonomy, while also conveying the message that no matter what, the TACS Psych team would be available to support him.)

Lane never spoke to staff again and minimally cooperated with care. He died of COVID a few days later, with the TACS Psych psychologist holding his hand as he passed. In addition to Lane's tragic outcome, staff faced significant second victim issues as they grieved with Lane, understood his anger, yet felt powerless to help him. The staff member who likely but unknowingly caused the COVID exposure was particularly aggrieved. She felt very guilty and struggled with sleep problems, intrusive thoughts, and difficulty completing tasks at work. With mentoring and support, she recovered fully.

Inpatient, outpatient, and community coordination

Randy was a 42-year-old male survivor of a serious vehicular trauma. He was driving on a two-lane road with his partner when a vehicle driving from the opposite direction struck his car. His partner was killed; Randy had minor injuries. Although he was not at fault, his partner's family blamed him. Randy was not suicidal at the time of discharge and was referred for outpatient trauma treatment in a community behavioral health program.

Two days after discharge, Randy presented to the emergency department with suicidal ideation, with intent and plan. He was evaluated by virtual psychiatry and again discharged to outpatient follow-up. He did not show for the appointment. As discussed in Chapter 15 (Breaking down barriers: addressing social determinants of health), our program structure dictates that every patient who has received TACS Psych services during their inpatient stay will be engaged in ongoing telephone check-ins to ensure that any ongoing recovery needs may be proactively addressed. Later that week, Randy was contacted by a TACS Psych trauma social worker, with whom he had a good relationship, for a routine phone check-in. In this case, the coordination between members of the treatment team and community resources was truly life-saving.

Care Coordination

Trauma Social Worker: Hi Randy, this is Allison O'Sullivan. I'm the trauma social worker you spoke with in the hospital. I wanted to call to check in to see how you were doing. How are you? (Randy may not have talked to an individual he didn't know, but he had a relationship with the inpatient trauma social worker.)

Randy: Not so good. I actually texted 988 today, but they weren't very helpful. Randy talked about his recurrent suicidality and his recent emergency department visit.

Trauma Social Worker: Why don't you go back? I can call ahead and try to make sure you get the help you need.

Randy: Ah, I'll be OK. The last time I went, they didn't do anything to help me anyway.

Trauma Social Worker: Are you having thoughts of wanting to hurt yourself now?

Randy: After a minute of silence, Randy stated,"I'd rather not say."

Trauma Social Worker: I'm really concerned, Randy. It's OK if you are having those thoughts. I'm here to help you. If you don't feel comfortable going to the hospital, would you feel more comfortable if someone from the mobile crisis team came to your house to see you? (The trauma social worker was very worried, though he knew the importance of validating his emotional experience, given the multiple recent invalidating experiences with other mental health providers. In the background, they had notified their trauma social work partner Amy Vinyard for assistance, who contacted the community mental health agency hotline to begin the process of dispatching the mobile crisis unit.)

(Continued)

Randy: Nah, I'm OK. My place is a mess. I don't want anybody coming in here.

Trauma Social Worker: They don't have to come in; they can talk to you outside. (Clinician tries to maintain rapport, leverage their existing relationship, and eliminate any obstacles or excuses.) Actually, I have them on the other line. Let's talk together on a three-way call.

Randy agrees to the crisis team visit. He is admitted for inpatient psychiatric treatment. A week later, he calls the TACS Psych trauma social worker immediately after his discharge from the psychiatric hospital, expressing gratitude for their intervention. "Thanks for sticking with me," he said. "I had a gun in my hand when you called and would have shot myself."

End-of-life issues: legacy work

Justin was a 27-year-old with a complicated hospital course after a gunshot wound. Justin had significant abdominal injuries, including a liver laceration and pancreatic injury. He subsequently developed peritonitis and multiple organ failure. Medical and surgical options became limited, and Justin decided to accept comfort care as medical and surgical options were limited and unlikely to be of benefit.

End of Life

Clinician: These are difficult times. I know you've been feeling very poorly. What thoughts and feelings have you been having?

Justin: I have so little time left. I know that. I really struggle with how to make sense of that and what it all means.

Clinician: Sometimes general, questions about what life means are hard to answer. It can be more useful to think about what your life meant and what it can still mean.

Justin: I want to leave something behind. I've done a lot of bad things, and I have a lot of regrets. It's my own fault that I got shot.

Clinician: Regrets are normal, but I've had the feeling during the times we've talked that you've done the best you could in situations that were sometimes very difficult. (Attempts to broaden perspective away from negative memories and guilt with genuine reflections on the patient's kind and caring manner.)

Justin: I have really tried to be good to my mom. And my son is so sweet. He's little, just 2. I'll really miss him.

Clinician: What can you leave behind? (At this point, legacy work could begin.)

Justin decided to write a long letter to his son, which he dictated to the clinician. He decided to also have a conversation with his mother in which he broached deeper issues of his regrets, but also his love for her. He became progressively more ill, developed delirium, and died 2 days later, peacefully, with his mother at his side.

Somatic therapy: using focusing

We met Chris in our discussion in Chapter 9 (Somatic therapies and acute trauma). He is a hiker and tennis player admitted for a prostatectomy, but awakened during surgery. He had been quiet and subdued but became more interactive after a somatic, focusing-style intervention.

Focusing

Clinician: I know you've been pretty quiet with the other staff and me. It can be hard to talk much after all you've been through. Sometimes it can help to talk to your body and see what it's feeling.

Chris: It's fine. It's all good.

Clinician: Sometimes those quick answers mean your head is talking, not your body. Give it a minute. Just listen and see what comes up. (Chris's response was quick and automatic, suggesting an overlearned, overpracticed response pattern, not a genuine answer from his body.)

Chris: I know what you mean. I just kind of automatically say that. (Chris pauses) I guess "alone" would be the word.

Clinician: Check it out again with your body, just to make sure that feels right. (Chris has identified a handle, "alone," but it is important to recheck whether that handle is just right or if there is a better handle.)

Chris: Actually, "betrayed" is a better word. I feel like I was betrayed by my body, and it betrayed me. There is hurt there.

Clinician: Does that word, "betrayed," feel right? (Checks out the new handle.)

Chris: Yes, that feels right.

Medical trauma: reporting an unwanted outcome

Jake is a 40-year-old male admitted after vehicular trauma resulting in extensive injury to his left leg. Prior to surgery, the surgical team was hopeful the leg could be saved, but unexpected technical issues during surgery made it impossible to save the leg.

Medical Trauma

Surgeon: We have some bad news. When we went to try to repair the damage to your leg, we weren't able to. The damage was too extensive. We had to amputate your leg below the knee.

Jake: What do you mean?

Surgeon: There was unfortunately no way to save your whole leg. Due to how severe your injuries were, we had to remove the bottom portion of your leg six

(Continued)

inches below your knee. (The surgeon realized they were a bit too abstract and not clear enough, trying too hard to soften the news. Repeats the message more clearly and directly.)

Jake: How is that possible? You said you could fix the leg. (Denial and shock are common responses. Jake struggles with acceptance.)

Surgeon: We hoped we could, and we thought we could, but the damage to the tissue was too severe. We did all we could. I'm sorry. I know we told you we thought we could repair the leg, but we couldn't. (Expresses genuine regret that the hopeful prediction was inaccurate.)

Jake: That can't be true, doc. No, I don't believe it. You guys must have screwed up with my leg!

Surgeon: I know it's a shock. It's something we hoped to avoid at all costs. But we just couldn't. (Surgeon is forthright in expressing genuine regret. He does not become defensive when the patient blames him but reiterates that all possible efforts were made. The surgeon could have made a simple explanation of the technical issues, but decided this was not what the patient really wanted or needed at this time. Detailed explanations can be experienced as defensive.)

Jake: What am I going to do with one leg? What is that going to mean?

Surgeon: We'll be with you for your recovery. You'll get the best care possible, both in taking care of the remaining leg and during the long-term work of recovery and prosthesis, and helping you function as best as possible. (Chooses to respond to the emotional content and fear of abandonment rather than the details of recovery. Emphasizes that the patient will not be abandoned but will be cared for. No attempt is made to minimize the difficulty of the trauma or sugarcoat the impact. A realistic promise of care is made.)

Addressing relational dynamics in support systems

Fred is 23-year-old who was shot while repairing his car. He had a lengthy hospital admission after the shooting. Fred's parents had divorced when he was 10. They both lived in the area and had significant contact with Fred, but rarely saw each other. After Fred's acute trauma, they decided to try to collaborate around his care. They would visit Fred frequently, and their visits would often overlap. Staff noticed that Fred would often be upset when either of his parents visited, but especially upset when he saw them both. Fred had a stoic demeanor and tended to minimize any emotional issues, a long-standing response since childhood stemming from having to be the emotional caregiver for his parents.

Support Systems

Clinician: So, how have you been doing?

Fred: Fine. (Looks very upset)

Clinician: Are you sure you're fine? You look upset. (Clinician labels visible affect.)

(Continued)

Fred: I'm fine.

Clinician: Looks like your parents were just walking out. How was your visit with them? *(Gentle confrontation.)*

Fred: I get so tired of them sometimes. They keep squabbling right in front of me. I feel like I'm 10 years old again.

Clinician: It's so easy for families to fall back into old patterns of behavior in a time of crisis like this. (The clinician carefully avoids siding with either party. To blame the parents might make Fred protective of them and end the opportunity to explore a new way of interacting with them. Instead of confrontation, offers psychoeducation.)

Fred: Totally. It becomes me taking care of them again, just like it always was. And I'm the one who is sick and needs help.

Clinician: That's very healthy, to focus on your needs. That's what we all need to focus on. What do you think could be handled differently with their visits? Remember, you are entitled to ask for what you need right now. (Encourages healthy self-care and assertiveness.)

Fred: I'm not sure. I really am grateful that they visit. I don't want to say anything that might upset them.

Clinician: You are the one in crisis now. They need to be able to handle you clearly, telling them what you want and need. (Education, support, encouragement.)

Fred: Well, one simple thing they could do is visit separately. Then I could actually talk to them. It goes much better when just one of them is here.

Clinician: That is a great idea. How would you like to tell them about that?

Fred: I guess the next time they come. But I'm afraid it won't go well. They are going to start blaming each other, then get mad at me.

Clinician: Would you like me to be there when you talk to them? (The clinician offers the concrete support of their presence during this difficult conversation. In longer-term treatment in an outpatient setting, the clinician might have encouraged Fred's independence and autonomy in having the conversation with his parents by himself. But in the short-term context of inpatient acute trauma care, the clinician decided that a more rapid change was more appropriate.)

Fred: That would be great, thanks. They are coming tomorrow at 2 p.m.

Clinician: Fantastic. I can be there. This can be a great chance to experience dealing with your parents in a different way and insisting on your own needs. (The clinician subtly emphasizes that their involvement is a transitional phase that can lead to a different interactive pattern with their parents, which would represent a form of posttraumatic growth.)

The family meeting went well. The clinician was able to model openness and direct communication and give Fred permission, by example, to do the same. Fred was able to express his appreciation for his parents' help and his frustration with their conflicts. They had not realized the impact of their behaviors and were genuinely remorseful. They promised to visit only separately and were able to tell Fred how much they care about him. Fred began to be more authentic in his communication with his parents.

Cultural humility

The term "cultural humility" describes the clinical approach to understanding and working with patients from a different culture. It implies a willingness to learn without stereotypes or biases.

We met Rosa in Chapter 16 (Considering cultural context). Rosa was raised in the Caribbean and grew up practicing Santeria. She was living with her daughter and slipped and fell down a few stairs. She told staff that a ghost pushed her and insisted that salt be sprinkled in front of the door to her room.

Cultural Issues

Clinician: Tell me about the fall.

Rosa: I was on the stairs, and it was like a ghost pushed me.

Clinician: What did you feel exactly? (Here, the clinician is seeking to understand the actual experience rather than the religious interpretation of the experience. The clinician is not judging the interpretation.)

Rosa: Well, I was hurrying. I had just gotten up. The dog had left a toy on the stairs. I had to step around it, and I stumbled. Felt so weird losing my balance like that. Damn ghost.

Clinician: That sounds scary. Do you have experiences like that a lot with ghosts? (The clinician has heard a very plausible story of a fall related to environmental issues, with a culture-bound interpretation made by the patient. Still, the clinician wants to clarify how pervasive the ghostly experiences might be to rule out potential psychosis.)

Rosa: Oh, I see ghosts a lot. Mostly, I can just feel them. They're like sudden flashes of cold, or they flicker past in the corner of my eyes, like shadows.

Clinician: Ah, I see. (Clinician is reassured that the perceptual experiences are not typical psychotic hallucinations and not associated with fear or dysphoric affect. With the subject's permission, collateral is obtained, which again confirms that the experiences are culturally normative.)

Transitioning to outpatient care

Jim has been in the hospital for about 3 weeks after multiple abdominal wounds from a drive-by shooting. Jim has done well psychologically throughout a long hospital course and has developed a strong relationship with the TACS Psych clinician. Now it is time for him to be discharged and to begin follow-up with outpatient behavioral health services. In this dialog a great deal is said with very few words.

A Warm Handoff

Clinician: Jim, I wanted to introduce you to Anthony. As I mentioned to you yesterday, Anthony will be your doctor in the outpatient program after you are discharged tomorrow. (Warm, in-person handoff with introduction.) Is it OK if I

(Continued)

share with him some of the general details of what we have been talking about? (The idea of continuity is very important to most patients. Many do not like to have to start from the beginning, especially with painful issues like acute trauma. The clinician adds the words "the general details" to emphasize the fact that although there will be continuity, the clinician's relationship with Jim has been individual, personal, and important. The two clinicians are not interchangeable, just as Jim will not just be interchangeable with another patient.)

Jim: Sure, doc, just tell Anthony whatever you think he needs to know. (Turning to Anthony.) Nice to meet you. Hope you can deal with all this stuff.

Outpatient Clinician: Glad to meet you too, Jim. I know you've been through a lot. David and I have been working together for a long time, and I understand some of the tough issues you have been facing. (Anthony takes over the conversation to initiate the new outpatient relationship, which in a sense begins now. He realizes from Jim's remark that he wants reassurance that he can deal with the suffering he is experiencing. Anthony doesn't give pat, naïve, global reassurance. Instead, he emphasizes his connection with David, using the positive relationship he has with Jim to facilitate the transition to the new relationship. In effect, Anthony is saying, "Like David, I have the capacity to be with you in your suffering.")

A Second-Best Handoff

Clinician: Jim, we talked yesterday about your upcoming discharge. As I told you, I would be setting up an appointment with Anthony, our outpatient psychologist. I have worked with Anthony a lot. If you'd like, I can fill him in on some of the issues we've been talking about. (The transition will be to a specific, named individual who knows the program and has a relationship with the clinician.)

Jim: Sure, that would be great. Does he "get it" as you do? Or will I have to explain everything to him?

Clinician: Anthony is very good. I think you will like him. He understands the kinds of issues trauma survivors go through, and, if it's OK with you, I will explain to him about the special issues you have with your sister. (Clinician assures Jim about the continuity of care by using a very specific example of an issue that he and David have worked on in the inpatient setting.)

Chapter summary

There is no perfect way to conduct oneself during high-stakes, and oftentimes unpredictable, emotionally laden conversations in acute care settings. The above collection of dialogues is meant to serve as an example of our distilled wisdom; to hopefully inspire different lines of thinking and plant a seed for change to enhance future clinical conversations. It is important to note that developing a personal style takes time, practice, and a considerable number of missteps prior to landing on "it." Many approaches are rooted in well-studied and widely accepted therapeutic modalities, though we must remember that the key ingredient to conducting successful challenging conversations doesn't always lie within a manual. An air of genuineness can oftentimes accomplish more than the most technically sound delivery. While a mirror may, indeed, be the most cruel object in the world as it accurately reflects that which presents before it, it is also a requisite for personal growth. Self-compassion, objectivity, and a willingness to navigate novel clinical scenarios will lead to substantial professional growth and ultimately better outcomes for those we serve.

References

Golden, B. P., Tackett, S., Kobayashi, K., Nelson, T., Agrawal, A., Pritchett, N., Tilton, K., Mills, G., Lorigiano, T.-J., Hirpa, M., Lin, J., Disney, S., Lautzenheiser, M., Huang, S., & Berry, S. A. (2022). Sitting at the bedside: Patient and internal medicine trainee perceptions. *Journal of General Internal Medicine, 37*(12), 3038–3044. https://doi.org/10.1007/s11606-021-07231-4.

Swayden, K. J., Anderson, K. K., Connelly, L. M., Moran, J. S., McMahon, J. K., & Arnold, P. M. (2012). Effect of sitting vs. standing on perception of provider time at bedside: a pilot study. *Patient Education and Counseling, 86*(2), 166–171. https://doi.org/10.1016/j.pec.2011.05.024.

Chapter 23

Trauma narratives: historical and literary examples

Stories of trauma and recovery

Personal, literary, and mythological narratives can help us understand different aspects of the trauma experience. Besides the case examples shared in previous chapters, the following narratives illuminate specific aspects of the human experience of trauma. The terrifying power of trauma has been recognized throughout history and is part of the fabric of human culture. Life histories and timeless stories show us that in studying acute trauma, we are continuing to revitalize an ancient but still living cultural tradition.

Posttraumatic growth and the why of living: Viktor Frankl

Viktor Frankl, the creator of what he called logotherapy, was a victim of serious trauma. His traumatic experiences colored his work and theories. Many of Frankl's ideas are at the core of existential therapy, narrative therapy, and acceptance and commitment therapy. As the title of one of Frankl's most famous books, Man's Search for Meaning, suggests, the central human need is not sex or power but a search for meaning (Frankl, 1962). Pain becomes bearable when it has a purpose or meaning; trauma becomes bearable when life has a purpose. In the face of ongoing torture and humiliation, only those who can hold on to a sense of a higher purpose of meaning can survive.

Frankl grew up in the Jewish sector of Vienna. He faced abuse and poverty, then, with the rise of fascism, he and his family were sent to concentration camps. His wife and parents died there; Viktor survived. His message is a crucial one and invokes the centrality of the lived experience of the trauma survivor. As Frankl put it, "Those who have a 'why' to live, can bear with almost any 'how'" (Frankl, 1962). Although logotherapy and existential therapy do not lend themselves readily to manualized therapies and efficacy trials, they are intuitively appropriate and evidence-informed.

The Psychology of Acute Trauma. DOI: https://doi.org/10.1016/B978-0-443-33212-8.00026-9

Survivor guilt: Maya Angelou

The great poet and activist Maya Angelou was raised in a context of family disruption. Early in her childhood, she was living with her grandparents and doing well, but then her father appeared unexpectedly and brought her back to her mother in St. Louis. At the age of 8, she was abused and raped by her mother's boyfriend. She told her brother, who told other family members. The rapist was jailed briefly, then released. Soon after his release, he was murdered, probably by members of Angelou's family, in revenge for the rape.

Angelou was overwhelmed by guilt after the murder. She felt that speaking the man's name caused his death, and she became mute. As she wrote in her famous autobiographical novel, I Know Why the Caged Bird Sings, "I thought, my voice killed him: I killed that man because I told his name. And then I thought I would never speak again." (Angelou, 1969). She was mute for almost 5 years, overwhelmed by guilt. Finally, with the encouragement of a loving teacher, Angelou began to speak again.

Angelou developed a deep love of literature and writing, transforming her traumatic experiences into highly influential autobiographical works. She read a poem to a nationwide audience at Bill Clinton's inauguration and was a prominent spokesperson for human rights causes.

Survivor, guilt typically involves a traumatic event with both survivors and fatalities, like a motor vehicle crash. The survivors sense the inherent injustice of the situation and feel responsibility for that injustice. Maya Angelou's experience of survivor's guilt is complex because it involves the death of the perpetrator of the assault. Angelou did what she should have done in informing her family of the assault, but her right action had serious consequences.

Moral injury and resilience: St. Paul

The story of St. Paul's conversion to belief in Christ is well known. As described in the Acts of the Apostles, Paul, then named Saul, was on his way to Damascus with writs of authority from Jewish religious authorities to arrest Jews in Damascus who were followers of Jesus. On that road, Paul was struck from his horse, a bright light filled the air, and a voice said, "Saul, Saul, why do you persecute me?" Paul was struck blind. His sight was restored by the Jewish healer Ananias, and Paul had a religious conversion. He changed his name to Paul to underline his change of heart. He not only became a Christian but one of the boldest, bravest, and most energetic of Jesus's disciples, with the new and radical idea of spreading Jesus's teaching to Gentiles. He is considered one of the founders of Christianity.

Just before the description of Paul's conversion, Acts describes another important event in early Christian history, the stoning of St. Stephen. St. Stephen was an early leader of the Christian movement and is considered the first Christian martyr. Saul had a central role in his stoning, having gathered the cloaks of those who would be hurling stones. Stephen, as he died this horrific death, begged God to forgive those who were stoning him. We might imagine the stoning of St. Stephen as an example of moral injury for Paul. Perhaps that moral injury and guilt about the death of Stephen set the stage for his later conversion.

After his conversion experience, Paul developed remarkable resilience. During his ministry, he was arrested, beaten, flogged, and stoned. He even survived three shipwrecks. With his new religious faith, he accepted all these traumas with remarkable equanimity, according to his letters. They were simply necessary sacrifices for his faith, offerings for the glory of Christ.

Posttraumatic growth: George Wallace

George Wallace was a prominent segregationist politician in the 1960s, 70 s and 80 s. He served as the governor of Alabama for 16 years. In his inaugural address as Alabama's governor in 1963, he declared, "Segregation now, segregation tomorrow, segregation forever" (Bishop, 2025). Wallace ran for president on four occasions. When he ran as an independent in 1968, he won five Southern states. While running for president again in 1972, he was the victim of an assassination attempt that left him paralyzed from the waist down. After the attempt, he seemed to display a genuine change of heart. He won the governorship of Alabama again in 1974 but renounced his former segregationist views. He attempted to make amends with the Black community and appointed several Black individuals to positions in his administration. He began to describe himself as a born-again Christian, and in a private letter to his would-be assassin, then in prison, he forgave him and wished for him to accept Christ so that the two of them could be united in heaven. His trauma and subsequent paralysis seemed to initiate posttraumatic growth (PTG).

Posttraumatic growth with posttraumatic stress disorder: Paul and Ludwig Wittgenstein

In Vienna in the early 1900s, the Wittgenstein family was one of the wealthiest in Europe, and one of the most intellectually prominent. Margaret Wittgenstein was an important patron of the arts and posed for Gustav Klimt. Paul Wittgenstein was an accomplished concert pianist. Their brother Ludwig was a brilliant theoretical logician and trained at Cambridge under the mathematician Bertrand Russell. He would become one of the greatest philosophers of the 20th century.

World War I was traumatic for the family. Paul was shot in the arm by Russian troops, the surgery was botched, and he lost his arm to amputation. Despite the challenges of being a one-armed pianist, he was determined to continue his career. Because of his wealth, he commissioned some of the great composers of his time, including Prokofiev, Strauss, and Britten, to develop pieces for a one-armed pianist. He continued to tour, eventually moving to the United States where he continued his career and lived on Long Island. This aspect of his recovery suggests PTG, but he, also seemed to experience posttraumatic stress disorder (PTSD). After his injury, he was irritable and demanding, alienating audiences and sponsors. He considered the works he commissioned to be his personal property and altered them at will, alienating his composer friends.

The philosopher Ludwig serves as another example of PTG plus PTSD. Although he himself was uninjured in World War I, he witnessed horrific events, describing them in his wartime personal journals, as well as suffering vicariously, the trauma of his brother's amputation. His academic work changed dramatically after the war. Instead of being a logician, he became a philosopher. His great work, Tractatus Logico-Philosophicus, written in a prisoner-of-war camp, was about the limits of language and logic (Wittgenstein, 1921). In that work, he redefined many of the traditional problems of philosophy as linguistic problems. He moved beyond philosophy, as well, to a philosophical mysticism. The final sentence in this short book is, "Whatsoever we cannot speak about we must pass over in silence." What did he need to pass over in silence?

Rereading Wittgenstein now, I am reminded of the words of Frida Kahlo about her acute trauma, quoted earlier in this book. She wrote, "If you knew how terrible it is to know suddenly, as if a bolt of lightning elucidated the earth. Now I live in a painful planet, transparent as ice, but it is as if I had learned everything in a few seconds" (Herrera, 1983). One feels that Wittgenstein suddenly grasped a similar mystery but could not speak about it. A scholar looking at a well-known photograph of Wittgenstein after the war noted that he had the "thousand-yard stare," which was a term coined by the U.S. Marine Corps to describe a certain faraway look that trauma survivors can have, where they look off into the distance, seeming to see something unseen (Santiáñez, 2018).

Wittgenstein made dramatic life changes after his traumatic war experiences. The changes were both positive and negative, suggesting PTG occurring simultaneously with PTSD. He was now a prominent philosopher and was offered the chairmanship of the Department of Philosophy at Cambridge University. Instead, he abandoned philosophy and became an elementary school teacher in rural Austria. He gave away all his money, feeling that he should live only on what he could earn. His bright students loved him and considered him a brilliant teacher, but he was ill-tempered and physically abusive with students who were less bright. Late in life, after he had resumed a career in philosophy, he returned to the rural town where he had taught to apologize, in person, to the students he felt he had mistreated.

Acceptance and reconnecting with the world: Rumi and the murder of his beloved

Rumi was a 13th-century Persian poet and Sufi religious figure whose popularity and importance cross national and religious boundaries still today. He has the unusual distinction of being the most popular poet in both the United States and Iran. Rumi's life was colored by a specific traumatic event, the murder or disappearance of his beloved friend and teacher, Shams Tabrizi.

Rumi met Shams in 1244, when Rumi was 37, and Shams was in his 60s. Rumi was an academic and a scholar; Shams was a wandering mystic. The two became inseparable in an intense, loving master–disciple relationship. In 1248, while the two were talking, Shams was called out to the back door of Rumi's home and never returned. Most likely, he was murdered by jealous members of Rumi's extended family. Rumi withdrew from the world and spent several years in intense grief. He emerged from grief and began to write the ecstatic mystical poetry for which he is now famous. One of these poems reflected on the loss of Shams:

Where did the handsome beloved go? …
He spread his light among us like a candle.
Where did he go? So strange, where did he go without me? …
If his heart and soul are joined with God,
And he left this realm of earth and water, where did he go? (Rumi, 2017)

One of Rumi's great works was called The Collected Poems of Shams, as if Shams's spirit became part of Rumi. The scholar became a poet and mystic. The Mevlevi Sufi religious order, known as the Whirling Dervishes, was founded by Rumi's followers after his death.

The stigma of trauma: Eloise and Abelard

Eloise and Abelard were 12th-century lovers haunted by assault and trauma. Abelard was a well-known teacher and scholar, one of the most respected of his time. He fell in love with one of his students, Eloise. He approached her father, offering to provide private tutoring to Eloise. Her father agreed, honored by the attention paid to his daughter by a famous scholar. Soon, Eloise and Abelard became lovers. Eloise then became pregnant, and the angry kinsmen of Eloise broke into Abelard's home and castrated him. Eloise was sent to a convent. The two continued to write frequently. Eloise, in her letters, pleaded with Abelard to visit her so that they could share their grief. Abelard wrote long and loving letters in response but refused to visit, partially out of fear and guilt, partially out of shame at his injury.

Many aspects of this sad and tragic story are worth pondering. To medieval audiences, the relationship between Eloise and Abelard was inappropriate because it involved fornication; to us, it is inappropriate because of the power differential of a relationship between teacher and student. Abelard lost social and academic status after the incident, not because of the sexual relationship, but because of his trauma. In the world at that time, to be castrated meant that one could not hold positions of power or authority in the Church. Although he was a victim of an assault, Abelard was stigmatized by the type of injury he had. As we have previously discussed throughout this book, in modern times, trauma survivors still face stigma sometimes. Victims of gunshot wounds, for instance, are sometimes assumed to have been somewhere they shouldn't have been or to have done something they shouldn't have been doing. Abelard's story reminds us that the idea of blaming the victim is an ancient one.

Trauma therapy: The Fisher King

The Fisher King is, of course, a mythological figure, not a real one, but his story beautifully illustrates several aspects of trauma, especially the deeper aspects of trauma therapy. The Fisher King, named Anfortas, is an important figure in the Arthurian legends (Jung & von Franz, 1970). He has a mysterious wound in his groin, inflicted by a magical spear, that can never heal. Sorely limited by his wound, he can only fish. Yet the wounded Anfortas is the guardian of the Holy Grail, one of the most sacred objects in Britain, sometimes described as the chalice of Christ, although that description is likely a Christianization of a more ancient myth. The Grail can only be attained, and Anfortas can only be healed, by a knight who asks the right questions. Anfortas lives in a magical castle that can only be found when one is lost. The knight Percival stumbles upon the castle, meets the Fisher King, and witnesses a great pageant involving the Grail. Percival foolishly remains silent through this experience, afraid of giving offense by being too inquisitive. When he awakens the next morning, he is in an empty field; the castle, the Grail, and the King are gone. He failed to attain the Grail and heal the wounded King, although success was within his grasp, because he failed to ask the right questions. The Grail can only be attained by a knight bold enough to ask of the Fisher King the three grail questions: "What ails thee?" "What do you need?" and "Whom does the Grail serve?"

The story of the Fisher King illuminates important areas of the trauma experience. First, Anfortas's wound is eternal yet sacred as it is caused by a magical spear. This reminds us of the concept of survivorship and that the process of recovery from trauma is a lifelong one. Second, recovery from trauma depends not on passive waiting but on asking the right questions. These questions address issues that a good clinician needs to address, but they are also, internally, the questions the trauma survivor must ask themself to facilitate recovery and, potentially, PTG. The final question, "Whom does the grail serve?" is a spiritual one and addresses the kind of existential and spiritual questions that trauma can raise.

Another posttraumatic growth story, with a traumatic brain injury and a near-death experience: Michel de Montaigne

Michel de Montaigne was a prominent French statesman and philosopher of the 16th century. He is most remembered now as a writer and as the inventor of the personal essay form. He wrote a large collection of essays, some of which are still considered among the most influential ever written. His style of writing, which would now be called narrative nonfiction, interwove personal anecdotes with philosophical reflection. His style was considered self-indulgent in his time but was also prescient, and his essays are now considered works of genius.

Montaigne became a writer after a serious traumatic injury. As he was riding his horse, it collided with another horse at full gallop, and Montaigne was thrown 15 feet in the air and tumbled to the ground. He was unconscious for an extended period of time and was carried to his home unconscious and assumed to be dead. But he began to stir, vomited, and became confused and agitated. Upon returning to consciousness, Montaigne described a vivid experience of floating above his unconscious body: "There the horse lay, bowled over and stunned, and I ten or twelve paces beyond, dead stretched on my back, my face all bruised and skinned … having no more motion or feeling than a log" (as cited in [Krulwich, 2013]). Montaigne described his feeling of impending death as one of intense peace, calm, and acceptance. He recovered from his fall as a changed man.

Montaigne abandoned his public life and retired to his castle to focus exclusively on reading and writing. In the 22 years that followed, he wrote his great work, called Essays, which still influential in psychology, philosophy, and education. Was Montaigne's dramatic change in career and discovery of a new literary form an example of PTG or the consequence of his near-death experience, or both?

The problem of evil: Fyodor Dostoevsky

The great Russian writer Fyodor Dostoevsky was a trauma survivor:

December 22, 1849

Today, the 22nd of December, we were all taken to Semyonovsky Square. There, the death sentence was read to us, we were given the Cross to kiss, the dagger was broken over our heads, and our funeral toilet (white shirts) was made. Then three of us were put standing before the palisades for the execution of the death sentence. I was sixth in the row; we were called up by groups of three, and so I was in the second group, and had not more than a minute to live. I thought of you, my brother, and of yours; in that last moment, you alone were in my mind; then first I learned how very much I love you, my beloved brother! I had time to embrace Plechtcheyev and Dourov, who stood near me, and to take my leave of them (Dostoevsky, 2003).

Fyodor Dostoevsky had been imprisoned for criticizing the Tsar. The event described above is his false execution, a torture technique made famous by the Okhrana, the tsarist Russian Empire's secret police. As Dostoevsky described, the prisoner was prepared for execution and the certainty of death, only to have the commutation of his sentence at the last instant.

In Dostoevsky's case, the commutation of his death sentence was followed by a 4-year imprisonment in Siberia, where he regularly faced and was exposed to vicious beatings and cruelty. The impact of the sadism and cruelties he faced was lifelong; his letters and novels are haunted by the impacts of his traumas. Dostoevsky was a devout Christian, and he struggled most acutely with the question of why a good and just God allows the presence of the horrors and evils of the world. The "Grand Inquisitor" story within The Brothers Karamazov is one of the most beautiful expositions in all of literature about the problem of evil (Dostoevsky, 2002). The "Why me?" question so often asked by trauma survivors is posed by Ivan Karamazov, the brilliant atheist of the brothers. He describes at length to his brother Alyosha, a novice monk, horrifying details of human suffering and cruelty. He insists that no good and just God could have created such a world. Alyosha tearfully assents yet maintains his powerful spiritual beliefs. As did Dostoevsky. Despite his suffering, he remained a devout believer, and his faith in spiritual transformation is the cornerstone of his literary works. "I believe like a child that suffering will be healed and made up for, that all the humiliating absurdity of human contradictions will vanish like a pitiful mirage" (Dostoevsky, 2003).

Cultural aspects of trauma: Camille Claudel

Camille Claudel was a French sculptor born in 1864. She worked for many years with Paul Rodin. They worked side by side, and sometimes the boundaries between their work were unclear. Claudel faced substantial gender discrimination as a female sculptor, and some of her work was undoubtedly appropriated by Rodin, who was a prominent sculptor at the time of their collaboration. Some of her sculptures explored sexual and intimate themes, and showing those works under her own name would have been seen as unacceptable.

In her 40s Claudel began to show behavioral changes (Ayral-Clause, 2022). She became more isolative, destroyed some of her works, and became suspicious that Rodin was stealing her ideas and trying to kill her. Her father continued to support her, but he died in 1913. She was not informed of his death, and 8 days later, at the insistence of her brother Paul, she was psychiatrically hospitalized. Considerable questions remain as to the nature of her illness and whether she needed to be hospitalized. The hospital, on several occasions, wanted to discharge her, but her family refused. She remained in the hospital for 30 years. Visitors from the artistic community described Claudel as rational and appropriate during hospital visits. Her mother never visited her, her sister visited her once, and Paul visited 6 times in 30 years.

In the American Psychiatric Association's (2022) Diagnostic and Statistical Manual of Mental Disorders, Fifth Edition, Text Revision (DSM-5-TR), incarceration is not officially considered a trauma unless it is accompanied by an event, like an assault, while in prison (American Psychiatric Association, 2022). The trauma of incarceration has been called "carceral trauma" or postincarceration syndrome. In Claudel's case, the cultural and gender issues clearly were involved in her tragic and possibly inappropriate hospitalization. Her hospitalization was involuntary; she was signed in by her brother and a doctor. Paul, who was a well-known writer and socially prominent, was able to keep her hospitalized despite the repeated recommendations of the hospital. Her delusions about her work being stolen likely had at least a kernel of truth in view of her complex artistic relationship with Rodin. Gender inequality was central to Claudel's tragic story. She was probably exploited by Rodin, then brutalized by her family. As discussed in the PTG discussion, cultural factors can preclude PTG in the contexts of poverty or discrimination.

Although forgotten in her time and despite her relatively brief period of artistic productivity, Claudel is now considered to be a major figure in modern sculpture, at least equal to, if not superior to, Rodin.

The internal experience of trauma: Job

The Bible's book of Job is an ancient exploration of the question that haunts so many trauma survivors and their families: "Why do bad things happen to good people?" The authorship of the book is unknown, although Jewish tradition insists that it is authored by Moses himself. It is probably a layered manuscript, with parts dating as far back as Moses's time, around 1500 B.C.E., but with many parts added after 500 B.C.E. It is the only book of the Bible written in the format of a dialog with various speakers, including Job, four of his friends and finally Yahweh himself, who addresses Job "out of the whirlwind" ((Edinger, 1992), p. 89).

The book begins with God and Satan discussing Job, who is universally acknowledged to be a good and just man, who is also wealthy and held in high regard by society. Satan wonders if Job would still be good if he faced calamities. They wager, and God grants Satan the freedom to visit Job with any means of horror, short of death, to test his faithfulness. Job loses his wealth, his flocks, his lands, and finally his children. He is beset by boils and other bodily ailments. He even begins to experience nightmares, perhaps related to his multiple traumas:

> When I think that my bed will comfort me,
> that sleep will relive my complaining,
> thou dost terrify me with dreams

and affright me with visions. ([The New English Bible, 1970], Job 7:13–14)

Believing in the just world hypothesis, Job's friends exhort him repeatedly to confess his sins, admit his errors, and insist that he must have done something terribly wrong to be punished as cruelly as he has been. Job is a proto-existential hero, and he insists on his truth, that he has done nothing wrong. He even demands a reckoning from God Himself.

take thy heavy hand clean away from me
and let not the fear of thee strike me with dread.
Then summon me, and I will answer;
or I will speak first, and do thou answer me. ([The New English Bible, 1970], Job 13:21–22)

God does answer and, as all trauma survivors come to know, does so in a way that is unexpected and overwhelming. God insists on his own "divineness" and inscrutability. In effect he asks Job a long series of riddles, that, like Zen koans, jar his complacency and sense of human understanding.

Where were you when I laid the earth's foundations?
Tell me, if you know and understand. …
Did you proclaim the rules that govern the heavens,
or determine the laws of nature on earth? ([The New English Bible, 1970], Job 38: 4–33)

This last question is a particularly important one. God reminds Job that the world runs by God's laws, not human law. Job is stunned into awe and silence. He replies "I knew of thee then only by report, but now I see thee with my own eye sees" ([The New English Bible, 1970], Job 42:5). Job points out in these words that the knowledge he has, through the actual experience of trauma, is of a different nature than any academic or philosophical understanding of God's role in the world. He has a flash of insight not unlike that experienced by Frida Kahlo, quoted earlier in this book, when she said that she had learned, in an instant, the true nature of the world. God vindicates Job, declaring that Job had been faithful to Him and that the horrors visited on him were not punishments for wrongs Job had committed. God was just being God, asserting His power, perhaps acting in accordance with some higher understanding of justice that supersedes our own.

In the end, the book of Job offers a symbolic version of PTG, or at least posttraumatic recovery. The conclusion of the book, which is probably a later addition to the work, offers an attempt at a restitution narrative (hearkening back to our earlier discussion of trauma narratives and the work of Arthur Frank). Job's health, wealth, and flocks are restored; his material possessions are actually doubled. The 10 children he lost are replaced by 10 more. Here, the attempt at a restitution narrative falters. I am not sure that from Job's perspective, his children are as interchangeable as his flocks. Job lives for another 140 years, time enough to ponder God's inscrutable ways.

The injustice of trauma: Monica Seles

In 1993, Monica Seles was the world's number one-ranked women's tennis player and the premier tennis player of her era. By that time Seles, although she was only 19, had won nine Grand Slam titles. In the middle of a match in Hamburg, Germany, a crazed fan of one of her main competitors, Steffi Graf, ran onto the court and stabbed Seles in the back with a steak knife. The tennis world was shocked and outraged. Although the knife penetrated deep into Seles's back, no vital organs were injured. Her physical recovery was uncomplicated, but her psychological recovery was not. She retired from tennis for 2 1/2 years, suffering from posttraumatic stress symptoms, depression, and an eating disorder. She described trauma-related anxiety.

The tennis court had been her safe space, but that changed after her assault. "When I stepped on the court, that's when I'd get angry…. The tennis court was my place. Anything that was happening in my private life, I could forget about it and think of the ball. I felt the safest there….. Suddenly that was taken away" ([Cart, 1995], para. 6) Seles credited psychotherapy for her gradual recovery and comeback. "If I hadn't done that, gone to a psychologist, it would have been bye-bye, Monica" ([Cart, 1995], para. 8). Although she was never again the dominant player that she had been, she returned to the court and even won one more major tournament, the Australian Open, before retiring from tennis.

Seles was particularly pained by the injustice, not only of the assault itself, but by the minimal consequences that her assailant faced. He never actually served jail time and was only briefly on probation. "Everything he wanted, he got. I never got anything. Justice does not exists. He got Steffi to be No. 1…. He can go anywhere, he can be anywhere" ([Cart, 1995], para. 13).

Injustice is prominent in Seles's story not only in the assault itself, but in the aftereffects. Seles points out that her life was radically altered, but her assailant faced minimal consequences. Many acute trauma patients feel a similar injustice, a radical imbalance between their suffering and the consequences faced by the person who caused that suffering. This sense of injustice was an important issue Seles had to face during her recovery.

According to those close to her, Seles has finally found peace outside of the tennis world. She returned to public life briefly after her retirement to appear on the reality show Dancing with the Stars. Her autobiography, Getting a Grip: On My Body, My Mind, My Self, describes her painful recovery and the role of psychotherapy in that recovery (Seles, 2010).

Blaming the trauma survivor: Medusa

Ovid's narrative of the story of Medusa is a powerful version of the blaming of the survivor that can occur in trauma, especially sexual trauma. Medusa is known for her horrific appearance; snakes cover her head instead of hair, and her appearance is so horrific that anyone who looks at her turns to stone. According to Ovid, Medusa was once a beautiful maiden and a priestess in the goddess Athena's temple. Poseidon, the god of the sea, became attracted to her and raped her in the temple. Athena was outraged at the desecration of her temple. She could not punish Poseidon, a powerful god, so she punished the victim instead. In punishment for desecrating the temple, Athena transformed the innocent maiden into a monster with snakes for hair. Medusa was slain by Theseus, who beheaded her. He avoided being turned to stone by locating her reflection in his shield, thereby looking at her only indirectly, as if the forces of the patriarchy cannot "face" the wrongs they have committed.

Medusa, who is powerful, innocent, and punished for the crime of which she was a victim, has become a feminist heroine. Her survivor story depicts the blame women so often face after they are assaulted. Despite the sad end of the story, an element of PTG is present. Out of Medusa's decapitated head is born Pegasus, the great winged horse that signifies poetry, creativity, and inspiration. Sometimes PTG must wait until the next generation to occur.

Resilience: Django Reinhardt

Jean Reinhardt, known as Django, was one of the great jazz guitarists of all time. A regular in the Paris club scene of the 1940s, he toured the United States with Duke Ellington. His recordings and compositions, like "Minor Swing", have become jazz classics. He has influenced rock guitarists like Willie Nelson, Jeff Beck, and Jimmy Page. Jerry Garcia of the Grateful Dead said of him, "There's a lot of guys that play fast and a lot of guys that play clean, … but nobody plays with the whole fullness of expression that Django has" ((Cross, 2025), para. 6). The Allman Brothers' song "Jessica"was written as a tribute to Reinhardt.

Django was Romani and in his youth traveled with his clan in a traditional Roma caravan. In 1928, when Django was 19, his wagon caught fire (his wife made flowers with highly flammable celluloid). He had serious burns over half his body. He was hospitalized for 18 months, and he lost most of the fourth and fifth digits of his left hand. Doctors told him he would never play guitar or walk again, and they insisted on amputating his leg. With the help of his friends, Django fled the hospital. Over time, he taught himself to walk with a cane. He relearned guitar on a steel-string guitar designed by his brother, who was also an accomplished guitarist. He did fret work with his remaining fingers, using the stumps of the last two fingers only for some chords (Dregni, 2006).

Django's story is one of resilience rather than PTG. He was a great guitarist before his traumatic injury and became an even better one after his injury. He continued to play just like he continued to walk, despite the opinions and predictions of others. The heart of his music was in his mind, not his fingers.

Tragically, Django Reinhardt died in Paris at age 43, suffering a brain hemorrhage while walking home after a performance at a Paris club.

The janus face of posttraumatic growth: Christopher Reeve

As mentioned in Chapter 18, Posttraumatic Growth and Survivorship, PTG can have a "Janus face." Janus is the Roman god of transitions, beginnings, and endings. He was typically invoked at the beginning of festivals and ceremonies. Janus had two faces, one looking to the past, one looking to the future. PTG has been described as Janus-faced because of its ambivalent nature. PTG looks to a new future but also back at the trauma and its impacts, with grief. Genuine healing can exist simultaneously with naïve hope.

Christopher Reeve was a prominent actor in the 1970s and 80s. After training at the Juilliard School, he worked on Broadway. He won the starring role in the film Superman and its sequels, as well as in Somewhere in Time. In the 1980s, he became involved in equestrian sports, eventually participating in competitive dressage. At a tournament in 1995, his horse balked at a jump, and Reeve fell headfirst, his hands tangled in the reins. He fractured his first and second vertebrae. He became paralyzed from the neck down, unable to breathe on his own without a ventilator.

Reeve initially experienced hopelessness and despair, and even encouraged his wife to let him die. After a long recovery, he was able to return to some acting and directing. He starred in a remake of Hitchcock's Rear Window, a classic film about a disabled man watching suspicious events out of his window from his wheelchair. Reeve also became a prominent activist, speaking passionately about spinal cord research and developing the Christopher Reeve Foundation to support spinal cord research. In an interview after his recovery, Reeve said, "Who knows why an accident happens? The key is what you do afterwards… you have two choices. One is to stare out the window and gradually disintegrate. And the other is to mobilize and use all your resources, whatever they may be, to do something positive" (Fay, 1998).

The Janus-faced aspect of Reeve's recovery lies in his focus on a cure for spinal cord injury and on his insistence that one was imminent. Disability advocates have argued that Reeve's focus on a cure distracted from more important and realistic work on disability access. Additionally, by focusing on a cure, issues related to living and coping with disability were avoided. Living with a disability is less glamorous than hoping for a cure, but at the same time, according to these voices in the disability community, more authentic (Brown, 1996). Sometimes naïve hopefulness may be the only way of coping with despair. As the two-headed god Janus reminds us, looking forward means looking backward at the same time. Acceptance and hope are in a complex and constant dialog. Perhaps there is no perfect way to be a trauma survivor.

Rural trauma: Mordecai Brown

Although we tend to associate trauma with urban settings, trauma is very common in rural environments. Machinery is used extensively in rural settings, and sometimes farm workers are poorly trained. In the past, farms were family operations where safety standards were minimal.

Mordecai Brown grew up on a farm in rural Indiana in the 1880s. As a child, he was feeding material into the feed chopper. His hand slipped and got mangled. Much of his index finger had to be amputated, and his damaged middle finger was set poorly and healed severely bent. Likely, many rural youths at the time, dreamed of being a baseball player. Despite his damaged hand, he practiced by tirelessly aiming rocks at knotholes in stumps.

Brown eventually worked in coal mines in rural Indiana but played semi-pro baseball as a third baseman. One day, his team had no pitcher, and Brown was called to fill in. His damaged hand created an unusual grip, and his pitches had a drop and spin that made them very difficult to hit. In 1904, he joined the major leagues, playing for the Chicago Cubs. Newspapers nicknamed him "Three Finger Brown," a nickname he despised but which caught on. He went on to become one the of great pitchers of all time. His career earned run average (ERA) of 2.06 is the best of any major league pitcher with more than 200 wins. Brown's signature pitch was his curveball with its unique spin from his misshapen hand, which was considered almost unhittable (Haugh, 2008). Rural trauma and poor medical care created a legendary Hall of Fame pitcher.

Reliving trauma at the end-of-life: Kurtz and Joseph Conrad

Joseph Conrad's book Heart of Darkness, which was adapted into the Vietnam Conflict film Apocalypse Now, is a rich study of trauma and moral injury. The central character in the book, Kurtz, is both a perpetrator and survivor of trauma. Kurtz was a highly successful colonial rubber trader in the depths of the jungle along the Congo River in what is now Zaire. His success was based both on his ruthless style and his immersion in indigenous culture. Kurtz brutalized the indigenous people and was himself brutalized. He also witnessed the great brutality of other Europeans, suffering both trauma and moral injury as he tried to meet the ceaseless demands for rubber from his colonial sponsors.

In the story, the narrator, named Marlow, meets Kurtz in the depths of the jungle, where he has been accepted by an indigenous community. Kurtz is dying of a fever. The climax of the story is Kurtz's end-of-life experience. Kurtz tries to flee the help and support to die alone. He is forcibly restrained on board the ship intended to rescue him, where he remains until his death. Onboard that ship he appears to relive his past traumatic experiences. His final, dying words, whispered to Marlow, were," The horror! the horror!"

In the final part of the book, Marlow must return Kurtz's personal effects to his fiancée in London, who knew nothing of the horrors Kurtz had faced. His fiancée begged to know Kurtz's last words, assuming he thought of her at the end of his life. Marlow struggles with a decision about how to handle trauma. Does he tell the fiancée the truth or lie? He lies, keeps the trauma secret, and tells Kurtz's fiancée that her name was the last word that Kurtz uttered.

Heart of Darkness is based on Conrad's own traumatic experiences. Conrad was a survivor of complex trauma. His parents were imprisoned and died when he was only 7. As a youth, Conrad was profoundly depressed and suicidal. He later served in the British merchant marine. In that capacity, he spent time in the Congo, and experienced first-hand the brutality, greed, and ruthlessness of the colonial world. In the Congo, Conrad developed malaria and dysentery. Recurrent bouts of malaria plagued him for the rest of his life. He died of a myocardial infarction at the age of 66.

Trauma and recovery are central themes of many of Conrad's works. His main characters, like Kurtz and Lord Jim, are haunted by the effects of trauma from which they never recovered. His stories are not about PTG, but about the pervasive and unavoidable suffering that often occurs when traumatic stress responses go unaddressed.

Chapter summary

Human experience is sometimes best understood through narrative. This chapter illustrates, through narrative, some of the key points described in theoretical terms in previous chapters. This final chapter also pays homage to powerful human stories of trauma coping, and resilience

References

American Psychiatric Association (2022). Diagnostic and statistical manual of mental disorders (5th ed., text rev.). American Psychiatric Association Publishing. https://doi.org/10.1176/appi.books.9780890425787.

Angelou, M. (1969). *I know why the caged bird sings*. Random House.

Ayral-Clause, O. (2002). *Camille Claudel: A life*. Harry N. Abrams.

Bishop, M. (2025). *George Wallace and the campaign for forgiveness*. Grateful American Foundation.

Brown, S. E. (1996). *Super duper? The (unfortunate) ascendancy of Christopher Reeve*. Independent Living Institute.

Cart, J. (1995). *A return to the light: 'I was for so long in such a dark place,' Monica Seles says of her 2 1/2 year struggle to escape stabbing trauma*. Los Angeles Times.

Cross, R. (2025, May 20). "Nobody plays with the whole fullness": The one guitarist Jerry Garcia said nobody came close to. *Far Out*. https://faroutmagazine.co.uk/guitarist-jerry-garcia-said-nobody-came-close-to/.

Dostoevsky, F. (2002). *The brothers Karamazov*. Farrar, Straus and Giroux.

Dostoevsky, F. (2003). *Letters of Fyodor Michailovitch Dostoevsky to his family and friends.* University Press of the Pacific.

Dregni, M. (2006). *The life and times of a gypsy legend.* Oxford University Press.

Edinger, E. F. (1992). *Ego and archetype*. Shambhala Publications, 1972.

Fay, F. (1998). *Our first interview with Christopher Reeve*. Ability Magazine.

Frankl, V. (1962). *Man's Search for Meaning Beacon Press.* Beacon Press.

Haugh, D. (2008, June 29). Celebrated farmhand. *Chicago Tribune*. https://www.chicagotribune.com/2008/06/29/celebrated-farmhand/.

Herrera, H. (1983). *Frida: A biography of Frida Kahlo*. Harper & Row.

Jung, E., & von Franz, M.-L. (1970). *The Grail Legend.* Princeton University Press.

Krulwich, R. (2013, March 25). *Death, but softly*. KCUR/NPR in Kansas City. https://www.kcur.org/2013-03-25/death-but-softly.

Rumi, J. A.-D. (2017, November). *Where did the handsome beloved go?* Poetry Foundation. https://www.poetryfoundation.org/poetrymagazine/poems/144612/where-did-the-handsome-beloved-go.

Santiáñez, N. (2018). *Wittgenstein after the eleventh.* Wilfrid Laurier University Press.

Seles, M. (2010). *Getting a grip: On my mind, my body, my self.* Avery.

The New English Bible. Cambridge University Press, (1970).

Wittgenstein, L. (1921). Tractatus logico-philosophicus. In C. K. Ogden (Ed.). Kegan Paul, Trench, Trubner & Co.

Appendix: clinical tools and worksheets

Event, thought, emotion, and physical feeling record

Recommendations for use: Initial in-session practice to explore the presence of novel emotions and physiologic arousal. Can assist with diagnostic clarity and promote insight into potentially distressing stimulus-response relationships during out-of-session practice (Fig. A.1).

Coping skill record

Recommendations for use: Builds off progress made via the event, thought, emotion, physical feeling record to incorporate a focus on active utilization of coping skills and the patient's responses. Typically deployed during clinical courses that allow for multiple sessions to assess the efficacy of interventions during both in-session and between-session practice (Fig. A.2).

Stoplight tool

Recommendations for use: Communication skills tool that aims at increasing the quality of communication between patients, their teams and support networks. Instructions for use are located on the top of the worksheet (Fig. A.3).

Personal values card sort

Recommendations for use: Cards are designed to be cut out and placed in a single deck, with the "Not Important to Me," "Important to Me," and "Very Important to Me" cards placed in front of the patient. The patient then reads each card and sorts it into one of three piles, allowing for exploration of their value system. May be completed in one or more sessions (Fig. A.4).

Event, Thought, Emotion, Physical Feeling Record

As soon as you notice a change in your emotions or physical feelings complete the worksheet below, practice at least twice a day.

Date and Time	Event	Thought(s)	Emotion(s)	Physical Feeling(s)
	What happened before your emotions changed?	What thoughts or mental images did you experience?	What emotions did you have?	How did your body feel?

Example events:
- Loud noises
- Nightmares
- Certain smells
- Seeing something that reminds me of the traumatic event

Example thoughts:
- I'm never going to get better
- The world isn't safe
- Someone might hurt me
- I'm a burden to my family

Example emotions:
- Sadness
- Anger
- Frustration
- Worry
- Fear
- Guilt

Example physical feelings:
- Heart beating fast
- Hard to breath
- Tightness in chest
- Tingling in hands or feet
- Sweating
- Hot or cold flashes

FIGURE A.1 Event, thought, emotion, physical feeling record.

Coping Skill Record

As soon as you notice a change in your emotions or physical feelings complete the worksheet below, practice at least twice a day.

Date and Time	Event	Thought(s)	Emotion(s) and physical feelings	Coping Skill(s)	Response
	What happened before your emotions changed?	What thoughts or mental images did you experience?	What emotions did you have? How did your body feel? How intense were they on a 0 to 100 scale?	What coping skill did you use?	What emotions and physical feelings did you have? How intense were they after you used your skill (0 to 100)?
	Example events: • Loud noises • Nightmares • Certain smells • Seeing something that reminds me of the traumatic event	Example thoughts: • I'm never going to get better • The world isn't safe • Someone might hurt me • I'm a burden to my family	Example emotions: • Sadness • Anger • Frustration • Worry • Fear • Guilt	Example skills: • Deep breathing • Meditation • Social support • Fun activity	Example physical feelings: • Heart beating fast • Hard to breath • Tightness in chest • Tingling in hands or feet • Sweating • Hot or cold flashes

FIGURE A.2 Coping skill record.

Stoplight tool

Red light: A topic that should not be discussed, stop conversation
Yellow light: A topic that is leading to discomfort and should be changed
Green light: Conversation has returned to a place of comfortability
(To use, cut circles out or fold paper on dashed lines)

Red Light

Yellow Light

Green Light

FIGURE A.3 Stoplight tool.

PERSONAL VALUES Card Sort W.R. Miller, J. C'de Baca, D.B. Matthews, P.L. Wilbourne University of New Mexico, 2001	**IMPORTANT TO ME**
VERY IMPORTANT TO ME	**NOT IMPORTANT TO ME**
ACCEPTANCE to be accepted as I am 1 9/01	**ACCURACY** to be accurate in my opinions and beliefs 2 9/01
ACHIEVEMENT to have important accomplishments 3 9/01	**ADVENTURE** to have new and exciting experiences 4 9/01
ATTRACTIVENESS to be physically attractive 5 9/01	**AUTHORITY** to be in charge of and responsible for others 6 9/01

FIGURE A.4 Personal values card sort.
(a-i) From Miller, W. R., C'de Baca, J., Matthews, D. B., & Wilbourne, P. L. (2001) Personal values card sort. University of New Mexico. In the public domain.

AUTONOMY to be self-determined and independent 7 9/01	**BEAUTY** to appreciate beauty around me 8 9/01
CARING to take care of others 9 9/01	**CHALLENGE** to take on difficult tasks and problems 10 9/01
CHANGE to have a life full of change and variety 11 9/01	**COMFORT** to have a pleasant and comfortable life 12 9/01
COMMITMENT to make enduring, meaningful commitments 13 9/01	**COMPASSION** to feel and act on concern for others 14 9/01
CONTRIBUTION to make a lasting contribution in the world 15 9/01	**COOPERATION** to work collaboratively with others 16 9/01

FIGURE A.4 (*continued*)

COURTESY to be considerate and polite toward others 17 9/01	**CREATIVITY** to have new and original ideas 18 9/01
DEPENDABILITY to be reliable and trustworthy 19 9/01	**DUTY** to carry out my duties and obligations 20 9/01
ECOLOGY to live in harmony with the environment 21 9/01	**EXCITEMENT** to have a life full of thrills and stimulation 22 9/01
FAITHFULNESS to be loyal and true in relationships 23 9/01	**FAME** to be known and recognized 24 9/01
FAMILY to have a happy, loving family 25 9/01	**FITNESS** to be physically fit and strong 26 9/01

FIGURE A.4 (*continued*)

FLEXIBILITY to adjust to new circumstances easily 27 9/01	**FORGIVENESS** to be forgiving of others 28 9/01
FRIENDSHIP to have close, supportive friends 29 9/01	**FUN** to play and have fun 30 9/01
GENEROSITY to give what I have to others 31 9/01	**GENUINENESS** to act in a manner that is true to who I am 32 9/01
GOD'S WILL to seek and obey the will of God 33 9/01	**GROWTH** to keep changing and growing 34 9/01
HEALTH to be physically well and healthy 35 9/01	**HELPFULNESS** to be helpful to others 36 9/01

FIGURE A.4 *(continued)*

HONESTY to be honest and truthful 37 9/01	**HOPE** to maintain a positive and optimistic outlook 38 9/01
HUMILITY to be modest and unassuming 39 9/01	**HUMOR** to see the humorous side of myself and the world 40 9/01
INDEPENDENCE to be free from dependence on others 41 9/01	**INDUSTRY** to work hard and well at my life tasks 42 9/01
INNER PEACE to experience personal peace 43 9/01	**INTIMACY** to share my innermost experiences with others 44 9/01
JUSTICE to promote fair and equal treatment for all 45 9/01	**KNOWLEDGE** to learn and contribute valuable knowledge 46 9/01

FIGURE A.4 *(continued)*

LEISURE to take time to relax and enjoy 47 9/01	**LOVED** to be loved by those close to me 48 9/01
LOVING to give love to others 49 9/01	**MASTERY** to be competent in my everyday activities 50 9/01
MINDFULNESS to live conscious and mindful of the present moment 51 9/01	**MODERATION** to avoid excesses and find a middle ground 52 9/01
MONOGAMY to have one close, loving relationship 53 9/01	**NON-CONFORMITY** to question and challenge authority and norms 54 9/01
NURTURANCE to take care of and nurture others 55 9/01	**OPENNESS** to be open to new experiences, ideas, and options 56 9/01

FIGURE A.4 *(continued)*

ORDER to have a life that is well-ordered and organized 57 9/01	**PASSION** to have deep feelings about ideas, activities, or people 58 9/01
PLEASURE to feel good 59 9/01	**POPULARITY** to be well-liked by many people 60 9/01
POWER to have control over others 61 9/01	**PURPOSE** to have meaning and direction in my life 62 9/01
RATIONALITY to be guided by reason and logic 63 9/01	**REALISM** to see and act realistically and practically 64 9/01
RESPONSIBILITY to make and carry out responsible decisions 65 9/01	**RISK** to take risks and chances 66 9/01

FIGURE A.4 *(continued)*

ROMANCE to have intense, exciting love in my life 67 9/01	**SAFETY** to be safe and secure 69 9/01
SELF-ACCEPTANCE to accept myself as I am 68 9/01	**SELF-CONTROL** to be disciplined in my own actions 70 9/01
SELF-ESTEEM to feel good about myself 71 9/01	**SELF-KNOWLEDGE** to have a deep and honest understanding of myself 72 9/01
SERVICE to be of service to others 73 9/01	**SEXUALITY** to have an active and satisfying sex life 74 9/01
SIMPLICITY to live life simply, with minimal needs 75 9/01	**SOLITUDE** to have time and space where I can be apart from others 76 9/01

FIGURE A.4 *(continued)*

SPIRITUALITY to grow and mature spiritually 77 9/01	**STABILITY** to have a life that stays fairly consistent 78 9/01
TOLERANCE to accept and respect those who differ from me 79 9/01	**TRADITION** to follow respected patterns of the past 80 9/01
VIRTUE to live a morally pure and excellent life 81 9/01	**WEALTH** to have plenty of money 82 9/01
WORLD PEACE to work to promote peace in the world 83 9/01	**Other Value:**
Other Value:	**Other Value:**

This instrument is in the public domain and may be copied adapted and used without permission.

FIGURE A.4 (*continued*)

Index

Note: Page numbers followed by "*f*" indicate figures, "*t*" indicate tables, and "*b*" indicate boxes.

B

C

U

V

W

Z

Printed and bound by CPI Group (UK) Ltd, Croydon, CR0 4YY
17/09/2026
02218538-0002